MIXED MESSAGES: MATERIALITY, TEXTUALITY, MISSIONS

Edited by

Jamie S. Scott

and

Gareth Griffiths

palgrave
macmillan

MIXED MESSAGES: MATERIALITY, TEXTUALITY, MISSIONS

First published in 2005 by
PALGRAVE MACMILLAN™
175 Fifth Avenue, New York, N.Y. 10010 and
Houndmills, Basingstoke, Hampshire, England RG21 6XS
Companies and representatives throughout the world.

PALGRAVE MACMILLAN is the global academic imprint of the Palgrave Macmillan division of St. Martin's Press, LLC and of Palgrave Macmillan Ltd. Macmillan® is a registered trademark in the United States, United Kingdom and other countries. Palgrave is a registered trademark in the European Union and other countries.

ISBN 0–312–29576–6

Library of Congress Cataloging-in-Publication Data is available from the Library of Congress.

A catalogue record for this book is available from the British Library.

Design by Newgen Imaging Systems (P) Ltd., Chennai, India.

First edition: May 2005

10 9 8 7 6 5 4 3 2 1

Printed in the United States of America.

CONTENTS

LIST OF CONTRIBUTORS

J. Marshall Beier teaches in the Political Science Department, McMaster University, Hamilton, Canada. He is the author of *International Relations in Uncommon Places: Indigeneity, Cosmology, and the Limits of International Theory* (New York: Palgrave Macmillan, 2005).

James William Coleman teaches in the Department of Social Sciences, California Polytechnic State University, San Luis Obispo, the United States of America. He is the author of *The New Buddhism: The Western Transformation of an Ancient Tradition* (New York: Oxford University Press, 2002) and with Harold R. Kerbo, the co-author of *Social Problems: A Brief Introduction, 2E* (Upper Saddle River, NJ: Prentice Hall, 2003).

Jeffrey L. Cox teaches in the Department of History, University of Iowa, the United States of America. He is the author of *Imperial Fault Lines: Christianity and Colonial Power in India, 1818–1940* (Stanford: Stanford University Press, 2002), and with Shelton Stromquist, the co-editor of *Contesting the Master Narrative: Essays in Social History* (Iowa City: University of Iowa Press, 1998).

Norman Etherington teaches in the Department of History, University of Western Australia, Perth. He is the author of *The Great Treks: The Transformation of Southern Africa, 1815–1854* (New York: Longman, 2001) and of "Missions and Empire," in the *Oxford History of the British Empire,* (vol. V. W. R. Louis and Robin Winks, eds. Oxford: Oxford University Press, 1999, pp. 303–14).

Gareth Griffiths teaches in the Department of English, University of Western Australia, Perth. He is the author of *African Literatures in English: East and West* (New York: Longman, 2000), and with Bill Ashcroft and Helen Tiffin, the co-editor of *Post-Colonial Studies: The Key Concepts* (New York: Routledge, 2000).

Isabel Hofmeyr teaches in the Department of African Literature, University of the Witwatersrand, Johannesburg, South Africa. She is the author of *The Portable Bunyan: A Transnational History of* The Pilgrim's Progress (Princeton University Press, 2004) and of *"We Spend Our Years as a Tale that is Told": Oral Historical Narrative in a South African Chiefdom* (London: James Currey, 1993).

Eliza F. Kent teaches in the Department of Philosophy and Religion, Colgate University, Hamilton, New York, the United States of America. She is the author of *Converting Women: Gender and Protestant Christianity in Colonial South India* (New York: Oxford University Press, 2004).

Klaus K. Klostermaier teaches in the Department of Religion, University of Manitoba, Winnipeg, Canada. He is the author of *Hinduism: A Short History* (Oxford: Oneworld, 2000) and of *A Concise Encyclopedia of Hinduism* (Oxford: Oneworld, 1998).

Jane Samson teaches in the Department of History and Classics, University of Alberta, Edmonton, Canada. She is the author of *Race and Empire* (London: Longman, 2004) and of *Imperial Benevolence: Making British Authority in the Pacific Islands* (Honolulu: University of Hawai'i Press, 1998).

Jamie S. Scott teaches in the Division of Humanities, York University, Toronto, Canada. With Alvyn Austin, he is the co-editor of *Canadian Missionaries, Indigenous Peoples: Representing Religion at Home and Abroad* (Toronto: University of Toronto Press, 2005), and with Paul Simpson-Housley, of *Mapping the Sacred: Religion, Geography and Post-Colonial Literatures* (Amsterdam and New York: Rodopi, 2001).

Jane I. Smith is Co-Director of the Duncan Black Macdonald Center for Christian-Muslim Relations, Hartford Seminary, Hartford, the United States of America. With Yvonne Haddad and John Esposito, she is the co-editor of *Becoming American: Immigration and Religious Life in the United States* (Walnut Creek, CA: Altamira Press, 2003), and the author of *Islam in America* (New York: Columbia University Press, 1999).

Peter van der Veer teaches Comparative Religion at the University of Utrecht, the Netherlands. With Shoma Munshi, he is the co-editor of *Media, War, and Terrorism: Responses from the Middle East and Asia* (New York: Routledge, 2004), and the author of *Imperial Encounters: Religion and Modernity in India and Britain* (Princeton: Princeton University Press, 2001).

PREFACE

Andrew Porter has recently noted that "Christian missions have long been associated both with the growth of empire and with colonial rule," and that "the nature and consequences of that association have provoked animated debate," notably around "questions of 'culture' and 'identity' " (Porter 2003, 1). This collection of essays began when we the editors agreed that despite this long association, with some notable exceptions, a couple of things seem often to have been downplayed or even entirely neglected in scholarly accounts of missions.[1] First, the study of Christian missions, like the study of religion itself, has more and more become located within the broader realm of religious and cultural studies, at once inclusive of, yet moving beyond the mainly theological concerns of traditional missiology and mission histories. In this respect, to adapt the words of Joel Robbins, what we might call the new mission studies attempts to resist the temptation to render "Christianity something less than cultural—something less, that is, than a system of categories and values with its own coherence" (Robbins 2004, 30). Second—and it is perhaps here that this book makes its most extravagant and adventurous claim—we feel that Western scholarship has too often tended to understand missions exclusively in terms of Christian proselytizing movements. This narrowness in matter and method prorogues two avenues of important research: analysis of the missionary impulse in a variety of other worldviews, both religious and nonreligious; and comparative studies in evangelism and proselytism.

Although these convictions have been strengthened both by research that has continued to emerge in other places and by the material that came in from some of the leading scholars in the field in response to our calls for contributions to this volume, two further considerations have shaped this collection. First, because we editors have both maintained a special scholarly interest in postcolonial societies and their concerns over many years, our aim in this volume has been mainly, though not exclusively, to "explore the budding nexus between Mission Studies, Cultural Studies and Postcolonial Studies," as one of our contributors puts it, with a strong emphasis on British missions, complicated by important, but only occasional examinations of American evangelicals based in British colonial and imperial territories. Second, these essays seek to address some of the many ways in which missions engaged and fashioned the peoples and spaces they encountered through the powerful transformative vehicle of the written text. Mission texts were not only powerful tools of control in themselves; as individual pieces of writing or as constitutive genres, they were also part of a new modality that privileged writing and the textual generally, both endorsing and in some cases creating the reality of dominant "sacral texts" in societies and cultures that had no such tradition of a monolithic and unified code of moral and religious authority. In this sense, the idea of writing was a crucial instrument in creating the modern forms not only of the postcolonial spaces it engaged, but also, in different ways, of the colonizing cultures themselves, helping to forge there new unified identities resistant to the possible radical dislocations of class and gender that emerged as Western societies entered the industrial age of mass-literacy. The production of texts was not, of course, confined to Protestant missions; as another of our contributors notes, Ultramontanist revivalism brought a new surge in Roman Catholic missionary activity with attendant increases in proselytizing literature and other kinds of Christian cultural production. But evangelical emphasis on the Bible and on personal salvation unmediated by anything beyond the personal faith of the believer meant that Protestant missions became crucially centered on the production and dissemination of texts as instruments of conversion and control.

It is not surprising, then, that the commissioned papers making up Part I of this collection have focused on Protestant missions, though we as editors did not explicitly require such a focus. For this first set of essays, we asked contributors to consider the roles texts of all kinds played in mission practice in accordance with their specific scholarly interests and regions of expertise. As a result, these essays cover many forms of mission textuality. Part I opens with a contextualizing account by Jeffrey Cox of the "master narratives" of missions. This essay is designed to provide a discursive historical framework for the more detailed case studies that follow. A second framing essay by Isabel Hofmeyr argues the need to reconfigure the existing split between studies of missions abroad and "at home" within a new more fluid, transnational model. Closing with two case studies of this process in practice, Hofmeyr's essay segues neatly into five more extended case studies of Christian missions and mission practices. Exploring interrelations among written, pictorial, and oral expressions of everyday evangelical activity and different forms of secular literature and life, these essays examine a range of topics having to do with the textual and material cultures of Christian missions: mathematical tables and texts as vehicles and indicators of religious experience; missionary adventure tales; the semiotic role of clothing in missionized cultures; missionaries, alien landscapes, and the tourist gaze; and the key part played by missions in the implementation of colonial educational policies. We should point out, however, that although we have tried to capture something of the geographical spread of Christian missions, as well as the audacious reach of evangelical ambitions, we do not make any claims to comprehensiveness in either of these respects; Part I might well have benefited from an essay on British missions in China, for example, or on evangelizing activities among Jewish and Muslim communities, both in Great Britain and overseas.

Part II seeks, first, to indicate how mission as a concept has had a broader presence beyond Christianity in other religious traditions. It offers accounts of mission as a force in Islam, Buddhism, and Hinduism. Clearly, the treatment of each of these religions might have been broadened to include a range of essays as extensive as those in Part I. In focusing on those non-Christian missions that engage with the "West," rather than the many missions within these religions themselves, we have sought to indicate that the processes of missionizing have flowed both ways across the contested spaces of the post-Enlightenment, postcolonial world, a fact often overlooked in earlier mission accounts with a postcolonial perspective. Sometimes religious individuals or communities rediscover and revive proselytizing tendencies deeply embedded with their own ideological and historical trajectories to consolidate and expand traditional domains of influence; in other instances, the encounter with Christianity prompts members of other religions to adopt, adapt, imitate, and in some cases improve upon the proselytizing technologies of imperial and colonial British and American missions in an effort to resist Christian missionary advances and to reestablish indigenous religious authority. Second, in a further extension of the idea of mission, the essay concluding Part II suggests that the modern institutions of Western, liberal democracy bear an uncomfortably close resemblance to religious missions, especially as represented in such structures and texts as the World Bank and the development narratives, which it at once embodies and expresses. Here, too, then, in this second group of essays, we have tried to expand and extend mission studies in and through a wide range of topics, though again, we make no claim to have been aiming at, still less to have achieved, complete coverage; essays on contemporary Jewish, Baha'i, or Sikh proselytizing would fit easily into Part II, for example, as would studies of the export of Marxist or Maoist ideas and practices from their cultures of origin.

Beyond their engagement with changing academic perceptions of missions and religions, these essays seek also to reflect the growing realization, so eloquently expressed by Peter van der Veer in his Afterword, that we may be on the verge of a major epistemic shift in which post-Enlightenment assumptions about the dominance of the secular is under considerable challenge. We see signs of this shift in the ways in which we now recognize that resistance to Euro-American models of social practice as constituting a new universal "world order" often find their focus through a revisited counter-discourse of the sacral, a counter-discourse that refuses to inhabit a different and separate space from civil discourse. This shift in perspective has also become true of Euro-American cultures themselves, as they respond both to the presence within their boundaries of a changing demography in which religious differences increasingly figure in the construction of personal and group identities within previously predominantly secular national frameworks, and as their own foundational cultures prove unpredictably resistant to the dominant post-Enlightenment, secular forms of social construction and engage in a renewed sense of religion as a factor in their own identity. As Jamie S. Scott has written elsewhere, "[o]ften ambiguous and complex, such [phenomena] represent and dramatize the contested processes of colonization, resistance and decolonization by which lands and landscapes may be viewed as now sacred, now desacralized, now resacralized" (Scott 2001, xxvii).

In the work of Martin E. Marty, R. Scott Appleby, and others, the focus of these changes has often been on the emergence of so-called fundamentalist forms within cultures as diverse as those of Asia, Africa, or the American heartland.[2] Yet these fundamentalist practices are really part of a broader recognition of the inseparability of sacral and secular concepts in the practice of these cultures, whatever the political, constitutional, or legal texts may have asserted during the "modern" period. The issue is not whether we should applaud or deplore the fact that the post-Enlightenment secular ideal has never been the actual practice for most people and cultures across the world; it is simply that this fact needs to be addressed more openly and more directly as we try to adjust to the realities of an increasingly globalized set of economic and political modalities and their cultural consequences for all societies in the period ahead. For this reason, the collection concludes with an essay that addresses the broader effect of the mission model on international practice in the twentieth century and after. Neither in the past nor in the present or likely future can we separate the practice of missions, narrowly conceived as a "religious" practice, from the influences this phenomenon has had and continues to have on secular national and international institutions and ideologies. Missions perceived themselves—and at the level of individual practices often were—well-intended. Nevertheless, in their systemic engagement with the world their results were frequently less than beneficent. This collection is a modest attempt to broaden the ways in which we think about the role of the concept of mission as we enter this new so-called global era.

Finally, let us say that we have not sought either to impose a consistent viewpoint or to force contiguity between the variety of practices and the range of views expressed in this collection. Rather, the book's purpose is to open up the discussion of issues, not close them down by establishing a new universal paradigm. It is therefore gratifying to us as editors that such a diverse group of contributors from such a wide range of disciplinary and regional backgrounds seem to us to have produced a collection that we believe achieves a remarkable degree of overlap in concern and of interaction in methodology, while still embracing difference as a positive goal of creative scholarship in this developing field.

Notes

1. There is no need to catalogue these exceptional voices here, since the essays in this collection invoke them as conversation partners and engage with them in a variety of ways.
2. See, e.g., Marty and Appleby (1991), and the exhaustive research into various forms of fundamentalist thought and practice in the world's religions which has constituted the numerous volumes of the Fundamentalism Project.

PART ONE

PROTESTANT MISSIONS, TEXTS, AND CONTEXTS

CHAPTER ONE

MASTER NARRATIVES OF IMPERIAL MISSIONS

Jeffrey Cox

The two most important stories about Western religion during the last 300 years are the progressive de-Christianization of Europe and the expansion of Western religion beyond the boundaries of Europe. In Europe the decline of Christian institutions, and the abandonment of religious faith, reached new and unprecedented levels in late twentieth century, requiring a reevaluation of the timing of the decline of religion in Europe. In *The Death of Christian Britain*, Callum Brown identifies the 1960s as the decade of secularization in modern British history (Brown 2001, chapter 8). Scholarly discussion over the de-Christianization of the Christian heartland has focused for the most part on questions of timing rather than fundamental explanations, largely because of the pervasiveness of the master narrative of secularization in both scholarly and journalistic discussion of the problem of decline.

Despite the virtual abandonment of the narrow, functionalist social theory of secularization used by sociologists and anthropologists in the 1960s and 1970s, there remains in place a largely uncontested master narrative that serves as a framework for both the description of, and the explanation of, the decline of religion in modern Europe: the master narrative of secularization. I am using the phrase "master narrative" in a relatively unsophisticated (and philosophically pragmatic) sense to classify the scale of narratives used by historians. A master narrative is a big story that makes smaller stories intelligible.[1] Because it is a master narrative, it is often partly hidden, lying in the background to be deployed selectively by the historian, and brought into play to explain things that cannot be dealt with explicitly. In the master narrative of secularization, religion is locked into a competitive struggle with modernity, and the latter holds a decisive advantage. The metaphorical graph that measures the fate of religion in modern Europe slopes inexorably downward.

When turning from the decline of religion in Europe to the expansion of European religion elsewhere, the master narrative of secularization becomes problematic. The twentieth-century global resurgence of religion, including Christianity, has caught many commentators by surprise. Secularization continues to be inscribed on to the non-Western world by some scholars and commentators, especially when Western interests are involved, in the form of a global struggle between modernity and "fundamentalism." Believers in secularization, when confronted with evidence of explosive religious vitality in the non-Western world, suggest that its religious decline is just a matter of time. It is well known that modernity happens first in Europe, and later outside of Europe, where modernization will eventually kill off religion just as it has in the West. In his review of David Martin's account of Latin American Pentecostalism in *The Times Literary Supplement*, March 29, 2002, Bryan Wilson asks: "May not the current of secularization, running powerfully in the West, overtake or eviscerate the Pentecostal Revival in the Third World?" The sheer complexity of new religious manifestations around the world, however, ultimately defeats the master narrative of secularization, at least for the time being. With new attention being paid to "the provincialization of Europe," secularization is increasingly seen as a projection on to the non-Western world of categories and experiences that belong to Europe (Chakrabarty 1992). The diversity of religious experience in the twenty-first century provides too much to explain by reference to a binary, global struggle between secular modernity and religious anti-modernity.

The Providentialist Master Narrative

In scholarship on the global expansion of Western religion, there is no single uncontested master narrative in play, but competing master narratives recognized to a greater or lesser degree by everyone involved, whether they are labeled "master narrative" or not. Secularization is one master narrative. In the history of foreign missions, there is another, the master narrative of the providential progress of Christian expansion that found its classic expression in the surprisingly durable work of Kenneth Scott Latourette. The master narrative of global Christian expansion is not inevitably triumphalist or celebratory or even heroic, but always focuses on the documentation of God's providential work in the world. The providentialist master narrative encompasses the foundational narratives of missionary history along with the newer mission studies narratives that are much more critical of past missionary practice. There is, for instance, the "sins of our forefathers" mission studies narrative, based on a lament for the imperialist, ethnocentric, and patriarchal attitudes of the predecessors of present-day missionaries.[2] The providentialist master narrative also encompasses the more recent scholarly studies of "indigenization," in the works of Lamin Sanneh and many others, that stress non-Western agency in the creation of non-Western Christianity almost to the point of eliminating Western influence altogether.[3] However liberal these narratives are, they all put the history of Christianity at the center of the story.

The providentialist mission studies master narrative, whether celebratory or critical, is rooted in the texts written by and about pioneer Western missionary heroes such as William Carey in India and Adoniram Judson in Burma. A Northamptonshire Baptist minister and former shoemaker, Carey provided the agenda for the modern Protestant missionary movement by outlining a practical bureaucratic mechanism to put the missionary impulse into effect, the voluntary missionary society. In 1792, Carey published his *Enquiry into the Obligations of Christians, to use means for the Conversion of the Heathens*, where he felt confident enough to argue that "the spread of civil and religious liberty" meant that for the gospel "a glorious door is opened, and is likely to be opened wider and wider" (Carey 1792, 79). For Carey, the expansion of true Christianity was only beginning, because for him true religious faith had to be voluntary religious faith. The forced conversions, backed with state power, of previous Roman Catholic mission efforts were of no interest to him, for "Papists are in general ignorant of divine things" (Carey 1792, 65).

For Protestants in the eighteenth century, the fundamental problem confronting enthusiasts of global Christian expansion was one of organization. Having abolished the religious orders, Protestants possessed no efficient mechanism for expansion beyond their national borders.[4] Carey proposed an innovative form of ecclesiastical organization, the voluntary missionary society. Carey assumed that ordinary ministers would be called by God to conduct their ministry abroad. But not every English minister was as committed as Carey, who left for Bengal in 1793 to begin an interesting career as a distinguished grammarian, translator, and printer of Bibles in various Indian languages. In his wake, though, the English-speaking world was populated by voluntary missionary societies. Carey played a crucial role in founding the Baptist Society for Propagating the Gospel Among the Heathen in 1792, which was followed by (to take the case of Great Britain alone) the interdenominational (later Congregational) London Missionary Society in 1795, the evangelical Anglican Society for Missions to Africa and the East (later known as the Church Missionary Society) in 1799, and the Wesleyan Missionary Society in 1813. With the gradual transformation in the early nineteenth century of the (Anglican) Society for the Propagation of the Gospel into an ordinary missionary society representing the interests of high church Anglicans, the major Victorian English religious denominations each had an efficient bureaucratic machine for raising money and supporting foreign missionaries. Dozens of smaller societies followed, and the pattern was repeated in the United States, Scotland, Ireland, and eventually the English-speaking colonies of Great Britain and other Protestant countries.

The struggle to create a new professional—the full-time missionary—was shaped by key mission texts that also did much to define the non-Western world for English-speaking readers: Thomas Coke's *History of the West Indies* (1808–1811), William Ward's *A View of the History, Literature and Religion of the Hindoos* (1817), John Williams's *Narrative of Missionary Enterprises in the South Seas Islands* (1837), Robert Moffat's *Missionary Labours and Scenes in South Africa* (1842), and the extremely popular works of David Livingstone, especially *Missionary Travels and Researches in South Africa* (1857) and *Narrative of an Expedition to the Zambesi* (1864). In these foundational narratives, male clerical heroes, assisted occasionally by unnamed women or "natives," move from the Christian heartland into a kind of global religious vacuum peopled by non-Christians who are sometimes portrayed as noble, sometimes as vicious, but always as ignorant of the benefits of the Christian gospel. By the time of the publication of *Jane Eyre* in 1847, St. John Rivers was a recognizable type, the clerical missionary hero, admirably high-minded, ascetic and learned, but somewhat unbalanced. Jane Eyre "saw he was of the material from which nature hews her heroes—Christian and Pagan—her lawgivers, her statesmen, her conquerors: a steadfast bulwark for great interest to rest upon; but, at the fireside, too often a cold cumbrous column, gloomy and out of place" (Brontë 1981 [1847], 375).

In the course of the twentieth century, writing about missions became a substantial academic enterprise, especially in the United States. Hundreds of dissertations have been written in North America on missionary topics, most of them in divinity schools or departments of religion. The *International Bulletin of Missionary Research*, and successive editions of David Barrett's *World Christian Encyclopedia*, stand as monuments to the massive scale of missionary research and writing. The nineteenth-century foundational narratives have been rewritten. Women were first put in the story, and then put at the center of the story (although I still encounter surprised looks when explaining that two-thirds of all British and American missionaries were women). Non-Western Christians—the nameless "native assistants" and "Bible women" of the foundational narratives—have been put in the story, and then put at the center of the story. It is fair to say that although the nature of the heroes has changed from white male to female to nonwhite, the heroes remain. Much academic work in the mission studies fields remains within the confines of an essentially providential master narrative, in which the focus is on the inexorable march of Christianity around the world.

It would be little exaggeration, and no surprise to many mission studies specialists, to say that much scholarly work on missions is invisible in the noneclesiastical academy. The mainstream scholarly disciplines of history, anthropology, and literary criticism operate with a very different set of assumptions about the agents of Western religious expansion. Secular master narratives about Western religious expansion are based on two assumptions, either the "presumption of marginality" or the "attribution of imperial agency." Like the characteristics of the providentialist master narrative, the presumption of marginality and the attribution of imperial agency are both rooted in historical rhetoric. As the first English Baptist missionaries to India were attempting to establish a foothold in Bengal and avoid being expelled by the imperialist East India Company, the Rev. Sydney Smith took aim at them in a widely read essay in the *Edinburgh Review* in 1808, dismissing these would-be missionary heroes as "little detachments of Maniacs" (Smith 1808, 179). In Smith's imperialist view, voluntarist Baptist missionaries of low social status were endangering the state in India with their ill-considered fanaticism. They were not in the mainstream of imperial history, but at the margins. His view was shared by the earliest ecclesiastical imperialists in India. The first Anglican Bishop in India (1814), Thomas Middleton, had in his early years no interest in missionary work in the broader sense, and limited his ministry to the nominally Christian European population among whom, he asserted: "We have work enough for years to come, without interfering with any species of superstition" (quoted in Cnattingius 1952, 75).

The Imperialist Master Narrative

This plotline is the master narrative of mainstream imperial history. Its central story is the expansion of the West throughout the world, bringing with it the benefits and/or evils of Western civilization variously defined to a non-Western world that is classified in the ever-shifting objective language of the detached Olympian observer, or in the durable, smug, and frequently defamatory figures of speech of Orientalism. At the center of the master narrative of imperial history is Western power, whether military, bureaucratic, economic, or cultural. In Rider Haggard's *She* (1887), Rudyard Kipling's *Kim* (1901), or in E. M. Forster's *A Passage to India* (1924), explorers, scholars, military officers, merchants, and imperial administrators are central to the imperial enterprise, and missionaries are marginal. This master narrative is very much with us today, steaming majestically along in the five objective scholarly volumes of the *Oxford History of the British Empire*, and rewritten for readers of the *New York Times* in columnist Thomas Friedman's global vision, at once liberal and defamatory, of a Middle East transformed into an American suburb.

In the master narrative of imperial history, Western missionaries and their domestic supporters are for the most part mindless humanitarian bumblers who get in the way of imperial progress and meddle in matters about which they know nothing. In *Bleak House* (1853), Charles Dickens's Mrs. Jellyby lets her children starve while she raises money for African missions; the racist Sir Richard Burton dismisses an African clergyman as "the missing link"; Kipling's bumbling Mr. Bennett is a menace to Kim and by extension, through his incompetence and poor judgment, to the stability of imperial rule in India. There are alternative modes of depiction, including the objective and the heroic, but the presumption of marginality remains deeply rooted. Imperial historians who are interested in missionaries, such as Andrew Porter, have established a foothold for the study of missions in the *Journal of Imperial Commonwealth History* and even in *The Oxford History of the British Empire*, but the overall presence of mission studies in those fields remains at the margins.[5] The comic mode is very widespread in twentieth-century cinematic depictions of missionaries. One thinks of Robert Morley in *African Queen*, wringing his hands while lost in the jungle and confessing that he only became a missionary because of his inability to make a living at home. Missionaries are perfectly suited for the full Monty Python treatment they receive in "Missionaries."

The Postcolonial Master Narrative

Modernity is at the center of the master narrative of secularization, and Christianity at the center of the providentialist master narrative. A focus on Western power, however defined, is at the center of the master narrative of imperial history. The presumption of marginality not only marks historical scholarship in imperial history, but also in the flourishing field of postcolonial studies, which despite its antithetical stance continues to share characteristics of its thesis: imperial history. In her justly influential *Burdens of History*, Antoinette Burton undermined the claims of secular English feminists to be advocates for the women of India by unmasking the images of helplessness and dependency that feminists used to bolster their own political claims in Britain (Burton 1994). These images were closely linked historically to an even more pervasive and influential body of literature, generated by the missionary movement, depicting Indian women with similar tropes of helplessness and dependency. It is likely that most people in Britain received their basic views of foreign cultures from missionary literature, especially at a time when almost every child in Britain attended a Sunday School. Missionary literature is not interesting to Burton, and appears not at all in *Burdens of History*. It is shoved to the sidelines by the presumption of marginality shared by the imperialist/postcolonialist master narrative.

Postcolonial scholarship shares other characteristics with the imperial history that preceded it. Dominating the field of postcolonial scholarship, whether acknowledged or not, is the work of Edward Said, whose sustained and persuasive analysis of the imperial complicity of Western scholarship about the non-Western world has been very difficult for his many critics to dislodge. Said's basic technique, used to very good effect by Burton, is that of unmasking. The universalist claims of Western scholarship are shown to be corrupted by the sheer historical fact of Western imperial expansion into the non-Western world in the nineteenth and twentieth centuries. The universalist claims of Western Christianity could easily be subjected to the same unmasking, but Western religion is at the margins rather than the center of the story in Said's most widely read books, *Orientalism* (1978) and *Culture and Imperialism* (1993). Western expansion in the Saidian master narrative is resolutely secular, as is its mirror image, opposition to Western expansion in the form of anti-imperialism. Following the publication of his two major works, Said was forced to come to terms with the resurgence of non-Western religion, and even criticized historians such as Eric Hobsbawm for being too secular in their outlook to evaluate "fundamentalism" (Said 1995). But writing in Cairo's weekly newspaper, *Al-Ahram*, December 19–25, 2002, Said confronts a world increasingly focused on religiously based ideologies, whether Zionism or militant Islam or the Christian Right, in sentences that could almost be taken directly from the writings of Karl Marx or Sigmund Freud: "How can it be acceptable to turn passively to another religion and look there for worldly salvation? Impossible. Human beings make their own history, not gods or magic or miracles."

Said provides an interesting example of why attention to master narratives is important. In the preface to her recent biography of V. S. Azariah, the first Indian Protestant Bishop in India, Susan Billington Harper launched an attack on the secular presuppositions of mainstream scholars of global Christianity. They have ignored Indian Christianity, she argues, because of a self-conscious, political bias against religion in general. The difficulties historians face in fitting religion into narratives of global Christian expansion are far more complicated than simple political, social, or religious bias. I once put this point directly to Walter L. Arnstein, a scholar of Victorian religion whose popular textbook on British history, directed to American college students, is now in its eighth edition (Arnstein 2001). When I asked him why religion hardly appears in his account of twentieth-century Britain, despite his own well-known interest in religion, his response identified the heart of the matter: "The question is, where do you put it in?"

For the postcolonial master narrative, a similar question might be asked. Where do you put Western religion in the master narrative? Said's story is one of secular Western expansion—from 35 percent of the earth's surface to 85 percent in the course of the nineteenth century—and the ways in which universalist Western scholarship on the non-Western world was distorted and corrupted by inescapable power relationships. The twentieth-century antithesis of Western imperialism, anti-imperialist nationalism, is a secular political movement with which Said explicitly identifies. If politics and power are central and religion marginal, then Western religion can only fit obliquely into the story of modern history. In a few paragraphs in *Culture and Imperialism*, Said acknowledges the mixed messages that Christian missions create when juxtaposed with Western imperialism. Western religion can only enter his story, however, through a personal reference.

Anyone who has read Said's memoir, *Out of Place*, can hardly fail to notice the importance of Western religion in his childhood and adolescence. He describes his great grandfather as "the first native Evangelical minister in Lebanon" (Said 1999, 15). His maternal grandfather was the Arab Baptist pastor in Nazareth, and received his theological education, or at least part of it, in Texas. Said's father was an active churchgoing Anglican in Cairo, who subjected his son to large doses of regimented religion: "For years, Sunday meant Sunday School; this senseless ordeal occurred between nine and ten in the morning at the GPS, followed by matins at All Saints' Cathedral. Sunday evenings took us to the American Mission Church in Ezbekieh, and two Sundays out of three to Evensong at the cathedral" (Said 1999, 22). After confirmation as an Anglican, Said was sent to an American prep school founded by a man whose name he appears to assume his readers will recognize, Dwight L. Moody. "And so it was with religion—the Sunday service, the Wednesday evening chapel, the Thursday noon sermon—dreadful, pietistic, non-denominational (I disliked that form of vacillation in particular) full of homilies, advice, how-to-live. Ordinary observations were encoded into Moodyesque sturdy Christianity in which words like 'service' and 'labor' acquired magical (but finally unspecifiable) meaning, to be repeated and intoned as what gave our lives 'moral purpose' " (Said 1999, 232).

Obviously religious socialization failed to take in Said's case, which might be included in an anthology of "Great Failures in Religious Education." But *Out Of Place* reveals that Said is interested in religion. It can only be put into a personal story, however, and it is the personal story that creates a space for mixed messages that creep into *Culture and Imperialism*, albeit so briefly that they are easy to miss. Said describes a visit by a relative from the Middle East, apparently a minister, who is on a mission to persuade the liberal Protestant bureaucrats in New York to desist from promoting the forced ecumenical merger of small, Arab Protestant denominations. Said takes some time to say a few good things about his own Arab Protestant tradition, a community he describes as resulting from "imperial competition for converts and constituents" that created communities that ". . . acquired their own identities and traditions, their own institutions, all of which without exception played an honorable role during the period of the Arab Renaissance" (Said 1993, 39–40). Having been created by Western missionaries as separate denominations, they are now aggrieved to find themselves under pressure from Western denominations to merge into one ecumenical denomination, erasing the separate and presumably authentic identities that had emerged over the course of a century.

Said briefly acknowledges the contradictory nature of the missionary, and non-Western Christian, relationship to imperialism: "One should note that this touching story concerns an experience of imperialism that is essentially one of sympathy and congruence, not of antagonism, resentment, or resistance. The appeal by one of the parties was to the value of a *mutual experience*. True, there had once been a principal and a subordinate, but there had also been dialogue and communication" (Said 1993, 40; emphasis added). Before reaching the end of the paragraph, however, Said reverts to structural determinism: "The implicit argument made by the Western missionary authorities was that the Arabs had gotten something valuable out of what had been given them, but in this relationship of historical dependence and subordination, all the giving went one way, the value was mainly on one side. Mutuality was considered to be basically impossible" (Said 1993, 41). Before completing this discussion, Said refers to the need to ". . . get beyond the reified polarities of East versus West," but before he proceeds with his narrative those polarities are reinscribed. Missionaries and Arab Protestants alike, it appears, are trapped in a structure in which, in Said's ringing words from *Orientalism*, "It is therefore correct [to state that] every [nineteenth-century] European, in what he could say about the Orient, was consequently a racist, an imperialist, and almost totally ethnocentric" (Said 1978, 204).

Said is not the only celebrated secular scholar with personal connections to the missionary movement. E. P. Thompson is the author of one of the best-known assaults on evangelical religion in twentieth-century British historical writing, the famous eleventh chapter of *The Making of the English Working Class*. "The Transforming Power of the Cross" pillories evangelical Methodism as a species of sexualized false consciousness, diverting the working class into the gratifications of "a ritualised form of psychic masturbation" (Thompson 1964, 368). Thompson's father was a Methodist missionary to India, although one who eventually left his mission to become a scholar and supporter of Indian nationalism. E. P. Thompson attended Kingswood School in England, populated by children of Methodist ministers and missionaries, where he once played the Angel Gabriel in the school pageant. Religion obviously no more "took" in his case than it did in the case of Said, and Thompson's post-Marxist historical master narrative is relentlessly secular. In his reflections on his father in *Alien Homage*, however, Thompson recognizes the mixed messages of religion in an imperial setting (Thompson 1993). The elder Thompson was author of *The Rise and Fulfillment of British Rule in India*, a pro-nationalist history that treats the Indian national movement as the natural outcome of the implantation of Western ideas of democracy and national self-determination. Unmasking the Orientalist presuppositions of a text that attributes the national movement to Western influence would be easy work, but in *Alien Homage* Thompson is interested in complexity, not the reified polarities of East and West. Like Forster, he examines the intricacies of friendship across imperial boundaries, concluding finally that he had come to abominate the "[a]bbreviated categories which too often close enquiry before it has commenced. Some in the West are prisoners of vast undiscriminating categories . . . and bring those ready-made slide-rules to measure, and often to obliterate, the complexities of the past" (Thompson 1993, 69).

It is impossible to tell any historical story without some larger story in the background, a master narrative that informs and makes intelligible the smaller story. No one can explain everything at once. As Thompson recognizes when dealing with the complexities of imperialism, it is important to unmask and examine critically the larger stories, the master narratives, with an eye on their vast undiscriminating categories that might obliterate the ambiguities and ironies of the past. In the postcolonial master narrative, Western religion is marginal, and appears only under the heading of the personal. What I have labeled for convenience the Saidian master narrative, with its technique of unmasking, predates Said's work by many decades; it is rooted in earlier texts that featured anti-imperialist unmasking of imperialist pretensions to neutrality, objectivity, and beneficence. There is a genre of anti-imperialist historical writing where the presumption of marginality is set aside, and Western religion brought into focus. The presumption of marginality is replaced by the attribution of imperial agency.

Nineteenth-century Indian critics of missions treated missionaries as self-evident promoters of British imperial rule. An early work of historical scholarship squarely within the nationalist, anti-imperialist tradition is Baman Das Basu's five-volume *Rise of the Christian Power in India*, published under the auspices of the Brahmo Samaj movement in 1923. Basu's work bases its indictment of British rule as specifically Christianizing on an exegesis of texts by Macaulayan improvers and missionary providentialists. With the recent resurgence of Hindu nationalism in India, these anti-missionary arguments have been given new prominence, especially by Arun Shourie. The role of imperial government was to create a vacuum, the role of imperial missions to fill it. "The clear object: to perpetuate British rule into the indefinite future. The definite instrument: to instruct the natives in western learning, to inculcate in them western values so that they come to perceive their own interest in the perpetuation of British rule" (Shourie 1994, 80). Likewise, the attribution of imperial agency often appears naturally and uncritically in secular scholarship on missions. In some cases attribution is almost offhand, as in Joseph Esherick's use of the number of Christian conversions in China as an index of imperial tension during the days leading up to the Boxer Rebellion (Esherick 1987, 91). In *Subaltern Studies I*, Ranajit Guha simply lists missionaries as one of a number of "dominant foreign groups . . . British officials of the colonial state and foreign industrialists, merchants, financiers, planters, landlords and missionaries" (Guha 1982, 8). Like Basu and Shourie, Esherick and Guha treat the imperial agency of missionaries as self-evident and even as self-conscious.

Sustained treatments of missions by notable anthropologists, on the other hand, treat imperial agency on the part of missionaries as latent rather than manifest, requiring a sustained unmasking in order to lay bare the imperialist functions of Christian ideology in an imperial setting. In his study of evangelical Anglican missionaries in East Africa, Thomas O. Beidelman concludes that "Christian missions represent the most naive and ethnocentric, and therefore the most thoroughgoing facet of colonial life . . . Missionaries invariably aimed at overall changes in the beliefs and actions of native peoples, at colonization of heart and mind as well as body. Pursuing this sustained policy of change, missionaries demonstrated a more radical and morally intense commitment to rule than political administrators or business men" (Beidelman 1982, 5–6). What had been consigned to the margins is put at the center, and declared to be even worse from an anti-imperialist point of view. And even in the sustained and highly sophisticated treatment of the appropriation of Christianity by South Africans Jean and John Comaroff, missionaries are defined ultimately by the binarisms of East and West (Comaroff and Comaroff 1991, 1997). Africans who collaborate with Western missionaries have their hearts and minds colonized. Only when Africans appropriate Christianity for their own purposes, in opposition to and resistance to Western missionaries, can their religious views be defined as authentic and genuinely African. The unmaskings of Beidelman and the Comaroffs provide clear examples of the unmasking techniques consistent with the Saidian master narrative. When missionaries are put at the center of the story, they are defined primarily as cultural imperialists. Insofar as they were not marginal to the missionary enterprise, they were even worse than the explorers, administrators, military officers, and scholars normally treated as central.

Mixed Messages and Personal Encounters

Mary Louise Pratt has supplied a number of useful phrases to describe the intersections between personal experience on the one hand, and on the other, the competing master narratives of missions—providentialist, imperial, and postcolonial. They occur in what she refers to as "contact zones" of clashing experiences, generating what can only be called mixed messages. Pratt describes contact zones as "social spaces where disparate cultures meet, clash and grapple with each other, often in highly asymmetrical relations of domination and subordination—like colonialism, slavery or their aftermaths as they are lived out across the globe today" (Pratt 1992, 4). The providentialist master narrative is well described by her phrase "narrative of anti-conquest," in which Western imperial expansion is treated as benign or accidental in its relationship to the expansion of Western religion, which is thus divorced from the brute realities of power and military force (Pratt 1992, 100).

Non-Western Christians in the nineteenth century would not have used the same language as Pratt, but they were often very much aware of being caught in a contact zone of clashing cultural expectations. Their voices should lead to some caution about the ultimate adequacy of a Saidian unmasking of missionary cultural imperialism. In their encounters with missionaries, non-Western Christians often took seriously an aspiration that the Comaroffs dismiss as "the multi-racial Christian commonwealth of missionary, fantasy" (Comaroff and Comaroff 1991, 32). At the same time, in their personal encounters with missionaries, they frequently recognized, and sometimes asserted, the truth of the Saidian critique that power is the basis of cultural inequality, which in turn generates further inequalities of power. Within the contact zones may be found what Said referred to as "an experience of imperialism that is essentially one of sympathy and congruence, not of antagonism, resentment, or resistance. The appeal by one of the parties was to the value of a *mutual experience*" (Said 1993, 40; emphasis added). Missionaries were often important and respected figures in non-Western Christian communities, and in some cases also in non-Western, non-Christian communities.[6]

One such contact zone was documented in great detail. In the wake of the traumatic military rebellion of 1857/58, missionaries and imperial administrators of the Raj convened a conference on missions in Lahore, the capital of the newly conquered and forcibly unified province of Punjab, and published the proceedings. The forms of orientalist defamation that accompanied the conquest of India were complex and sophisticated, but they did not include stereotypes of ignorant, unlettered, and uncultured Indians. The deficiencies attributed to Indians were identified primarily as moral and religious. Missionaries and imperial administrators were well aware that in Punjab they were dealing with several ancient and highly sophisticated cultures, and they were also aware that the handful of early Christian converts were educated men and women who could not be ignored in the task of building up an indigenous Indian Christian church, one that would survive the demise of the British Empire. One of the purposes of the Lahore Missionary Conference of 1862 was to lecture Indian Christians on their rights, responsibilities, and obligations. Another purpose was to allow them to speak directly to missionaries and their supporters in the colonial administration, and document their words (Lahore Missionary Conference 1863).

The competing master narratives of Western religious expansion were on display in the personal experiences of conference participants. The triumphant colonialists of the Punjab School of Indian Administration believed firmly in the benefits of Western expansion into the non-Western world. Missionaries, on the other hand, never treated their own mission explicitly as subordinate to that of British imperial rulers, however much they might support imperialism in their political views. They regarded themselves as agents of God's providential work in the world, a timeless mission of global expansion that extended beyond the boundaries of time itself. When presenting their views to Indian Christians, theirs was a narrative of anti-conquest—a "concessionary narrative," to coin a useful phrase Pratt borrows from Peter Hulme (Pratt 1992, 100). Such a narrative, in Hulme's words, "goes some way towards recognizing a native point of view and offering a critique of European behaviour, but can only do this by not addressing the central issue" (Hulme 1986, 253). Thus the missionaries conceded the grievances of Indian Christians and Indians in general, especially in the mission world, but denied the link between those grievances and the brute realities of military conquest and cultural aggression. Addressing a group of Indian Christians later in the nineteenth century, the pioneer Anglican evangelical missionary to Punjab, Robert Clark, outlined the assumptions of the concessionary narrative of anti-conquest with a denial that he had any motives at all: "It is not merely we, who are only a few teachers from a foreign country, who are seeking to interfere with the old religions of India. It is the Truth itself which commands men everywhere to repent and to believe in Christ. Our great power as missionaries in India, is that we have no personal motives; that we seek nowhere for our own profit in the people's conversions" (Punjab CMS Native Church Council 1883 [unpaginated]).

Clark was continuing a conversation with Indian Christians, and non-Christians that had begun as soon as missionaries set foot in newly conquered parts of India. It was a conversation that rarely appeared in the defamatory or humanitarian missionary literature about India distributed in the imperial metropolis. Long before the advent of postcolonial scholarship, Indian Christians set out to demolish missionary pretensions to neutrality at the

Lahore Conference in 1862. At a conference panel dedicated entirely to the topic, "Sympathy and confidence: How can foreign missionaries secure, in the highest degree, the sympathy and affectionate confidence of their native brethren?" missionary after missionary lamented the lack of warm friendship and spiritual equality in their relationships with their Indian coreligionists. An Indian Presbyterian, the Rev. Golak Nath, responded with what amounted to an early Saidian analysis of the entire missionary enterprise:

> I have failed to discover how an European or American missionary *can* secure the *full* sympathy of Native converts: for sympathy must be considered a sort of substitution, by which we are placed in the situation of another, and are affected, in a good measure, as he is affected. . . . But the social position of a missionary, his intellectual and spiritual attainments, his highly civilized ideas, and his cultivated, refined feelings, must place him so far above his converts, generally, that there can scarcely be any fellow-feeling between them. A missionary would hardly find any *loveliness* in the character of his converts, to excite much kind feeling towards them. They are necessarily objects of his compassion and pity, but hardly worthy of his friendship, or capable of communion with him, except on religious subjects. (Lahore Missionary Conference 1863, 166–67; emphasis in the original)

If it were not for the phrase "except on religious subjects," the conversation might have ended right there, with missionaries condemned as racist, imperialist, and totally ethnocentric in what they could say about the Orient. But Golak Nath was an ordained Christian minister in full charge of a mission. His daughter would soon become one of the first independent women missionaries in India. He was committed to a partnership with Western missionaries dedicated to the building up of an indigenous Indian Christian church in which men and women could treat each other as spiritual equals across the imperial boundaries. He had not solved a problem, but identified one, and the problem was imperialism—the genteel imperialism of professional advantage, cultural access, the power of the clergyman, the teacher, and the educational administrator. Golak Nath could not stop at identifying the problem, and duly proceeded to outline a series of measures that might generate the sympathy between missionaries and Indian Christians that he had just declared impossible.

In the 1860s contact zone in Lahore, Golak Nath outlined the terms of an ongoing negotiation that remained remarkably durable throughout the subsequent history of colonial India, and appeared over and over again throughout the non-Western world as soon as there was a body of educated non-Western clergymen and Christian professional women. He was attempting to negotiate his way among conflicting master narratives, and the result was a set of mixed messages about the relationship between religion and imperial power. Later in the century, the Rev. Wadhawa Mall addressed the annual meeting of the Punjab Church Council, another contact zone created for the purposes of allowing

Western and non-Western Christians to speak to each other. He observed: "Not only the Gospel but English ways and wealth have come with them into this country. Thus we have two gospels here; that of our Lord Jesus Christ, and that of English customs. Now we are between two stones of a grinding mill. Christ's gospel and His Spirit in us press us on one side; on the other English civilization. Which shall we choose?" (Punjab CMS Native Church Council 1898, n.p.). In these words, Wadhawa Mall recognizes the prison of vast undiscriminating categories that defined the competing master narratives of imperial history and providentialist Christian history. The question he posed would remain unanswerable without a fundamental challenge to the reified polarities of East versus West. He was speaking among friends, Western and non-Western, who were committed to the missionary fantasy of a multiracial Christian commonwealth, but he also confronted the realities of imperial power that were embodied in those personal relationships. The struggle to sustain those relationships became an imperial struggle, one acknowledged as such. For Forster, the central, humanist issue was friendship. For missionaries and non-Western Christians, there was even more at stake, for they were committed to spiritual relationships that transcended mere friendship.

The defamatory categories used to classify the non-Christian world in Victorian missionary literature can obscure the realities of personal encounter and ongoing conversations in the giant contact zone known as "the mission field." When building Christian institutions in a non-Western setting, missionaries and non-Western Christians alike discovered that master narratives clashed and messages became mixed. When the Rev. Samuel Azariah (later Bishop Azariah) traveled to Edinburgh in 1910 for the World Missionary Conference, he delivered a celebrated appeal to Western missionaries, after acknowledging the many benefits brought by Western educational and medical institutions: "We also ask for Love. Give us Friends!" (quoted in Williams 1994, 400). To a Western world only beginning to come to terms with anti-imperialism, he was bringing a conversation that had been going on in the non-Western world for decades in thousands of disparate settings.

Notes

1. I depend here on Allan Megill's essay, " 'Grand narrative' and the discipline of history," which classifies narratives as narrative, master narrative or grand narrative (Megill 1995). There are other ways to classify narratives, and other terms, that would serve the same purpose.
2. See, e.g., Jeff Guy's book on John William Colenso (1983) and Daniel O'Connor's on Charles Freer Andrews (1990), which represent two very good studies of liberal Protestant missionary heroes.

3. See, e.g., the work of Lamin O. Sanneh (1989, 1993). In fact, Norman Etherington was lamenting that missionaries were being left out of African church history as early as 1983.
4. The small Moravian church was an exception. See J. C. S. Mason (2001).
5. It seems that this neglect of missions by scholars of imperialism is about to change. A full volume on "Missions and Empire" edited by Norman Etherington is now in preparation for the New Oxford History of the British Empire.
6. In a celebrated essay, Homi K. Bhabha introduces the concept of hybridity as a means of dealing with interactions in what Pratt calls contact zones, but his attention is entirely on non-westerners, not on missionaries or the Indian Christians associated with them (Bhabha 1985).

CHAPTER TWO

INVENTING THE WORLD: TRANSNATIONALISM, TRANSMISSION, AND CHRISTIAN TEXTUALITIES

Isabel Hofmeyr

In a series of recent articles, Achille Mbembe points to the ways in which analyses, at once nativist and Marxist, have dominated the field of African Studies and outlines the intellectual legacies and consequences of these traditions of scholarship. As he makes clear, these paradigms have relied on a conception of subjectivity strongly tied to race, location, slavery, and other forms of colonial oppression. The consequence of such analyses is, first, to confer "on Africa a character so particular that it is not comparable with any other region of the world" (Mbembe 2001, 1), and second, to obscure an understanding of the continent's most significant contemporary developments, like war, epidemic, global crime networks, charismatic religion, and consumerism, which are transnational in character. Mbembe comments:

> Indeed, the "world" as a category of thought is one of the most impoverished concepts of African philosophical reflection. To a very large extent, the confinement of Africa to area studies and the inability of African criticism to think in terms of the "world" go together. (Mbembe 2001, 4)

Following Mbembe, I propose we understand missions in Africa as a site for inventing "the world."

Such an understanding of missions in Africa builds on and reconfigures two existing historiographical traditions of studying missions. The first of these traditions is the field that has grown up around understanding African Christianity (Maxwell 2001). This body of scholarship has in part defined itself against older nationalist forms of analyses, which have construed missions and Christianity as foreign imperial impositions and conversion as a regrettable form of "false consciousness." In opposition to these forms of explanation, much contemporary work on African Christianity understands it as a phenomenon spread primarily by Africans. Missionaries were, as one of their number put it, "too few, too expensive, too European, too shortlived" and the day-to-day business of evangelization was done by African evangelists (Miller 1948, 16). A second historiographical tradition comprises forms of analysis that situate missions as transnational phenomena, which impact as much on their "home" societies as on the societies to which they travel. In such analyses, missions become a critical factor in metropolitan politics and are deployed by a number of actors to advance their interests (Thorne 1999; Viswanathan 1989, 1998).

Both historiographical trajectories have been extremely important in deepening and sophisticating our understanding of missions. However, the two traditions are seldom brought into close alignment and articulation. Transnational studies of mission, perhaps best exemplified by Susan Thorne's excellent book, *Congregational Missions and the Making of an Imperial Culture in Nineteenth-Century England*, assert the importance of the "foreign" mission field for politics in the metropolis. But the "foreign" portion of the equation is generally understood as a remote and undifferentiated phenomenon, a broad backdrop against which political debates in the metropolis unfold. The precise intellectual activities, projects, and political struggles of African Christians in those "foreign" missions do not register as significant factors in this transnational equation. Studies of African Christianity, by contrast, tend to focus heavily on such local activities and projects. The transnational mission world is invoked, but again, as a remote off-stage presence. The metropolitan sites of mission and their internal struggles register as a factor that moulds African Christianity. They are less frequently considered as a dimension in how African Christians reckon and project themselves into an international arena. True, there is a considerable body of revisionist work on empire that has implemented the type of dialogical approach to mission studies suggested here. This scholarship rejects divisions of "home" and "abroad," "metropolis" and "colony," and seeks rather to understand empire as an unequal but intellectually integrated domain (Cooper and Stoler 1997; Prakash 1995; Stoler 1995). But this research has a tendency to over-focus on the metropolis and its colonial apparatus, too. As a recent commentator notes, "the emphasis is so strongly on internal tensions among the colonizers and their problems in boundary-maintenance vis-à-vis the colonized that the latter have a somewhat shadowy existence as actors" (Geschiere 2001, 168).

How, then, this chapter asks, might these two fields—transnational studies of mission and studies of African Christianity—be more productively configured?

How might we reimagine the mission field in such a way that the "chemistry" of African intellectual formations can be factored more meaningfully into transnational equations? Focusing on ideas of evangelical text and textuality produced in the Protestant mission domain, I argue that the conceptualization of religious texts produced in the mission world represents an "archive" of strategies for reading and interpretation from across the mission arena. Within this "archive," various intellectual agendas could be billeted, apparently supporting the same set of objectives, even if they were at times contradictory. Equally, textual strategies from elsewhere could be taken over to support or strengthen one's own hermeneutic procedure. The chapter explores these ideas in relation to two case studies: the first unfolds between Madagascar, England, and a broad international mission audience; the second is set between the Eastern Cape in present-day South Africa and a broad transnational tract-reading public. But before we turn to these case studies, let us begin our investigation with some stories about the working of perhaps the most classic nineteenth-century evangelical genre, namely, the tract. These short texts generally took the form of a single sheet or a small pamphlet suitable for popular distribution. As the stories below suggest, this was a form to which extraordinary powers were attributed.

Magical Textualities

In our first narrative, a man is given a tract that he tears up in a rage and throws down on the carpet, expecting that the servant will sweep it away. The next day, the torn scraps still lie on the carpet. The man summons the servant to enquire why the offending scraps have not been removed. She explains that she saw the word "ETERNAL" written on one of the pieces of paper and felt afraid to sweep it away. The man sticks the pieces of torn paper together, reads the tract, and is converted (Watts 1934, 8). In this story, the tract itself is an object capable of exerting extraordinary force and influence in the world. Even when shredded, the tract functions like a mesmerizing billboard that transfixes those who encounter it. The tract appears to have powers of remote control that capture all who come within its range. This idea is endlessly enacted in narratives that tell of tracts cast aside in hedges, in holes in the wall, in coal grates, or left in pockets of laundry, or on park benches, ensnaring passersby who chance upon them (Watts 1934, 13).

Tellingly, this power of the tract can be writ on a much larger scale. Consider, for example, two accounts of how major events in world history are precipitated by tracts. In the first account, Admiral Gaspard de Coligny, leader of the Protestant Reformation in France, is converted by a tract that was placed on the coverlet of his hospital bed. A nurse also reads it and passes it on to a "Lady

Abbess," who subsequently flees to Holland, there to influence the man who becomes her husband, namely William of Orange. One tract precipitates extraordinary consequences in world history, notably the Protestant Reformation in France, while implicitly securing Protestantism in England, since it is the descendant of William of Orange who will lead the "Glorious Revolution" of 1688 (Watts 1934, 3). The second account of a tract's cosmic capabilities concerns the seventeenth-century Puritan, Richard Baxter, who encounters a tract, *The Bruised Reed* (1630), by Richard Sibbes, which influences him to write a devotional classic, *The Saints' Everlasting Rest* (1650). This book in turn converts Philip Doddridge, who writes *Rise and Progress of the Religion of the Soul* (1745). William Wilberforce encounters this last text, is converted by it, and is moved to write his celebrated *Practical View of the Prevailing Religious System of Professed Christians* (1797), which in turn influences Leigh Richmond, who authors *The Dairyman's Daughter* (1811), a successful tract subsequently translated into more than fifty languages (Watts 1934, 3–4). In short, these parables convey a sense of texts invested with quite extraordinary powers of possession and enchantment, exercising a knock-on effect across centuries and shaping major developments in world history. The text itself appears to possess an authority through which it compels dramatic conversions and events across time and space.

At some level, of course, this theory of textuality is recognizably evangelical. As the numerous studies of the phenomenon indicate, it stresses the centrality of powerful conversion and religion as an emotional experience (Bebbington 1982, 1989; Thorne 1999; Viswanathan 1989, 1998). Texts, and education more generally, are seen to play an important part in conversion and religious experience, and texts are seminal agents for precipitating and sustaining belief. That said, the political, social, and religious aspects of evangelicalism have been extensively studied, but its theories of textuality have attracted less attention. Where they have been studied, their provenance has been attributed to a layering of literary influence. This archive includes the literary forms of dissent and nonconformity (Cutt 1979); a late eighteenth-century use and "colonization" of popular forms of storytelling like the chapbook and ballad (Pedersen 1986); and the techniques of the sentimental novel (Cutt 1979; Gilmont 1999). As one commentator notes:

> Rooted in *The Pilgrim's Progress*, the Puritan sermon and the writings of Dr Watts, [the tract] drew its theories of education from those of the Wesleys, Mrs Trimner and Hannah More, and its calculated appeal to the emotions from Richardson and the novel of sentiment. (Cutt 1979, 183)

Such explanations are of course illuminating in suggesting the broad contours of how evangelical literary genres are shaped. Their focus, however, is exclusively on

England, despite the fact that any evangelical genre is explicitly transnational, since it is intended to speak to all Protestant or would-be Protestants across the globe. That tracts were intended for global broadcast is apparent from even a cursory look at the history of tract organizations. An historian of the Religious Tract Society (RTS), the major Nonconformist organization for tract production and distribution "at home" and abroad, comments, "the impulse which drove [the RTS] to give the Christian gospel . . . to the heathen in distant lands drove them also to take counsel together about the heathen at home" (Hewitt 1949, 17). Like other evangelical genres, the tract, then, is imagined as transnational in its address, intended for distribution across a vast domain, often in several languages. The question that thus arises—and the key issue for our purposes—is: What do this broader distribution and reception mean for the genre and how it is understood? As we shall see, the way in which religious texts were interpreted and received overseas played a role in how they came to be defined and understood as evangelical instruments, and at least some of the powers attributed to evangelical literary genres, and hence the ways in which they are conceptualized and imagined, derive from their circulation and reception in "foreign" mission fields.

Charms of Life: Evangelical Texts in Madagascar

Let us turn to our first case study. The efforts of the London Missionary Society (LMS) to establish a mission in Madagascar in the 1820s are well known (Gow 1979; Larson 1997). Invited in 1829 by Radama, king of the Merina court, the LMS missionaries were brought in with a view to acquiring their skills for the expanding kingdom. These skills included Roman literacy (Arabic literacy existed in small pockets in Madagascar), technological capacity, and bureaucratic know-how. The king, however, died in 1828. The new monarch, Queen Ranavalona switched strategy. She ordered the missionaries off the island and turned on the converts, ordering punishment for anyone who had taken up the new religion (Gow 1979, 1–38; Larson 1997).

This saga of persecution, which evoked the missionaries' own inheritance of hounded dissent, was extensively propagated in LMS and evangelical mission publicity. Books and pamphlets, many carrying lurid illustrations of martyrdom, poured from mission presses, exemplified in heroic titles like *A Narrative of the Persecution of Christians in Madagascar with Details of the Escape of the Six Christian Refugees Now in England* (1840), by Joseph John Freeman and David Johns, and William Ellis's *Faithful unto Death: The Story of the Founding and Preservation of the Martyr Church of Madagascar* (1876; see also Ellis 1838, 1870). These accounts soon migrated into the mainstream of the LMS's historiography and appeared almost *de rigueur* in its subsequent histories, annual reports, pamphlets, tracts, books, plays, and pageants.[1] Traveling "road shows" of converts who had managed to flee Madagascar attracted excited British crowds (Budden 1923, 46–47; Ellis 1876, 122).

One sub-theme of this bigger picture concerned John Bunyan's *The Pilgrim's Progress*, which had played a part in the sensational story of the persecution. In the 1830s, Madagascar was one of the first African sites for the translation and distribution of this key text of Protestant evangelical mission work, which had been distributed in Britain and elsewhere in abridged form as a tract since the 1820s (Anderson 1991, 34). As a—if not *the*—key text of dissent and nonconformity, Bunyan's story was close to the heart of Nonconformist evangelical missionaries and was propagated wherever they went (Hofmeyr 2004). Virtually as he was about to flee Madagascar, one of the missionaries, David Johns, wrote out a Malagasy translation by hand of part of *The Pilgrim's Progress*. The Malagasy Christians then transcribed between six and eight copies, and these were circulated amongst the embattled community of converts (Ellis 1838, 516; 1870, 107; 1876, 93; Freeman and Johns 1840, 148). Bunyan's story soon gained currency amongst the Malagasy Christians and sections were often referred to and invoked by the converts as an analogue for their own suffering (Freeman and Johns 1840, 166, 167, 169, 231, 253, 256, 257, 259, 264, 273; LMS, Madagascar, Incoming Correspondence). Funds were raised in Britain for further printings of the Malagasy translation, which were produced as small, and hence easily concealed volumes, in some cases bound together with sections of the Bible.

It did not take long for these stories of Bunyan's miraculous powers to percolate into the Nonconformist world, and stories of the Malagasy translation of *The Pilgrim's Progress* were endlessly broadcast in evangelical mission publicity (Green 1899, 63; Hewitt 1949, 44). These stories included accounts of the fragile manuscript copies being passed lovingly from hand to hand; of Christians on the eve of their execution, citing sections from *The Pilgrim's Progress*; of the small printed copies being surreptitiously passed around (Brown 1900, 470; Ellis 1838, 516; 1870, 107; 1876, 93; Freeman and Johns 1840, 165). Such stories chimed in well with Nonconformist attitudes to *The Pilgrim's Progress*, seen by many to be as important as the Bible and possessed of equally miraculous power. The text's astonishing potency was further evinced in the fact that it could pass with apparent effortlessness across the barriers of language, race, and culture, to be received readily by the Malagasy converts. This idea was to become a staple trope for discussing Bunyan's power in the mission domain. George Offor (1787–1864), an early Bunyan editor and dissenter of the old school, noted in an introduction to Bunyan's collected works,

> *The Pilgrim* has been translated into most of the languages and dialects of the world. The Caffrarian and Hottentot, the enlightened Greek and Hindoo, the remnant of the Hebrew race, the savage Malay and the voluptuous Chinese—all have the wondrous narrative in their own languages. (Offor n.d. (a), lvii)

Another commentator, talking at the unveiling of Bunyan's statue in his hometown, Bedford, in 1874 expressed a similar sentiment:

> Travel whether you choose, along the stream of the Ganges—through the rich groves of Ceylon—by the sparkling shores of Polynesia—or underneath broad-leaved bananas of New Zealand, you shall meet thousands who rejoice and tremble over the vicissitudes of "Christian." The African chief who throws aside his spear, joined the group of Christian listeners, and obtained his first glimpse of redeeming love through the veil of the parable; while in Madagascan forest the persecuted flock of God, by pondering it in the manuscript volume which they had written in their own hands, have fitted their souls for the steel, the poison, the precipice, and the martyr's crown! (Birrell 1874, 108)

This idea was frequently re-iterated in discussions of *The Pilgrim's Progress* (Offor 1847, cxlvi; Punshon 1882, 69; Williams 1888, 66). At times, it was expressed via the metaphor of "the pilgrim" assuming different "disguises," the more effectively to travel into far-flung societies. When completing the Tswana translation of Bunyan in 1837, Robert Moffat observed, "I am at the present moment dressing Bunyan's Pilgrim in a Sichuana [Tswana] garb, and if he does not travel this land through and through I shall be much mistaken" (Religious Tract Society 1846, 37).

Of course, the notion of a miraculous text that traveled across language, race, and culture to "seize" its new readers conforms to evangelical notions of textuality, in which texts are endowed with astonishing power and authority. But to explain Bunyan's "successes" in Madagascar in this way is to consider only part of the story. What did Malagasy Christians make of the text and did this play any part in how the book came to be understood? Piers Larson's recent account of the reception of LMS evangelism in Madagascar provides us with some answers. In his analysis of how Christianity in the island was vernacularized by its recipients, he demonstrates how the ideas and practices of nonconformity were reshaped by existing ideas and intellectual frameworks. Central to his analysis is the idea that mission tracts and books, in keeping with extant sacred practice, became treated as protective objects and charms. As Larson notes, this practice appears the most credible way of explaining the quite disproportionate desire for reading matter amongst converts, many of whom were not fully literate. By the early 1830s, the LMS press in the capital, Antananarivo, was producing 20,000 items per year for a "reading" population of at most 5,000. This understanding of documents as protective objects brushed off on missionaries, too, who gained a renewed understanding of scriptures as a "charm of life" (Larson 1997, 994). The persecuted converts' adoption of *The Pilgrim's Progress* as a charm and guide must similarly have given missionaries, and the audiences to whom these stories were relayed, a revitalized grasp of the book's extraordinary powers. Part of this perception hinged on the apparent power of the book to cross the barriers of language, race, and culture. This perception in turn was enabled by the Malagasy understandings of documents as talismans, a set of interpretive practices that accounts for the spectacular popularity of printed texts in Madagascar.

One way then to think about the Malagasy case is that its mission depictions are contingently inflected by Malagasy understandings of documents as protective charms or "fetishes." Such representations of the text "far away" rebound back on the text "at home," and resonate with evangelical audiences who themselves hold premodern theories of textuality and texts, which are capable of "seizing" and utterly transforming readers. For further evidence of such "magical" practices, one need only look at the inscriptions and introductions to British editions of *The Pilgrim's Progress,* urging readers not only to read, but also to act.[2] Ideal readers are hence those who position themselves in such a way that the text compels them. The text is consequently something that, fetish-like, moves its readers to particular forms of action in the world. Offor, in one of his numerous introductions to *The Pilgrim's Progress,* comments: "It seizes us in childhood with the strong hand of its power, our manhood surrenders to the spell of its sweet sorcery. . . . There was never a power which so thoroughly possessed our hearts. . . ." (Offor n.d., 5).

As Susan Thorne has indicated, Nonconformists at home were quick to seize the opportunity of using the fashionable, exotic, and glamorous foreign mission endeavor as a political card to enhance their own standing, and hence redress the political disabilities they faced "at home." Their use of mission translations of *The Pilgrim's Progress* conforms to this pattern (Hofmeyr 2002). As one of their key cultural possessions and a text that articulated their theology and social outlook, *The Pilgrim's Progress* was dear to the hearts of all Nonconformists. However, it was a book regarded with disdain, contempt, or indifference by the Established church and the social classes aligned with it. By energetically advertising the book's appeal to thousands in the mission domain, Nonconformists at home could add value to their most beloved text and underline the apparently universal appeal of their views and values. While such a view does much to widen and internationalize the parameters within which a text like *The Pilgrim's Progress* is seen, it cedes little explanatory value to the "foreign" intellectual formations within which the text is taken up. The case study presented here has suggested some of the ways in which one might begin such a process of factoring in such intellectual activity. As this study has demonstrated in relation to Madagascar, evangelical forms of reading, of which *The Pilgrim's Progress* was often an exemplar, were shaped both by Nonconformist notions of inspired textual agency and by Malagasy perceptions of texts as containing talismanic or charm-like powers. This convergence in turn promoted an apparently shared set of understandings around the book as a magical object. In this terrain, differing agendas and ideas could be pursued, whilst still apparently conforming to the same set of objectives. Likewise, forms of interpretation, like the Malagasy view of texts as a "charm of life," could be used to buttress and enhance Nonconformist hermeneutic procedures. As Rafael has indicated in the case of seventeenth-century Jesuit–Tagalog interactions, mission activity often produces such zones of strategic misreading, in which competing spiritual and intellectual understandings must be managed. In the case of Malagasy–Nonconformist interaction, one jointly created intellectual category for such management cohered around the idea of the text as a magical object. This category in turn could absorb and contain competing and at times contradictory spiritual orders of explanation.

The Malagasy case, which involved the first mission translation of *The Pilgrim's Progress* in Africa, in turn came to have wider ramifications. Its widely publicized success as a mission tract exemplified the power of Bunyan's text, and possibly acted as a further incentive, if one was required, for further mission translations. These translations, of which there were ultimately to be 80 in Africa, in turn underlined the text's "miraculous" ability to cross the barriers of language, race, and culture with apparent ease. Together, these mission translations, publicized in a variety of forums, particularly missionary exhibitions, generated the notion of *The Pilgrim's Progress* as a "universal" story (Hofmeyr 2002, 99–101). This idea of a text holding universal appeal, which was subsequently absorbed from Nonconformist thinking into the emerging academic discipline of English Literature (Hofmeyr 2002), emerges from the contingencies of the mission domain, in which a variety of intellectual traditions play a part in creating a form of reading and interpretation that is transnational in its orientation.

Internationalizing the Tract: John Knox Bokwe and Ntsikana

Let us turn to consider our second example of such transnationally made ways of reading and interpretation in the mission domain. The backdrop is Southern Africa, and the precise setting is the Eastern Cape, home of one of the oldest missions in the subcontinent, namely the Scottish Presbyterian Lovedale Missionary Institute, established in the 1820s. Our protagonist is an alumnus of this "ivy league" institution, John Knox Bokwe (1855–1922), remembered today as a composer and hymn writer. He was also a writer, and we consider here a tract that he produced, entitled *Ntsikana: The Story of an African Hymn* (n.d.). *Ntsikana* tells of a noted Xhosa prophet and hymn writer, and by some accounts, the first Xhosa to adopt aspects of Christian belief. In this analysis, we demonstrate how Bokwe uses the tract form as a way of projecting an élite version of African Christianity into an international domain, a move that allows him to "speak" over and around both the white-dominated mission establishment and the colonial state. In undertaking this examination, we analyze how Bokwe utilizes the tract's capacity for international address by making it a "hinge" by means of which he might articulate different spiritual traditions and insert African Christianity into an international narrative.

With its octavo format and 30-odd pages, the tract itself is small. But it does come encased by a series of paratexts that attempt to organize readers' expectations and to provide them with a way in which to receive and interpret the text. As these paratexts provide insight into how this field of expectation and reading is internationally organized, they are worth considering in some detail. To begin with, the cover of the booklet gives the title and author, and indicates that the tract is "sold at the Bookroom, Lovedale, South Africa," at a price of 4d. Over the page, however, we gather that the tract itself is published by the International Bible Reading Association (IBRA), and the frontispiece provides a full-page picture of its offices at 56 Old Bailey, London. After this image, there follows a short introduction on the IBRA, written by its Honorary Secretary, Charles Waters. It tells us that the IBRA promotes daily reading of the Bible "and makes such reading profitable and interesting by the association of the daily portions with a weekly topic." This topic in turn forms the subject of the International Sunday School Lesson for the following Sunday. This method of reading "secures for the Bible a place in every-day life, interests parents in the Sunday School teaching, and is equally helpful to others not connected with the Sunday School." The membership subscription, "if connected with a Branch using English cards," is one penny annually. A Branch comprises at least ten members, and the Branch secretary conducts correspondence, issues cards and monthly hints, and keeps a register of members. Each member gets a "pretty Card of Membership, monthly leaflets containing shorts hints on each day's reading, and quarterly illustrated circular letters." English cards "have been issued to more than 600,000 members in all quarters of the world, and have been translated into twenty other languages, including Kaffir."[3] Cards, we are told, are given only to those who "read the daily portions regularly." The monthly hints and circular letters are issued in English only. A Cape Town name and address is given for those seeking English cards. "Kaffir cards (membership subscription $1\frac{1}{2}$d) may be had of Mr. J Knox Bokwe, Lovedale."

This prefatory piece is then followed by an Introduction, again by Charles Waters. He tells us that the tract was written at his request and first appeared in *The IBRA Messenger*. "Through this channel it has been read by members of the International Bible Reading Association in all quarters of the world." Waters mentions that he had met Bokwe during the latter's visit to England in 1892, and "was much pleased with his ready and intelligent grasp of the subjects discussed, and his eagerness to adopt any plan promising to be of benefit to his fellow countrymen." Bokwe was keen to spread the IBRA method of Bible reading, and "with his prompt and effective help Kaffir cards were printed and issued early in 1893." Bokwe has continued to act as Secretary for his Branch, and "has had the pleasure of seeing his work increasing and proving helpful in Sunday School work, and to those who have been brought under its influence." Waters concludes: "I very cordially commend this little narrative, and have no doubt it will prove as interesting to others as it has already done to many in England and elsewhere. I look upon it also as a proof of the valuable work done at the Lovedale Mission, with which Mr. Bokwe has been so long associated."

What these paratexts do is announce that the tract one is about to encounter forms part of an elaborate field of internationally organized reading. The cover tells us that the book is sold at Lovedale but, we soon learn, it has been published in London as part of the IBRA. This organization coordinates a field of simultaneous and international reading, which traverses different languages. Through this network, members will read the same thing on the same day, and follow a similar theme that will be explored in Sunday School. Entire social networks, like families, for example, will hence be keyed into the daily and weekly reading activities. One's reading will also be organized by similar bureaucratic procedures involving membership cards, registers, and periodic circulars. By subscribing to the IBRA, one announces oneself as part of an international textual web in which one is part of a broad Protestant confederacy of apparently equal readers. Yet, as the introduction makes clear, this confederacy is also controlled by relations of power and patronage. Charles Waters is the one who invites authors to write, makes suggestions, and endorses their efforts, often in condescending tones, as the above excerpts indicate.

By the time we reach the body of the pamphlet, it is clear that Bokwe is a key node in this international web of reading, a point reiterated in his byline, which appears again on the first page of the story itself: "By J. K. Bokwe, IBRA Kaffir Secretary" (Bokwe n.d., 7). This byline provides a useful entry point into the text, since it summarizes Bokwe's chosen position as a node in a crosslinguistic and international network of shared reading and textual organization. In this capacity, he coordinates a set of biblical texts, translating and disseminating them among new Xhosa audiences in the Eastern Cape. This method of working is broadly reproduced in the tract itself, where Bokwe likewise "co-ordinates" a set of texts and re-broadcasts these to a new international audience. The "texts" he draws together in the tract are diverse and include mission ethnography, *The Pilgrim's Progress*, Xhosa praise poetry, and the nineteenth-century South African novel, *The Story of an African Farm* (1883), by Bokwe's celebrated contemporary, Olive Schreiner.

Mission ethnography is the first of the texts that Bokwe deploys, and the opening section of the narrative provides us with an ethnographic account of a Xhosa-grouping, the Gaika (Nqgika in current orthography). Bokwe's descriptions tell us of their customs, beliefs, architecture, styles of personal adornment, and "primitive" forms of belief in God and superstitious belief in witchcraft (Bokwe n.d., 6–12). His descriptions are interspersed with pictures illustrating some of these practices, for example, "Gaika Kaffir Women, painted in their heathen clay," and "Painted Heathen Kaffirs, in full ornamental dress" (Bokwe n.d., 10, 16). In his descriptions, Bokwe employs a standard feature of mission ethnography, namely a stark before-and-after story; the "before" scenario depicts a heathen state of affairs, the "after" a desired, but yet-to-be fully realized Christian order.[4] In this regard, Bokwe draws certain clear distinctions between "heathen" and convert. One of these distinctions concerns the use of clay for personal and ritual adornment, a practice that in both the text and its accompanying images signifies heathenness. Washing off the clay, a practice instituted by the protagonist Ntsikana, will come to betoken conversion. Likewise, the practices of witchcraft are held up as evidence of superstitious belief that needs to be eradicated and supplanted by Christianity.

However, Bokwe's ethnography does not conform in all respects to standard mission ethnographies, and there are several complicating factors. One of these factors emerges as he concludes the introductory ethnographic section: "Such was the state of this African tribe, typical also of other tribes, before the truths of the Gospel penetrated the land. The story of 'Ntsikana' forms a connecting link between the days of utter darkness, such as I have described, and the now apparent marks of civilization" (Bokwe n.d., 12). Rather than a straightforward before-and-after picture, Bokwe complicates this periodization by inserting Ntsikana as an interregnum into the story. We now have a beginning, middle, and end: the beginning is heathen; the middle is led by an African prophet; and the ending characterized by "civilization" and its "marks." Significantly, Bokwe sets out what he considers this civilization to be:

> The Sunday School Union has, since 1893, generously helped the spread of the Gospel in South Africa by printing the IBRA cards in the Kafir language. These are now penetrating into hundreds of homes, and the daily readings are being found very helpful. The Biblical passages are being read with more interest, and a knowledge of the Gospel truth is thus being gained by the people. In the days of Ntsikana such advantages did not exist.

> No missionaries had settled in the country, and it was the falling of only one precious seed from a stray traveler which took root in Ntsikana's heart. The ever-careful Husbandman tended it, and fruit has been reaped abundantly. (Bokwe n.d., 12–13)

The teleological ending toward which the narrative drives is not one of glorious mission triumph, but rather an order of IBRA-led scripture readings in which Bokwe plays a leading part. The line of development in the story is hence one that passes from Ntsikana to Bokwe; both are hymn writers and both receive and disseminate the seed of the word, whether orally or in print. Bokwe is the person who passes on the baton of Ntsikana's story and the one who forms a living link with him. At one point in the narrative, Bokwe mentions a large shady tree under which Ntsikana preached. Bokwe himself has visited this spot, pointed out to him by an "aged informant" who was one of Ntsikana's followers. Bokwe likewise makes Ntsikana's hymn known to a wider audience by including his own English translation and arrangement of it in tonic solfa notation at the end of the booklet. In this way, Bokwe positions himself in an informal line of "apostolic succession" that starts with Ntsikana and then stretches forward via his followers to Bokwe, and thence into the lineage of African Christianity in the Eastern Cape. This lineage in turn is interpellated via Bokwe into the transnational realms of Protestantism.

What the remainder of the narrative makes clear is that Ntsikana is in fact the major agent for spreading Christianity amongst the Xhosa. European missionaries feature, but only in walk-on parts. Johannes van der Kemp, the LMS missionary who arrived in 1799, is referred to as a "traveler" from whose preaching Ntsikana first hears the gospel. Indeed, in some subsequent versions, Ntsikana receives the message directly from God with white missionaries playing no role at all (Hodgson 1980). In foregrounding Ntsikana in this way, Bokwe realigns the mission narrative as one directed by Africans. This stress on African Christianity is also apparent in the tract's emphasis on the hymn, signaled in the subtitle: "The Story of an African Hymn." This formulation consciously invokes Schreiner's novel, *The Story of an African Farm* (1883), perhaps as a familiar point of reference for a British audience, perhaps as an indication that unlike Schreiner's novel, which is about a loss of faith, Bokwe's narrative is about the increase of faith. Whatever the intention, the invocation does remind us of the international audience to which Bokwe orients his text.

At this point, another issue arises. In speaking to this international audience, it is the hymn form that Bokwe chooses to highlight. Why? One possible answer is that the hymn proved not only to be an extremely popular form amongst African Christians, it was also one area in which Africans could win some space to compose and write in a white-dominated mission world. Indeed, many of the subcontinent's most enduring hymns, like those of Ntsikana, have been

African-composed.[5] In southern Africa, this popularity can be further seen in the figures for mission book sales, which were usually topped by hymnals. What is more, the hymnals were generally bought voluntarily, unlike other consistent sellers, namely bibles or school textbooks (Hofmeyr 2001, 103). By highlighting Ntsikana's hymn, Bokwe foregrounds a major cultural form of African Christianity. In addition, privileging the hymn form sidelines other genres of African Christianity to which Bokwe's élite Christianity had a more ambiguous relationship. The most notable of these forms is prophecy. Ntsikana is renowned as a prophet, and sections of Bokwe's text are taken up narrating his prophecies.

One of these prophecies concerns "the land being taken from the Gaikas and divided out to white men, and cut up into roads" (Bokwe n.d., 22–23). Bokwe provides an account of this prophecy in direct speech:

> A time is coming when you will see people whom you have never seen before. Be careful of these people; do not receive them to dwell among you, but let them pass unmolested. If you receive them they will raise the dust off their feet and leave it lying on you, that is if you do not accept this word. I see this country white with waggon roads. I see flocks of sheep grazing on it. I see this land studded with white houses. There are witnesses who will bear me record; but beware of strange doctrine—it will mislead many. (Bokwe n.d., 23)

Another prophecy, again in direct speech, runs as follows:

> To show that sin will have increased in the world, there will smoke even a child. I see the plumes of the Gaikas waving on the borders of the Kei. I see the forests full of roads, and the trees split into splinters or planks. In the distance there comes a great war of races, which will cause men to wade almost knee-deep in blood. There will be fighting and fighting, and then a time of respite in which there will be friendly giving of tobacco to each other. Then at last there will be a general rising, in which a mother will quarrel with her own daughter; the son will rise against his father, and friend against friend. Men will stab each other's shoulders, and there will be such crossing and re-crossing as can only be likened to ants gathering stalks of dried grass. Then the end will come—the beginning of peace, for which there had been no preconcerted council or arrangement of man. The reign of BROAD-BREAST (*Sifuba-Sibanzi*) will commence and continue in the lasting peace of the Son of Man. (Bokwe n.d., 24–25)

Bokwe adds the following note to the prophecy: "The name of Broad-Breast for the Saviour may be compared to Bunyan's Great-Heart," the latter being the knight-at-arms who in the second part of *The Pilgrim's Progress* conducts the heroine, Christiana, and her party safely to heaven, where her husband Christian awaits her. As with the invocation of Schreiner, Bokwe pulls different texts into alignment, asking us here to place and hence compare the folkloric dimensions of Bunyan alongside those of Xhosa prophecy.

Hodgson notes that Ntsikana is remembered today primarily in his role of prophet, but that in his depiction, Bokwe presents these prophecies as ambiguous, enigmatic, and difficult to decode and follow (Hodgson 1980, 24). In some senses, of course, the prophecies have strategic use, in that Bokwe can provide a critique of the violence underpinning the colonial order by placing these words in Ntsikana's mouth. At the same time, though, Bokwe does not endorse such prophecies with the same degree of enthusiasm as he does the hymn. Prophecy was and is a major feature of African Christianity, particularly of its more demotic strains. But Bokwe speaks from a much more élite tradition of African Christianity, and this subject-position may help explain his arm's-length approach to prophecy, which he holds in suspicion as a manifestation of "primitive" Christianity, in every sense of the phrase.

Bokwe, then, makes the tract deliver on its international claims by turning into an international reading field. Not only is this turn signaled in the protagonist and theme of the book, but also by the method suggested by his ideal, implied reader. Such a reader is one who compares and contrasts texts. This reader must compare *The Story of an African Farm* to *The Story of an African Hymn*, liken Bunyan's Great-Heart to Ntsikana's *Sifuba-Sibanzi*, and so on. In asking his reader to undertake such work, Bokwe illustrates an important international reading principle, namely that to read internationally is to undertake tasks of comparison. As Brigit Meyer reminds us, African converts often of necessity had to compare religious systems, particularly when it came to questions of translation (Meyer 1999, 82). Bokwe, as an African Christian and as a translator himself, would no doubt have been acutely aware of the requirements of such incessant comparative work. The ideal reader of Bokwe's pamphlet is likewise called upon to undertake these comparative labors. The tract then implies that such comparative work is the ideal reading mode of all Protestants, since they are involved in an international religion into which numerous different traditions flow.

Of course, it might be countered that such an arena of comparison can never exist, given the racist and evolutionist bias of mission Christianity, in which non-European societies are coded as "primitive" and belated versions of "developed" nations. In such a framework, comparison can only ever be a reinforcement of an existing inequality, as different traditions must necessarily be structured in relations of racialized dominance. Not surprisingly, parts of Bokwe's booklet do conform to this template. His use of mission ethnography, for example, invites us to contemplate "heathen" society from a "modern" vantage point that renders the former "primitive." Ntsikana's prophecy is likewise read as an "early" manifestation of a later and more "proper" Christianity. In some views, then, Bokwe's tract can be no more than a performance of African primitivity and belatedness for a metropolitan audience.

At the same time, however, Bokwe's tract is susceptible to a more complex reading, too. One route into such a reading is to pay close attention to the types of juxtapositions that he sets up. These comparisons, we notice, do not always involve contrasts between "advanced" and "primitive" societies. Instead, Bokwe complicates the time and space of such comparative maps. By comparing Schreiner with Ntsikana—and also implicitly, therefore, with himself—he contrasts a series of southern African voices and asks what their similarities and differences might mean in opposition to a view of the world rooted in metropolitan definitions. By invoking Bunyan, Bokwe also blurs the vectors of mission imperialism: where does one place a prophetic ancestor of evangelical Nonconformist—and Presbyterian—missionaries? Could Ntsikana be their Bunyan; and Bunyan the Xhosa Ntsikana? In this way, Bokwe creates a confederacy of Protestant readers who are expected to think "outside the box" of social Darwinism and evolutionism. Just as he functions as IBRA secretary, "collating" and distributing texts with a view to establish a shared field of reading, in his tract, Bokwe does the same in relation to a novel "library" of texts that he aligns in a strategic manner. In so doing, Bokwe strives to establish a transnational field of reading in which a variety of forms can take their place, be they Xhosa praise poetry, biography, mission ethnography, or Bunyan's *The Pilgrim's Progress*. At the same time, though, as "secretary" of this textual universe, he can also align and distribute his "texts" strategically, so that he can present his élite version of Christianity as representing all African Christianity. Finally, Bokwe achieves all of this intellectual work through the genre of the tract, which he turns into a "screen" for international projection. Rather like the Latin American theorists whom Kraniauskas discusses, Bokwe "take[s] charge of the intersection of different historical temporalities and attempt[s] to elaborate a global project with them" (quoted in Kraniauskas 2000, 126).

Conclusion

Both of the case studies presented here illuminate the complexity of the mission "archive," understood as a textual zone, stretched across time and space. As this chapter has attempted to demonstrate, this transnationally made "archive" opened up novel possibilities for international addressivity, which allowed people to think, read, and write *as if* they were addressing a vast international Protestant public, even if in reality they only reached a limited actual or potential audience. The zone offered different groups—Nonconformists in England, new converts in Madagascar, the African élite in the Eastern Cape—an opportunity to project their micro-politics into an international arena, often over or around their own local states. This international projection in turn meant that their texts utilized the international resources of the mission arena in different ways. Evangelical Protestants could use Malagasy forms of reading and interpretation to strengthen their own hermeneutic procedures, while John Knox Bokwe could draw on the genre of the tract in order to "amplify" his account of African Christianity in the Eastern Cape. Each of these strategies in effect drew on textual and interpretive resources from elsewhere to make a virtue of local necessities. Conceptualizing the textual arena of the mission domain in this manner enables us to configure its intellectual formations in more interesting ways. Rather than reading African Christianity either in largely local terms or as a remote backdrop to the workings of metropolitan missions, we can insert its intellectual projects more meaningfully into a global arena and so, "world" it in the way that Mbembe suggests.

Notes

1. See, e.g., the writings of Anthony (n.d.), Griffiths (1920), Ridgwell (1921), and Patten and Shillito (1935).
2. Inscriptions in the following editions of *The Pilgrim's Progress* in the Bunyan Collection, Bedford Library, Bedford: item 22621 (1823); item 22738 (1776); item 33801(n.d.); tear-out post-card edition, item 56699 (n.d.[a]).
3. A nineteenth-century term for Xhosa, the predominant language of the Eastern Cape, "Kaffir" has since become an epithet of extreme racial abuse. At the time that Bokwe wrote, its connotations were different and as used here, it refers to the language, Xhosa.
4. Or as a Scottish missionary said in a different context: "Let me remind you that there are two Manchurias, two Old Calabars, two Jamaicas, two Grand Caymans. There is the one you will find when you land there, and the other which you labour to realize" (United Presbyterian Church 1890, 284).
5. See also Sandilands (1955), Phiri (1975, 24–25), and Muller (1999, 88–119).

CHAPTER THREE

THE MISSIONARY WRITING MACHINE IN NINETEENTH-CENTURY KWAZULU-NATAL

Norman Etherington

Nicholas Thomas has called attention to the way the power of the colonial state "turned upon inscription, upon the absorption of events into a prodigiously dispersed writing machine" (Thomas 1994, 111). Missionary societies also functioned as writing machines, but for different reasons and with different results. They generated mountains of inscribed paper that make the work of historians difficult even in regions where only a single society was at work. There is simply too much to read. A great deal of this output was designed to raise the spirits and loosen the purse strings of supporters at home. Other papers reflect concern at headquarters to make their agents accountable. But by far the greatest outpouring of the missionary writing machine aimed to change, and after a fashion, to empower the objects of their attention: "converts from the heathen." This chapter surveys many different forms of writing in one of the most heavily missionized regions on earth. It deals not only with the role of language in the colonization of African souls, but also with the material paraphernalia that marked the evangelical enterprise as distinctively as the colonial state was marked by the pass, the police register, and the tax collector's receipt book. Missions to Natal and the Zulu Kingdom began in the 1830s at a time when disease still made most parts of Africa inaccessible to European preachers. The absence of the most deadly fevers and the presence of hundreds of thousands of unconverted people attracted missionaries from Germany, Scandinavia, France, Britain, and the United States.

In the beginning was, of course, the word. There was also the costume, the picture, and the song. Allen Gardiner, a British ex-naval officer turned freelance missionary, presented himself in full dress uniform at the court of Dingane, the Zulu king, in 1835. He launched his pioneer mission with a demonstration of the magical properties of writing. While Gardiner stood outside, his interpreter took notes as various articles were secreted in the royal enclosure. With the paper as his guide, the missionary plucked one after another from their hiding places. Using pictures in a book, Gardiner showed the king London buildings, women's fashions, and the English court. When the subject of singing came up it was the missionary's turn to be amazed that last year's songs were scorned in favor of new compositions, many of the king's own devising. Missionaries would be the first to introduce hymns intended to be sung in precisely the same four-part harmony year after year. Gardiner topped off his performance by producing "The Book" that had made the British "a great people." It would, he promised, teach the Zulu "to know the words that they might become greater" (Gardiner 1836, 14, 32–33, 37, 39, 42–43, 52–53, 57, 67–68, 71, 77, 122, 127, 131–34, 151, 161–63, 169–71, 177–80, 213).

Hard on his heels came American Congregational missionaries, Methodists, Lutherans, Roman Catholics, and Anglicans, each with their own favored set of books, costumes, pictures, and songs. Unlike the colonial state, whose first care was to survey its dominion, the missionaries scrambled to turn Africans into readers. All the societies realized that the shortest route to that goal was to put books into local languages. That required hard decisions to be made about alphabets, spelling, and grammar. Apart from the Methodists, most of the missionaries had been trained in the scriptural languages of Hebrew, Greek, and Latin. Lewis Grout of the American mission measured the local language against these models and did not find it wanting. "So far as I have yet seen," wrote Grout, "the language of this people appears very simple and yet highly philosophical in its structure; & with the exception of a few clicks, it seems to be very mellefluent and euphonic. Both its euphony and precision is highly promoted by a striking characteristic of the language called the Euphonic or alliteral concord. In this respect I think it may be regarded as equal if not superior to the Greek language" (American Board of Commissioners for Foreign Missions [ABCFM], Grout to R. Anderson).

Working out the grammar was relatively easy for classically trained clergy. Deciding what to call the language was more difficult. Methodist missionaries in the Eastern Cape had called the people's language "Kaffir," the same name settlers gave to all the African farmers of that district. There was no sharp division between that language and the language spoken at the Zulu court. Rather, dialects spoken along the coast shaded into each other. For several years, the

Methodist missionaries of Natal tried to force upon their congregations books printed in "Kaffir"—the language of the various groups today known as Xhosa (Wesleyan Methodist Missionary Society [WMMS], Gaskin to the Secretaries). Other societies decided against experimenting with a common language, choosing instead to make a new grammar that they called "Zulu," after the name of the ruling lineage of the Zulu kingdom. Such apparently trivial linguistic decisions led in time to the much sharper division between Xhosa and Zulu that exists today.

How to write the language was another question. The English language had no characters for the clicks and several other sounds peculiar to Zulu. Grout believed that the only way the language could be correctly transcribed was to use the complex system devised by the German Egyptologist, Karl Richard Lepsius. His fellow missionaries rebelled when they realized its implications for printed texts. Andrew Abraham complained: "If dz is better than j then it would be an improvement to write Dzohn instead of John, or dzuddze for judge" (ABCFM, Abraham to Anderson). Rufus Anderson, Secretary of the American Board in Boston agreed:

> Mr. Grout's plan of a syllabic language strikes us very unfavorably. A syllabic alphabet is not necessary; it looks outlandish, and isolates the language & people, and I fear we should never be willing to get the type [fonts for printing]. There is no intelligent man, I presume, who knows anything about the matter, who does not regret that the Cherokees should have been carried by their national vanity into the use of Guess's syllabic alphabet. I hope the idea will be relinquished at once, and at any sacrifice. (ABCFM, Anderson to Zulu Mission)

The clincher was that the other missionary societies opposed the new alphabet; if the Americans went their own way, their converts would be writing a language that no one else could understand. The upshot was that the various societies agreed to use the English alphabet, reserving the consonants c, q, and x to represent clicks, and employing hl and ts to render other sounds common to the Zulu language.

Having made that decision, missionaries at once began to worry that by reading Zulu texts produced by their rivals their converts might fall into theological error. Bishop John W. Colenso, a theological and philological autodidact, created huge controversies with his choice of the word *Unkulunkulu* for God, and a few years later with his questioning of the literal truth of the first five books of the Old Testament.[1] Other missionaries eventually acquiesced in Colenso's choice for the awesome name of God, but some refused to use his other translations. One of his own clergy revolted when he discovered that the bishop's baptismal service "left out, not only the *saving of Noah* and his family and the passage through the Red Sea but even Our Lord's Baptism in the River

Jordan" (Society for the Propagation of the Gospel in Foreign Parts [SPG], Tönnesen to the Secretary; emphasis in the original). Colenso proved that he could give as good as he got when he pulled up the American missionaries on a Zulu expression used in one of their school texts:

> . . . as some sharp things were said against the Bishop, he would naturally be ready to embrace any occasion of speaking against the American Missionaries. Unfortunately, one little expression in this primer gave him such an occasion, & he was quick to see it. The expression is this, "*Utixo wa ti, Ma ba bujiswa.*" God said, Let them be destroyed. It occurs in the answer to this question, "How" (did Jesus by his death atone for our sins) Ans. "When all men were sinners, God said, Let them be destroyed. The son arose & said, Let them be saved, let me die in their stead." We must admit that this is an unhappy expression. Too much is understood. It represents God the Father as differing from the Son, and desiring the death of the sinner. Against such erroneous doctrine he [Colenso] warned his people. (ABCFM, Abraham to Anderson)

In another era, these would not have been minor quibbles but cause for religious warfare. However, the missionaries working in KwaZulu-Natal were conscious that their need for books and tracts in Zulu outweighed the risk of denominational heresy. More and more, they used each other's translations. Methodists bought elementary school books "in good Zulu" from the Americans at the discounted price of 10 pence each (WMMS, Pilcher to Osborn). In 1867, the Americans voted to use Anglican Archdeacon Henry Callaway's books in their advanced Boys School at Amanzimtoti (American Zulu Mission [AZM], *Minutes, 13 February 1867*). At the same time, they sent drafts of their first complete translation of the New Testament to other missions for comment and criticism (ABCFM, *Annual Report, 7 June, 1867*). Their reward for this ecumenical approach was Methodist approval for their own schools to use that translation (WMMS, Hayes to the Secretaries). French, German, and Norwegian missionaries were able to use those same books, because Zulu was the language common to all their converts.

The volume of publications required in Zulu led all the missions to request printing presses and printers. It would have been impractical to send manuscripts in Zulu home for printing and proofreading. Writing on behalf of the whole American Zulu Mission, James Bryant complained that the people were running out of reading matter:

> What is the use of teaching them, if when taught, they have nothing to read? We wish not merely to create a taste for reading, but also to furnish reading which may gratify that taste; and how can we do this without books?
>
> So urgent is our need of the Hymn Book, Catechism, & Arithmetic, that we may perhaps make an effort to print one or more of these works at our own press, & with our own hands, tho' from our ignorance of the business, & the pressure of other duties, we can only prosecute the work of printing slowly & at great disadvantage. . . .

> We are trying to introduce the English language into our schools, but this work is necessarily a slow one & many years must pass before the mass of this people can be taught to read the English Language intelligently. We greatly need a supply of Zulu books on scientific subjects which may prepare the way for the introduction of more important English works on the same subjects. (ABCFM, Bryant to Anderson)

The next year the Americans, got their printer (ABCFM, *General Letter for 1850*). Within a few years the Anglicans, Methodists, and Lutherans had also acquired presses. All the presses began printing substantial runs of texts. By 1865, the Berlin Missionary Society had finished translations of the gospels of the four evangelists, and was arranging with fellow Lutherans of the Norwegian and Hermannsburg Lutheran missions to share the cost of printing them (Berlin Mission Society 1866). The first productions of the American press in Zulu included 1,500 72-page hymn books, 1,000 32-page catechisms, 800 8-page tracts, 1,000 48-page arithmetic books, 850 82-page copies of Matthew's gospel, 1,500 copies of an edition of 37 psalms, and 375 8-page copies of *Inhanyezi Tohusa* (ABCFM, *General Letter for 1850*). This outpouring of printed texts went not just to mission station residents, but to city churches and even to prisoners serving terms in gaol (AZM, *Minutes of a Mission Meeting, Durban*).

No department of the colonial state in South Africa began to rival the missions in production of texts in African languages until well into the next century. For that reason, the decision of the mission societies to print a variety of texts was vitally important to the development of African education. Some of these texts are long-forgotten religious tracts. In 1852, Josiah Tyler began to work on a translation of Leigh Richmond's *The Dairyman's Daughter* (1811); 12 years later, the work was finished by an African woman and published in an edition of 1000 (AZM, *Minutes of Mission Meetings*).[2] The Anglican Colenso and the Methodist minister Joseph Jackson, Jr. brought out separate editions of *The Pilgrim's Progress* (1678) in the late 1860s.[3] The Methodist version was printed and published by the American mission. As more students grew competent in English, books on secular topics were ordered in substantial numbers. In addition to the predictable books on the lives of missionaries, temperance tracts, and pious magazines, missionaries ordered a variety of texts for teaching purposes, including Homer's *Odyssey*, William Robertson's *History of the Reign of the Emperor Charles V* (1749), Hugh Blair's *Lectures on Rhetoric and Belles Lettres* (1783), James Rennell's *Geographical System of Herodotus* (1800), Sir Archibald Alison's *History of Europe during the French Revolution* (1833–42), Lowell Mason's *The Manual of the Boston Academy of Music* (1834), Thomas K Arnold's *Henry's First Latin Book* (1839), Blaise Pascal's *Provincial Letters* (1847 [1656]), Ebenezer Cobham Brewer's *Guide to the Scientific Knowledge of Things Familiar* (1848), Thomas W. Redhead's *The French Revolution from 1789 to 1848* (1848–49), *The London*

Quarterly Review, and Otto Schulz's German elementary grammar and the writings of German scientist, Baron Justus von Liebig, on animal and vegetable chemistry (*Whatever 101 Is*; SPG, Illing to Secretaries).

Although it was not to be expected that very many African adolescents advanced to the reading of these texts, it is remarkable that such books were read at all. Despite the regular demands by settler representatives in the Colonial Legislative Council that African education be limited to simple vocational and manual instruction, the mission schools were for a long time beyond the reach of their power. Even the Methodists, whose clergy were drawn mainly from the artisan class, demanded relatively high standards of achievement from African students contemplating careers in preaching or teaching. In 1871, for instance, Jackson reports that the course of study for Jeremiah Dhlamini and Hosea Wakwankosi embraced "English and Kafir [Zulu] reading, English Grammar, Arithmetic, & Translation." He goes on to describe the conditions of these young Africans, who are both being taught and being trained as teachers:

> Jeremiah has advanced as far as Simple Proportion in Arithmetic and Hosea has got as far as Compound Multiplication. Both have been twice through the first Conference Catechism, and are now at work on the second. The great object kept in view has been to give them such a knowledge of English as will enable them to read it with profit to themselves; & in order to [secure] this, much of their time has been devoted to translation. They receive a part of their instruction in the Day School from the Missionary; the rest of the morning is devoted to Teaching in the Day School. Their afternoons have been wholly occupied in study, with the exception of an hour for manual labour as exercise. (WMMS, Report of Two Students)

As there were no secular schools for African children, the little state aid that was available went to the missionaries. In 1869, a disgruntled critic remarked with evident exaggeration that Colenso's clergy were "simply Government Schoolmasters ordained by him" (SPG, Macrorie to Bullock). In 1865, the books supplied included 400 readers from the Irish Series, a further 800 readers for advanced students, 300 copies of McLeod's Explanatory English Grammar, and 200 introductory texts in Geography (Secretary for Native Affairs [SNA], Inspector Mann, List of Required Books). The enthusiasm of parents for the instruction shows in the gradual increase of private subscriptions to the schools and their willingness to pay for family Bibles (ABCFM, Pinkerton to Clark; WMMS, Schedules).

In addition to this cornucopia of printed books and tracts, the missionaries generated other texts whose importance has been generally neglected in conventional histories. For the benefit of authorities at home they produced a flow of statistical tables or "Tabular Views" packed with columns of numbers. Theology held that Christ's "Great Commission" would be fulfilled when the Gospel had been preached to all the world. But the inevitable shortage of worldly resources meant that mission officers wanted the efficacy of their work confirmed by numbers. The tables themselves constituted a discourse of progress. The Berlin Missionary Society collected and published annual charts showing the number of stations, missionaries, station residents, the population in the neighborhood of each station, candidates for baptism, baptisms performed, and communicants received.[4] Such tables were accumulated by all the societies working in Natal except for the Anglican and Roman Catholic missions, who did not draw the bulk of their funds from overseas sources.

Methodist statistics are particularly interesting because the eponymous "method" spread a paper trail over regions much wider than those served by conventional mission stations. Every station was the centre of a cluster of "preaching places," each of which would be visited only periodically by a European missionary. African lay preachers conducted services on other Sundays. The preaching places might be no more than clearings in the bush. Every Sunday those attending would be issued with "tickets" confirming their membership in the society. After the pioneering period, the tickets were also accompanied by cash contributions, and so became a kind of receipt. Table 3.1 gives a Methodist "Tabular View" of 1851, not long after the first missionaries arrived. Table 3.2 gives a "Tabular View" of the same as it looked thirty years later.

Whether viewed at mission society headquarters, in print in the mission magazine, or displayed at the local chapel, the tables gave indisputable evidence that the work was going forward. So did the tables of school attendance, recording every advance through the lessons in arithmetic, reading, penmanship, scripture, Dutch, English, and Zulu. Other charts recorded the names and salaries of assistant ministers, teachers, and vocational instructors. In 1876, John Vimbi was paid £10 as a catechist; Joshua Dhlanuve, more senior, received £20; and Mangena Ngoya earned £24 as a night school teacher. Saul Msane, a day school teacher who would one day lead a deputation of militant African workers to meet General Botha at Pretoria, received £42, only a little less than the white female school mistresses Mary Thurston and Lucinda Mendenhall (Etherington 1978, 174).[5] The tables in their delicious materiality signalled transition of Africans to the world of quantification, grading, and competition.[6] Every day in every way things were getting better and better.

In the early days of mission work, Africans were the objects rather than the owners of the writing machine. Even their names were not their own. Being "born again" through baptism in many cases meant receiving new names. So, in 1860, four young girls in Zululand, who had been Umfuzi, Unomlandu, Unomtyadula, and Nongazi, became Charlotte, Augusta, Margaret, and Agnes

Table 3.1 Tabular View of the Natal District, 1851

Stations	**Durban**	**Maritzburg**	**Kwangubeni**	**Indaleni**	**Palmerston**
Chapels	7	2	2	1	1
Other preaching places	7	3	3	5	14
Missionaries and assistants	1	2	1	1	1
Catechists, readers, and interpreters	2	1	3	2	3
Day school teachers		1			1
Sabbath school teachers	23	18	8	6	6
Local preachers and exhorters	16	10	1	2	4
Accredited church members	163	122	29	38	63
On trial for membership	45	11	4	1	16
Sabbath Schools	7	3	2	2	1
Sabbath scholars of both sexes	250	200	50	60	126
Day schools	4	1		1	1
Day scholars of both sexes	60	12		25	80
Total scholars deducting those attending both sunday and day	250	200	50	60	126
Regular or occasional attendants on public worship	1250	350	800	500	2000

(*Net Cast in Many Waters* 1870, V: 144). The Secretary of the Free Church of Scotland Mission suggested to Natal missionary James Allison that

> it might greatly help to increase the interest of the young people if . . . one of the young men, in particular, who may be contemplating returning to his own country [Swaziland] as an Evangelist, could be selected. One whom we might regard as *our* protegé, whose name we knew, and respecting whose history, etc. some little information might be furnished. Were a selection made, we could send him a letter occasionally and perhaps hear from him in return. And even after leaving Maritzburg, we could follow him with our prayers, and, it might be, in other ways. (United Free Church of Scotland; emphasis in the original)

Perhaps, it was suggested, the boy might be adopted by the Sunday School at Skirling and named Skirling, or perhaps Isaac Barrett, after the pastor of that church.

Not only did the baptised receive the names of such Old Testament patriarchs as Solomon, Abraham, Reuben, Job, and Daniel, or New Testament worthies

Table 3.2 Tabular View of the Natal District, 1882

Stations	Durban English	Durban Native	Indian Mission	Maritzburg English	Maritzburg Native	York English	Ladysmith etc.	Ionono's Kop	Telapi etc.	Verulam English	Harrismith Native	Edendale	Zwaartkop	Indaleni etc.	Stuart's Town	Verulam Native	Endwedwe	Lower Tugela etc.
Chapels	8	1	1	7	1	6	3	1	1	4	1	4	1	3	2	4	1	1
Other preaching places	6	9	15	3	14		10	7	7	1		5	1	4	6	6	5	1
Missionaries and assistants	4	1	1	3	3	1	2	1	1	1		1	1	2		1	1	1
Catechists			2				1					1						
Day teachers	1	2	4	2	4		2		1			5		1		1		
Sabbath teachers	102		4	60	8	4	14	4	2	52	1	12		9		5	4	4
Local preachers	16	9	2	20	22	4	17	8	5	9	3	25	2	8	6	11	6	1
Members	314	77	38	265	210	60	266	76	116	100	20	255	47	103	49	87	72	8
On trial	21	46	5	140	120		162	129	111	6		116	31	24	12	26	9	1
Sabbath schools	7	1	1	7	2	1	4	3	1	4	1	2		2		2	1	1
Sabbath scholars	689	20	27	500	100	26	156	40	50	228	20	155		97		51	60	34
Day schools	1	2	4	1	4		2		1			4		1		2	1	
Day scholars	73	84	142	60	210		76		53			180		73		44	23	
Total scholars deducting those attending both sunday and day	739	84	148	450	198	26	202	40	83	228	20	215		73		17	47	34
Attendants on public worship	1600	600	2000	2500	1000	160	1770	500	590	550	140	950	250	600	400	420	300	160

like Mary, Joseph, Thomas, Margaret, Barnabas, and Timothy, but they also often received surnames of notable mission officers and dead missionaries. Thus Jabez was named, not for the Biblical figure, but for Jabez Bunting, one of the secretaries of the Wesleyan Methodist Missionary Society. The name of Champion, which was born by many important religious and political leaders of the twentieth century, commemorated an American missionary who died young. Space is too short to allow a complete listing of comparable cases. Often the historian's only clue to the ethnicity of people mentioned in the tables of ecclesiastical employees is the low annual wage recorded in the salary column.

While their roles were generally passive in the first instance, Africans soon began to own parts of the process and output of the missionary writing machine by accumulating pieces of paper in their own names. In addition to the weekly tickets issued by the Methodists, there were receipts for school fees, charitable donations, and sales of Bibles (ABCFM, Umvoti Annual Report; SNA, Jackson to Shepstone). There were school certificates, too, and printed copies of the laws of the church were distributed to members.[7] There were written pledges to remain pure, abstain from alcohol, and to say no to drugs. Writing home to Boston in 1856, William Ireland boasted of his achievements:

> You have already had accounts from members of our mission, in reference to the alarming extent, to which the heathen of this land consume their time in beer-drinking—to say nothing of the brutalizing otherwise injurious effects of the practice. There is also another practice to which these heathen are addicted, which in the opinion of many is quite as besotting as injurious—*viz.* That of smoking a drug called "Insangu" [dagga or cannabis]. . . . it is only recently that I have established a temperance society here. . . . I have drawn up an anti-drinking and anti-smoking pledge—which has already received the signatures of almost all at the station who are of a suitable age to sign it. (ABCFM, Ireland, Annual Report of Ifumi)

In an opposite case, the Anglican missionary at Ladysmith in 1859 "had the satisfaction of seeing the last pack of playing cards possessed by my people committed to the flames" (SPG, Joseph Barker Journal).

Junior catechists received printed forms:

> This is to certify that ________________ has passed satisfactorily an examination before the Committee of the A.Z.M. in Personal Experience and Bible Truth, and is hereby licensed to preach the Gospel for one year from date, and is recommended as a suitable candidate to be employed by the churches of the A.Z.M. (ABCFM, Minutes of Annual Meeting of the AZM)

Increasingly, Africans printed these forms and all the other output of mission presses. In 1860, Colenso recruited Magema Fuze as his printer, and continued to employ him in that capacity for the next 25 years. Finding that the volume of work had grown too great for their white printer to handle, the American missionaries successfully applied to the Natal government in 1865 to fund the training of a Zulu assistant (SNA, Mann to Shepstone). Other missions followed suit because the work of proofreading could be done so much more easily by men who could read and write Zulu. African printers set the type for the first newspaper produced in the Zulu language, launched by the American mission in 1876. Initially named *Ubaga*, it was the lineal ancestor of *Ilanga lase Natal*, one of the most important South African newspapers of the twentieth century.

It is of the utmost significance that the early printers and print media were associated with dissident political and religious activity. Colenso's printer, Magema Fuze, was briefly gaoled by the Natal government for presenting the "Christian Natives Petition" on behalf of Chief Langalibalele, who had been exiled for "rebellion" in 1874.[8] Later, he accompanied the Zulu paramount Dinizulu into exile on St. Helena. Fuze wrote histories of his own people, most importantly, *Abantu Abanyama*, and was a key informant to Alfred T. Bryant, whose *Olden Times in Zululand and Natal* still stands as a landmark in early twentieth-century African history. Mbiana Ngidi, who once had been the American ideal of a black missionary, grew weary of being treated as a second-class clergyman and broke away to found his own church. He called his first independent station "Newspaper" (ABCFM, Rood to Clark). The real newspaper, published by the American mission, eventually died because Zulu Christians complained that it carried too little commercial news (AZM, Hance). The newspaper founded at the turn of the twentieth century by John Langalibalele Dube, after his return from education in America, was full of the commercial and political news that go-ahead Africans wanted to read. It would be at the center of resistance to the colonial state for decades to come (Brookes and Webb 1965, 296).

At this point, it is worth recalling that Captain Gardiner came not only with the book, but also with the picture, the song, and the costume. Anyone familiar with contemporary churches in South Africa will know how central pictures, songs, and costumes have become to popular religious life. Every mission brought pictures of Western cities, holy places in Palestine, and fancied scenes from the life of Christ. Colenso used a magic lantern to entertain a group of "refugee chiefs" who had fled to the colony of Natal after a civil war in 1856–57. The bishop reported that they "were, of course, overwhelmed with the exhibition, which, besides some wild animals, with which they were familiar, included some excellent views of St. Paul's, the Houses of Parliament and the Tower [of London]." He next preached them a sermon, which concluded with more pictures sent by the Anglican mission headquarters:

> English *before* Christianity: (1) *Augustine preaching to the Saxons*, with some account of their superstitious practices of our English forefathers, and their habits of life, not so very different from those of the Kafirs themselves.

> English *after* Christianity: (2) Capetown with its buildings, commerce, & *Churches*; Christian Charity sends Missionaries to white settlers (3) Newfoundland Church Ship, (4) to men at diggings, many of whom, like some white people in this country, have lived wickedly as if they knew not God, & unless they repent, will have a fearful account to render. Now let us see what effect Christian teaching has upon other nations, besides the English, upon nations, just like yourselves in the present day.
>
> Pictures of Natives of various kinds engaged in their ordinary occupation, without any special marks of superstition or cruelty; including, of course, the Zulu kraal.
> Instances of Native superstition.
> Ditto of Native Cruelty.
> First arrival of Missionaries—astonishment of natives—welcome of returning Missionary, &c.
> Converts frequenting Divine worship.
> Converts discharging the duties of domestic life.
> Converts suffering for Christ.

Colenso also conducted an evening service, so the chiefs could hear "our 33 boys and their teachers take their part in the responses and the hymns with great spirit" (SPG, Colenso to Secretaries).

All the missions at work in KwaZulu-Natal devoted considerable effort to the translation and printing of hymns. To save trouble, the Methodists "Zuluized" the hymns already translated into Xhosa by their brethren down the coast. By 1880, another Methodist had completed a translation of 60 hymns, mostly from Ira David Sankey's *Sacred Songs and Solos* (1874) (WMMS, Kirby to Kilner). James Langley longed to have the whole English hymnal translated into Zulu "for the sake of its system of Theology" (WMMS, Langley to Boyce). In the long run, it was not the theology embodied in the hymns that mattered, but the system of printing music and the four-part harmonies in which they were set. From the African Jubilee Choir, which sang for Queen Victoria in 1891, to Ladysmith Black Mambazo, which featured at the South African Freedom Day concert in Trafalgar Square on April 29, 2001, modern South African black music is unthinkable without the four-part missionary hymn.[9]

The costume was from the first part of a missionary crusade against "nudity," by which they meant the scanty clothing worn in daily life. Early missionaries, recalling the "anxious seat" where repenting sinners sat during revival services in rural America, remarked that "the shirt is the anxious seat of the Zulu" (ABCFM, Tyler to Clark). Shirts were given away to young men and women in the early days of the mission. They became the outward and visible sign by which the converted set themselves apart from the traditionalists. Much historical literature correctly identifies clothing as part of a larger complex of "soap and water Christianity." As Bernard Cohn has demonstrated, clothing was also an important instrument of creating and ordering difference (Cohn 1996, 106–62). But it was not a simple system of signification imposed from without. From the beginning, clothing was at the centre of a dialogue about power in which Africans made choices. Chiefs accepted and wore military uniforms and top hats presented by visiting travelers, long before they accepted missionary teaching about clothing. While the missions strove to clothe their congregations in the most respectable dress, settler politicians tried to confine servants to light shorts and shirts as a signal of their subservience (Etherington 1988, 44). Dressing for church became more than just a matter of pleasing missionaries or putting on the raiment of the Lord. It affirmed one's membership in a community in which all were equal in the sight of God. It functioned as a badge of denominational affiliation in a land where the diversity of churches reflected the diversity of mission societies at work. Methodist women, for example, could be picked out by their red blouses, black skirts, stockings, and white hats. Other dress identified other groups (West 1975, 39). Throughout the era of *apartheid* the splendor of Sunday morning costumes spectacularly denied the drab uniforms imposed by most white employers.

The influence of the missionary writing machine eventually extended far beyond the churches they founded. It lives today even in the independent churches founded by indigenous rebels and prophets. Many of these are too poor to print books and keep rudimentary records. But the word, the hymn, the costume, and the picture are omnipresent. In 1968, I witnessed a dialogic display of costume at the annual gathering outside Durban of the prophetic church founded by Isaiah Shembe. At one point in the proceedings, four groups of dancers advanced upon each other from the sides of square marked out in the red dust. One group comprised women dressed in beaded skirts and bras. From across the square danced men clad in animal skins and carrying tiny versions of the traditional Zulu leather shields. Adjacent to them were men wearing khaki safari suits and pith helmets, while a throng of women in blouses and full black skirts carrying parasols completed the ensemble. At one level, the dance recapitulated the collision of colonial power and traditional authority; at another, it symbolised the world Shembe's followers had left behind, for none of those costumes are worn to church services. Another set of quite different uniforms identifies the faithful.

Other founders of independent churches witness in striking ways to the power of the mission heritage. In *Zulu Zion and some Swazi Zionists*, Bengt Sundkler has described several of these churches with unparalleled skill. He tells the story of George Khambule, who came from a relatively well-to-do Methodist family. After a supernatural vision accompanied by an out-of-body experience, Khambule was inspired to found a church, which flourished in the interwar years. He infused his followers with his own preoccupation with texts and signs. He discovered new letters of the alphabet, secret names of saints, and a heavenly telephone. He made charts and kept a journal. He found written messages in the arrangement of stones in riverbeds. All these texts were worked into his services in a literal and material fashion. As in other churches, men and women came to his services clad in distinctive gowns: purple, white, black, green, and red. The presiding priest and congregation would begin with an antiphonal set of sayings and responses. After prayers, they would chant the doxology, followed by further chanted sayings and responses, ending with the choral singing of a hymn, "The Song of the Telephone" (Sundkler 1976, 119–60). Readings of such churches as at once survivals of tradition and challenges to constituted authority have a considerable and respectable academic pedigree. Their rituals and texts undoubtedly convey mixed messages. But viewed against the background of mission history, they can equally well be seen as distant descendants of the great missionary writing machine.

Notes

1. Colenso's choice of *Unkulunkulu* for God is still a live issue at the beginning of the twenty-first century.
2. For the original text, see Richmond (1811).
3. Colenso titled his work, *Incwadi ka Bunyane*. See Colenso to Shepstone; WMMS, Jackson; and AZM, *Minutes of Mission Meeting*.
4. See, for example, Berlin Missionary Society (1880).
5. See, for example, WMMS, Schedule of subordinate paid agents.
6. See, for example, WMMS, General school schedules of the Natal District.
7. See, for example, the Umsunduzi Rules accompanying the ABCFM Annual letter for 1880. Here is the text of the Rules in abridged form:
   Rule 1. No one who is a polygamist shall be received into any of the churches.
   Rule 2. No member of any of the churches . . . shall be allowed to *lobolisa* [i.e., give cattle as a marriage present to the father of the bride].
   Rule 3. In no church . . . shall a man who is a widower be allowed to live with any woman, as his wife, before he has been formally married to her . . .
   Rule 4. No member of any of the churches . . . shall be allowed to participate in, or encourage in any way, the making of 'beer-drinks . . .'
   Rule 5. No member of any of the churches . . . shall be allowed to use as a beverage any intoxicating drinks whatever.
   Rule 6. No member of any of the churches . . . shall be allowed at any time to smoke the *Insangu* [cannabis].
8. On these matters, see also Guy (1983, 212–14).
9. For the African Jubilee Choir and its American missionary connections, see Campbell (1995, 128–33).

CHAPTER FOUR

POPULAR IMPERIAL ADVENTURE FICTION AND THE DISCOURSE OF MISSIONARY TEXTS

Gareth Griffiths

Mission travel and the idea of adventure are inextricably bound up in late Victorian imperial discourse. Victorian heroes included evangelical warriors, such as "Chinese" Gordon, the secular Martyr of Khartoum, who fortified himself daily with biblical reading, and missionary-explorers, who saw themselves as Christian soldiers against paganism and slavery, such as Livingstone. In the high period of late nineteenth-century expansionism, imperialism and missionary aims were essentially the same. In this chapter, I want to examine a number of late nineteenth- and early twentieth-century mission narratives, which incorporate elements of these popular secular aims to show how they developed and to suggest that they were important in two ways. First, they were a significant part of the popular material, which helped shape and sustains imperial mythologies well into the twentieth century, and second, they began in the same period to be appropriated to anticolonial ends by the emerging, anticolonial leadership of the colonized peoples.

It has long been recognized how important popular tales of imperial heroism and adventure were in shaping the ideologies of Empire in this period (see Bristow 1991). But we also need to recognize how the influential mission presses employed these popular heroic genres to deliver their message, despite the inherent dangers and contradictions they involved for the Christian message of peace and brotherhood. Despite an increasing interest in the role of missions in imperialism, this is still a neglected part of the larger story of imperial textual control. The output of mission presses was a much more significant overall part of the huge growth in publishing characteristic of the period from 1867 to 1914 than has generally been recognized. They also persisted, as I show, for much longer than

"HIS HAND CLOSED ROUND THE OTHER'S NECK AND HE HURLED HIM ACROSS ONE OF THE BARRELS."

we might assume. The nature of the new class of readers emerging in the last decades of the century with the growth of lower-class literacy following the Board School Act of 1870 made them an unlikely market for the multi-volume novel, which had been produced to meet the demand of the upper middle-class

"THE TERROR."

By H. M. WARD.

THEY GRIPPED EACH OTHER, SWAYING BACKWARDS AND FORWARDS

readers of the first three-quarters of the century. The market place after 1867 was in need of a new kind of text—short, pithy, and targeted at more specific interests. Magazines of popular short stories such as *The Strand Magazine* were designed to appeal by format, price, and content to audiences with lower literacy skills and less available money and leisure time. They won their audiences with a diet of short, sensational tales accompanied by thrilling illustrations.

The simultaneous immense growth of popular missionary publications in this same period was designed for a complementary audience to that serviced by the new secular forms. In fact, they were in direct competition to win the hearts and minds of the new readership away from the secular press of the day and bring them back to Christianity. Every possible form of publication from short illustrated tract, through pamphlet, weekly or monthly mission journal and newsletter, to mission memoir and autobiography emerged to serve this new project.

They matched the popular genres in price, and their formats often eerily echoed them, with covers and illustrations that make them hard to distinguish at first sight from the secular publications of the same period. The covers of the pamphlets in the many series published by mission presses in this period are identical to those illustrations employed by the secular magazines. With the indicators of provenance removed, it would be impossible on the evidence of the covers or illustrations alone to assign them to one or other of these sources.

In the same way the very popular secular adventure tales of exploration, soldiering, and hunting in various far-flung parts of the Empire were also increasingly influential on the mission publications competing for the new readership. The tale of missionary adventure and exemplary heroism was employed to represent many regions of mission endeavor, notably India, the South Seas, and China. But the long public fascination with the exploration of the so-called Dark Continent from the1840s onwards, the success of a large body of best-selling secular exploration and hunting journals, and the rapid expansion of imperial interests in Africa from the mid-1870s all ensured that Africa was the region most frequently represented in both secular and mission texts by this genre of the heroic, adventure tale. So it is on Africa that I want to concentrate.

The texts produced by white missionaries in Africa in the late nineteenth and early twentieth centuries were, as I have suggested, frequently indistinguishable from those of the popular adventure tale. For example, the published posthumous letters of the martyred Bishop James Hannington present him as indistinguishable from the boy heroes of popular, secular tales like his own *Peril and Adventure in Central Africa* (1886). We are told that he was called Mad Jim when a boy and was fearless. As a young man he is hopeless at business but fond of "riding, shooting and all athletic exercises." The stress on heroism and peril in these late imperial narrative journals and letters serve to occlude any reference to the commercial nature of imperialism. In such tales the imperial planters, box-wallahs, and settlers of the late imperial world are displaced by a simplified world of imperial adventurers, soldiers, and hunters. This phenomenon contrasts with the detailed accounts of commercial enterprise such as coal mining, or the planting of cash crops as an intrinsic part of mission endeavor, which are a notable feature of David Livingstone's journals, and his missionary vision, at least in the earlier period. This shift further illustrates the shift in later mission discourses from the mid-century Livingstonian emphasis on the civilizing influence of mutual commerce to the stress on the direct colonizing practices of armed settlement.

Similarly the mission goal of conversion seems often equally subordinated. Hannington's letters, for example, have many descriptions of exotic African customs, of hunting for game, and of perilous crossings of rivers and mountain ranges, but hardly any descriptions of evangelizing and education. Missions are exciting is the message for adventurous boy readers (of whatever age!). Thus the secular values imported from the boy's adventure tale genre overrides its Christian purpose or, at the very least, disrupts it significantly. Here is a typical passage from Hannington's text:

> My boy then said to me, "If you want to kill monkey, master, you should try buckshot," so returning him my rifle, I took my fowling-piece. Perhaps it was fortunate I did so, for about a hundred yards farther on the riverbed took a sharp turn, and coming round the corner I lighted on three fine tawny lions. They were quite close to me, and had I had my rifle my first impulse might have been too strong for me to resist speeding the parting guest with a bullet. As it was, I came to a sudden halt and they ran away. (Hannington [1886], 40)

At first we might assume as we read this that the Bishop is glad that his first bloody impulse was frustrated by having selected the wrong gun, as a good Christian should be, but his subsequent actions clearly belie this. The text continues:

> In vain my boy begged me to retreat. I seized the rifle and ran after them as fast as my legs would carry me; but they were soon hidden in the dense jungle that lined then river banks; and although I could hear one growling and breathing hard about ten yards from me, I could not get a shot. (Hannington [1886], 40)

Such fractures between an overall discourse of Christian charity and forbearance and the rhetoric of the hunter/adventurer seeking to conquer and subdue the worlds he encounters is a common ideological and discursive rupture in these texts.

The journals of earlier African missionaries like Robert Moffat and his son-in-law Livingstone also contain scattered episodes of peril and danger, such as Moffat's account of his ground-breaking journey to the *kraal* of the Matabele chief Mzilikazi or Livingstone's famous, almost fatal encounter with a lion, when his left arm was severely mauled before the lion was shot (Livingstone 1963; Moffat 1855). But even Livingstone, who is arguably the most adventurous of all the early missionaries, exhibits a far more complex, humane, if paternalistic, tone toward Africa and Africans. He does not engage in the sort of excess, which I have illustrated from the letters of the later Hannington. But by the 1870s this "adventure" element dominates the texts, overwriting the more complex accounts of the mid-century journals of Moffatt and others like him. In fact, even the stories of these early explorers is recast to fit the new discursive mode demanded by the changed market place for mission texts, illustrating the increasing and often totally false elision between hunting stories and mission narratives in the period after 1870.

The posthumous, celebratory *Scenes and Services in South Africa: The Story of Robert Moffat's Half-Century of Missionary Labours* (1876) recounts Moffat's experiences as one of the earliest missionaries in the interior of southern Africa, where he worked from his first journey out of the Cape in 1821 to his death in 1870. This late text contains numerous pictures of wild animals such as hippos and elephants, suggesting that this sedentary missionary was akin to the explorer figures, who had followed in the footsteps of the journeying explorations of his better-known son-in-law Livingstone. In other words, this mission-published text, released after Moffat's death, reflects the shifting discourse of mission texts in the last quarter of the century. The material contained in Moffat's own journals that recount his hard and mostly sedentary work, the unexciting and disappointing nature of which drove his son-in-law, Livingstone, into his doubled life of mission and exploration have been reshaped by judicious editing and the addition of illustrations to the taste of the new age.[1] The sources on which these late revised accounts draw are also surprising, as this 1876 text illustrates.

Scenes and Services in South Africa recounts what purports to be an accurate account of Moffat's famous visit to the *kraal* of Mzilikazi—"Moselekatze," as he transcribes it—and contains an image of a party of missionaries and their black bearers being attacked by buffalo. The illustration in the 1876 text is, in fact, reproduced without acknowledgment of the source, which is Henry Morton Stanley's journal of his 1874 expedition. Thus an illustration from the journal of the most publicity-conscious and least Christian explorer of the late Victorian age—the journal of a journey undertaken well after Moffatt's death—is used to illustrate Moffatt's far less self-consciously "adventurous" journey to visit Mzilikaze, which had taken place decades earlier. Of course, the source of the illustration is not acknowledged, and the readership is encouraged to assume that this exciting and dangerous event occurred as illustrated to Moffatt and his companions.

By the mid-1870s, then, mission presses have totally elided the secular adventure and mission history forms, even importing actual images and events from the former to cater for the taste of its audience for exciting and stirring images and stories. By the end of the century, the Africa presented in the earlier and more complex journals of missionaries like Moffatt and even Livingstone, the original missionary-explorers, have been indelibly overwritten by the much more explicit imperialism of late Victorian exploration and the discourse of late nineteenth-century adventure fiction.

A good example of such late mission adventure journals is *Winning a Primitive People*, by Donald Fraser, published after his retirement in 1914, but recording the experiences of this young missionary in Nyasaland from 1896. Here is Fraser's account of the beginning of his journey to the mission:

> Towards the close of the year 1896 I landed from a little Portuguese coasting vessel at the Chinde mouth of the River Zambezi, on my way to the Livingstonia Mission. . . . [A]t last I had entered at the gateway of the Africa of wild romance which has always appealed to everyone who has the heart of a boy.[2] In a day or two a little flat-bottomed stern-wheeler, in which I was one of three or four passengers, was slowly threading its way between the

TOSSED BY A BUFFALO.

Stanley's 1874 expedition. 'The travelling procession interrupted'

> sandbanks of the great shining river and every hour of the hot day was full of new order and interest. Sometimes we passed a school of hippopotami, whose heads were showing above the water, sometimes rifles cracked at crocodiles that were sunning themselves on a sand-spit, and every day we spent hours digging ourselves out of some shallow in which the little steamer had run aground. (Fraser 1914, 17)

This description of the practice of shooting animals seems especially disingenuous. Again it reveals the fracture between the text's conflicting rhetorical postures, a fracture revealed in the trope of the passive rifles that "crack" with no apparent agency or assistance from a narrator whose grammatical disassociation from the act is only matched by his rhetorical fascination with it.[3]

These adventurous, heroic missionary accounts were not restricted to England and English publishers. The Welsh-American adventurer Stanley was, if anything, even better known by the 1890s than even earlier heroes like Livingstone, whose highly publicized "rescue" had made Stanley's initial reputation. An American example shows how widespread this imperial myth of Africa had become by the turn of the century. *Sketches from the Dark Continent*, by Willis R. Hotchkiss, was reprinted in London in 1903 from the American edition published in Cleveland in 1901. Hotchkiss was a missionary of the Friends Industrial African Mission, established at Kaimosi, Kavirondi, British East Africa. The fact that Hotchkiss was a Quaker and an American makes the presence of this heroic, adventure discourse in his journals even more interesting and contradictory than in the case of an Anglican such as Hannington. Hannington at least had the excuse of working for a church that has always been prone to consider the realms and interests of God and the English throne as virtually identical.

Again, Hotchkiss's text closely resembles Stanley's many accounts of travel and exploration in Africa, which he has clearly read. It is filled with almost identical, highly detailed Stanleyesque accounts of the organization of caravans and marches, and of the shooting of game for the pot or for self-defense. Such accounts are indistinguishable from those of the adventurer/explorer narratives except for the Christian moral tags that are simply added on. For example, Hotchkiss offers a long account of coming across a baby rhino with its mother. The mother fails to scent them, but hears them. Preventing a porter from firing his shotgun at her, Hotchkiss is still attacked:

> Finally with head up and snorting as only a rhino can, she dashed for us. None of us had our rifles in our hands, for all were pretty well used up, two having had fever the night before and the rest were destined to have it yet that day. There was the sound of falling boxes as the men dropped their loads and dashed for the scrubby trees around. But fortunately the animal did not keep on its course across our line; if she had someone would have been hurt or killed. But she swerved and went down the line parallel with the caravan. The askari recovered themselves and after firing some fifty rounds succeeded in bringing her down. (Hotchkiss 1903, 21–22)

The moral tagline sits uneasily at the end of this rousing tale. "This day was really the end of the long tramp in quest of service for the Master" (Hotchkiss 1903, 22). Or in quest of rhinos? Nor is this instance an isolated example. There is also a detailed description of how Hotchkiss later kills a rhino plaguing some villagers (Hotchkiss 1903, 51–55). At one point, Hotchkiss refers to himself openly as a "hunter," illustrating his confused self-definition within the available frames of narrative reference: "The first care of every rhino hunter is to look about for means of escape" (Hotchkiss 1903, 53).

It is not only animals that pose a threat. As for his explorer hero Stanley, "hostile" natives are encountered and have to be dealt with. Stanley was renowned for the ruthlessness with which he thrust aside hostiles on his heavily armed journeying. The influence of this discourse can be seen in the description Hotchkiss offers of attacks on his men by hostile natives:

> Day after day, my men would be driven from their work . . . I returned with the men, but no one was to be seen. No sooner had we begun to work, however, than we were surrounded by a band of natives who skulking from tree to tree, arrows fitted to the bowstrings, and swords in hand, threatened our lives. The situation was critical, and I did something for which I was ashamed at the time, and have been increasingly so ever since. Having a revolver in my pocket—a thing of rare occurrence—I drew it out, opened it, and then in the sight of the angry mob, took some cartridges from another pocket, filled the chambers slowly and deliberately, closed the weapon and then returned it to my pocket. All this without saying a word. But the act seemed sufficient, for there was a hasty consultation among our foes and then they suddenly withdrew. Why I did this I cannot tell, because I am strictly opposed to the use of fire-arms to quell disturbances of the natives, both from motives of principle and expediency. It is contrary to the Spirit of Christ, and that ought to be sufficient for any one who follows Him. (Hotchkiss 1903, 40–41)

Although Hotchkiss cannot come up with an explanation for himself it may not be beyond our powers to speculate. If a landscape and a people are cast into specific roles, and if the "hero" of this drama has a self-conception rooted in a romantic vision of himself as hunter/explorer, it may be hard not to act out this myth even in situations where the behavior contradicts his conscious ideological self-perception. After all, as I noted earlier, Stanley's accounts are uncannily echoed in Hotchkiss's work. Stanley's journals are full of battles with hostile natives, so much so that he was the subject of public censure even in his own day for the excessive violence and cruelty of his response to native threats. That such censure often came from missionary sources makes the collusive and corrosive interpenetration of the discourses of such texts even more ironic and fascinating. In fact, Stanley may only have been a little more honest about his violent practice than others in the late nineteenth century, not least the missionaries themselves.

Hotchkiss is not alone in recording the contradictions that these ideological and discursive models engendered in the minds of many of these later missionary adventurers. This observation can be further illustrated by the writings of the Anglican Bishop, Charles Mackenzie. In Mackenzie's journal of the first, disastrous Universities Mission to Central Africa (UMCA) expedition to establish a mission on the upper tributaries of the Zambezi, the bishop struggles with the issue of whether or not he should use arms against hostile natives. As a good imperialist as well as a good missionary, he resolves the issue by evolving a policy, which justifies such violence when it is in defense not of himself, but of his followers. This debate as to whether the appropriate response to such hostility is justified self-defense or a Christian submission to martyrdom is a recurring feature of many late nineteenth-century texts. For a view contradictory to Mackenzie's, though, we might turn to the pamphlet written by the UMCA missionary, Bishop Chauncy Maples. The pamphlet deals with the famous Mangwara raid on the mission at Masasi in 1883.[4] Maples is insistent that, despite the dangers faced during the raid, he refused to fire upon the attackers. Although here, as in other accounts of the raid in the mission press, it is emphasized that converted, freed slaves were captured and re-enslaved by the raiders, a situation that Mackenzie had clearly identified as one in which armed defense was justified. Another UMCA account published in 1855, only two years after the raid, refers to "the famous attack upon the Mission Station itself at Masasi in 1883 (when they carried off many of our people)" (*African Tidings* 1885, 18). This account concludes: "this fierce tribe [the Mangwara] has not lost its love of war and plunder, but they have at least learnt to respect our missionaries and Mission Stations" (*African Tidings* 1885, 18). How this respect was achieved in such a brief period and whether by employing Mackenzie's policy of just defensive violence where mission followers were threatened, or through Maples policy of absolute Christian forbearance is never made clear. The reader is left to speculate that perhaps not all missionaries were quite so easy as Maples on the Magwangara and other "hostile" tribes.

Of course, both practices could be rendered into the stuff of popular fiction, either in heroic mission martyrdom accounts, or in more secular tales of mission heroism. When Rider Haggard published *Allan Quatermain* in 1887, only five years after the Masasi raid, he included a graphic account of a Masai attack on a mission station. The mission is defended not only by Quatermain and his adventurer friends, but also by the well-armed missionary and appropriately named Mr. Mackenzie.[5] This description is accompanied in the first and subsequent editions by a woodcut showing the heavily armed missionary:

> In his hand was the Winchester repeating rifle we had lent him; and stuck in an elastic cricketing belt, like those worn by English boys, were first a huge buckhorn-handled carving knife, with a guard to it, and next a long-barreled Colt revolver.
>
> "Ah, my friend," he said, seeing me staring at his belt, "you are looking at my 'carver.' I thought it might be very handy if we came to close quarters; it is excellent steel, and many is the pig I have killed with it." (Haggard 1887b, 70–71)

Clearly for Haggard, the gap between adventurer and missionary is easily closed. I need not stress, of course, how huge an influence on the late Victorian world Haggard's tales exerted.

Slowly, but perhaps inevitably as time went on, it became almost impossible to distinguish the genres and themes of the secular texts from mission texts. By the second decade of the twentieth century, many of the missions were beginning to separate themselves from the effects of imperial adventuring in their actual practice in the field. Missionaries increasingly found themselves at odds with government policies, and especially with the attitudes and aims of settler groups in British East Africa and southern Africa generally. But at the same time as this gap between mission ideologies and the ideologies of settlers was opening up, the mission presses were continuing to produce a body of texts reproducing the stereotypes of the high imperial period. The persistence of the adventure genre and its continuing popularity in the home market was a major factor in this contradiction between the practices of the missions in print and action. In fact, if anything, this textual contradiction increased and deepened as the new century went on.

By the end of the first decade of the twentieth century, mission presses were actively producing adventure narratives tales, which had little or no connection with Christian life. One such text was *Sinclair of the Scouts; or, with Bayonet and Barricade in West Africa*, by "J. Claverdon Wood," a pseudonym for Thomas Carter. This novel was issued by the Religious Tract Society and published in the first decade of the century, along with a series of such adventure tales, as the advertisement from the inside cover shows (see Wood [1911]).[6] The titles in The Religious Tract Society advertise in its series, "The Boy's Library of Adventure and Heroism," and include two novels by William Gordon Stables, *Allan Adair*; *or Here and There in Many Lands* (1900) and *Wild Life in Sunny Lands; a Romance of Butterfly Hunting* (1906). The latter advertises itself as "full of adventure all over the world with savage tribes of more or less appalling ferocity and hideous habits," and the former is described thus: "Among may exciting episodes may be mentioned shooting 'rattlers' in the Sierras, encounters with narwhals and bears in the Arctic regions, a hairbreadth escape on the terrible ice-river of Spitzbergen, and adventures among the savages of Patagonia" (Stables 1900, 1906).

This influence of popular adventure narratives on missionary publishing persisted well into the twentieth century, as did their continuing popularity with the home readership. This popularity is reflected in the sales figures recorded in the papers preserved in the mission archives, and it indicates that they remained a profoundly influential form, shaping the average Europeans perception of Africa and Africans, however transmuted by ideology and generic influence, long after their authors could have had any direct experience to transmit. The first-hand "factual" accounts by missionaries I discussed earlier, however disrupted by the contradictions generated by their intertextuality with popular secular forms, are replaced over the first three decades of the twentieth century by even more distorted, purely fictionalized accounts, based not on actual experiences but derivative of the original examples of the nineteenth-century journals and accounts I have described above.

I can only give some brief examples here of the persistence of these discursive features in texts published for the home market as late as the 1950s, and of how successful they were in terms of sales. Still, I trust these examples will serve to show the ongoing ideological purchase and popular appeal of these missionary published adventure narratives well into the twentieth century. One especially intriguing series is the Edinburgh House Publication, the Yarn Series, which came out with 22 volumes from 1913 to 1940.[7] The prolific and popular mission author, Basil Mathews, produced no fewer than five of this series on areas such as the Near East, Africa, the South Seas, and India, as well as two others entitled *Yarns on Heroes of the Deep* (1922; with Arthur E. Southon) and *Yarns on Heroes of the Day's Work* (1932). Mathews is an example of the emergence of mission writers with an output and sales rivaling those of the popular writers for secular presses. For people like Mathews, mission story-writing came close to being a full-time profession. By this time, the adventure story has lost its claim to authenticity as a true tale or a journal and has become a genre, pure and simple. There is no sense of these being "reports from the field," in the sense of the early tracts. How could they be unless Mathews was remarkably well traveled for the period? What such writers are doing is recycling into the genre tales and stories from a variety of sources in journals, mission reports *et cetera*, and marketing them through the form of the now highly popular adventure story to the increasingly large mass readership of the mid-twentieth century.

Sales figures I have gathered from archival records suggest why such professionalized mission text writers were able to emerge.[8] The average first print run for the Yarn Series was 5,000, with none less than 3,000 and some as high as 10,000. The press account records in the mission archives show that the majority of tracts in this series, which ran from 1913 to 1940, went to two or three editions. These figures illustrate the ongoing success of accounts of "heroic" mission adventure, even into the 1940s. By 1915, specific series aimed at girls have emerged, mirroring the growth of the girl's "tales" to match the earlier boy's adventure "tales," that developed in the same period in popular secular narratives.[9] These numbers and their late dates suggest that the powerful audience created by the mission presses in the late nineteenth century remained in place much later than we might imagine and continued to influence domestic imperial attitudes much later than we might imagine.

Titles in a mission series such as Edinburgh House's Torch Adventure Series, which published 98 titles between 1928 and 1936, suggest the extent of the ongoing collusion between missionary texts and popular genres in the interwar period, when nationalist movements were already beginning to stir in the colonized world. Many titles in the series have sales of 15,000 to 16,000 recorded, and significantly, the sales figures rise steadily from 1928 until the mid-1930s, when a decline in sales numbers is recorded, as if the initial market has been saturated. But significantly, in July 1939, the whole series is revived and all 92 titles are brought out in a second edition, the sales of which average 3,000 to 5,000. The date of this reissue and its relationship with a renewed nationalist fervor just prior to the outbreak of World War II must remain speculative, though there is evidence to support this association in other material I have assembled, but not yet fully analyzed. That and much else that can be gleaned from these archives must wait for a larger and more extensive argument than I can muster here.

However, the pernicious persistence of these outdated stereotypes in mission-published texts is only one side of the story. In their 1991 book, *Revelation and Revolution: Christianity, Colonialism and Consciousness in South Africa*, anthropologists and cultural theorists Jean and John Comaroff emphasize the importance of these early missionary discourses in the formation of self-ascriptive ideological modes of resistance within the native communities themselves (Comaroff and Comaroff 1991). In a similar spirit, I have argued elsewhere that many mission genres were quickly appropriated or modified to subversive ends by colonized African subjects (Griffiths 2001). The mission presses offered emerging African leaders, themselves often mission-educated, an important means of communicating with a powerful group of potential supporters, the local English-educated readership, a class crucial to the development of early nationalist resistance.

Jomo Kenyatta's text, *The Life of Chief Wangombe* (1942), is as an example of the appropriation to these ends of the missionary genre of the heroic life—a form in which there is a strong intertextuality between the idea of the exemplary life and the idea of the heroic warrior, an intertextuality still rooted in the tropes of imperial adventure fiction. The young Kenyatta, who of course, was to become in due course the first president of an independent Kenya, is able to exploit this imperialistic genre in the presentation of Wangambe as an exemplary figure, whilst using it to develop a highly politicized subtext. In effect, he has exploited the same gaps and fissures within the original discourse I discussed earlier, but for a different and subversive end. This text offers a classic example of the possibilities for discursive mediation, subversion, or mimicry that critics such as the Comaroffs and others have argued are always implicit in the supplementary excess these imperial genres generate.

Kenyatta published his *Life of Chief Wangombe* in a series put out by the United Society for Christian Literature. The narrative illustrates the increasing tension that, by the 1940s, was part of the process of missionary patronage of the African text. Kenyatta's book, the first in the series, immediately and uncompromisingly announces its nationalist project in its dedication to "the members of various tribes in Africa who died in the service of African peoples" (Kenyatta 1942, Preface). Although *The Life of Chief Wangombe* follows the classic exemplary life narrative form, it is clearly also designed to counter the many imperial narratives that present precolonial tribal life as "short, brutish and nasty." It uses the discourse of the heroic hunter/adventurer prevalent, as we have shown, in such texts to present a very positive image for this early precolonial Gikuyu leader, emphasizing the courage and dignity of the protagonist, for example when, as a young man, he is shown killing a leopard stealing a goat from his father's herd:

> In its death-agony the beast leapt forward, and had not Wangombe retreated quickly it would have fallen upon him. He ran for help, and when he came back with his comrades they found the leopard lying dead on the spot where he had stood, with a big gash in his throat and the top part of Wangombe's spear protruding from its heart. (Kenyatta 1942, 36)

The text goes on to describe how the mature Wangombe led a successful war against the Masai, but the war is presented as meaningful and heroic, not brutish and barbarous, analogous to European or American wars whose historic heroes figure as positive role models in European narratives. It is the defense of the Gikuyu people and territory that Wangombe successfully leads that is emphasized, and his warrior action, like his Christian mission models is tempered with mercy when Wangombe realizes that one of the Masai enemy was once a playfellow. On discovering this Wangombe calls a truce, and from that time onwards trading with the Masai is initiated. When disease attacks the Masai the group who trade with the Gikuyu are the only ones able to survive. The contemporary message of the virtues of intertribal unity in the face of an outside threat is clearly implied. That the Europeans represent such a threat is also clear from the ending. When the Europeans (or Athongo) arrive, he gives them building sites. But the Europeans are presented not as the saviors, but as an unknown factor that a sensible people will treat with caution:

> On his deathbed he summoned his councilors, and warned them to be very watchful in their relations with the Athongo. "Remember how many battles we have fought to protect our country from invaders," he said in a slow sinking voice. "Don't forget that you have a great task in front of you. You may not have to fight with spears, shields or bows and arrows, in the way with which you are familiar. But in the short time I have had contact with the Athongo, I have seen how hard it is to deal with them. They know how to dazzle your mind

> with praise, when they know that by doing it they will achieve their ends. Learn their clever way of talking for it is by using your wisdom that you may safeguard your country." (Kenyatta 1942, 63)

Kenyatta's text turns to his own use "the clever way of talking" represented by his appropriation of the form of the missionary text and the institutional power of the mission press. Thus, while these genres continue in their unmodified forms to replicate and sustain the ideological formations of late imperialism within the home market, they are simultaneously becoming appropriated to a radical and subversive anti-colonial usage by the emerging mission-educated leadership of the African colonies. Ironically, then, the products of mission presses exercise two radically different functions in the later period, from the 1930s onwards.

In conclusion, the late nineteenth and early twentieth centuries, as I have tried to show, saw the growth of a powerful, persistent, diverse, and influential industry, producing missionary pamphlets, tracts, journals, and books. Yet it is only recently that detailed notice of the range, ubiquity, persistence, and influence of such texts has been taken by postcolonial literary scholars. It seems incontestable that the product of these powerful and long-lasting patrons of writing in the colonized world, and their influence on the representation of colonized peoples to themselves and to others, deserves far closer attention than it has so far received.

Notes

1. Moffat did, of course, make one famous journey to the *kraal* of the Matebele king, Mzilikazi, in what is now southern Zimbabwe. But the greater part of his life was spent with his wife at their mission at Kuruman. As in the case of most early missions, their conversion successes were few and Livingstone's initial journeys were undertaken to test his theory that only by venturing among uncontacted Africans and converting their leaders directly could this poor showing be improved.
2. The connection of the idea of boyishness and of innocence of heart has its roots in the late Victorian obsession with sexuality as the root of sin. It is for this reason that the world of the boy or girl is perceived as closer to the world of the true Christian than that of the adult. Of course, the boy's world is also one of violence and bloodshed, but that is easily overlooked in a period when war and conquest could be justified in the name of the civilizing mission.
3. The passage recorded here also opens up some further interesting lines of enquiry into the complex relationship with other rather better-known texts of the same period. I am sure the reader will have noticed the close resemblance between Fraser's account and Conrad's in *Heart of Darkness*, both in its descriptive details, and in the similarity between the attitudes of the narrators, who share a complex model of involvement in, yet detachment from, and moral superiority over the enterprise of colonialism.
4. Entitled *The Magwangara Raid upon Masasi*, this pamphlet is hand-dated October 16, 1882. Clearly, this date is in error, since the raid had not taken place at that time (UMCA Archives Rhodes House Library TC E41–F7).

5. Norman Etherington, mission historian and author of a book on Haggard, identifies Mackenzie with a German missionary known to be involved in gunrunning. But when I pointed out the Masasi incident to him, he agreed that it might well have also been an important influence on Haggard.
6. The edition I own is inscribed as a gift in pencil and the gift is dated 1911, suggesting a publication date sometime in the early years of the century.
7. School of Oriental and African Studies (SOAS) Missionary Special Collection Box 166 H/up 14.
8. SOAS Missionary Special Collection Box H/up 12 No 164 FBN 4 contains useful Budget and Production Programmes. Box H/up 14 16614 contains log books of editions, titles in chronological and alphabetical order, royalty agreements and paste-ups of reviews. The logbooks of monthly records also give sales figures. Box H/up 50 202 15 contains *inter alia* textbooks and pamphlets, 1911–1912. Box H/up 60 212 FBN 16 contains lists of the many titles in the various series, as does H/up 61 213 FBN.
9. Clearly the whole issue of the gendering that this discourse institutionalizes is a subject that deserves a fuller and separate treatment. The fact that the form is extended to girls in this late period, with suitable amendments for Edwardian ideals of suitable womanly virtues, does not negate the fact that, as Bristow's title, *Empire Boys* indicates, this discourse is predominantly masculinist and "adventures" are part of the construction of what is seen as predominantly a "man's world."

CHAPTER FIVE

BOOKS AND BODICES: MATERIAL CULTURE AND PROTESTANT MISSIONS IN COLONIAL SOUTH INDIA

Eliza F. Kent

Historians of nineteenth-century Christian missions have frequently noted the tension between the impulse to convert and the temptation to civilize. To the extent that the conditions under which British missionaries lived and worked in India were already overdetermined by the fact of British colonial rule, these two impulses were, in practice, deeply intertwined. However, one can discern two distinctive strains of argumentation in the discourse generated by missionaries to describe, define, and justify their goals and the means for achieving them. Advocates of the Christian mission in India mostly agreed that Indians were in a degraded state that could be remedied by the teachings to which the missionaries had privileged access, but they differed in their diagnoses of the problem, as well as in their solutions for remedying it. One argument was that the "gospel alone" was what Indians needed to save them from their unregenerate state. Implicit in this argument was a particular understanding of the person, as being essentially determined by the state of his or her "soul," that immaterial, immortal, and deeply interior center of being that was described dichotomously as either dark with sin, or pure, light, and free. According to this soteriology, the problem was sin, an inborn predisposition to compulsively transgress God's law. Sin was a universal malady with which all humans were inherently afflicted, and its solution was faith in Jesus, whose death on the cross had opened the floodgates of redemption, so that all who took refuge in him would be saved.[1]

The other argument was that until Indians had reached a certain degree of "civilization" they would not be able to appreciate the value of Christian teachings about sin and salvation. This line of thinking understood "civilization" primarily in terms of education, but it encompassed a wide range of values, tastes, beliefs, and practices associated with the lifeways of the Protestant middle classes in England. A very different understanding of human nature was implicit in this soteriology, one deeply influenced by social Darwinism. According to this view, all members of the human family were advancing, generation by generation, toward the perfect realization of human potential, but some nations—particularly the Protestant, English-speaking ones—were closer to this pinnacle than others. Moreover, it was the duty of the former to help the latter in achieving this goal by accelerating the rate of their evolution. British advocates of mission regarded the educational work of missionaries, in its many varied contexts, as a powerful catalyst that could render a people suitable for salvation by the gospel.

One popular view that combined the two theories of mission was that the work of the civilizing mission helped to *complete* the process of regeneration initiated by the testimony of faith, which was itself brought about by preaching the gospel. However, so long as these two soteriologies coexisted in the ideological underpinnings of nineteenth-century British missionary institutions, they led to a curious situation. On the one hand, British missionaries preached with passion a stripped-down concept of Christianity, which held that "accepting Jesus" was all that was necessary for salvation; on the other, they were obsessed with changing the ways in which Indian Christians lived, dressed, worked, thought, and spoke. What W. R. Ward has written about the "missionary church" in England could also be said about the missionary societies in mid-nineteenth-century India: "Those who most beat the drum about the depravity of mankind and the all sufficiency of grace were now the most committed to hectic programs of works and to the construction of rational organisations for their accomplishment" (Ward 1994, 272).

These two emphases within missionary discourse are particularly evident in the material instruments by which missionaries sought to convey their teachings to Indians. I hope to shed some new light on the old issue of the tension between conversion and civilization by closely examining the material instruments that missionaries used to convey their messages, with a focus on the British missions in south India. In the first part of this chapter, I examine one of the tools used by Protestant missionaries to convey what they took to be the central meaning of Christianity as understood through the doctrine of the atonement: the belief that salvation was possible for all people through the faithful recognition that Jesus Christ had died for their sins. Along with painted story scrolls, tracts, books, and a multitude of songs and hymns composed in vernacular Indian languages, missionaries made use of a preaching tool known as "Wordless Book." Characteristic in its simplicity and undiluted by talk of hygiene or financial prudence, this device consisted of four plain pieces of colored cloth or paper—black, red, white, and gold or yellow—sewn or glued together along one side to form a book. Each field of color stood for a different component of the doctrine of atonement: human sin, the redemptive blood of Jesus, the state of souls cleansed from sin, and the golden palaces that await the saved in heaven. By means of the wordless book, a missionary of even limited linguistic skills could communicate the core message of the faith in an efficient manner to a wide variety of audiences, literate and illiterate.

If, however, this highly compressed version of the Protestant message suggested that all that was necessary for salvation was repentance and a testimony of faith, in practice missionaries were very rarely satisfied with such abbreviated displays of adherence to Christian doctrine. The second part of the chapter investigates another type of material instrument: clothing. Through clothing, missionaries and Indian Christians sought to instill in converts the refined, proper behaviors worthy of people calling themselves Christian. In particular, I examine the so-called breast-cloth controversies that took place in the princely state of Travancore. This controversy gives us an opportunity to explore why Indian Christian converts responded so differently to two different means of meeting the requirements of the missionaries that Christian women dress modestly—the sewn blouse, or "jacket," specially designed for Indian Christian women by the wives of missionaries, and the "breast-cloth," a length of cloth brought over and across the shoulder, so that the bosom was covered. As we shall see, the latter style was characteristic of how the women of the locally dominant caste dressed.

The Age of Atonement

One of the conditions necessary for the notion that one could or ought to preach the gospel alone was the ascendance within British Protestantism of the doctrine of the atonement, a particularly concise rendering of Christianity. The nineteenth-century British missionaries who came to evangelize Indians brought with them a spectrum of theological positions. By 1850, at least four different British missionary societies operated in India. The oldest society was the Society for the Propagation of Christian Knowledge (SPCK), which later became the Society for the Propagation of the Gospel in Foreign Parts (SPG), a High-Church body affiliated with the established Church of England; the Church Missionary Society (CMS), also affiliated with the Church of England, but deeply influenced by evangelical ideas; the London Missionary Society (LMS), a nonconformist interdenominational body; and the Wesleyan Methodist Missionary Society (WMMS), a nonconformist British group composed mostly of followers of John Wesley's fiery brand of Protestantism.

While these groups were grounded in very different theologies, particularly with respect to the significance, function, and organization of the church as an institution, they shared a basic commitment to the doctrine of the atonement (Hilton 1988). Glossing this doctrine in shorthand terms like "the cross," "the Christ event," or the "crucifixion," these mission organizations shared the belief that Jesus' sacrificial death on the cross had created the means of salvation for all human beings. Drawing on different images from the New Testament, divergent interpretations of the doctrine clarify how Christ's death actually accomplished this salvation: Christ was killed as a ransom fee that paid for the lives of all sinners; or through his perfect, sinless life Christ accumulated enough virtue to compensate for the sins of all humanity; or he was the only sacrificial offering capable of satisfying God's justified wrath at human sinfulness (Hilton 1988, 7–8). But each interpretive condensation of the gospel served as the lynchpin of a mission's theology, because it emphasized the universal nature of salvation via the path of Christianity, transcending the particulars of culture, language, or history. It made possible the hope that social borders marked and reinforced by such differences could ultimately be dissolved. Sin, judgment, mercy, and salvation were the key themes in this story, which was recast and retold in innumerable ways. Whether or not such themes struck a chord with Indian hearers is something we explore in a moment.

British evangelists began arriving in India in large numbers in the years after 1813. Intense campaigning by a politically influential group of evangelicals based in Clapham, London, pressured the British parliament into adding a "missionary clause" to the charter of the East India Company for the purpose of introducing "useful Knowledge and . . . religious improvement" to the "Native Inhabitants of the British Dominions of India" (Grafe 1990, 30). These evangelicals, men and women alike, were fresh from the intensely emotional evangelical revivals that had swept through England, Ireland, and Wales during the eighteenth century (Holmes 2000). Given their background, missionaries from Britain were disappointed by the level of religious enthusiasm they found among existing Indian Christian congregations in south India, which had been founded by German Pietist missionaries in the eighteenth century (Hudson 2000). Some devoted time and resources to the cultivation and "reform" of Indian Christian communities, but the majority styled themselves as pure evangelists: they were there to spread the "Word" as far and as fast as possible, by any means necessary.

Debates arose amongst the missionaries in India about the better strategy for accomplishing evangelical goals—itinerant preaching or education. Antony Copley has provided an incisive analysis of these debates. He argues that it was not until the 1880s that missionaries on the whole came to embrace the concept of education as a means of "preparing the soil" for conversion, as opposed to simply preaching in homes or in public markets, regional *melas* (fairs), and along streets and lanes (Copley 1997, 13–27). Before that time, itinerant preaching held a privileged place among the various methods of evangelizing, whether in homes or in the open air. Missionaries believed that the time of "harvest" was so ripe that simply announcing the core of the gospel message in familiar language would turn non-Christians away from their "heathen" beliefs.

Even this relatively simple program for action, however, required several conditions to be successful: missionaries would need to learn the local language in order to convey the core message in recognizable terms; they would have to gain and keep an audience long enough for the information to be delivered; and they would have to deliver their message with enough urgency that Indians would feel compelled to act, either by accepting or by rejecting Christian claims about Jesus. The difficulties missionaries encountered trying to master the vernacular languages of India are too various to deal with here. Instead, I would like to focus on one of the techniques missionaries used to attract an audience and convey the message in spite of linguistic barriers, namely the teaching tool referred to as the wordless book.

Books and British Power

References to the wordless book appear in the detailed descriptions of their work that missionaries wrote in the late nineteenth and early twentieth centuries for the benefit of their supporters in England. Praised as "a most useful text for an impromptu sermon," this book could be as large as a flag, capable of attracting the attention of a large crowd (Elliot 1987, 146), or small enough to fit in the palm of the hand, a size useful for evangelizing in homes.[2] Its simplicity made it flexible enough to be used in the wide variety of preaching venues in south India: bazaars, *melas*, homes, verandahs, side streets, and lanes, in the shade of a large tree, or off the back of the wagon in which the missionary traveled. The book consisted of nothing more than four pieces of cloth or paper, each "page" standing for one component of the core Christian message—sin, the blood of Jesus, redemption from sin, and heaven.

Books as material objects in and of themselves carried a great deal of symbolic resonance for both missionaries and Indians. In one sense, the colored pages of the wordless book play on the theological notion that the revealed word of God contained in the pages of the Christian Bible was not necessarily the literal speech of God addressing his people, but rather a message carried by writings that were felt to have a divine origin (Graham 1987, 121). In India, as elsewhere, Protestants held out the promise that through the painstaking process of learning to read one could gain direct access to the scriptures and the powerful salvific message they contain. This promise might have had appeal for individuals from lower castes, since they were strictly prohibited by the laws of Hinduism from reading the Vedas, sacred books attributed with similar salvific properties. The historical record indicates that for many Indian Christians, the Bible served as a powerful symbol of their distinctive identity. For example, female Indian evangelists, known as Bible women, carried enormous cloth-bound Bibles, which virtually became part of their uniform (Kent 1999, 147). Moreover, the basic literacy that missionaries disseminated widely among the population through their innumerable schools was an instrumental part of the civilizing mission. Books opened up a whole world of knowledge. Geography, history, and astronomy were all enlisted in the task of extirpating "superstition," so that modern, enlightened forms of knowledge, both religious and secular, could take root.

In addition, the book stood metonymically for the formidable administrative power of the British state, capable of encompassing the cultural, geographical, historical, and linguistic diversity of India within its printed pages (Cohn 1996, 4–5). Printed books thus became a signifier of British sovereignty, easily distinguishable from Indian books, which consisted of strips of palm leaves bound together with a thorn or a thong, the brittle surfaces of which were inscribed with the letters of Malayalam, Tamil, Telugu, or Sanskrit. On the other hand, as a metonym for British power, the book was also vulnerable to misuse, so that its meaning was inverted. Like any signifier that comes to stand for an entire nation, way of life, or governing body, the book was vulnerable to violent appropriation. Missionaries reported with chagrin that some Bibles found their way into the salt, snuff, and rice market, where they were torn up and their pages used as packaging material (Bhabha 1994, 92, 122). Then again, some Indians saw a correlation between the size of the book and the power of those who wielded them. Samuel Mateer records a Brahman once saying, "I have seen that Christianity is declining and losing its strength. Up to this time you were giving us large books; now you have begun to bring books of a single leaf" (Mateer 1871, 337). Seen in this light, the wordless book might have been seen as a particularly flimsy and weak form of book. But perhaps it was a more effective sign of British and Christian power than the hefty tomes distributed by missionary Bible societies precisely because it could not be reduced to mere paper through an act of subversive dismemberment. In short, books could mobilize sentiments of affinity through identification with the Christian British, or of estrangement through alienation from and contempt for the British (Lincoln 1989).

While ostensibly designed to assist nonliterate audiences in understanding the Christian message, the wordless book also helped missionaries compensate for their frequently inadequate training in local languages. Missionary anecdotes extolling the capacity of the wordless book to dispense with the trappings of language elide this potential embarrassment. In 1898, a teacher from the Church of England Zenana Missionary Society's (CEZMS) school for deaf children in Tirunelveli reported enlisting the help of one of her students to quiet an unruly village Sunday school class. Miss Swainson wrote: "One of the dumb girls was told to explain by signs the 'Wordless Book' which was being shown, and all that the heathen children learnt that day was from her" (Church Missionary Society 1899, 121). Such missionary accounts attest that the wordless book was helpful both for nonliterate teachers and audiences, just like the scrolls and story-boards used throughout India for disseminating religious narratives and doctrines among nonliterate groups.

Having reduced the teachings of Christianity to the bare minimum, however, so that they were stripped of any cultural or historical baggage, the wordless book became too abstract to make concrete sense to those otherwise unfamiliar with a Western cultural milieu. Of course, people can and do learn new symbol systems; over time, Indian Christians have become among the most influential theologians and interpreters of Christianity in the world. But in these nineteenth-century direct encounters, missionaries repeatedly ran up against the wall of mutual incomprehension. The wordless book illustrates aspects of this difficulty. It was essentially a symbol that pointed to other symbols. Red, for example, stood for the blood of Jesus, which itself was a symbol evoking the redemptive power of Jesus' death. The blood of Jesus was not to be taken as "real," ordinary blood, but rather as having the properties of a cleansing agent, capable of dissolving sins, themselves understood metaphorically as sensible entities like dirt or stains. The more literal-minded inquirer might ask about the "real" referents to which these symbols pointed, to which the missionary might answer that the Atonement was ultimately a divine "mystery," incapable of explanation in mechanistic terms. One had to *experience* salvation for oneself. In the context of religious revival in England, a preacher's public performance skillfully and passionately manipulated these symbols to induce such experiences in audience members prepared, it was believed, by the Holy Spirit to receive them. But the performance fell flat when the symbols that missionaries relied on to convey the richly imagined narrative of salvation so characteristic of Protestantism—the deep, interior self, stained with sin, and the awesome mercy of God's sacrifice—were simply not shared with their Indian audience.

Referring to the use of the wordless book during her early days with the CEZMS, Amy Wilson-Carmichael suggests that such simple props were helpful at initially attracting the interest of listeners, but did not always facilitate a direct connection with the audience. When a missionary focused exclusively on the "souls" of the audience, they often pulled them back to the somatic realities of the social order, where the body was the field upon which individual destiny was inscribed and lived out. Wilson-Carmichael's classic work of missionary reportage, *Things as They Are* (1904), describes in detail the difficulty of getting Hindu villagers interested in the fate of their souls. Here, she describes a typical variety of interruption:

> I was in the middle of [my sermon], and thinking only of it and their souls, when an old lady with fluffy white hair leaned forward and gazed at me with a beautiful, earnest gaze. She did not speak; she just listened and gazed. . . . And then she raised a skeleton claw, and grabbed her hair, and pointed to mine. "Are you a widow too," she asked, "that you have no oil on yours?". . . Her question had set the ball rolling again. "Oil! no oil! Can't you even afford a half-penny a month to buy good oil? . . . Don't any white Ammals ever use oil?" (Wilson-Carmichael 1904, 8–9)

The fluffy, un-oiled hair of white women was one object of fascination that commanded the attention of Indians more than the contents of a sermon. Others were the pith helmets (or sola topis) worn for protection against the sun, the absence of jewels, and other markers of respectable married status, and of course, white skin. "What sort of soap do you use to make your skin white?" asked one hearer, and Carmichael noted, for the benefit of her readership back home, that "most of them would far rather be told that secret than how to get a white heart" (Wilson-Carmichael 1904, 10). This exchange, repeated numerous times in evangelical literature—especially in the writings of women evangelists—reflects the efforts that Indians made to fit the exotic figure of the missionary into a familiar taxonomic framework for ordering the different groups in society. All over India, the way in which one adorned and clothed the body revealed a great deal about a person's place in the social order, most notably their caste and marital status.

Clothes and the Civilizing Mission in the "Land of Charity"

Popular conceptions of the relationship between dress and missionaries include the impression evangelists foisted Western-style clothes upon converts that missionaries tried to force the converts to dress in Western styles in an effort to create a generation of "mini-me's" in the colonies. A good deal of recent scholarship challenges this view, arguing that a lot of subtle jousting went on between missionaries and converts, when desires and ambitions were bound up in dilemmas over what to wear (Comaroff and Comaroff 1997, 218–273; Harper 2000, 139–145; Tarlo 1996, 23–61).

In colonial south India, missionaries displayed a good deal of ambivalence about the transformation of Indian customs and manners after those of the West. While "civilization" was heartily encouraged, "imitation" was feared and condemned; it was thought to lead to living beyond one's means and indebtedness, arrogance and putting on airs. At the same time, commitment to the concept that salvation came through God's grace alone faltered when British churchmen confronted the economically depressed and socially marginalized masses, who consistently responded with the most enthusiasm to Christianity. When faced with the large numbers of poor Indians who entered the church in the wake of mass movements, a tendency among many British missionaries to see themselves as spiritually, culturally, and racially superior brought merely verbal confession into suspicion; it rarely served as sufficient proof of a convert's actual spiritual regeneration (Dirks 1996, 125). Although there were notable exceptions, I would argue most missionaries wished to see the lives of Indian converts reshaped, and they focused much of their reform efforts on those practices that seemed in direct violation of Christian scripture, like polygamy, dishonesty, petty theft, and so forth. Sometimes, however, both missionaries and Indian Christians were liable to conflate "Christian law" with Western custom.

The notion that the care and presentation of the body, along with the organization of the living environment, were reliable indices of the state of the soul constituted a key component of the ideology informing the civilizing mission. A speech about church work among the lower classes, for instance, delivered at the Third Decennial Missionary Conference, stressed that "the tendency of regenerate souls to keep the body and its surroundings pure is easily observable" (*Report* 1893, 13). At the same time, however, Protestants from England and the United States had no monopoly over the idea that the surfaces of the body revealed something about the moral state of the depths. In nineteenth-century south India, too, visual presentations of the self were key components of the assertion of self-worth and social status, although the scale of values according to which such worth or status was measured differed considerably. In this respect, the sartorial styles that nineteenth-century Indian Christians adopted or rejected in the princely state of Travancore are revealing. The so-called breast-cloth controversies illustrate how the civilizing mission could become very complicated when Indians appropriated the objects that symbolized its values, interpreted them according to local scales of values, and used them to mobilize latent sentiments of affinity and estrangement between themselves and their Indian neighbors.

In 1828–1829, and again in 1858–1859, outbreaks of violence rocked the princely state of Travancore, on the southern border of the Madras Presidency and now part of Kerala. In the 1820s, Indian Christian women of the low Nadar caste started covering their torsos in public with a particular style of garment.[3] This garment was associated with the women of the dominant local caste, the Nayars. In response to the perceived transgression of their caste's customary privilege, male Nayars burned down chapels, destroyed gardens, and poisoned wells. They also publicly stripped the women of Indian Christian communities, tearing from their bodies the disputed breast-cloth, a length of material drawn across the bosom and over the shoulder. Several scholars have investigated the historical background to these events, but none asks why Indian Christian women initially resisted the jacket designed for them by missionary wives (Cohn 1996; Gladstone 1984; Gnanadason 1990; Hardgrave 1968; Yesudas 1975). Here, I would like to relocate these disturbances more specifically within the context of the south Indian tradition of attributing meaning to garments and adornments.

London Missionary Society evangelists found a suitable field for their efforts in Travancore, known to Indians as *Dharmabhumi*. The LMS missionary Samuel Mateer glossed this Sanskrit name as the "Land of Charity," translating *dharma* as "charity" (Mateer 1871). At root, *dharma* means to sustain or uphold, and the word comes to denote notions of law, religious duty, and even the socio-moral order of the cosmos. Missionaries and colonial administrators regarded Travancore as one of the most conservative and staunchly Hindu regions of the subcontinent, where the traditional Hindu social order was firmly upheld (Jeffrey 1994, 36). The Raja of Travancore presided over an unusually diverse population. Extremely old Muslim (*Muppillai*) and Syrian Christian communities, founded by immigrants from the Middle East, had been living in the region since the first millennium of the Common Era. A large community of low-caste fisher people, the *Mukkuvars*, converted to Roman Catholicism in the mid-sixteenth century. But the majority of the population was Hindu, comprising three main status levels: several castes of heavily indebted or enslaved agricultural workers (Pariah, Pulaya, Ezhava, and Nadar); a Brahmin landholding and priestly élite; and a Nayar military caste, many of whose members owned land or worked as managers for Brahmin estates.

Based on notions of purity and pollution, a strict ideology regulated contact between the members of different castes. According to Mateer's frequently cited testimony, distance taboos preventing polluting contact between members of different castes were finely calibrated:

> A Nair, for example, may approach, but must not touch a Nambudri Brahman. A Shanar [Nadar] must remain thirty-six paces off, and a Puleyan slave must stay at a distance of ninety-six paces. Other intervals, according to a graduated scale, are appointed to be observed between the remaining castes; thus, for instance, a Shanar [Nadar] must remain twelve steps away from a Nair, a Pulayan sixty-six steps away and so on. (Mateer 1871, 32)

In order to prevent polluting contact between castes from happening inadvertently, a plethora of rules and customs ensured that members of each caste were visibly distinguishable from each other. A council of *sudra* (probably Nayar) leaders, called the Pidagaikarars, was responsible for enforcing these rules, as well as for adjudicating disputes that arose over their transgression. Each year, villages would send two or three delegates to an annual meeting of this body in Sucindram. According to church historian C. M. Agur, "One of the chief topics discussed in this annual council was whether all the individuals of their caste and other castes had duly observed their respective caste customs and manners, and whether any one class had adopted the costume, food, speech (provincialism or brogue) and general habits of the other class, and if the council discovered that any individual violated or trespassed his caste rules and limits, it took the law into its own hands and brought him to judgement and carried everything with a high hand" (Agur 1903, 570).

One striking feature of the region, which it shared with other areas of India, is that the distinctive sartorial style of each caste or religious community marked its place within the social hierarchy. In the estimation of Western observers, none of the indigenous residents of this hot, tropical region wore very much clothing. But one must bear in mind that this assessment comes from people who were advised to wrap themselves in a thick layer of flannel undergarments to protect them from the disease-carrying tropical "miasma" of south Asia (Cohn 1996, 153–156). In one of his popular books about the customs and habits of Travancore, Mateer described the various styles worn by women of different castes:

> Children perfectly naked are playing about in the blazing sun, and from hence southward one sees great numbers of women going about in nature's garb from the waist upwards. Indeed, one of the first signs of having entered Travancore territory is the sight of half-nude Chogan [an "untouchable" caste] females watering trees, or otherwise engaged on the banks of the backwaters. Muhammadan women, on the contrary, seem rather cumbered with clothing, wearing both jacket and upper-cloth, often black with filth, or the greater portion dirty, then partly covered with one clean white cloth, making the others appear but the worse by contrast. The Brahman women are always nicely dressed. The inelegant but decent dress of the Roman Catholic fisherwomen appears to be the result of a curious compromise between barbarous laws and female modesty—they cover the bosom straight across with a cloth which runs under each arm. But we are struck with the fact that the Christian jacket seems to occur but too rarely in proportion to the number of converts, and are obliged to hope that this mark of propriety and refinement is not getting forgotten in these days of peace and prosperity. The Christians seem to prefer the respectable "upper cloth," but it is insufficient as a garment for females. (Mateer 1883, 15)

Other literary sources, along with paintings and drawings from the period, allow us to enlarge upon this economical, if deeply condescending description. Below the waist, women of all castes wore some kind of unstitched long cloth, wound numerous times around the waist, with one end sometimes drawn up between the legs to allow for greater mobility. The women of the Nayar caste sometimes drew the other end of the cloth up across their breasts and over the shoulder, in a style much like the present-day sari. More frequently, at home, they did not cover their torsos at all. And in semi-private settings, such as a posed sitting for a photograph or painting, they pulled a very thin, bordered cloth over their breasts and secured it around the chest (Nandakumar 1996). Nambudri Brahman women had to be much more scrupulous in covering their bodies than women of other castes, as might be expected given the intense concern for women's sexual purity generated by their kinship system, in which only the eldest brother in a family had the right to marry and father the family's heirs (Yalman 1963). They not only drew one length of the cloth across their chests, they also complemented this garment with an undergarment, a blouse of colored cloth that tied in the front. On the very few occasions that Nambudri women left the seclusion of their homes, they further obscured their bodies from sight by traveling under huge umbrellas. As Mateer mentioned, the women of Muslim and Syrian Christian communities wore a long-sleeved blouse of white or colored cotton, while the low-caste fisherwomen, the Mukkuvars, wore a strip of coarse cloth tied around their chests, covering the breasts but leaving the shoulders bare. According to the customs of the region, enforced by local caste councils, women of the ritually polluting low castes—including the Nadars—were forbidden to wear anything above the waist or below the knees.

In one way or another, historians of this period agree that the breast-cloth stood as a symbol of the social aspirations of the Nadars. Traditionally, they harvested the sap of palmyra trees to produce a mildly alcoholic beverage, toddy. This activity rendered the Nadars too ritually polluting to enter Brahmanical temples. Along with other even more degraded castes, they were subjected to numerous restrictions within the Hindu social order: they were forbidden to carry umbrellas; to carry pots of water on their hips or milk cows; to wear sandals or gold or silver jewelry; and significantly, to wear any garments above the waist or below the knees. At once reflecting and reinforcing the inferior place such groups occupied in the caste hierarchy, these prohibitions systematically denied members of low-caste groups the use of widely recognized symbols of social worth.

In the nineteenth century, however, lower castes often benefited from local economic changes attendant upon British colonization. Some Nadars became quite wealthy. As Dick Kooiman has shown, the establishment of coffee plantations in the hills of Ceylon (Sri Lanka) (from 1824) and the Nilgiris (from 1838) helped to spur this economic turnabout. Many members of the Nadar community in Travancore improved their incomes as plantation workers, supervisors, labor contractors, and even owners (Kooiman 1989, 117–143). Also, as Nadars in Travancore and in the neighboring district of Tirunelveli left the palmyra fields to work in the plantations, those who stayed behind were able to earn a much better living by immigrating from one region to another in concert with the alternating months of the tapping season, since the trees in Tirunelveli exuded sap during March and August, and in Travancore, between September and February (Kooiman 1989, 155). In addition, Nadars in Travancore became involved in trade, dealing in commodities such as jaggery, tamarind, and cotton, and plying their wares along the trunk roads built down the center of the Madras Presidency by the British (Hardgrave 1969, 94–96; Kooiman 1989, 156). All of these factors conspired to make the ascribed status of Nadars as a low, ritually polluting caste incommensurate with their perceived self-worth.

In this context, the appropriation by Nadar women of Mateer's "respectable breast-cloth" associated with Nayar women becomes understandable as a strategy for claiming higher status through the medium of dress. Emma Tarlo rightly argues that because of its proximity to the body, clothing is particularly susceptible to symbolic elaboration. Existing at the boundary between self and nonself, clothes are frequently perceived as expressions of the wearer's identity or nature, like the detachable ornaments of jewelry, or cosmetics (Tarlo 1996, 16). Moreover, like other symbols, clothing is a multivalent sign, liable to be interpreted in a variety of different ways. For this reason, clothes remain an unstable form of symbolic communication, because a given audience may fail to perceive what the wearer seeks to convey by donning a particular garment for a particular occasion. This ambiguity worked to the advantage of Nadars. While missionaries vociferously asserted to Travancore authorities that the breast-cloth meant nothing more than the Christian women's desire for modesty, Nayars and Nadars shared an understanding of the style as a significant marker of high-caste status. Fashion became an important staging ground for social aspirations because controversial claims could be made under the cover, as it were, of quotidian forms of practice. If the interest of Nadar women in the breast-cloth is fairly evident, however, the reasons behind their lack of interest in the Christian bodice are more obscure.

Bodices and Breast-Clothes: Raiments of the Soul, or Emblems of Status?

Within at least six years of their arrival, it appears that missionaries were urging the female half of their congregations to cover their bosoms in accordance with Western notions of female modesty. In 1812, Colonel John Munro, a British resident at the Travancore court, was acting as Dewan for the young and politically weak indigenous ruler, Rani Lakshmibai. Munro issued a proclamation guaranteeing Indian Christian women the right to cover their bosoms, although sources do not indicate with what form of dress (Kooiman 1989, 149). In the 1820s, the wives of LMS missionaries designed a distinctive garment for Indian Christian converts to wear to meet the demands of Christian decency. They modeled this garment on the Muslim style of blouse, but with shorter sleeves, similar to the present-day *choli*, or sari blouse. Sources from the period refer to it either in English as "the Christian jacket," or by reference to other local garments, like the Brahmin woman's *ravakkay* (the upper garment) or the Muslim woman's *sappayam*.

Nineteenth-century documents portray the desire for modesty as the only reason for introducing this innovation, but Indian Christian converts do not seem to have taken to the jacket immediately. The LMS missionary, Charles Mault, reported that the Nadars looked upon it as "an invidious badge of distinction from which the people turned away with as much abhorrence as respectable farmers in England would from a badge worn in a parish workhouse" (Kooiman 1989, 158). By about 1856, though, the missionaries had succeeded in getting Christian women to wear the garment on a large scale. As Rev. F. Baylis wrote to the missionary board in London,

> It has been exceedingly difficult to introduce what to them is a strange custom . . . the women generally have been content with putting their cloth over their heads and folding it in front, when they come to service, which is not sufficient covering even then, and on other occasions going about as the heathen women. . . . At our last celebration of the Lord's Supper, *for the first time*, every one of the female members, old women as well as young (and the old generally have a great objection to these new-fangled customs) had on the jacket and were thus decently clothed. (quoted in Jeffrey 1994, 54; emphasis in original)

This victory was achieved only through a concerted campaign the year before, when the hardworking girls in an LMS boarding school made 500 jackets, 150 of which were given away, with the rest sold to recover the cost of the material (Jeffrey 1994, 54).

In stark contrast to the recalcitrant women of the Indian Christian congregation, boarding school students were, at least in missionary representations, exemplars of feminine Christian virtue. In photographs, they are shown very modestly dressed in both saris and blouses. The girls boarding school in Nagercoil was founded in 1823 by Mrs. Mault and Mrs. Mead, wife of another LMA evangelist, Charles Mead, for the education of the so-called lower castes of the region (Mateer 1871, 271). In the "total" environment of these institutions, missionaries were able to regulate closely the diet, dress, sleeping habits, behavior, and comportment of the students (de Alwis 1997). In the Nagercoil boarding school, the girls learned the disciplined arts of lace-making and embroidery, themselves exercises in cultivating dainty femininity. The emphasis on needlework in these schools served multiple purposes. Not only did it train workers capable of producing the stitched garments that Indian Christians were encouraged to adopt; it was also, more importantly, a key component of the boarding school's efforts to instill "civilized" values in their students. In addition, as Malathi de Alwis argues in her study of Christian boarding schools in colonial

Sri Lanka, "Sewing played a crucial role in the very molding of Christian women, in the construction of a particular moral demeanor. It was a practice that insisted on neatness, orderliness, concentration, patience, and precision" (de Alwis 1997, 119). Some of the money that students earned through their labors was put toward purchasing their freedom, and some evidently went to the support of the school, as well as that of a neighboring seminary for boys (Kooiman 1989, 78; Mateer 1871, 275).

Educated, well-dressed, financially self-supporting and skilled in needlework, the girls at the Nagercoil boarding school served as a powerful symbol of the civilizing effect of Christianity. When LMS missionaries petitioned the Rajah of Travancore to intervene in the riots of 1858–1859, they held up as evidence of the civilized status of Nadar women the bronze medal that the boarding school girls had won in London, at the Great Exhibition (1851), for "pillow lace" made with embroidered threads of silver and gold (*Parliamentary Papers* 1859, 39). Having become so thoroughly distinguished from their Indian compatriots, however, these girls experienced great difficulty fitting into Nadar Society again. Kooiman writes, "They could not be reabsorbed into their community and consequently had to be settled on mission compounds" (Kooiman 1989, 78). Becoming too closely identified with the values, tastes, and culture of the missionaries had its dangers as well as its advantages.

The plight of the girls in the LMS boarding-school sheds some light on the question of why Indian Christian women with more scope for choice persistently refused to adopt the garment sanctioned by the missionary seal of approval, preferring to wear the breast-cloth, even over the advice and warnings of their patrons. According to Kooiman, LMS records suggest that some women were afraid to wear the Christian jacket, lest this item also be viewed as a transgression against the laws of the country (Kooiman 1989, 158). Given the intimidating and punitive practices of the Pidagaikarars, this interpretation seems reasonable. As Baylis suggested, elderly women resisted it on the basis of their suspicion of any "new-fangled" custom. But perhaps another explanation suggests itself, if we examine the jacket through the lens of indigenous traditions of assigning meaning to particular garments. Viewed in this context, adopting the Christian jacket appears not only as a distinctive marker of Christian identity, and thus, insofar as virtually all Travancoran Christians were from the lower castes, as a new marker of caste status; it also indicates a certain absorption into the nimbus of power of the foreign missionaries.

In addition, the significance of clothing in the status hierarchies of nineteenth-century south India was deeply influenced by the institution of kingship, in which symbols such as clothing and articles of adornment were used to honor those people who best approximated the moral ideal. Kings and other more local rulers promoted their loyal followers within the local status hierarchy by bestowing on them the honor of wearing a special garment, or carrying a certain banner, or being carried in a palanquin, and so forth. While historians of the princely state of Pudukottai, in what is now Tamil Nadu, have provided the closest analyses of this phenomenon, it seems not improbable that the monarch of Travancore, along with subsidiary ruling bodies such as the Pidagaikarar council, policed the boundaries of the social order in a similar way by regulating the use of emblems, material objects that both signified and embodied the patronage, and approval of the sovereign.[4] As we have seen, clothing was a mechanism for marking and enforcing social divisions within Travancore society. This practice was not merely a semi-conscious matter of tastes being shaped by class and status; it was regulated by law and violently enforced. At the same time, though, we should avoid the Orientalist error of assuming that because the regulation of social borders was highly systemized, it was impervious to change.

However much colonial ethnographers tried to represent Indian society as static and rigidly hierarchical, numerous avenues for social change and social mobility made nineteenth-century Indian society extremely complex, fluid, and dynamic. The king's ability to recognize merit in his followers and bestow honors on them provided important opportunities for social mobility, and also constituted an arena for intense conflict. Emblems were gifts that a sovereign would give to loyal subordinates in recognition of feats of valor performed in the king's service, such as killing wild animals or defeating the enemies in battle. Flags decorated with the special insignia of the king, fly whisks (a symbol of kingship), and swords were typical emblems. But the concept of the emblem extended to the right to display such objects in formal processions, along with other perquisites, such as the right to a ride in a palanquin and be served by specialist dancers, musicians, and torchbearers. Titles—paradigmatically one of the royal names—formed another category of emblem.

As Nicholas Dirks rightly observes, emblems may be seen as human counterparts of the honors (*mariyatai*) a god distributed among his followers in the central ritual of Puranic Hinduism, *puja* (Dirks 1988, 47, 100). Emblems were to the king as honors were to the god—material objects that transmitted the substance of the sovereign from himself to his followers, and thereby allowed the followers to partake of a portion of the king's or the deity's sovereignty. Besides standing as a sign of the king's pleasure, these objects also gave recognition that the subject was acting in a way that approximated the king's heroic, courageous conduct, and further, allowed the recipient to approximate the king's conduct even more. An honored subject, by acting virtuously, would get to use a special umbrella or flag, or decorated palanquin, just as the king did. In other words, emblems signified a subject's proximity to the moral center of society, the king, both by recognizing virtuous action and by allowing for more exact imitation of the sovereign. In each case, whether garments, jewelry, flags, or other objects were conferred by kings, the objects themselves can be seen as more than just marks of honor. As Joanne Waghorne argues, these objects helped to build up a new "body," a substantially new identity for the recipient, transforming him from what he was into a new, honored, and honorable companion of the king (Waghorne 1989).

British colonialism, however, brought an influx of new rulers, with new concepts of the moral ideal to be emulated. The riots that erupted over women's clothing in mid-nineteenth-century Travancore may be attributed in part at least to the ways in which local missionaries, intentionally or unintentionally, arrogated to themselves the role previously monopolized by kings and Pidagaikarars. By insisting that female members of their congregations change their style of dress, they were usurping the right of local leaders to reshape social borders through the assignment of emblems of status. At the same time, evidence exists that indigenous codes of dress governing the behavior and appearance that marked social standing were capable of change. Rulers in Travancore had, in fact, previously bestowed on an élite fraction of Nadars the privilege of wearing the breast-cloth (Hardgrave 1968, 62; Petition from the Shanars of South Travancore).

Traditionally, prohibitions were placed on low castes in Travancore against carrying umbrellas and wearing sandals or clothing above the waist, but I would argue that these prohibitions functioned as *negative emblems*. Exposed breasts, sun-darkened skin, and callused feet were badges of shame, not honor. These badges of shame built up a body that placed low-caste Nadars *outside* the respectable social order, at a distance far removed from the ordering center of society, embodied in the king. When Nadars began to aspire toward a better station in Indian society, aligning themselves with new centers of power in the emerging political landscape of colonial south India, they began to enjoy opportunities for acquiring emblems of their own, from new sources.

It is remarkable that, at least initially, Indian Christian women refused these signs of allegiance. Embodying the civilizing mission of the LMS in Travancore, the Christian jacket seems definitely to have mobilized sentiments, but of estrangement rather than affinity. Insofar as virtually all converts to Christianity came from the lower echelons of the caste hierarchy, it seems likely that the jacket was interpreted as one more signifier of degraded social status. As much as LMS missionaries preached a gospel of equality, what converts wanted was a way to distinguish themselves from the roles and associations of the past.[5] Rather than identifying with the new British rulers at this particular historical juncture, Nadars favored the strategy of identifying with the higher castes. They thus appropriated the Nayar style of dress in order to elicit recognition of their improved status, in a manner that Kooiman likens to the process of Sanskritization (Kooiman 1989, 203–208).

The Consolidation of Indian Christian Identity

Objects introduced into Indian society by British missionaries evoked a wide range of emotive responses, from bafflement to desire, from outrage to contempt. These objects were thus instrumental in reconfiguring the social borders that distinguished the Indian Christian community. It seems appropriate to conclude by providing an account of the outcome of the disturbances in Travancore. After about two years of increasingly violent and disruptive clashes between Nadars and Nayars, the dispute over the breast-cloth reached a legal resolution. The legal side to the affair took the form of a contest between modernity and tradition. The Nayars, supported by the royal government of Travancore, argued that the breast-cloth was a part of a customary system of caste-markers that helped to differentiate the population into their respective hereditary classes. It was thus crucial to preserving the "way of life" of the region. On the other hand, the British government in Madras, impelled in part by the pressure put on them by the English-language press and the LMS missionaries, insisted that basic human decency was at issue. The governor of Madras conveyed the gravity of the colonial government's responsibility to reform this "barbaric" transgression of natural human liberty in a letter to the British resident in Travancore: "I have seldom met with a case, in which not only truth and justice, but every feeling of our common humanity are so entirely on one side. The whole civilized world would cry shame upon us, if we do not make a firm stand on such an occasion" (*Parliamentary Papers* 1859, 43). On July 26, 1859, the Raja of Travancore issued a proclamation: "We hereby proclaim that there is no objection to Shanar women either putting on a jacket, like the Christian Shanar women, or to Shanar women of all creeds dressing in coarse cloth, and tying themselves round it as the Mukkavattigal [Mukkavar fisherwomen] do, or to their covering their bosoms in any manner whatever; but not like the women of high caste" (Hardgrave 1969, 69).

The presence or absence of the breast-cloth across the bosom of a low-caste woman generated many different meanings: to missionaries it connoted modesty deriving from heightened moral sensibilities; to Nayars insolence; and to upwardly mobile Nadars, it was a means of conveying defiant self-respect. The very multiplicity of meanings attached to this object, to this gesture, is indicative of the historically and socially volatile climate of the times, as this somewhat isolated corner of the subcontinent became more and more thoroughly enmeshed within global flows of capital and commodities, as well as so-called modern ideas and attitudes. During such turbulent times, signifiers do not have a transparent, univocal meaning, equally apparent to every audience member. The material objects that missionaries brought with them to the "field" of south India, or invented, built, or devised once they arrived, became embedded in a web of meaning. But as scholarship on the reception-history of Christian missions demonstrates, the symbolic import that missionaries attributed to any one of these objects was by no means inevitably the same one that indigenous people invested in them (Comaroffs 1991, 1997; Rafael 1988). Such scholarship makes clear that missionary efforts to control what their hearers took away from their presentations was fraught with difficulty.

Examinations of the wordless book and the Christian bodice reveal that the failure to communicate across the cultural abyss that separated Indians and British can be understood in terms of the dynamics of assimilation and differentiation. In order to attract Indians, missionaries had to assimilate their message to local context, but still retain the theological specificity of the Christian teachings. Those who sought to preach the gospel alone frequently erred on the side of differentiation, and thus never did gain the interest of their audiences, because they failed to make the Christian teachings relevant in the Indian context. Their reports to Christians in England were filled with hopeful accounts of hearts moved and truths accepted through preaching, education, and the liberal distribution of tracts and Bibles. But the rates of conversion were infinitesimally small, except among the low castes and "untouchables," who were marginalized from the centers of power and influence within Indian society. For these converts, who embraced Christianity in groups bound together by caste and family connections, conversion was seen, at least in part, as a way to escape the stigma and exploitation that came along with their low social status (Forrester 1980; Hardgrave 1968; Kooiman 1989; Oddie 1975). For many of these converts, becoming Christian served as a way to reconfigure social boundaries. In this way, they could differentiate themselves from other low-caste groups, as well as distance themselves from the social roles to which they had been confined in the past and create alliances with powerful newcomers offering new social roles.

Among many other things, religious conversion is a strategy for reconfiguring the social borders that divide and unite groups of people (Viswanathan 1998). Conversion to Christianity frequently necessitates the transfer of allegiances from one group to another, since the church maintains that one can only have true commitments to one faith at a time. How are the invisible, yet deeply felt lines that divide one group from another constructed? As Bruce Lincoln has argued, many factors may help to "mark and enforce" social borders, including "differences in language, topography, diet, patterns of economic and marital exchange, habituated behaviors (customs), normative preferences (values in the moral sphere, aesthetics or tastes in others), and so forth" (Lincoln 1989, 9). But seen from a broader analytic perspective, these factors are not in and of themselves responsible for creating these boundaries. Rather, they are instruments that evoke something more basic and directly constitutive, what Lincoln calls the "sentiments . . . of affinity and estrangement" (Lincoln 1989, 9).[6] These two terms encompass, he continues, "all feelings of likeness, belonging, mutual attachment, and solidarity—whatever their intensity, affective tone, and degree of consciousness—and, on the other hand, those corresponding feelings of distance, separation, otherness and alienation" (Lincoln 1989, 9–10). Material objects collectively constitute another item I would add to Lincoln's list of instruments capable of mobilizing the social sentiments that construct social boundaries, especially those material symbols that become closely associated with a particular group, such as a national flag or a cleric's collar.

Lincoln's thoughts on discourse and the construction of society are of interest to scholars studying the history of missions. Given the vast cultural and linguistic differences between missionaries and the Indians they sought to persuade, it is somewhat astonishing to consider how they ever did manage to evoke sentiments of affinity sufficient to motivate Indians to ally themselves with the mission. In cases where they were successful, particularly among the economically depressed and socially marginalized fractions of society, one can see that the discourse of missions mobilized the latent sentiments of estrangement between Hindus from the so-called low-castes and the élites of traditional Hindu society. And yet the discourse of missions was very rarely successful in generating sentiments of affinity sufficient to overcome the sense of alienation between foreign missionaries and Indian converts. Certainly, Western feelings of racial superiority proved remarkably intractable, even among those people with the most familiar, cooperative contact with Indians. But Indians, too, had their own reasons for desiring to see themselves as distinct, on some level, from the British.

This chapter has explored how some of material objects that missionaries used in their evangelical and "civilizing" efforts succeeded or failed in generating the sentiments capable of softening the rigid social borders that separated British missionaries from the Indians to whom they preached. I have argued that while the strategy of converting Indians by the "gospel alone" would seem, on an ideological level, to generate more sentiments of affinity between the British and Indians, since it regarded both of them as equally capable of sinning or being saved, symbolic objects associated with the civilizing mission attracted considerable interest from Indians. While the civilizing mission, as is well known, held out the promise of eventual equality, it was based on a profound sense of superiority and difference. In the hands of Indians, however, objects that carried the weight of

British civilization ended up serving as markers for a new social group, distinct from Hindu Indians or the Christian British, that is, Indian Christians.

Notes

1. Research for this project was made possible by grants from the American Institute for Indian Studies and the Fulbright Foundation, who are gratefully acknowledged. For further elaboration of this research, see Kent (2004).
2. While conducting fieldwork in India in 1996–97, I met an elderly female Indian evangelist, or "Bible woman," who demonstrated to me how she would teach the rudiments of Christian salvation using a miniature version of the wordless book. See Kent (2004).
3. In nineteenth-century sources, people from this community were referred to as Shanars. In part because of the historical developments I describe in this chapter, they have come to regard that term as offensive, preferring to be called "Nadars." Earlier, the title "Nadar" was reserved for an élite faction within the community, the "Lords of the Soil," who owned property and exploited the labor of their less fortunate caste peers. Faced with the dilemma of being anachronistic or potentially offensive, I have chosen the former option.
4. Several scholars have dealt with the subject of emblems, known as *pirutus* in Tamil-speaking south India. See, e.g., Dirks (1988) and Waghorne (1989, 1994). Bayly briefly discusses the importance of emblems among Paravar Roman Catholics (Bayly 1989).
5. This interpretation raises another, strictly speculative question: If the missionary wives had designed a garment that resembled their own dress, as missionary wives were later to do with the long-sleeved ruffled blouse worn under the sari, would the Nadar converts have responded any differently?
6. As Lincoln is well aware, the language of sentiment is likely to arouse alarm in some social scientists (Lincoln 1989, 176). But if we recognize that kinship patterns, languages, values, and taste are socially constructed, however well naturalized and taken for granted, "sentiment" seems an adequate term to designate those affective–cognitive factors that make them seem real and worth defending.

CHAPTER SIX

LANDSCAPES OF FAITH: BRITISH MISSIONARY TOURISM IN THE SOUTH PACIFIC

Jane Samson

The materiality of Europe's encounter with the Pacific has only lately been addressed by scholars, and it has tended to focus on the collection and interpretation of material culture. Adrienne Kaeppler's pioneering work on Captain Cook's ethnographical collections has been enhanced by recent studies in the theory of museum acquisition and display, which emphasize the connection between collection and imperialism (Barringer and Flynn 1998; Coombes 1994; Kaeppler 1978; Pearce 1989). Anthropologist Nicholas Thomas has examined a range of these issues in the Pacific context, and included missionaries in his superb book *Entangled Objects: Exchange, Material Culture, and Colonialism in the Pacific*. In a chapter titled "Converted Artifacts: The Material Culture of Christian Missions," Thomas underscores the mutability of material culture: objects can be exchanged, appropriated, or renounced and their significance transposed in what he calls "the dialectic of reification and consumption" (Thomas 1991, 176). This transposition can be described as conversion in the context of Christianization, not only because the meaning of objects is convertible, but because objects can be surrendered or reinvented as signs of conversion to Christianity. One example is indigenous clothing, which was given to missionaries (and others) after islanders began wearing European cloth. These items were not merely objects of acquisition, however; the surrendered clothing "marked a moment of social transformation, and could have been read as artifacts of the history of conversion" (Thomas 1991, 169). I would like to highlight Thomas's focus on objects as subjectivities. He stresses that

> material culture types do not have stable identities within particular cultures, and their renaming and recontextualisation may be motivated in a variety of ways: ironically, the

> assumption that displacement amounts to parody presupposes the essentialist tenet that I have tried to displace—that an original identity is salient to recontextualization. (Thomas 1991, 187)

Thomas is talking about European objects or practices adopted by islanders, and also about island objects or practices adopted by Europeans. He is right to say that the use of "mimicry" or "parody" as terms of analysis is misleading, implying an original authenticity that is being misappropriated or subverted. The essence of Thomas's argument is that there is no such thing as authenticity. Objects are entangled in histories that change with ownership, exchange, or the passage of time.

In this chapter, I want to apply the notion of entanglement to a study of missionary attitudes toward the Pacific landscape. An investigation of mission materiality must surely include the environment itself, and the way that missionaries constructed geographies and landmarks. I am mindful of Greg Dening's thoughts on relics:

> Relics of what happened in the past are cultural artifacts of the moments that produced them, but they also become cultural artifacts of all the moments that give them permanence. In a familiar pacific metaphor, the relics of the past are always cargo to the present. Things that cross cultural boundaries lose the meaning encapsulated in them and are reconstituted in meaning by the cultures that receive them. (Dening 1991, 354)

I find the first part of this analysis more useful than the second, however. Artefacts (or landmarks) can become layered with meaning, but do not necessarily lose prior meanings in favor of new ones. Different meanings can attach themselves to the same objects or landmarks at the same time. The linear image of Dening's artefacts moving through time is not always a helpful metaphor; in this case, it fails to appreciate the full complexity—the "mixed messages"—of missionary responses to the material world of the South Pacific. To make such a claim is not to say that appropriation or reinvention is never present; missionaries often interpreted what they saw in inevitably Eurocentric terms, and in some cases it is clear that islanders wished to make a permanent break with objects that were no longer meaningful to them, or which contained meanings that were now considered inappropriate. There are also more ambiguous situations to invite analysis. Missionaries conducted tours of their own stations, becoming tourists themselves in certain contexts, the chief of which was a site of missionary martyrdom. Through a discussion of John Williams's death and commemoration, I show how missionary materiality became entangled with indigenous significance, and I suggest that a new vocabulary is needed if we are to describe situations like this with full sensitivity to all of the types of meaning involved.

Let me begin with an overview of missionary interactions with geography and landscape in the south Pacific. I use the word "landscape" deliberately here, even though the Pacific Ocean itself was often considered empty by visiting Europeans. The long ocean voyage served to emphasize the literal and figurative distance being traveled; the sea was a transitional space of reflection on past and future. Of particular significance was the appearance of the constellation of the Southern Cross. The proclamation of Christian salvation seemed to be inscribed on the sky itself in the southern hemisphere. All constellations are subjective constructions, but for missionaries traversing the vast and unfamiliar Pacific they were welcome points of reference. Presbyterian missionary George Gordon recalled his last glimpse of the Northern Star in 1864: "The sinking of the northern constellations in the horizon, reminds me that I am fast receding from the land dearer to me than all others on earth" (Patterson 1882, 76). At the same time, when gazing on the Southern Cross amid the new southern stars, "a variety of sacred associations came home to my mind" (Patterson 1882, 78–79). For Gordon, "home" was beneath the cross, however far he traveled from the land of his birth. The Southern Cross validated the mission quest and symbolised the universalism inherent in the Christian message.

Once ashore, missionaries found that the natural aesthetics of the south Pacific spoke to their faith, and they mapped the geographies around them using metaphorical and theological cartographies drawn from the Bible. Of all their potential south Pacific destinations, the landscape of Australia seemed to be the most alien. As the *Quarterly Review* noted in 1825, "There is something so strangely different in the physical constitution of Australia, from that of every other part of the world;—we met with so many whimsical deviations . . . from the ordinary rules and operations of nature" (Heathcote 1976, 31). For missionaries, the disjunction was more than "whimsical." The landscape seemed barren and threatening despite (or perhaps because of) its spiritual significance for the indigenous population. These feelings held especially true of the more remote, desert areas of the continent. The brothers of the Benedictine mission at Pago in the Kimberley district explored the area with help from Aborigines, noting landscape features such as caves that were believed to be places of spiritual activity: "Their horror knew no bounds, when they saw our boys, who were ahead of us, going into the caves" (Perez 1977: 29). The brothers observed men's bones interred in these caves, and in clefts of rock, and their Aborigine companions explained that the spirits of the dead men could choose either to move on, or to remain near the bones. Deep pools of water were also sites of spiritual significance. They could house animal spirits, or the spirit of rain, and could also be the source of human conception; baby spirits dwelt in some of these pools and would latch on to a passing man, migrating from him to his wife when she dreamed at night. For these reasons there were few names for rivers as a whole; each pool and meander had its own name and significance. Rock and cave paintings added a human gloss to the story the landscape itself was telling.

But these were Aborigine beliefs. For the Pago brethren, and for most missionaries in the Australian outback, the landscape was alienating. Insufficient water supplies, poor land for agriculture and grazing, and plagues of grasshoppers reinforced the image of a hostile geography. Geoffrey Bolton has used the phrase "A Timeless Land" to indicate the view that "before 1788 the ancient, bony, scoured-down Australian continent had no history" (Bolton 1981, 1). George Seddon and Mari David explain that when British observers called Australia "worn out" or "reversed,"

> they meant that it was strange, harsh, rugged—unlike the green and gentle, temperate homeland. If Australia had been settled by Spaniards, for example, the responses and behaviour might have been very different. . . . But whatever might have been, it was the Anglo-Saxons (and Irish) who came, thus generating the central paradox, that of a people whose cultural traditions and aspirations derive from a fundamentally different physical environment. (Seddon and David 1976, 11)

At Killalpaninna in northern South Australia, the German Lutheran missionary Wolfgang Reidel learned his first Aboriginal word, *nilanila*, which was Diyari dialect for the water mirages that beckoned enticingly on the desert's horizon. In Reidel's mind, the word reminded him of the Latin *nihil*, or "nothing" (Stevens 1994, 172).

For many missionaries, God was not to be found in the empty landscape, but instead in the schoolrooms and chapels of their mission stations. They realized that for Aborigines, conversion would have to be a physical as well as a spiritual process, symbolized by an end to wandering in the bush. Where Pacific islanders were encouraged to surrender their "idols," Aborigines were invited to renounce their migratory lifestyle. Conversion thus had a geographical dimension. The Pago brethren accepted the need for Aborigine converts to gather food in the bush; in times of famine "even the Christians were asked to go." Nevertheless, they insisted that converts had to seek prior permission, fearing that they might "dispense even with the requirements of natural law to make their feasting in the bush complete" (Perez 1977, 91–92).

Restrictions on bushwalking cut Aborigines off from their sacred places, severing them from their spiritual geography. Even the Pago brethren eventually realized the depth of the connection between Aborigines and the land, admitting that at times nothing else but going walkabout could resolve physical or psychological ill health: "The bush is part of their aboriginal life, and often their best medicine. It would be, therefore, both cruel and imprudent to deprive them of it altogether. They need it now and then; in any case, if not given them, they will simply take it" (Perez 1977, 92). Neil Gunson has suggested that one of the reasons for the widespread failure to make Aborigine converts was the inability of Europeans to provide a meaningful alternative to the indigenous landscape of faith: "Christianity as preached to the Aboriginals was simply a new mythology which seemed to have less bearing on their environment than their own traditional religion. . . . their awareness of the universe was too real" (Gunson 1974, I 9). Samuel Marsden of the Church Missionary Society (CMS) frequently recorded his disappointment when a series of Aborigine boys remained at the mission for a while, appearing interested, but then went bush: "The natives however young when taken by the Europeans, will not submit to any Restraint, as soon as they can range the woods" (Gunson 1974, I 11). In this sense, missionary constructions of the bush as obstacle were accurate, and Marsden's views discouraged the expansion of Australian missions for decades. Thus it seemed that Australia's landscape, and the intimate relationship the Aborigines had with it, was a foe to be resisted, an enemy to be conquered.

We must not forget, however, that the Bible also supplied missionaries with geographical metaphors inviting hope for the future, enabling them to construct landscape as a space awaiting fulfilment—a geography of redemption. Although a large literature exists on missionary appropriations, conquests, and colonial discourses, I find that these terms permit only a partial analysis of complex historical material. Their focus on material power—whether textual, economic, political, or cultural—marginalizes human spirituality and the role of religious belief in influencing attitudes and actions. Many Western academics today may not be religious themselves, and therefore may prefer to concentrate on materialist and rationalist historical analysis, but in this age of reflexivity we should question those preferences. I contend that belief must be taken seriously in any analysis of missionary activities or, to put it another way, that religion matters in the history of religion.

Wilderness metaphors in the Bible produced a profoundly missiological geography, encouraging the construction of desert or bushland as empty space waiting for revelation. "The wilderness and the solitary place shall be glad for them" wrote the prophet Isaiah, "and the desert shall rejoice, and blossom as the rose" (Isaiah 35.1). This verse and others like it were often quoted as missionaries blended their aesthetic response to landscape with their mission calling. Although such metaphors may function as literary tropes in a colonial discourse, this function is not the sum total of their significance. Missionaries did not choose them because they were functional tropes; they used them because they came from what they believed was the word of God. The metaphors are entangled with, but not limited to, a material world of power relations. To see the Australian bush as empty was certainly to appropriate it and to deny the legitimacy of its significance for Aborigines. These attitudes have powerful implications for colonization and dispossession. But the wilderness metaphor is also a statement of faith—of belief that, in time, the desert would rejoice.

It was also a sign of the influence of romanticism, especially the belief that nature could inspire spirituality. Romanticism was often problematic for missionaries, especially evangelicals, who were anxious to avoid the taint of deism. Lancelot Threlkeld of the London Missionary Society (LMS) realized that he had to accompany Aborigines into the bush, at least occasionally, as "being the only plan I can conceive of to have an opportunity of hearing their conversation and being among them" (Gunson 1974, II 186). This approach gave Threlkeld some interesting experiences, and in one particular instance it became clear that his aesthetic appreciation of the landscape was growing. Going through the bush by night to witness an Aboriginal ceremonial dance, Threlkeld recalled that

> the moon shone in all its splendour. . . . The wind whistled mournfully through the fir-like trees, and the roaring of the ocean wave sounded like distant thunder. . . . The sensations produced, as we wended our way through the bush, were of a pleasing melancholy nature, every thing appeared highly romantic, but deeply deplorable, when viewed by divine light, as showing the degradation of poor humanity in consequence of the fall. (Gunson 1974, I 52)

Then, appearing to shake himself out of a romantic daze, Threlkeld sternly reminds himself of the moral contamination of the land's inhabitants. Even when Australia appealed to his senses, he was unable to forget the spiritual dimension that rendered it "deplorable."

There were some missionaries whose lives became much more intimately linked with the Australian environment. One of these was Johann Ernst Jacob, the stockman of the Lutheran mission at Killalpaninna. Jacob lived under canvas with his wife and son, sharing the seasonal, nomadic life of the Aborigine families, who camped with him and helped to tend the flocks. He died in 1907, during an absence from the station, and could not be buried, as he had wished, among the graves of his many Aborigine friends. Clearly, Jacob and his relationship with the land and its peoples cannot be seen in isolation from the activities of the rest of the mission, and missions themselves need to be located within the wider story of European expansion in Australia. Nevertheless, Christine Stevens claims that Jacob was simply one of those who "raped the landscape" (Stevens 1994, 265). The Killalpaninna mission was entangled in the story of increasing European settlement and control in Australia, to be sure, but is condemnation really the only way to approach Johann Jacob's individual experience? I would have liked to know much more about Jacob's own construction of the landscape and the way it related to his faith; for him at least, the Australian bush was anything but empty. I wonder whether, like Threlkeld, he struggled to control the landscape's theological impact, or whether he might have allowed it to surprise or challenge him.

Unlike Australia, New Zealand's landscape was rather easier for missionaries to engage with at first glance, and Alfred Crosby has used it as a prime example of the process of Europeanization by which biological and ecological exports transformed non-European lands. New Zealand had many similarities to Britain and, to early explorers and settlers, it seemed to be a country waiting for progress and development. Crosby explains that

> like the British Isles, New Zealand sits in the path of prevailing westerlies. . . . its weather is warm to cool and as soggy as that of England, and its foliage [greener] . . . than the native English have known since pre-Celtic and Celtic farmers culled her forests. . . . In climate, New Zealand is ideal for the kinds of agriculture and pastoralism, especially the latter, that have been characteristic of Europe for the last few millennnia. (Crosby 1986, 220)

Because of its obvious potential for Europeanization, and the enthusiasm of the Maori for trade, missionaries and others saw it as a new Britain in the southern hemisphere. Samuel Marsden, who was last seen expressing his exasperation about mission work in Australia, became a pioneer of the New Zealand CMS mission. As early as 1836, he wrote, "I am fully convinced that New Zealand, from its local situation, its rivers & harbours & from the natural character of the natives will become a great nation & will have great influence among all the islands in these Seas" (Marsden 1836). Here, New Zealand is already being constructed as a site of commercial and imperial significance. William White, arriving in 1823 with stores for the fledgling Methodist mission at Whangaroa, wrote that "the scenery which burst upon our view was the most Grand, Majestic, Romantic and pleasing that I had ever seen," though he also noted that the best part of the scenery was the extent of cultivated land (Owens 1974, 39). The Methodist farms prospered; by 1824 Nathaniel Turner was getting "better than 12 bushels [of barley] from a very small patch of land" and "about 20 bushels of good wheat," while instructing Maori workers in the use of the sickle and other European agricultural techniques (Owens 1974, 58). He was especially pleased when, in addition to working on the mission farms, they began growing their own wheat for sale.

Crosby has emphasized the important role of missionaries even when conversions to Christianity were few, and the missions themselves under threat during the first decade of their operations:

> their early influence was enormous—and deeply ironic in its secondary effect. They multiplied New Zealand's attractiveness to the pakeha [non-Maori] by accelerating the process of Europeanization. . . . The Christians brought plants and animals with them—wheat, various vegetables and fruit trees, horses, cattle, sheep, and other animals—and instructed the Maori in how to raise them and benefit from them. (Crosby 1986, 235)

The young Charles Darwin was observing this process in 1835, when he wrote at the Bay of Islands that

> [t]he lesson of the missionary is the enchanter's wand. The house had been built, the windows formed, the fields ploughed, and even the trees grafted by the [native] New Zealander. At the mill, a New Zealander was seen powdered white with flour, like his brother miller in England. Cricket fields completed the picture of an idyllic English village. (Crosby 1986, 245–246)

With tours like this one being offered to naval and scientific visitors, it is no wonder that New Zealand became the focus of interest for emigration societies in Britain, and as a result, became a British colony only five years after the time of Darwin's observations.

New Zealand was beautiful in its own right, too. CMS missionary William Yate felt the presence of God in its "sublime" landscape, writing about "the sweet solemnity" of a favourite retreat near a waterfall at Papakauri, where "if God be felt as present, the soul may enjoy an undisturbed contemplation of the wisdom and love of the Most High, in the works of Creation" (Yate 1970, 3, 13). Such sentiments were dangerously close to deism, but Yate liked to live dangerously, and was eventually driven from the mission amid allegations of sodomy. Even for Yate, however, the primary message of the landscape was the conventional one of agricultural potential. "Every diversity of European vegetable and fruit flourishes in New Zealand," he wrote, stating that the CMS farm at Waimate was "very neatly kept; and the plough and six horses going in this distant part of the world and managed entirely by the once-savage aborigines, is a sight which cannot fail to gratify every friend to civilisation, and to the welfare of man" (Yate 1970, 76, 78–79). But those "once-savage aborigines" engaged both Yates's sexuality and his intellectual interest, and like a handful of missionaries in New Zealand and elsewhere in the Pacific, he fell from grace. Did the landscape tell a different story to him then?

Missionary responses to the tropical islands were varied. Sailing across the Pacific on the LMS's first missionary voyage in 1796, captain James Wilson of the *Duff* described the passengers' boredom with the empty horizon, and the way they all looked "with eager expectation of descrying a South-Sea island; which, even in the minds of those whose reason and intelligence informed them better, fancy had figured as differing from all the lands or islands on which they had ever fixed their eyes before" (Wilson 1966, 50). Almost a century later, H. A. Robertson, describing his motives for leaving Nova Scotia to become a missionary in the New Hebrides (now Vanuatu), recalled "a longing . . . to know more of the myth-like isles of the south, the scenes of perpetual summer, of sunny skies and tropical seas" (Robertson 1903, 83). Once in the islands, missionaries perceived a landscape that was alien, yet compelling. Unlike Australia, the unfamiliar surroundings appealed to European aesthetics, and for missionaries the picture seemed to be one of an

Eden-like paradise. In 1860, the *Church Missionary Gleaner* told its readers that

> [i]t would be difficult for the strongest imagination to conceive an earthly paradise more lovely than is to be found in some portions of the South-Sea Islands. Freed from the usual power of the tropical heat, and fanned by the soft breezes of a perpetual spring, these delightful regions present to the eye extensive and beautiful views. . . . a lovely part of God's creation, as they came from the hand of the Creator. (Church Missionary Society 1860, 45)

The Pacific islands were being inscribed with a spiritual as well as a physical aesthetic, as earthly paradises that recalled Eden.

The Pacific islands seemed to exemplify the familiar biblical metaphors of wastelands and gardens, too. The *Church Missionary Gleaner* also told its readers that "The Pacific washes many a spot which might become the garden of the Lord. Shall not these sweet and fruitful isles, capable of sustaining a vast population, be secured to Christ as a part of his inheritance? Why are they left so long waste?" (Church Missionary Society 1860, 45). The contradiction between isles that were "sweet and fruitful," but also "waste," would have been obvious to readers: the landscape was fruitful, but its human inhabitants were not. Exceptions were made, however, for those who had converted. At Fiji in 1850, Methodist mission superintendent, Walter Lawry, was shown round the Bua station by missionaries who "drew my attention to a well-cultivated yam and tarro garden, and to the clean and cheerful-looking cottage which stood in the midst of it" (Lawry 1850, 95). This cottage was the home of Nathaniel, a convert. Because of this context, Lawry found that "all things around him seemed to smile, and the 'trees of the wood' which he then providently set in the ground for food, such as the banana and bread-fruit, these 'trees of the wood clap their hands'; enriching and adorning the joyful and beautiful home of this industrious and praying servant of the Lord" (Lawry 1850, 95–96). With slight misquotation, Lawry was invoking a scriptural passage describing the way that "all the trees of the field shall clap their hands," once Israel returned to the path of God (*Isaiah* 55.12). Demonstrations of bucolic bliss had helped LMS missionaries to impress Royal Navy visitors in the early days of the mission to Tahiti and the other Society Islands (Samson 1998, 14), and they represented the spread of Westernization, but they were also part of a religious narrative about the signs of redemption: the spread of a spiritual grace that would transform the landscape itself.

Missionaries did not write only about transforming the unfamiliar tropical islands into miniature versions of rural England, however. They also had more complicated responses to island environments, which suggest that some of them were able to find spiritual inspiration in the natural beauties of the Pacific world. Contemplating the flora of Fiji, Lawry found release from his consciousness of the moral darkness of Fiji, and enjoyed "a zest of delight only to be enjoyed in circumstances like mine, and by a person such as the Psalmist describes: 'The works of God are great, sought out of them who have pleasure therein.' Here every thing is luxuriant and grand: the tree, the shrub, the flower, the leaf, are all fresh, strong, and brought to perfection" (Lawry 1850, 70). Lawry's vision of perfection in nature is perfectly in tune with romantic sentiments, and Lawry used this romantic sensibility to frame the inferiority of Fijians. The fact that the islanders did not take similar aesthetic or scientific interest in plant and animal life was proof of backwardness:

> It may serve to show the *grade* which these people hold among Adam's children, to observe that, with very few and rare exceptions, they seem not to have the least idea of the loveliness of their trees, shrubs, and flowers. Entymology and geology have no charms for them. (Lawry 1851, 25; emphasis in the original)

This passage makes an interesting contrast with Threlkeld in Australia, whose romantic response to a moonlit night prompted him to remind himself of the heathenism of the landscape's human inhabitants, as though the natural world could not be enjoyed until the human world was redeemed. Lawry did not share this problem, preferring to see the enjoyment of nature as a privilege of civilization. The reason for this difference might lie in missionary ethnography. As Threlkeld was keenly aware, Australia's indigenous people were intimately connected with the land, and he had to venture away from his mission station if he wished to spend much time with them. For an Aborigine convert, to "go bush" was to jeopardize sanctity. Fijians, on the other hand, already cultivated crops and lived in villages, enabling their natural surroundings to be constructed as sites for recreation or scientific study, rather than as threatening obstacles to proselytization.

Where does all of this leave us? Current theoretical approaches to the study of southern landscapes are laid out by Kate Darian-Smith et al. in their collection *Text, Theory, Space*, where they note that the literature is still dominated by the English-speaking academy's ongoing devotion to theories of discursive structuralism. Landscape is usually defined as a construct based on unequal power relations, especially in the colonial context, as in the work of W. J. T. Mitchell and Paul Carter (Carter 1988; Mitchell 1994). In this interpretation, landscape is "a site of visual appropriation" (Darian-Smith, Gunner, and Nuttall 1996, 3). Most of the examples discussed can easily bear this reading: they feature attempts to impose European meanings and aesthetics onto an alien environment. This appropriation was more successful in New Zealand and the tropical islands than in Australia. Such an interpretation is clearly not the whole story, however. Postmodern theorists have suggested that "The map is a liminal thing, associated with thresholds and marginal zones, burdened with dangerous powers . . . a potent fetish helping colonials negotiate the perils of margins and thresholds in a world of terrifying ambiguities" (Ashcroft, Griffiths, and Tiffin 1989: 24). How can cartography facilitate negotiation, if everything is ultimately about European power? Negotiation implies an exchange of some sort, and having learned much about discursive power in the last 20 years or so, scholars should spend as much time on its "terrifying ambiguities" as on its colonizing structures.

My point here is that the messages about the landscape were bound to be mixed. British missionaries demonstrated the way in which aesthetics, science, romanticism, and theology—to name only a few—emerged in different ways and in various combinations to yield a range of responses to south Pacific landscapes. Simon Schama has pointed out the essential ingredient in modern European attitudes toward landscape: the phenomenon of urbanization. He demonstrates the way in which "*both* kinds of arcadia, the idyllic as well as the wild, are landscapes of the urban imagination," and "as irreconcilable as the two ideas of arcadia appear to be, their long history suggests that they are, in fact, mutually sustaining" (Schama 1995, 525). This deeply ambivalent cultural history helps to explain the paradoxical dichotomies in missionary descriptions of landscape: empty and rich; wilderness and garden; dark and light. Just as Schama's wild and idyllic arcadias served different, but mutually dependent aesthetic and cultural needs, so did landscapes that were, for missionaries, full of spiritual significance. Without a void, there would be no gospel to preach; without evidence of transfiguration, there could be no validation of salvation. The same landscape could be a desert or a garden depending on its spiritual status. These insights emphasize the importance of accepting paradox when considering the role of Christian belief in history (Samson 2001, 102, 122). Just as Schama's landscapes require both wild and idyllic arcadias, so missionaries required interdependent and mutually sustaining geographies of conversion and heathenism. As suggested with reference to Dening's theory of artefacts as cargo, both artefacts and landscapes can best be seen as embedded in a matrix of interpretation, rather than as part of a linear process of appropriation and reinvention. Within this matrix, a number of meanings can be held in tension.

Nowhere is this sort of interpretive tension more apparent than in the story of John Williams's death in the western Pacific, and the creation of a landscape of martyrdom on the island of Erromanga. On March 31, 1840 a solemn funeral took place at Apia in Samoa. The remains of LMS missionary, John Williams, and of his assistants James Harris, were laid to rest with all of the ceremony that could be provided by the visiting officers and crew of HMS *Favourite.* The two men had formed part of a landing party visiting the western Pacific island of Eromanga with the hope of leaving Polynesian teachers there. Although initial contacts with the islanders seemed peaceful, trouble began after Williams and

Harris began walking inland from the beach. Harris was struck down first; islanders then pursued Williams as he ran for the water. While the captain and crew watched helplessly from the mission ship offshore, islanders stripped the bodies and dragged them away. Unable to land safely to recover their remains, the captain sailed for Sydney, where he pleaded for a warship to help him to retrieve the bodies of his friends. HMS *Favourite* was dispatched, but found that the bodies had been dismembered and dispersed. The Eromangans offered two skulls and a few bones, which they claimed were those of Williams and Harris, and *Favourite* departed with them for Samoa.

There is so little academic interest in missionary deaths that we have no debate about why Williams and Harris were killed, let alone anything resembling the publishing industry that surrounds the death of Captain Cook. I must therefore confine my discussion to the way in which later missionaries, and other visitors, responded to the geographical site of Williams's death. I say "Williams'" because, rightly or wrongly, the death of James Harris never received the same attention. Harris was not yet an ordained missionary, and had accompanied Williams to test his vocation. Williams was already famous, having been one of the earliest missionaries to the south Pacific, and his book, *Missionary Enterprises*, set out the vision of a bold adventurer who built his own ships and sailed them into uncharted waters in the name of Christ. In Victorian Britain, he was a hero. Although later missionaries would be killed on the same island, notably Mr. and Mrs. George Gordon in 1861, and in 1872, George's brother, James Gordon, constructions of Eromanga as "The Martyr Isle" revolved almost entirely around Williams and the events of 1839.

The first outcome of these events was the valorization of Williams as a martyr. Missionaries, teachers, and converts were inspired by the story of his death; Pacific mission stations reported an upsurge in conversion. In England, "the missionary martyr became the center of a sort of Protestant cult. Color prints of Williams being clubbed to death were sold. When the book was brought out in a cheap edition, sales doubled" (Daws 1980, 66). Tributes poured from the presses making Williams seem like a combination of St. Paul and Christopher Columbus. These claims to significance, however exaggerated they appear today, reveal an underlying purpose that Gavan Daws explains:

> The evangelical Christians of England were sure that the future was theirs, that in "ages to come" the period they were living through would be remembered as "the era of modern missions." The LMS was on the way to converting the whole world. So to LMS people Williams now appeared as a great man showing the way to the promised land, who died before the promise could be fulfilled, but whose death made fulfillment all the more certain. (Daws 1980, 67)

Daws identified the cultural issues that came together in the process of valorizing Williams, especially the intense Victorian consciousness of history, and the ability to contemplate the historical significance of the present. For Victorian missionaries, the future held no terrors. It was the site of the fulfillment of scripture, firmly located in a narrative that began with creation and would end with the day of judgment. Williams's death could be celebrated with confidence as part of a story already told: martyrdom as history-in-the-making.

For later missionaries visiting Eromanga, this intense consciousness of history made them nostalgic, even while they were making their observations. The LMS had a new ship, the *John Williams*, and on board during her 1852 voyage was the Presbyterian missionary, George Gordon, recovering from fever. As the ship landed Samoan teachers at Dillon's Bay, where Williams had been killed, Gordon watched from the deck, musing:

> I shall never forget the scene as I stood looking at it through a glass. It would form a worthy theme for the painter and the poet. I had longed and prayed for the day when the messengers of mercy should gain a footing on Eromanga's blood-stained shores, and I thank God that the day has come, and that I have been a witness of it. (Patterson 1882, 328)

In such passages, Williams's death began to define Eromanga. It was "the one never-to-be-forgotten occurrence which has given Eromanga a world-wide notoriety" (Murray 1863, 172). And thus began the shadowing of Eromanga's landscape. On an 1846 voyage to the New Hebrides, William Gill of the LMS noted that the island of Vate, where mission teachers had been welcomed, was "a land of hope," where "all nature seemed to animate and encourage us." At Eromanga, however, "thick clouds were resting on its mountains, and thicker clouds of heathen delusion and degradation enveloped its savage population" (Gill 1880, 189). But missionaries were optimists; they knew the history of the future. In 1852, Gordon watched a spectacular sunrise with Captain Morgan, the same captain who had watched Williams and Harris meet their deaths on the same beach years before. The two men were struck by the contrast between the cloud-covered mountains of Eromanga and the blinding rays of the sun. Captain Morgan "recognised something emblematical in it, and he said that it led his mind forward to the time, when 'the Sun of Righteousness shall arise with healing in His wings,' to illuminate and save the inhabitants of this dark isle" (Patterson 1882, 325).

There was also an intimate connection between Williams and the landscape through the spilling of his blood. Blood is a central feature of Christian iconography, although for Protestants the redemptive blood of Christ was less immediately material because of the rejection of the Roman Catholic doctrine of transubstantiation. Nevertheless, a powerful cultural history remained, which can be linked with descriptions of the impact of Williams's blood on the geography of Eromanga. Despite Protestantism's ambivalent response to relics, it is clear that the issue of the martyr's blood was of great importance. How did Williams's commemorators deal with this in the absence of the blood itself? Displacing it from a material to a symbolic existence was one solution, and the significance of Williams's blood was usually explained by transposing it onto the landscape of "The Martyr Isle" itself. For the eyewitnesses of his death, this transposition was simply a matter of observation; Captain Morgan and the others had seen the body of Williams lying on the beach, "where a crowd of heathen boys had so cruelly beaten it with stones, that both the stream and the shore were red with blood" (Gill n.d., 107). For later visitors, however, none of the actual blood remained, nor did any need to be sought, because its presence was everywhere. References to Eromanga's "blood-soaked" shores abound in accounts of Williams's death, and such images multiplied after later missionaries were also killed. The island's geography became literally steeped in martyr sacrifice. James Paton, missionary biographer, explained: "Thus were the New Hebrides baptized with the blood of Martyrs; and Christ thereby told the whole Christian world that He claimed these Islands as His own" (Paton 1965, 75). Blood could speak.

Missionaries and other visitors to Eromanga liked to retrace Williams's steps and reconstruct the story of his death, comforting themselves by faith. As John Campbell put it, "for the reputation of Mr. Williams, and for the purposes of history, he died in the proper manner, at the proper place, and at the proper time" (Campbell 1842, 251–252). Everything from the search for Williams's remains to the investigation of reasons for his death reveals the way in which his colleagues and supporters sought a fitting narrative with which to give his death meaning. This need for meaning became more urgent when it was discovered that the bones brought away by HMS *Favourite*, and solemnly buried in 1840, were not the bones of Williams at all. In Campbell's scheme of things, this revelation was actually an advantage, and comparisons with Captain Cook were inevitable:

> Then there is Cook, Albion's glory, and the world's wonder; was it to be endured that the bones of Cook should moulder in Westminster Abbey? What place so fit for their repose as an island of his own discovery. Was not Owhyhee their proper place of sepulture? His was a death worthy of his matchless maritime glory. (Campbell 1842, 249–250)

He went further, declaring that "The laws of harmony require the end to be in accordance with the way. The history of true greatness ought, therefore, like itself, to form a climax" (Campbell 1842, 248). The words "proper," "fit," and "worthy" indicate the nature of Campbell's "laws of harmony," namely, the search for meaning and justice in human death. Such rationalization was important, if reverence for Williams was to be maintained in light of the fiasco about his remains. It also helped to invest the Eromangan landscape with a much more specific significance than generalized references to "The Martyr Isle."

The first landing of LMS missionaries after Williams's death was in 1841, when Mrs. Williams visited Eromanga with friends who "approached with very peculiar feelings the land which had so recently been the scene of the mournful tragedy" (Murray 1863, 91). These "peculiar feelings" sought and found a material focus in a variety of landmarks and artefacts that would become a veritable tourist trail. In 1852, when Captain Morgan brought the ailing George Gordon and three Samoan-trained Eromangan teachers to the island, they sailed into Dillon's Bay and took a boat toward shore to "have a still better view of that spot, which has now become invested with a kind of immortal interest." Seeing no one on the beach, they landed the boat and admired the beauty of the scenery, drinking together from the stream now called "Williams River" in melancholy communion. Morgan recited the story of the 1839 disaster "on the blood-stained beach" itself. Walking in Williams's very footsteps, he bent down to touch the past and "gathered a number of pebbles as nearly as possible from the spot where Mr. Williams was killed" (Patterson 1882, 326). Missionaries walked the Williams trail, often in the company of the Eromangans who had confessed to his murder, reveling in the intimacy of history and the symbolism of the human geography of Dillon's Bay:

> On the Monday, he [Kauiaui] and Oviallo walked about with us, showed us the place where Mr. Harris was first struck, the place in the stream, a few yards from it, where he fell, and the course along the road, and down to the beach, where Mr. Williams ran right into the sea. . . . Mr. Gordon has erected a little printing-office and teacher's residence close to the spot where the first blow was struck at Mr. Harris. (Turner 1861, 489)

Later tourists would come with cameras, capturing the landmarks for those unable to visit the island itself (Robertson 1903, 126).

George Turner, who visited the island in 1859, took particular pains over the Williams trail. "Every direction is associated with the tragic scenes of November, 1839," he wrote. And he continues:

> At the foot of the hill on which the chapel stands is the stream in which Mr. Harris fell, and the beach where Mr. Williams ran into the sea. Down the hill, below Mr. Gordon's study window, is the spot where the oven was made in which Mr. Williams's body was cooked. Over in another direction is the place where the body of Mr. Harris was taken. (Turner 1861, 486)

Turner actually produced a map of Dillon's Bay with each of the martyr's landmarks labeled, and created new landmarks of his own, as when he planted a date palm "in a line towards the stream with the spot where Mr. Harris was struck, and in a line towards the sea with the place where Mr. Williams fell" (Turner

1861, 489). While Turner was describing the Williams trail to his readers, he made one particularly intriguing observation:

> But the most striking and permanent memento of that sad day is a great flat block of coral on the road up the hill, about a gunshot from the place where Mr. Williams fell. There the natives took the body, laid it down, and cut three marks in the stone to preserve the remembrance of its size. The one mark indicates the length of the head and trunk, and the other the lower extremities, thus: -
>
> /// Head and trunk, 37 inches /// Extremities, 25 inches ///
>
> A native lay down on the spot, and, laying on his right side, with his knees somewhat bent, said that was how it was measured. (Turner 1861, 489–490)

In the 1870s, Robertson obtained accounts of this extraordinary stone from Eromangans involved in the attack on Williams and Harris, noting that Kauiaui had ordered Williams's body to be traded for pigs at one of the inland villages. The men carrying the body had needed to rest, putting it down on a large rock,

> and while doing so "amused" themselves by measuring the body as it lay there, and cutting small holes in the rock to indicate its length. Two such holes are to be seen on the top of this rock still, which the natives affirm are those made when the body of John Williams was measured. (Robertson 1903, 58)

Robertson's informants told him they had been curious about the body's stoutness; perhaps this fact explains why they decided to keep a record of its dimensions. Williams had certainly presented a striking appearance: "massive rather than muscular . . . his chest one of unusual breadth, the shoulders considerably rounded, and the whole frame bulky and broadly set" (Campbell 1842, 216). Turner's account of the stone contains a particularly interesting feature: a reenactment, by an Eromangan man, of the placement of Williams's body on the stone. The fact that the man had to draw up his knees might have helped authenticate the scene for Turner; Williams's best-known portrait shows a man with a very stout body and remarkably short legs. We can never know exactly what was in the Eromangan's mind as he performed for Turner; we cannot define the Williams stone's significance for his people, yet we can be sure that significance existed.

There is no doubt that Williams's death and its outcomes represent a prime case of entanglement, where memories and meanings were being contributed by both Eromangans and Europeans, but do we have an adequate way of theorizing *conscious* and *simultaneous* entanglement in a spiritual context like this? In his study of culture contact on Tanna, Eromanga's neighbour in the New Hebrides group, Ron Adams uses the concept, "dialogue by accident," to explain the way in which Tannese and Europeans both visited Tanna's volcano, seeing it as the central focus of the landscape, but for different reasons. He believes that "Because they shared a religious orientation to the world, both the Tannese and the missionaries interpreted all that the other said and did as expressions of a sacred reality . . ." (Adams 1984, 66). This observation takes us a step closer to finding a way of defining shared sacred description, although there was nothing accidental about the dialogue that took place at the Williams stone; all visitors there were memorializing Williams in some way.

Another historian of Tanna, Joel Bonnemaison, has used the theories of linguist and ethnographer, Georges Dumézil, to describe Tannese constructions of a sacred landscape. Dumézil coined the word *hiérophane* to describe "all worldly manifestations of the sacred. For *homo religiosus*, water, land, sky, fire, a volcano, a mountain, or a rock are not simply natural elements but *hiérophanes*, because they reveal the sacred dimension of the world" (Bonnemaison 1994, 113). I think that the Williams stone was a *hiérophane*, and that what happened there, as Eromangans and Europeans told their stories and shared their memories, was a hierophany. This term describes the perception of sacredness in the material world.[1] As Bonnemaison suggests, "Myths indicate great logical continuity and are replete with topographical details and place names. Here toponymy has a sacred dimension; it represents a cryptic script, a language that structures space, time, and society" (Bonnemaison 1994, 114). Although Bonnemaison is speaking of Tannese mythmaking, why should not the same process apply to the myths that Europeans made about island landscapes? At Eromanga, the result was a piece of sacred geography, which generations of pious visitors would invest with all of the reverence that they could no longer pay to Williams's official gravesite in Samoa. If the location of Williams's remains was uncertain, there were at least tangible signs of his body's presence in relics like the Williams stone. And through toponymy such as "Williams River," they were creating a homeland that spoke of their mission's origins and its ancestral heroes. We need to remember that this process took place in the context of increasingly unbalanced power relations, and that Eromangans did not participate in much of this mythmaking process until after they had accepted the presence of missionaries among them; it would be naive (or worse) to suggest that the Europeans appropriated an "authentic" Eromangan mythology. What I suggest instead is that we take seriously the way in which Europeans invested geography with sacred meaning, and acknowledge the fact that, under special circumstances, a hierophany could take place in which both Europeans and islanders participated.

Here we should return to John Campbell's observation about the "proper" way in which Williams had died. What was it that seemed so fitting about the Williams stone? For one thing, it spoke of cannibalism, an issue that provided a *frisson* of disgust for readers of missionary accounts, and that formed a familiar part of the generalized picture of savagery and immorality in the south Pacific. Europeans believed that they understood this aspect of Eromangan culture, and the stone provided iconic evidence of the dismemberment and cannibal feasting that gave accounts of Williams's martyrdom so much drama. Above all, it provided a permanent memorial that could be contemplated, described, photographed, and otherwise inscribed with meaning by its pious visitors. It was of Eromangan significance, too. Williams's body had been important enough to the Eromangans to warrant a long, exhausting trip into the interior, and a subsequent explanation of the stone's markings. We do not know whether the stone already possessed spiritual significance; this seems unlikely, given the determination of the missionaries to discover anything that might give additional meaning to Williams's death. But we do know that sacred stones were sometimes handed over to the missionaries, after Christian conversion began in the southern New Hebrides (Lawson 1994, 78). These "converted artefacts," to recall Thomas's term, were surrendered by islanders and collected by Europeans as signs of change. The Williams stone sends a different message. Whether or not it was ever a *navilah*, it was not renounced by the Eromangans; on the contrary, they helped to show it to visiting Europeans, and even, in at least one case, reenacted its role in the Williams martyrdom. They used the stone to help articulate part of their own story of Williams, at the same time as missionary tourists, imbued the stone with their spiritual imperatives. Dening has suggested that "Things that cross cultural boundaries lost the meaning encapsulated in them and are reconstituted in meaning by the cultures that receive them" (Dening 1991, 354). In a hierophany, however, cultural boundaries do not necessarily have to be crossed. It is difficult to see in the case of the Williams stone that Eromangan significance was "lost" and reconstituted by European meanings. Instead, the stone became a site of meaning for both groups.

The issue of Williams's final resting-place, however, was more of a "dialogue by accident." Turner was particularly anxious to set the record straight about Williams's remains, and on his tour of the island in 1859 he believed that he had solved the mystery:

> Inland is a grove of cocoa-nuts, underneath one of which the skull of Mr. Williams was buried. The bones taken to Samoa by Captain Croker, in H. B. M.'s ship, "Favourite," in 1840, were *not* the remains of Williams and Harris. He had no proper interpreter. The natives thought he wanted to *buy human bones*, and took off for sale whatever was handy from one of the adjacent caves, where they deposit their dead. One of the skulls was that of the father of a lad we had for some time with us in our institution in Samoa. It is difficult, at present, owing to hostility among the tribes, to get at the precise tree under which the skull of Mr. Williams was buried; but there let the remains of the martyr rest, and still form part and parcel of that palm which waves its foliage in every breeze, emblematic of the Christian hero's triumph! (Turner 1861, 486–487; emphasis in the original)

Dissatisfied with Turner's measures, George Gordon continued looking for relics. He gathered what he believed were some pieces of Williams's skull, and planted his own date palm where Williams's bones were supposed to have been scattered (Gordon 1859). He did not accept Turner's identification of the grove, and Turner had added a footnote to his account of it when he wrote up his original journals for publication:

> In a letter just received from Mr. Gordon, it appear's that after I left Eromanga last year, he got some further light on these sad transactions, and is now led to think that the body of Mr. Harris was cooked in Dillon's Bay, and that the body of Mr. Williams was taken to a place a few miles distant, and divided among three different settlements. (Turner 1861, 486)

Why, then, did Turner retain his account of Williams resting in an Eromangan grove? Why did both he and Gordon plant palm trees in places where they believed Williams had been?

Writing about the widespread growth and use of coconut palms in the Pacific islands, Methodist missionary superintendent, Walter Lawry, had noted the wide range of uses of the tree and its fruit. "But there is another tree," he reminded his readers, "it is 'the tree of life, which bare twelve manner of fruits, and yielded her fruit every month: and the leaves of the tree were for the healing of the nations.' Sublime emblem of Christ the Restorer!" (Lawry 1851, 76). The *Church Missionary Gleaner* of 1866 drew exactly the same parallel:

> [T]hus from isle to isle, and from group to group, this palm has reproduced itself, until its presence is almost universal throughout the numberless groups of the South-Sea Islands. It seems to typify the remarkable and interesting way in which Christianity is extending itself throughout these island homes of man, which are set in the midst of the great Pacific waters. (Church Missionary Society 1866, 119)

It was fitting for Williams to lie amid the palms, and this appropriateness explains why Turner left intact his original description: "part and parcel of that palm which waves its foliage in every breeze, emblematic of the Christian hero's triumph." John Campbell would have approved, because Williams was being given the burial he deserved.

We must wonder, however, about the possibility of "dialogue by accident." Presbyterian missionary, John Geddie, stationed on the island of Aneityum in the New Hebrides group, noted that islanders in the New Hebrides worshipped in groves, and this custom reminded him "of that which was followed by the idolaters in the days of ancient Israel," as in the Old Testament, where "Manasseh reared up altars and made a grove" (Patterson 1882, 130). George Gordon noted that on Tanna

> [t]he places usually selected for worship are groves, and not temples. These in all ages have been favourite spots for the worship of idols, or spirits. . . . The practice of these islanders reminds me of that which was followed by the idolaters in the days of ancient Israel. A small

> spot is cleared in the midst of the luxuriant foliage of these regions, and an altar of rude construction is erected, on which to place the offerings to the Natmasses. (Patterson 1882, 130)

Did these ethnographical speculations prompt missionaries to seek Williams in a grove, or failing that, to plant a grove where they believed his remains to lie? We have no record of Eromangan information on the subject of Williams's bones, although one may lie in oral history. In this respect, it is my hope that this essay might prompt more interest in the subject of Williams's death and its multiple meanings. As for the missionaries, they believed that it was fitting for their martyr to lie in a liminal space that included both indigenous and Christian spiritual significance. Eromangans appear to have played no direct role in this particular hierophany, but perhaps further research can reveal whether or not this was true.

Missionaries interpreted, reinvented, and reshaped south Pacific landscapes. In New Zealand, they helped to initiate a process of cultural and biological transfer that produced a Britain of the southern seas. In places of less malleable geography, or where there were too few settlers to Westernize the landscape, they interpreted what they saw through patterns established in scripture. At times, they sought a more direct relationship with their environment. They found that Pacific aesthetics spoke to their faith, and they used these geographical "lessons" to create hierophanies. Their response to the Pacific world was more than a one-way process of appropriation, however. Most often it was based on a dialectic drawn from the cultural legacies of wild and idyllic landscape aesthetics. These powerful traditions were both contradictory and mutually sustaining, creating a tension that complemented the theological distinction between deserts and gardens. Both were necessary if each was to be understood, and for missionaries, both were necessary to tell the story of salvation.

One of their hierophanies was created to commemorate the martyred John Williams. The toponymy of "Williams River," the "blood-soaked shores" and the bones in the grove helped to build one of the great foundation myths of Pacific Christianity. Here in "darkest" Eromanga, the pioneer missionary, John Williams, was killed and consumed, his remains scattered to join the island itself and to consecrate it to God. This mythology both completed and undercut the European appropriation of Eromanga; the sacred geography was traced on Eromangan landmarks and made necessary by Eromangan actions. A Williams safely buried in Samoa would not have given the same meaning to the landscape as a Williams consumed by the land's inhabitants. Because Eromangans had forced Europeans to seek their martyr in the island itself, Williams became an immediate presence: "Williams 'being dead yet speaketh,' and his voice will be heard throughout these realms for ages yet to come" (Campbell 1842, 248).

Missionaries both described the south Pacific landscape and were embodied in it: the ultimate material presence.

Note

1. The term "hierophany" is not a commonly recognized English word, though it appears as a translation of *hiérophane,* a basic category in the widely read phenomenology of religion associated with the Romanian scholar, Mircea Eliade. Closely allied to Dumézil's work, Eliade's celebrated analysis of *homo religiosus* is rooted in an understanding of hierophanies as physical manifestations of the sacred in religious symbols, myths, and rituals. Any phenomenal entity carries the potential to reveal the sacred, that is, to be a hierophany. See, e.g. Eliade (1959). In response to my suggestions, the *Oxford English Dictionary* has agreed to include the term "hierophany" in future editions.

CHAPTER SEVEN

PENITENTIAL AND PENITENTIARY: NATIVE CANADIANS AND COLONIAL MISSION EDUCATION

Jamie S. Scott

Introduction

Of Revelation and Revolution: Christianity, Colonialism, and Consciousness in South Africa, the first volume of Jean and John Comaroff's exhaustive study of nonconformist London Missionary Society evangelists among the Tswana of southern Africa, drops some tantalizing remarks about the ways in which "[s]chooling actually provided the model for conversion; conversion, the model for schooling" (Comaroff and Comaroff 1991, 233). The Comaroffs return to this theme in the closing paragraphs of their second volume, *The Dialectics of Modernity on a South African Frontier*. Of modern Protestant evangelizing, they write: "If the whole world was its parish, it was also its classroom. The civilizing mission was above all a pedagogic crusade" (Comaroff and Comaroff 1997, 412). At the same, they indicate that this "pedagogic crusade" implicated a third party—the state—and they go on to draw a key distinction between the way educational policy developed in southern Africa and the way it evolved in the mother country. "While the state took control of mass schooling in Britain during the nineteenth century," the Comaroffs note, "in South Africa missions long remained *the* major source of Western learning for indigenous peoples" (Comaroff and Comaroff 1997, 412; emphasis in the original). This chapter explores analogous issues in the Canadian colonial context, where a peculiar partnership developed *between* clergy and government on the issue of education for Native peoples.

Focusing on the incarnation of this partnership in the imagining, establishing, and maintaining of a residential school system for Native children, the chapter outlines the development of missionary attitudes toward the education of Native Canadians, then examines the formalization of these attitudes in terms of the reformatory ethos that came to dominate nineteenth-century industrial school theory, notably what I call "the doctrine of congregate schooling." A third section considers the role of Native leaders in this process, as well as the recent work of Native writers who passed through the residential school system, without whose testimony no consideration of these issues could claim a judicious sense of analytical balance. Adopting a Foucauldian perspective on the relations between power and knowledge defining this educational economy, the chapter concludes on an ironic note: the discursive exchange between schooling and conversion to which the Comaroffs allude results in Canada in new indigenous Christianities that seem at once more faithful to Native spiritual traditions and more reflective of evangelical understandings of biblical interpretation than the missionary pedagogical policies that spawned them.

Mission Education and Native Canadians

European colonial efforts to school Native North Americans out of their traditional ways began as early as 1620, when French Récollets missionaries established a boarding school at Notre Dame des Anges, near Québec. Six Native boys joined three French, "all of whom received instruction together in catechism, reading and writing," but the school closed for lack of suitable Native recruits (Jaenen 1986, 55). In 1633, Jesuits arrived in New France with a plan "to establish a Seminary for little Savages, to rear them in the Christian faith" (Thwaites 1896–1901, 7. 265; quoted in Jaenen 1986, 55).[1] According to Cornelius J. Jaenen, French attitudes toward Native Americans included efforts to "educate the children in the mission field as a means of reaching the older generation and rearing up a generation of converts who would eventually rise to positions of influence in the band or tribe," "to educate an elite, which would serve as Native examples and instructors, by sending chosen candidates to France," "to educate the youth in the controlled atmosphere of the reserves under the guidance of the missionaries and converted Native chiefs and *dogiques* or catechists," and "to francize [*sic*] both girls and boys in the socially controlled atmosphere of the boarding schools" (Jaenen 1986, 47, 48). In 1673, however, Bishop Laval shut the doors of the seminary, because, he reported, Native parents were often unwilling to yield their offspring without some kind of material compensation, making them twice as costly as French children to educate (Jaenen 1986, 56).

In 1763, the Treaty of Paris ceded New France to the British. Like the French Roman Catholics, the first British Protestant missionaries in North America also sought to school Native peoples in non-Native ways. In eighteenth- and early nineteenth-century Ontario, for example, the Anglican Society for the Propagation for the Gospel, Moravians and Methodists set up day schools on or near Native territories. As J. Donald Wilson has noted, "[b]y 1830, the Methodists had established an extensive educational mission among the Indians with eleven schools, eleven teachers, and 400 students" (Wilson 1986, 69). Since Protestant theology argued that personal knowledge of the biblical word of God was the key to salvation, the missionaries focused on translating sacred texts into Native languages and, conversely, encouraging a working knowledge of English. At the same time, however, missionaries began to accede to the civilizing agenda of the British colonial authorities, who were keen to replace this Christianizing policy of bicultural literacy with a modernizing programme of economic and social assimilation.

There is evidence of this intensification of missionary "civilizing" efforts as early as the 1820s. The Church Missionary Society (CMS) cleric, John West (1778–1845), is an important figure here. Posted in 1820 to the Red River settlement—later Winnipeg, in the province of Manitoba—West became the first CMS representative in British North America. Appointed by the Hudson's Bay Company as chaplain to the settlers and traders of the Red River colony, he showed just as much enthusiasm for converting Native peoples. Published in 1824 after his return to England, West's *The Substance of a Journal During a Residence at the Red River Colony, British North America, in the Years 1820–1823* (1824) gives a firsthand account of the efforts of early nineteenth-century "British Christians" to export "the advantages of civilized and social life, with the blessings of Christianity" (West 1824, v, vi).[2] To achieve these "civilizing" goals, West advances an argument in two stages. First, education in nonNative ways is the key to the "civilizing" process; in the *Journal*, West describes his evangelical mission as an attempt "to seek the instruction, and endeavour to meliorate the condition of the native Indians" (West 1824, 2). Second, for education to succeed, Native children would have to be removed from the corrupting influences of indigenous social and cultural traditions. Missionaries must "establish the principle," West writes, "that the North-American Indian of these regions would part with his children, to be educated in the white man's knowledge" (West 1824, 14–15).

This sort of thinking soon typified Protestant missionary approaches to the "civilizing" of Canada's Native peoples, regardless of denomination. By the 1880s, education claimed pride of place on evangelizing agendas. In 1886, for example, the CMS missionary, John A. Mackay, stressed the paramount role of schooling in the conversion of the Native peoples at the Battleford mission, Saskatchewan: "Schools, if efficiently conducted, with systematic Christian teaching," writes Mackay, "I consider about the most valuable agency we can employ" (Mackay 1886, 317). William Carpenter Bompas, Bishop of the Mackenzie River diocese, expresses similar sentiments in his *Diocese of the Mackenzie River* (1888). A chapter titled "Church of England Missions" includes the conviction that "education is here the main hope of Missionary success, for the minds of the natives need to be trained and enlarged by education to appreciate better the spiritual truths of the Gospel" (Bompas 1888, 33). Questions remained, however, about what form such boarding schools should take. Reform schools championed by philanthropic societies in the United Kingdom and the United States offered a likely model.

As early as 1788, the London Philanthropic Society had opened such a reformatory in St. George's Fields for "the encouragement of industry and the culture of good morals amongst those children who were training up to vicious courses, public plunder, infamy and ruin" (Leigh 1818). Significantly, the British reformers soon adopted a kind of open-door policy, "ignoring the distinction between vagrants and criminals" (Schlossman 1995, 365). In 1825, John Griscom, a Quaker reformer and leading member of the New York Society for the Prevention of Pauperism, presided over the opening of the New York House of Refuge. The American institution developed along similar lines to the British. In Steven Schlossman's words, "[t]he founders of reform schools assumed that their clientele would not be exclusively serious offenders, but a motley group of lower-class children" (Schlossman 1995, 365). Echoing this attitude toward the education of "marginal children," the mixed-blood convert, Peter Jones (1802–1856), campaigned for a boarding school for the Ojibwa in Upper Canada (Neff 1994, 171).[3] He argued that this institution should "provide a lot of ground for the boys to work," that "the girls be taught needle work & all sorts of domestic duties," and that "Religion, Education and manual labour go hand in hand" (quoted in Miller 1996, 80).

The Methodists established such "schools of industry" at Grape Island, Credit River, Alderville, and Alnwick (Wilson 1986, 72). As Methodist cleric, Robert Alder, wrote to Lord Glenelg, Secretary for War and the Colonies, in 1837, Native children could be taken "from their imperfectly civilized parents" to such institutions, where they might gain what the Wesleyan Methodist leadership later described as "a religious, literary, mechanical and agricultural education" (Hodgins 1893–1908, 4. 122; Wesleyan Methodist Church in Canada 1846, 160; both quoted in Wilson 1986, 72). By 1845, Jones himself had raised enough funds to establish the Mount Elgin Industrial Institution at Munceytown Reserve, in Upper Canada, which opened in 1847. By the 1880s, the missionary educational policy of all Christian denominations showcased such schools. Making settled citizen farmers of Native peoples, perceived, rightly or wrongly, as errant nomads, figured importantly here. The Anglican Bompas, for example, was keen to transform existing boarding schools into industrial institutions. "In connexion with the diocesan school," he writes, "it appears very desirable to set on foot an industrial farm for the purposes of encouraging the Indians to agricultural pursuits by setting an example of it, and training some of the youths to this work" (Bompas 1888, 33). Writing in 1909, John W. Tims echoes Bompas, informing the CMS readership in the United Kingdom "that so much of the industrial school should be embodied in the reserve boarding-school, as would, besides giving the pupils fair instruction in the three 'R's', enable them to get sufficient knowledge of the use of tools to build their own barns and dwellings, and become thoroughly acquainted with the management of stock and all that goes to make a good farmer" (Tims 1909, 350).[4] Nor were the Protestant missions alone in this venture. Spurred by Ultramontanist enthusiasm and unwilling to be left behind in the rush to civilize Native Canadian souls, the Roman Catholic Oblates of Mary Immaculate adopted similar policies, opening their first industrial school in 1884, at Qu'Appelle, at Lebret, in Saskatchewan.[5]

The churches recognized no conflict between this "civilizing" mandate and their evangelical responsibilities; rather, they saw the former as constituting the latter in a working partnership between Christian pedagogy and federal policy. In 1886, for example, the Anglican cleric, John Mackay, celebrated the "prospect of the Government making more liberal arrangements for the support of school-teachers, which, I trust, will enable us to extend the work, if we can get suitable agents" (Mackay 1886, 317–318). Ideally, the public purse would enable the churches to instill a Native culture characterized by "idleness and debauchery" with a sense of Christian industriousness (Wilson 1890b, 28). Thus Tims's remarks about making "a good farmer" appear in an essay titled, "Evangelizing the Canadian Indians" (Tims 1909). Describing "The Indian of Today" in 1890, the Anglican educational reformer, Edward F. Wilson, who founded the Shingwauk and Wawanosh industrial schools at Sault Ste. Marie in 1873, writes: "He must now be educated to labour" (Wilson 1890b, 28). "He does not need the higher education that the white is striving for," Wilson continues, with a characteristically imperial sense of racial superiority, "but he does need the virtue of industry and the ability of the skilful hand . . . [a]nd not only should he be taught to work, but that it is his duty to work; that labour is necessary to his well-being" (Wilson 1890b, 28).

In these respects, many missionaries held that church and state should aim at nothing short of the total transformation of Native identity. Elsewhere, Wilson puts on a developmental anthropologist's hat to talk about helping Native peoples "in the most beneficent way to work out their future, and, if practicable, to hybridize, if we may use the word, their nature to an adaptation of the habits of the white man" (Wilson 1890a). Such "hybridization" is the joint responsibility of the pastoral and political powers. In 1900, C. E. Somerset's brief note on "Indian Industrial Schools," in *The Missionary Outlook*, a Methodist periodical, celebrates the fact that "[b]oys and girls who have left industrial schools after having spent a few years in them are altogether unlike their brothers and sisters who have not had the same advantage" (Somerset 1890, 131). "Money spent by both church and state," concludes Somerset, "has been well spent" (Somerset 1890, 131).

Similarly, in a pamphlet titled "The Chootla Indian School, Carcross, Yukon Territory," Isaac O. Stringer, who succeeded Bompas as Anglican Bishop of the Yukon Territory, casts church and state as partners in the "civilizing" process (Stringer 1911). "Printed by the Boys of the School," the pamphlet describes the educational work of the churches as "essentially missionary" (Stringer 1911). But this missionary work would not have been possible without the support of government, Stringer argues. "[E]rected by the Department of Indian Affairs, and, in 1911, placed at the disposal of the Church of England, to be used as a boarding and semi-industrial school for Indian children," the Chootla's "commodious building" represents the happy outcome of a successful partnership between pastoral and political interests (Stringer 1911). The curriculum at Chootla reflects this seamless merging of secular and sacred responsibilities. In the morning, the "children are given, whenever possible, an ordinary common school education"; in the afternoon, "they are taught the things most necessary to uplift them and their friends at home to something nearer the Christian standard of cleanliness and industry" (Stringer 1911). The girls learn domestic skills, "the boys gardening, rough carpentry and blacksmith work," their whole education undertaken in the twin conviction that "knowledge of Jesus of Nazareth and trust in Him" will "alone save the decreasing Indians of the Yukon, and make them good and useful citizens of the greater Canada of the future" (Stringer 1911).[6] In Wilson's words, "When Indian children shall have acquired a taste for study, and a love for work, the day of their redemption will be at hand" (Wilson 1890a, 6).

Colonial Administration and the Doctrine of Congregate Schooling

As John Milloy has shown, the idea of boarding or residential schools for Native children originates in early nineteenth-century government thinking about industrial schools. In 1820, the Governor of Upper Canada, Sir Peregine Maitland, proposed to Lord Bathurst at the Colonial Office that Native children be removed from their communities to "School Houses of instruction and industry," where "they would be taught the precepts of religion, the social manners of polite settlers, and the basic skills of reading, writing, and arithmetic" (Milloy 1999, 15). Boys would be employed at "trades or on the farms and girls in making clothes, taking care of Dairies etc" (Milloy 1999, 15, quoting Maitland 1821). In 1845, Lord Elgin, Governor General of the Provinces of British North America, and Egerton Ryerson (1803–1882), Superintendent of Education for Upper Canada, publicly promoted such schools for Native children. Ryerson argued that these "industrial schools" should be "schools of learning and religion," where Native children should receive "a plain English education adapted to the working farmer and mechanic," noting that "nothing can be done to improve and elevate his character and condition without the aid of religious feeling" (Ryerson 1898, 73).

Such provisions combined two aspects of Ryerson's thinking on public education: first, as his "Report on a System of Public Elementary Instruction for Upper Canada, 1846" spells out, free and universal education goes a long way toward achieving social cohesiveness; and second, government must demonstrate a political willingness, however regrettably and reluctantly assumed, "to get vagrant 'street arabs' into institutions where they could be reformed and turned into useful members of society, and hence rescued from the slide into vagrancy and begging to petty crime and worse" (Neff 1994, 173). In a telling discursive circulation, such thinking in effect equates Native children with the Dickensian waif of mid-Victorian London by means of the racialized intermediary of the nomadic, and therefore uncivilized, "arab." As the Comaroffs have noted of analogous encounters between British colonial operatives and the indigenous peoples of southern Africa, to be settled in one place and firmly anchored there out of economic self-interest is to be redeemed from the temptations besetting "shifting populations . . . of shifty, shiftless people wandering about *sans* property, propriety, or a proper place in the body politic" (Comaroff and Comaroff 1997, 123). And for Ryerson, as for the British in southern Africa, education is central to this redemptive enterprise.

It is important to recognize that these ideas about the education of Canada's Native children did not appear in a discursive vacuum. The notion of a system of residential schools for Native children reflects the influence of theories of education current in mid-nineteenth-century Great Britain and the United States. Industrial schools were seen "as mechanisms for segregating, treating and socializing marginal populations" (Neff 1994, 174). Canada was by no means innocent of such influences. We find a revealing instance of this thinking in

Ontario in the 1870s. In 1871, William Barclay McMurrich and Emmerson Coatsworth toured industrial schools in Massachusetts and New York as representatives of the Toronto School Board. Keen to introduce such institutions to Ontario upon their return to Canada, McMurrich and Coatsworth promoted such a programme in their report to the school board. Submitted in 1872, the report outlines the economic, social, and cultural reasons for establishing industrial schools: "To reach [the vagrant class] not yet provided for by our City Schools and complete the system of natural education"; "To enable the Board properly and efficiently to carry out the truant system, or compulsory attendance at our Schools, and thus to ensure the education of all at the expense of all"; "As a matter of self-defence and gain, to add to the wealth of the community by rendering the vagrant and neglected class industrious, teaching them to earn an honest livelihood, and thus lessen the enormous expenditure required to keep them from doing us harm, or punishing them for harming us"; and "As a matter of philanthropy, to house the homeless, reclaim the vagrant, elevate the debased, reform the vicious, and prevent pauperism, from which this Province is so happily free" (McMurrich and Coatsworth 1872 [1908], 275–285; quoted in Neff 1994, 187–188).

Recognizing the political need to garner public support for these ideas, McMurrich also published an article on industrial schools in the widely read periodical, *Canadian Monthly and National Review*. The article recapitulates the economic, social, and cultural reasons informing his proposal. He asserts, for example, that industrial schools were conceived as a way of providing jobs training for " 'the Juvenile Vagrant Class'," which "our present system of School Education, more especially in the cities, fails to reach" (McMurrich 1872, 424). But then he goes on to make a key distinction between "the congregate system," which is "constructed on the plan of the penitentiary," and "the family plan," which consists "of a number of detached houses . . . forming a separate family under a matron or superintendent and assistants" (McMurrich 1872, 426). McMurrich recommends the introduction of the former in the Canadian cities of "Toronto, Ottawa, Hamilton, Kingston and London" (McMurrich 1872, 428). His reasons for this preference are several:

> [The congregate system] is in a condition from its extensive resources, sanitary, educational, industrial and moral, to receive a large number at any given time within its walls, so that a great diminution of juvenile crime and evil influence may be secured in the vicinity. It allows of a better classification and, from its organization, must have better discipline. It admits of an earlier distribution of its inmates, because if the experiment of their discharge prove unsuccessful, it has room enough to receive them again. (McMurrich 1872, 426)

Extrapolating upon this disciplinary rhetoric of "classification and organization," McMurrich goes on to laud the benefits of "systematic labour" in "the shop, with its carefully adjusted stints, with its delicate labours, requiring constant and absorbing attention, with its daily recurring duties, always demanding faithfulness," for the boys "hate work," being "naturally lazy" as a result of "truant, vagrant and vicious lives" (McMurrich 1872, 427). Finally, argues McMurrich:

> One great necessity, in the establishment of such a school, is not only that compulsory attendance be made the law of the land, but that power should be given to retain children committed to the school during their minority, or until such time as they may be discharged. Experience has shown that the commitment of a child for a definite period, rarely if ever, has any beneficial effect, as the child knows that when his term is up, he must go free. But when a child feels that everything depends upon himself, as to the length of time he is to remain as an inmate; that it is by the advances he makes in industry and education only, that he can expect to secure his discharge—then he is led to apply all his energies to the work before him—and his ambition and better feelings being roused, he benefits from the course of study he receives. (McMurrich 1872, 427)

Here, the penitentiary language of "law," "committed," "term," "free," "inmate," "discharge," and so forth demonstrates the extent to which "[t]he governance of childhood was aimed at the induction of a docile citizenship, the creation of a disciplined soul" (McGillivray 1997, 146).

It is this penitentiary model of congregate industrial schooling that comes to define and determine many of the conditions of nineteenth- and twentieth-century Canadian education for Native children. In 1879, the Conservative government of the father of Canadian confederation, John A. MacDonald, commissioned Nicholas Flood Davin to confirm the general suitability of industrial schools for Canada's Native communities. Like McMurrich and Coatsworth, Davin in large part based his *Report on Industrial Schools for Indians and Half-Breeds* upon his experiences visiting the United States, where meetings with Secretary of the Interior, Carl Schurz, Commissioner of Indian Affairs, E. A. Hayt, and a number of Cherokee leaders convince him of the success of President Ulysses S. Grant's assimilative policies of "aggressive civilization" toward Native Americans (Milloy 1999, 7–8; see also, Miller 1996, 101–103). Hayt introduces Davin to some "principal men" from "the five 'civilized' nations, the Cherokees, the Chickasaws, the Choctaws, the Creeks and Seminoles" (Davin 1879, 5).

In these Native American men, Davin sees "[t]he happy results of Industrial Schools strikingly shewn" (Davin 1879, 5). He reiterates the familiar ecclesiastical and government view that "the day school did not work, because the influence of the wigwam was stronger than the influence of the school" (Davin 1879, 1). In a shrewd rhetorical move, rather than adducing proofs for this position himself, he reports the views of the Native Americans: "All the representatives of the five civilized nations declared their belief that the chief thing to attend to in dealing with the less civilized or wholly barbarous tribes was to separate the children from the parents" (Davin 1879, 7). Similarly, it is not Davin himself, but the Cherokee Colonel Pleasant Porter who asserts that "[w]hat the Indian needs most is to be taught to work, and to apprehend values" (Davin 1879, 6). According to Davin, these opinions confirm the experience of missionaries working among Canada's Native peoples, whose received wisdom it is that "[t]he children must be kept constantly within the circle of civilized conditions" (Davin 1879, 12). In order to achieve such comprehensive conditions of social and cultural transformation, Davin makes 13 recommendations, among them that the government should implement a system of rewards for parents and children who support the new educational initiatives, eventuating in some form of compulsion to attend, once "Bands become more amenable to the restraints of civilization [*sic*] education" (Davin 1879, 15).

Finally, Davin stresses the key role missionaries will play in the programme. To begin with, the churches already operate a number of schools for Native peoples, thus providing a pool of experienced teachers and a way of saving government money. Not only have the missionaries "already demonstrated their commitment to 'civilizing' Canada's Indians," however; they constitute the ideal vehicle for the total transformation of Native society and culture (Barman, Hébert, and McCaskill 1986, 6). If, in Davin's words, "[o]ne of the earliest things an attempt to civilize them does, is to take away their simple Indian mythology, the central idea of which, to wit, a perfect spirit, can hardly be improved on," then "to disturb this faith, without supplying a better, would be a curious process to enlist the sanction of civilized races whose whole civilization, like all the civilizations with which we are acquainted, is based on religion" (Davin 1879, 14). In other words, Davin recognizes quite explicitly that educational efforts to transform Native social and cultural identity will succeed only with a total assault upon the deep structures of their everyday life, and it for this reason that church and state must combine their resources to impose the uniformly disciplined environment of the congregate industrial school upon Canada's Native peoples at their most vulnerable and impressionistic—as children.

Federal and ecclesiastical officials received a good deal of public support for this policy, too, particularly in the influential press. Popular magazines applauded the wisdom of bringing to bear the combined authority of church and state on the chronically troubled issue of relations between Canada's Native and nonNative communities. In the last decades of the nineteenth century, these magazines continued to trumpet an industrial school model for Native education. In 1891, for example, an article on "The Government and Indian Education" in *The Week* argues that reserve day schools are not enough to solve "the Indian problem" ("Iota" 1891, 378). "How can he [the Indian] become civilized unless he work," asks the author, "and how can he work unless he be taught?" ("Iota" 1891, 378). The answer: "industrial schools" ("Iota" 1891, 378). "To some this may seem an unnatural system," the author continues, since "[i]t takes a child from his home and parents and forces him suddenly into unaccustomed ways" ("Iota" 1891, 378). But "the boarding industrial school" has "overruling advantages" ("Iota" 1891, 378):

> In the first place the children are always present; they get their lessons every day, not once or twice a month; they are taught to love cleanliness and punctuality, things impossible in their own homes. They have a constant example of the unremitting work with which the white man purchases his success. They are given sound constitutions by good food and sufficient clothing, bathing and ventilation. They are given a good practical knowledge of that great civilizer the English tongue, and with this and the bringing together of various tribes in one school, the old tribal enmities are broken up and the child that came into the school a filthy, ignorant little Cree or Ojibway or Sioux, thinking his language, his village, his tribe, the perfection of all creation, is sent out an English-speaking Canadian. Besides this he has the benefit of the example of good living set before him by Christian men and women and his mind is still further braced by the hand training which he receives. ("Iota" 1891, 378)

Above all, "[t]he combination of Government and Missionary Society seems to work well, and the pupils turned out feel the white man has done what is fair by him, and that he henceforth must earn his own living" ("Iota" 1891, 379). In 1892, an essay on "The Indians of Western Canada" in *The Colonist* boasts in celebratory tones of "a great change in the character and customs of a whole race of people . . . being wrought silently and steadily" through "the Industrial Schools of the present day" ("Anon." 1892, 2).

In 1867, the British North America Act ceded wardship over Native peoples to the government of the new Dominion of Canada and guaranteed equal educational rights to Roman Catholics. "As consolidated in the Indian Acts of 1876 and 1880, Indian self-government was abolished, and finance and all social services, including education, were placed under federal control" (Barman, Hébert, and McCaskill 1986, 4–5). Throughout the nineteenth century, Anglican, Methodist, Presbyterian, and Roman Catholic missionaries continued to run day schools in smaller Native communities, but the churches also built and staffed a number of boarding schools on many of the larger reserves. In 1868, a year after confederation and the founding of the new Dominion of Canada, Ottawa's funding for 57 schools for Native children included support for 2 industrial schools in Ontario—Mount Elgin and Mohawk (Milloy 1999, 52). In 1879, Shingwauk and Wikwemikong were added. Created in 1880 by MacDonald's Conservative government, the Department of Indian Affairs, under the authority of Commissioner Edgar Dewdney, implemented the proposals contained in Davin's *Report*, and by 1891, the churches had entered into agreements with Ottawa to administer 19 industrial schools. According to Department of Indian Affairs statistics, "[b]y 1900, out of a total population of about 20,000 aged between six and fifteen, 3,285 Indian children were enrolled in 22 industrial and 39 boarding schools and another 6,349 in 226 day schools" (Barman, Hébert, and McCaskill 1986, 7). Low attendance figures convinced the Department of Indian Affairs "that, in general, day schools could not educate Aboriginal children" (Milloy 1999, 24). At the same time, "between 1891 and 1911 boarding schools were growing steadily and surpassed their industrial counterparts in both the number of institutions and students enrolled" (Titley 1986, 147). In 1923, the nominal distinction between boarding and industrial schools was abandoned for the preferred term, "residential schools," of which there were 71 scattered across Canada, housing 5,347 Native children (Milloy 1999, 52). In 1931, there were 44 Roman Catholic, 21 Anglican, 13 United Church, and 2 Presbyterian schools dotting the Canadian landscape, mostly in the prairies (Milloy 1999, 307).[7]

In many cases, church and state cooperated to locate these schools without regard for the ability of Native families to visit their children, or of the children to spend holidays with their families—a geographical expression of West's "principle, that the North-American Indian of these regions would part with his children, to be educated in the white man's knowledge." In 1884, Dewdney, reiterated this principle with great confidence in its efficacy for the future of Canada's Native peoples and the improvement of their society and culture:

> Experience has taught that little can be done which will have a permanent effect with the adult Indian, consequently, to create a lasting impression and elevate him above his brethren, we must take charge of the youth and keep him constantly within the circle of civilization. I am confident that the Industrial School now about to be established will be a principle feature in the civilization of the Indian mind. . . . By the children being separated from their parents and properly and regularly instructed not only in the rudiments of English language, but also in trades and agriculture, so that what is taught may not be readily forgotten, I can assure myself that a great end will be attained for the permanent and lasting benefit of the Indian. (quoted in Jaine 1991, 43)

Despite shifts in official educational policy, the disciplinary ethos, at once penitential and penitentiary, of the industrial school prevailed in the residential schools for over a century. Only in the 1970s were the last residential schools closed or transferred to Native administration.

Essentially, the ideology informing these government policies drew upon the same English common law doctrine of *parens patriae* ("parent of the country") invoked in Great Britain and the United States to justify the public institutions built to house, hide, and tame the increasingly large numbers of destitute children cast up in the wake of late eighteenth- and nineteenth-century urbanization and industrialization.[8] If the state deemed natural parents incapable of providing the essential elements of an appropriate physically and morally healthy upbringing, so the *parens patriae* argument went, then the state must assume these responsibilities. Reciprocal benefits flowed from such an arrangement: state intervention served the best interests of disadvantaged children, who were fed, clothed, and prepared for constructive roles in civilized society, as well as the best interests of civilized society, which might reasonably expect to profit economically, socially, and politically from the rehabilitation of a generation of youngsters otherwise condemned to wasted lives of petty crime and chronic incarceration. Only in 1966, did a government report at last begin to reflect the true picture of Native education in Canada: "Discontinuity of socialization, repeated failure, discrimination and lack of significance of the educational process in the life of the Indian child result in diminishing motivation, increased negativism" (Hawthorn 1966, 130).

Native Peoples and NonNative Educational Policies

As nonNative settlement expanded westwards across the Canadian prairies, Native leaders and Ottawa signed a series of seven treaties between 1871 and 1877, "in which the goal was to compensate Native peoples for land cessions and to assign them to reserves" (Fowler 1996, 45). Native leaders insisted that the treaties include provisions for education, "although they likely had day schools in mind" (Miller 1996, 98). The role of Native communities in the implementation of these educational programmes varied. A pattern of ambivalence toward nonNative schooling recurs under the British and Canadian dispensations. Perhaps Native peoples were at risk of being swept away in an irresistible historical current, but it is important to understand that many Native leaders strove to swim in this current.

At first, many Native leaders favored schooling in nonNative ways. As early as 1784, we find the Mohawk chief, John Deserontyon, writing to Colonel Daniel Claus, Deputy Superintendent of Indians in Montréal: "We have been long thinking about a Schoolmaster to go with us . . . [and] . . . we wish that the General would consider our case, and appoint such a person, as we never had more occasion for one than at present for the teaching of our Children who have been much neglected in that respect since we left home" (Petrone 1983, 38). Deserontyon also expresses the desire "to be instructed in religious Matters" (Petrone 1983, 38). Christian Native leaders often played a leading role in this educational process, too. In 1835, Jones was recommending to the Ojibwa of Upper Canada that "all the children be placed entirely under the charge and management of the teachers & missionaries; so that their parents shall have no control over them" (quoted in Miller 1996, 80). By 1844, Toronto's Bishop John Strachan writes about parents "anxious to have their children educated," and their children "as apt to learn as those of the Whites" (quoted in Wilson 1986, 68). Similarly, at a Native General Council meeting in Orillia, on July 21, 1846, the Mohawks of the Bay of Quinte argued for the abandonment of traditional ways, even though they understood clearly how and why these ways had come under threat. "[T]he chase of the Deer and the Beaver" were no longer "profitable," they declared, since "[t]he White man's labour is fast eating away the forest, whilst the sound of his Axe in summer and his Bells in winter is driving the game far away from their old haunts" (Hodgins 1893–1908, 5. 297).

After Canadian confederation, too, many Native leaders actively promoted education in nonNative ways. Epitomizing this position, in 1871 Ojibwa leader Augustine Shingwauk addressed Anglican missionaries in Toronto:

> I told the Blackcoats I hoped that before I died I should see a big teaching wigwam built at Garden River, where children from the Great Chippeway Lake would be received and clothed, and fed, and taught how to read and how to write; and also how to farm and build houses, and make clothing; so that by and bye they might go back and teach their own people. (Shingwauk 1991, 7)

Echoing Shingwauk's sentiments, Native treaty negotiators on the prairies drove hard bargains on the matter of education. Of the forging of "Treaty Number One," Miller writes: "[T]he draft that Canada's negotiator presented to the Indians at Lower Fort Garry in 1871 said nothing about education, but the text that emerged a few days later included a promise 'to maintain a school on each reserve hereby made, whenever the Indians of the reserve should desire it' " (Miller 1996, 98; quoting Morris 1991, 315). Reading and writing skills were valued especially highly. Dan Kennedy, for example, recalls a late nineteenth-century conversation among Assiniboine Elders:

> "And furthermore," he continued, "our children and grandchildren will be taught the magic art of writing. Just think for a moment what that means. Without the aid of the spoken word our children will transmit their thoughts on a piece of paper, and that talking paper may be carried to distant parts of the country and convey your thoughts to your friends. Why even the medicine men of our tribe cannot perform such miracles." (Kennedy 1972, 48)

Miller has suggested, however, that Native leaders "likely had day schools in mind" when they insisted that education guarantees be a key element of the treaties with Ottawa, not boarding schools, and still less the industrial school (Miller 1996, 98).

In recent years, a number of residential school testimonies have been published, many of which seem to bear out Miller's supposition. In *Geniesh: An*

Indian Girlhood, the Cree writer, Jane Willis, describes the monochrome sterility of the "St. Philip's Indian and Eskimo Anglican Residential School of Fort George, Quebec": "The walls [of the junior girls' dormitory] were painted the same greens as the playroom and classroom . . . The denim curtains were green, to match the walls and the linoleum" (Willis 1973, 27, 37). School staff treat pupils not as children, but as numbers:

> Miss Moore pointed to compartment 64, marked every piece of clothing she had issued to me with that number in black indelible ink, and showed me how to stack everything neatly into the small compartment. She hung my Sunday coat on clothes-hook 64. After setting aside the clothes she wanted me to put on, she led me out to the washroom and showed me which toothbrush, plastic cup, and towel to use. They were all marked 64. (Willis 1973, 38)

Upon arrival, children are processed, including disinfecting with kerosene, for "[i]t was assumed by the whites that all Indians entered the school infested with lice and all sorts of revolting creatures" (Willis 1973, 39). All the junior girls receive "Dutch-boy haircuts" (Willis 1973, 45). "Shorn of my long, flowing hair," Willis writes, "I felt completely naked" (Willis 1973, 46). In a welcoming address, the Reverend Dawson, an Anglican cleric and the school principal, reminds students: "[T]he most important reason you are here is to learn all about God and His son, Jesus Christ" (Willis 1973, 45). "Since your ancestors were heathen," Dawson continues, "you must try harder than other people to get into the Kingdom of God, for as it says in the Bible, 'The sins of the fathers shall be visited upon the sons' " (Willis 1973, 45). "Our school," writes Willis, "being run by the church, placed more emphasis on the fourth 'R'—religion—than on the other three" (Willis 1973, 33). A reading of the school's 12 cardinal rules follows the address, though Jane soon discovers "there were other rules, made up on the spur of the moment, usually when the supervisor was in a particularly foul mood" (Willis 1973, 48).[9]

The school Willis entered "with such great expectations," she concludes, "turned out to be a prison" (Willis 1973, 121). Elsewhere, Willis describes "those years in Indian boarding-schools" as "ten and a half years of boot camp" (Willis 1973, 195). In fact, whatever else they might have to say about their time at residential schools, a number of Native writers recur to this sort of carceral imagery. In a generous gesture, for instance, Ojibwa Basil Johnston trusts that his recollections of life at St. Peter Claver's School, "covering two periods, 1939–44 and 1947–50, is as accurate as memory and effort and bias will allow"; of the memoir, *Indian School Days*, "I hope as well that it is fair," he writes (Johnston 1988, 11). Still, imprisonment is the dominant trope for life at this Roman Catholic institution in Spanish, Ontario. The second chapter of the book is entitled "Sentenced to Spanish"; the title of the third chapter, "A Day in the Life of

Spanish," recalls Alexander Solzenitsyn's celebrated portrayal of the Soviet Gulag, *A Day in the Life of Ivan Denisovich*; words like "committal" and phrases like "served their term" pepper the narrative; and the boys constantly express hopes of "release" or being "sprung loose" (Johnston 1988, 78).

The disciplinary ethos of the residential school meant that Native children often suffered cruel punishments. On one occasion, for example, Dawson straps the seven-year-old Jane ten times across her bare bottom and back for talking back to her supervisor: caught playing off-limits, Jane was accused of being "sassy" for stating quite honestly that she did not know she was off-limits (Willis 1973, 62). "With my back full of welts," Willis writes, "I found I could lie in one position only, and that was on my stomach" (Willis 1973, 63). But Tomson Highway's novel, *Kiss of the Fur Queen*, takes this perspective to an extreme, raising feelings of outrage, guilt, and pity in its fictional portrayal of the physical and sexual abuse heaped upon the Cree brothers, Champion and Ooneemeetoo Okimasis. Like Willis, Highway describes the school in carceral terms—in terms of "steel-mesh fences and curfews that chained you to your bed by 9.00 P.M." (Highway 1998, 102). And as in *Geniesh*, so in *Kiss of the Fur Queen*, Native children suffer horrible abuses at the hands of nonNative Christian ecclesiastics. In Highway's narrative, this litany of abuse culminates in a reverie, as a repressed memory of sexual abuse returns:

> By the light of a moon full to bursting, the now eight-year-old floated down an aisle lined with small white beds, cradles filled with sleeping brown children. Out a door, and up and down corridors, the long black robe swaying like a curtain, smelling of cigar smoke, incense, sacramental wine.
>
> By the puffy armchair of pitch-black leather, Father Roland Lafleur, oblate of Mary Immaculate, unbuttoned his cassock, unzipped his trousers. So white, thought Champion-Jeremiah, so big. Black and white hair all around the base, like . . . a mushroom on a cushion of reindeer moss.
>
> Now he remembers the holy man inside him, the lining of his rectum being torn, the pumping and pumping and pumping, cigar breath billowing somewhere his cold shaved head.
>
> What had he done? Whatever it was, he promised that, from now on, he would say the prayer in English only: "Our Father, who art in Heaven, hallowed be thy name. And make me bleed. Please, Father, please, make me bleed."
>
> Back in bed, it was too dark to see what kind of chocolate bar it was. Sweet Marie? Coffee crisp? Mr. Big? (Highway 1998, 287)

Interviewed about the novel, Highway remarked that "writing *The Fur Queen* was an exorcism, a way of writing through the agony of being taken away from home at six years old, of being forced to speak English, of having the ugly, slobbering priests paw and kiss him, and watching his beautiful brother go deaf and blind before he finally died at age 35" (Martin 2001, R1).

It would be misleading to suggest that negative images totally govern Native accounts of the residential school experience. Micmac Rita Joe, for example, offers a more nuanced picture:

> [I]f you think that for two, sometimes three generations, people, families were being broken up, and they don't even *learn*, some of the kids, that their parents love them! What do you expect them to do when they are parents?
>
> So, I think some of the problems, or a lot of the problems that we see today, are really the result of the residential schools. And that must never happen again! . . .
>
> But let me tell you about the positive part that I have tried to research. The positive part of the residential school—and I will say that across the nation!—the positive part was: the people that came from it, the good ones, learned a lot from there. And so many people have gone on, and they have become chiefs, counsellors, and social workers, and they went on to learn! (Lutz 1991, 257)

Rita Joe here articulates an autobiographical perspective neither nostalgic nor perplexed. Fully aware of missionary abuses, she nonetheless refuses to permit past ills to dictate the kind of future that Native peoples will inhabit. Instead, she celebrates the accomplishments of "chiefs, counsellors, and social workers," accomplishments that constitute an ethos of Native self-determination. Then again, though, Jeannette C. Armstrong uses terms like "totalitarianism" and "indoctrination camps" to signify her conviction that an unofficial policy of cultural genocide was in force throughout the government-funded, church-run residential school system (Armstrong 1998, 239). Under this policy, Armstrong writes, "our language, our religions, our customs, our values, and our societal structures almost disappeared," even if that one word "almost" reveals a glimmer of hope and the determination to fuel it into reality (Armstrong 1998, 239).

Afterword

If we take at face value the trope of incarceration permeating Native residential school testimonies, we do not have to look far to discover its origins in the historical discourse, at once penitential and penitentiary, of nonNative educational theory. When Native writers vividly refigure the residential school experience in disciplinary and carceral terms, this imagining exactly echoes the language in which nineteenth-century nonNative colonial scions like McMurrich, Davin, and "Iota" articulated the evangelical ethos of the industrial reformatory, an ethos that continued to pervade the residential school system throughout its history. Canadians have seen a plethora of academic and popular publications about this system over the past several years. Mainly historical in emphasis, few of these studies take theoretical account of the carceral reality of residential schools. As Dian Million has noted, "[t]he residential schools were sites at the intersection and articulation of many powerful public narratives (Catholicism, Anglicanism, Canadian nationalism, etc.) embedded in a set of spatial relationships and practices that Foucault, in his early work *Discipline and Punishment*, called 'carceral space' " (Million 2000, 94). She continues:

> Carceral space defined by Foucault is social power invested into spaces designed to form individuals deemed outside a particular social order by surveillance and practice, like schools, the military, prisons, and mental hospitals. Residential schools were quintessential carceral spaces since they were organized to discipline both bodies and minds with the order socially invested in them. (Million 2000, 94)

Expressed in its least offensive terms, in Michel Foucault's own words, "if we take educational institutions, we realize that one is managing others and teaching them to manage themselves" (Foucault 1984, 369–370).

As Aimee Howley and Richard Hartnett have argued, however, Foucault suggests two "diagrams" for defining the "micro-physics" of power relations within major institutions: the paradigm of the disciplines and the paradigm of the pastorate (Howley and Hartnett 1992, 214; citing Foucault 1982, 214). Associated with the Christian churches, pastoral power exhibits more of a concern with improvement than containment; it is "normative rather than carceral power" and its "essential character is not disciplinary" (Howley and Hartnett 1992, 271). Pastoral power is concerned with personal salvation in the next world; prefers self-sacrifice to absolute control; cares for individuals as individuals, not just for the community as a whole; and values the inner life, not to convert the soul, but to cultivate the conscience and the value of personal identity (Howley and Hartnett 1992, 272). Hence techniques of pastoral power include "a complicated interplay of coercion and freedom," at the heart of which lies the power of the confessional, which enables "the pastor to know and control every member of the community" (Howley and Hartnett 1992, 272). "Pastoral power represented a transaction: the individual revealed the truth about him or herself, and the pastor guaranteed the individual's salvation," but "the pastor exercised this power only insofar as it was necessary to restore individuals to a state of grace—or, in more contemporary parlance, to the state of being normal" (Howley and Hartnett 1992, 272, 273). For Foucault, pastoral power "ensures, sustains, and improves" lives, seeking "voluntary compliance" to the norms it espouses (Howley and Hartnett 1992, 272, 271; citing Foucault 1988, 67).

Over against pastoral power lie the "main disciplinary institutions—prisons, mental hospitals, and public schools" (Howley and Hartnett 1992, 271). For Foucault, disciplines are "the collective set of techniques that different institutions use in order to establish and maintain control" (Howley and Hartnett 1992, 278; citing Foucault 1977, 137). In schools, ranking and observation are the key disciplinary techniques. On the practical level, ranking enables the mechanical imposition of order and establishes "criteria for identifying and requiring compliance"; on the symbolic level, it reifies "power relations and, thereby, legitimize differences" (Howley and Hartnett 1992, 278–279). Techniques of observation enable schools to make distinctions among students thus socialized to accept the norms by which they are ranked and judged. Here Foucault reflects upon the geography of the classroom: "Thus, the classroom . . . form[s] a single great table, with many different entries, under the scrupulously 'classificatory' eye of the master," whose ranking and grading "has a double role: it marks the gaps, hierarchizes qualities, skills and aptitudes; but it also punishes and rewards" (Foucault 1977, 147, 181). Other methods of observation include the examination, "a normalizing gaze, a surveillance that makes it possible to qualify, to classify and to punish," as well as evaluation, a "confessional technology" that inculcates "the belief that one can, with the help of expert interpreters, tell the truth about oneself" (Foucault 1977, 184; Howley and Hartnett 1992, 281).

The management of Native children in the residential schools constitutes a complex interweaving of these two paradigms. Here, when I talk about the "penitential and penitentiary" aspects of nonNative approaches to the education of Native children in residential schools, I am talking about the coupling of Foucault's understanding of power and its exercise as pastoral with Foucault's notion of disciplinary or carceral power. Both paradigms are present in the residential school system, but pastoral power begins to yield to carceral power once the missionary agenda gets tied to the government agenda and the disciplinary model of the industrial reformatory comes to permeate the everyday life of Native children removed from their familiar, familial environments. As the Methodist missionary, William Elliott, notes in 1895, in a telling discursive inversion of Native domestic and nonNative institutional identities, "[i]n the daily routine of the [Coqualeetza Indian] Institute . . . there is a strong smack of *home*" (Elliott 1895, 135; emphasis in the original). "That is the secret of its power," Elliott continues, "and power when it is seen what a change has been wrought in these Indian children since coming under the influence of the Institute" (Elliott 1895, 135). Schlossman's interrogative hits the nail on the head: "Could any institution that incarcerated young children against their will for several years' duration . . . truly be considered a substitute family or home?" (Schlossman 1995, 370).

What is more, missionary and government authority combine to extend and increase the panoptical techniques of classroom discipline in several ways. Native children were expected to work the school farms and gardens, the ordered rows of plantings both in the communal fields and in the individualized plots of the children's gardens recapitulating the disciplinary order of the classroom in the agricultural taming of nature. Similarly, the geography of the dormitory extends the daytime discipline of classroom and field into the night, as the lines of beds, the rigidly imposed times of going to bed and getting up, and the careful arrangement of bedclothes and toiletries ranks and orders the lives of Native children even as they sleep, creating a totalizing ethos of observation and judgment, with concomitant rewards and punishments for keeping or breaking the order of the night. Third, however, and most disturbingly, we can pinpoint the shift from pastoral to disciplinary power in and through a Foucauldian understanding of the notion of the canon of acceptable knowledge and behavior assumed in the residential schools. Literally "a cane or stick for measuring the worth of something, a canon is the standard against which all forms of knowledge are gauged" (Howley and Hartnett 1992, 276). As we have seen, church and state alike discount Native knowledge as not productive of normal individuals, or worse, productive of abnormal or sub-normal individuals. Native children must therefore be removed from their traditional environments, to save them from the abnormal or sub-normal selves they would otherwise become. But the exercise of this pastoral authority metamorphoses into the infliction of disciplinary power, as missionaries collude with government to enforce cultural conversion upon Native peoples.

This move from pastoral to carceral includes a move from reliance on the voluntary aspect of the former to reliance on the disciplinary and coercive aspect of the latter. In 1920, for example, Ottawa amended the Indian Act to make school attendance compulsory for every child between the ages of seven and fifteen, and in 1921, a delegation of Protestant and Roman Catholics representatives insisted to Charles Stewart, Minister of the Interior, that "the Government put into force the Compulsory clause of the revised Indian Act and secure an attendance of the maximum number of pupils at each and all Indian Residentiary Schools" (quoted in Milloy 1999, 71). "In 1933," Miller reminds us, "officers of the Royal Canadian Mounted Police were explicitly made truant officers," and in 1951, in a final rounding of the circle of carceral discipline, further amendments to the Indian Act "made a child who had been expelled or suspended, or who was defiantly truant, 'a juvenile delinquent within the meaning of *The Juvenile Delinquents Act, 1929*' " (Miller 1996, 170, 469 n.71). Worse still, as Native residential school testimonies make clear, the figurative canon of moral and spiritual authority metamorphoses into the physical realities of corporal punishment; the kind of caning that Willis recalls with such poignancy, for instance, represents the literalization and materialization of the canon—the "cane or stick" of authority—in acts of physical coercion and abuse. In the worst cases, this transformation in the techniques of disciplinary power eventuates in its most perverse forms in the actual incorporation of the rod of authority into the very body of the disciplined in the sort of sexual acts of oral and anal penetration that Highway writes about.

Taken to the extreme, as Maurice Blanchot has argued, such disciplinary procedures lead to the concentration camp, the logical outcome of a dominant social and cultural authority's absolute refusal of personal space to those who do not belong—to those who are constructed as abnormal or sub-normal—in and through the dissolution of personal identity in a totally regimented social space (Blanchot 1973, 60). In such contexts, the violated learn to become still, silent, and anonymous amidst the conditions of their own violation; to be recognized in the concentration camp is to risk annihilation (Blanchot 1973, 38). As we have seen, it is to these sorts of conclusions that Jeannette C. Armstrong has been driven. On the other hand, as the residential school testimonies of Willis, Johnston, and Highway also make clear, "even within this order, alternative narratives and acts already existed" (Million 2000, 94). In Million's words, "[a]s children, and most certainly as adults, these individuals continued to articulate that they belonged to different cultures—ones that had historically challenged, produced, and continued to produce knowledge that countered and interrupted the whole process that residential education was supposed to ensure" (Million 2000, 94). It would be misleading, therefore, to suggest that church and state were always and everywhere successful in their shared policy of cultural assimilation, sustained though it was over many decades across the geographically diverse regions of the developing nation of Canada.

In this respect, Stephan Collini has reminded us of "the complexity of culture" (Collini 1999, 263). There is no question but that we need to be aware of unequal distributions of power and influence of one kind and another in relations between European colonial and imperial officers and their cultural others, Collini argues, but we also need to keep in mind the dangers of slipping into too easy an opposition between marginalized Native peoples and their silencing oppressors, between a dominant centre and an alienated periphery. Just as "the centre" is not monolithic in its intentions, so too, different marginal groups "in a culture are never self-contained or purely oppositional, but share concepts and values and engage in constant commerce, often intelligible and profitable commerce, with their cultural neighbours, including the most powerful ones" (Collini 1999, 263–264). In other words, the complex entanglements of historical process produce inevitably ambiguous results, even under the most apparently one-sided conditions of cultural encounter, conflict, and occasional accommodation. According to a recent Canadian National Defence report, *Religions in Canada*, the "majority" of Native Canadians claim membership in one kind or another of Christian church (National Defence 2003, 70).

But the Christianities practiced among these various communities assume an increasingly Native flavor, their various expressions of spirituality revealing complex marriages of nonNative religious ways and Native Canadian traditions. In particular, the residential schools and their legacy continue to provoke such complexities. The Anglican Council of Indigenous Peoples, for example, has described the church's alternative dispute resolution protocols for addressing Native residential school grievances as "too bureaucratic and somewhat dehumanizing" (de Santis 2003). The process, argues the council, should include the indigenous tradition of "talking circles . . . which allow all persons present at a gathering to speak in turn" (de Santis 2003). In the self-addressed words of Laverne Jacobs, a member of the Ojibway First Nation of Walpole Island who has served as national coordinator for Native ministries for both the Anglican and United churches of Canada: "This is you—both Native and Christian" (Jacobs 1996, 240).

Notes

1. In 1639, an Ursuline girls' school opened, under Mother Marie de l'Incarnation (Jaenen 1986, 57).
2. Fast (1979) points out that the published text of West's journal is an edited version designed to serve as a fund raiser for CMS missions. The full text reveals West to have been less generous in his opinions of Native peoples, and less optimistic about the likely success of missionary efforts to convert them to nonNative ways. This discrepancy raises the important issue of audience. When we presume from reading missionary writings the effects of missionary policies upon Native peoples, we may be jumping the gun. As Nicholas Thomas points out, missionaries were quite capable of expressing themselves differently on the same subject to suit different audiences (Thomas 1994, 126).
3. For an account of the life and ministry of Peter Jones, see Smith (1987).
4. In a tidy discursive solipsism, cultivating Tims's "three 'R's' " and "use of tools"—things spiritual and things corporal—in missionary schools together constitute the cultivated yeoman citizen so valued by the state, either as laborers on settler farms or as subsistence farmers on reserves. For an analysis of federal government policies toward Native Canadian prairie farmers, see Carter (1990). On the trope of cultivation in the discourse of Christian missions to Native Canadian peoples, see Scott (2005).
5. As Jacqueline Gresko points out, although Qu'Appelle's founder, Father Joseph Hugonnard, also "saw schools as the civilizing part of the Christianizing process," he was less willing than his Protestant counterparts to discourage contact between his wards and their parents, since "[h]e intended to promote parental conversion through school visits" (Gresko 1986, 91, 93). Before long, however, cutbacks in government funding forced the school to curtail a number of programmes, including "ongoing links with parent groups" (Gresko 1986, 94).
6. For an analysis of tropes of female domestication in Canadian missionary discourse, see Rutherdale (2005). As Walter J. Wasylow has noted, to make them suitable candidates for domestic service or supportive partners for yeoman husbands, female pupils received "a rudimentary English education and training in all the chores and household work performed by a pioneer wife" (Wasylow 1972, 40).

7. For representative statistics on the dispersal of residential schools and attendance by province, see McGillivray (1997, 154–155).
8. For a useful account of role of *parens patriae* in the development of the reform school movement in nineteenth-century Europe and North America, see Schlossman (1995, 366–367). For a detailed analysis of transformations in the legal and political status of Native children in Canada in the nineteenth and twentieth centuries, see McGillivray (1997).
9. The first cardinal rule bans the speaking of Cree, though pupils exercise a kind of passive resistance by "refusing to speak either Cree or English when any of the staff were around" (Willis 1973, 46). Other cardinal rules apply to staying outdoors; chores; talking back to the staff or questioning "any statements or requests"; "noise, crying, or loud talking in the playroom" or "noise or talking" after lights out; eating every morsel of food served; immediate obedience; taking care of issued clothes and shoes; the use of inside portable dormitory toilets; intercourse between boys and girls (Willis 1973, 46). Failure to observe any or all of these rules risked severe punishment.

PART TWO

WORLD RELIGIONS, GLOBAL MISSIONS

CHAPTER EIGHT

DA'WA IN THE WEST: ISLAMIC MISSION IN AMERICAN FORM

Jane I. Smith

Spreading Islam

The impulse to "spread the faith" by whatever means available has been present in the community of Islam since the Prophet Muhammad received his first revelations in the early years of the seventh century of the Common Era. Though propagation by means of the sword was not incidental to the rapid spread of Islam across Asia, North Africa, and the Iberian Peninsula, far more peaceful means of bringing individuals and communities into the fold of Islam usually prevailed.[1] In many cases, the spread of Islam really meant the adoption of a way of life and faith practiced by merchants, traders, and itinerant teachers, or the willing replacement on the part of resident populations of an oppressive overlordship. While the political and financial rewards of the spread of the religion were not insignificant to the young community, the religious or theological goal was to make known the original message received by Muhammad of the uniqueness of God and the reality of the day of judgment.

The religious impulse to share the message of God's revelation has much in common with the missionary enterprise of Christianity, as described in the gospel of Matthew in the New Testament, which urges believers to make disciples of all people (Matthew 28.19). Throughout the more than fourteen centuries in which Islam has existed as an organized faith, Muslims have understood it to be part of their religious duty to bring as many people as possible under the umbrella of Islam. It comes as no surprise, then, that this kind of "missionary" activity constitutes an important component of the religious life of Muslims in the West in the twentieth and twenty-first centuries.

That Islam is the true faith of all monotheistic peoples of all times and places is a basic tenet of the religion of Islam. All of the prophets from the first man, Adam, to the last messenger, Muhammad, are understood to have been Muslims insofar as they were submitters to the one true God. Islam is thus the natural human response to God, and it is on the basis of that recognition and response that Muslims believe all people will be brought to a final accounting at the end of time. Qur'an 7.172 describes a kind of primordial covenant between human beings and God, in which all of humanity testifies to the lordship of God. Muslims have taken this text to mean that by their essential nature all people are really Muslim. Many Muslims, particularly in the current American context, emphasize that if one comes to recognize his or her real identity as Muslim, that person actually goes back to the original state of Islam. Thus Americans who adopt the faith are often referred to as "re-verts" rather than converts.

The Meaning of *Da'wa*

In Islam, the term for inviting people to Islam is *da'wa*, from the Arabic verb "to call."[2] Of the many variations on the basic root form found in the Qur'an, with their range of meanings, the actual word *da'wa* appears four times: 2.186 describes God's willingness to listen to the *da'wa* (call) of the faithful one calling on Him; 13.14 talks of God's calling all people to truth; 30.25 seems to imply the calling by God of all people at the day of resurrection; and 40.42–43 refers to the erroneous call of unbelievers tempting believers to reject their faith. Calling, therefore, is done by God, by those who wish to subvert the true religion, and by the faithful themselves. It is the last connotation that is most commonly referred to by the word *da'wa*, and it is seen as an important element of the religious responsibility of Muslims in America.

Da'wa is described in current Muslim literature as having a variety of forms. Most often, probably, it refers to the active persuasion of Christians, Jews, or persons of other or no faith that their current lives and their future destinies are at stake, and that it is urgent to understand and accept the message of Islam. Somewhat more subtle, but nonetheless very real for faithful American Muslims, is the importance of bringing those who have lapsed in their practices back to more scrupulous observance. Of the approximately six million Muslims currently estimated to be resident in the United States, for example, many do not attend the mosque on Friday or Sunday, pray regularly, or fast during the month of Ramadan. *Da'wa* is intended to help remedy that situation. A third variety of *da'wa* is what might be termed "the quiet call," as opposed to the more vocal reaching out to unbelievers or to the lapsed. It means simply living in as exemplary a way as possible, so as to make it evident that Islam is a way of life that brings comfort, joy and peace.

None of these interpretations of *da'wa* is new to Islam, but it is only fairly recently that they have come to be identified, spoken, and written about by American Muslims. To these three understandings might be added a fourth, which has been discussed a great deal since the terrorist attacks in New York and Washington on September 11, 2001. This fourth sense of *da'wa* has to do with education, specifically, telling the American people that Islam is a religion of peace and not of terror, and that the Islamic understanding is of a God of mercy and compassion, not a God of revenge.

Da'wa Comes to America

The attempt to bring others to Islam is, of course, not new to America. The fact that some 30–35 percent of Muslims in the United States are African American is due to the fact that they, or their forebears, chose to relinquish some other identity to adopt a form of Islam. Thus they have converted to such movements as the Nation of Islam, the Ahmadiyya, Sunni and Shi'i movements, and many other groups identifying themselves with Islam. Sometimes, that Islam has been "orthodox," and sometimes not. Many African American Muslims heard the message of Islam while incarcerated, the most famous case being that of Malcolm X.[3]

From the early days of the twentieth century, immigrant Muslims have sponsored efforts to convert Americans to Islam, although until recently they were fairly minimal. Starting in the 1920s, the most active missionary movement in America was that of the Ahmadis, from what is now Pakistan. Although Ahmadis are currently accused by other Muslims of being errant in some of their beliefs, they have been active in the propagation of Islam through teaching and translations of texts throughout the world. Many African Americans converted through the efforts of such Ahmadi missionaries as Mufti Muhammad Sadiq, one of the first Muslims to attack the blatant racism of American society. Alexander Russell Webb, founder in 1893 of the American Moslem Brotherhood in New York, the first documented Islamic institution in the country, is acknowledged as the pioneer of *da'wa* to white Americans. Webb was himself a convert from Presbyterian Christianity (Posten 1992, 162–163, 174–177).

In recent decades, a number of revivalist movements from other countries, particularly Pakistan and Saudi Arabia, have been visible on the American scene. They are active not only in making converts from the general public, but particularly in working within the Muslim community itself to propagate a particular ideology or interpretation. Often, they promote this kind of Sunni *da'wa* by targeting American Muslims to be the recipients of financial assistance. Among these are the Salafiyya movement, supported by the Dar al-Iftar in Saudi Arabia, and the Tableeghi Jamaat movement, which originated in Pakistan. American Shi'ites receive direction and assistance through such institutions as the Kho'i Foundation, formerly under the leadership of Imam Kho'i, from Najaf in Iraq. These kinds of efforts illustrate both the range of foreign-supported *da'wa* activities and some of the ideological differences that serve to pull the American Muslim community in different and often conflicting directions.

Da'wa in America today is carried out in a variety of other contexts. In May, 2001, a recent past-president of the Islamic Society of North America (ISNA) commented at a meeting of Muslim leaders that when he goes to a shopping center or other place where there are crowds, he envisions it as a potential arena of conversion to Islam.[4] The late Isma'il al Faruqi, professor at Temple University, said on many occasions that he considered his work in academia as the venue for doing *da'wa*, and that he looked forward to the time when all of America would be Muslim. Al Faruqi was the founder of the International Institute of Islamic Thought in Herndon, Virginia, which has been active in the *da'wa* enterprise. The Islamic Circle of North America (ICNA), second in size only to ISNA, has published "A Manual of Da'wah for Islamic Workers," which details concepts and techniques of outreach to the non-Muslim West (Posten 1991). Occasionally, the Islamic Society of North America sponsors *da'wa* training opportunities in countries such as Pakistan to provide instruction for young Muslims in an international context. In 1999–2000, for example, the Da'wah Academy of the International Islamic University in Islamabad organized a training camp of this kind.

The website of the Institute of Islamic Information and Education (III&E), which describes itself as "dedicated to providing the most accurate look at Islam in America," provides links to "Upcoming Dawah Training," a "Dawah List Order Form," and a site called "How Can You Help Dawah?"[5] In 1997, the III&E began *da'wa* training programs under the title "TRAIN-THE-TRAINERS COURSE (TTC)." These programs, which have taken place in Los Angeles, Houston, New Jersey, and Chicago, espouse the twin goals of reaching out to non-Muslims with the message of Islam and of training more *da'wa* workers like themselves. Viewers are encouraged to help the effort by making monetary donations—the form is available online—and by distributing free brochures, talking with non-Muslims and participating in various other outreach strategies.

A great deal of missionary effort takes place in the prison context. This kind of *da'wa* is carried out primarily by African Americans, both members of the current Nation of Islam and Sunnis eager to preach true or orthodox Islam, distinct from what they believe to be the perverted message of the Nation with its so-called racist ideology. Numerous people from the Muslim community work as chaplains, missionaries, and teachers, both in prisons and outside, to help rehabilitate new Muslims when they are released from incarceration. According to some sources, the number of persons in prison who have adopted Islam has grown from 25,000 inmates in 1987 to over 350,000 at the close of the twentieth century.[6] Whatever the numbers, there is no question that those working to propagate Islam in the penal system, as in other arenas, are acutely aware of the growing need for Islamic materials such as copies of the Qur'an, translations of religious texts, and basic information about beliefs and practices. Muslims have also mounted organized efforts to attend to the legal rights of Muslims to practice their faith appropriately in the prison setting.

The ISNA, largest of the American Muslim organizations, sponsors national conferences on Islam in American prisons. These conferences bring together people who have been involved in *daʿwa* and encourage assistance to the incarcerated. Efforts are also being made by groups of young Muslim converts in prison to create a sense of solidarity and responsibility. The Junior Association of Muslim Men (JAMM), for example, was established in 1994 at Sing Sing prison, as part of the ministry of the Muslim American Society's Imam Warith Deen Mohammed. Members of this association train new converts in the elements of Islam and help them to reenter American society. Emphasis is put on Islam as a structure through which converts can transform their lives, and on training these young Muslims for leadership positions in Muslim American society when they are released from prison. American Shiʿite Muslims are also active in prison *daʿwa*.

Some Sufi groups have been active agents in the dissemination of Islam, appealing to Americans who respond to the use of music, dance, chanting, and other means of bringing the supplicant into closer relationship with the divine. In some cases, members of the new generation of Muslims born in America to immigrant parents are joining white converts to Sufi movements. Many Sufi orders in the United States and Canada currently have very active *daʿwa* and educational programs, promoted and supported through publishing houses and other forms of information distribution. The Naqshbandi-Haqqani Order, for example, is said to have grown considerably in the United States as a result of the opening of a "Daʿwa Convention Center" in Fenton, Michigan, in 1993.[7] This center attracted hundreds of disciples and visitors (Hermansen 2000, 165). In addition, wearing particular kinds of Islamic clothing is a general characteristic of American Sufis, who can be said to be "doing *daʿwa*" by their very visibility.

Young American Muslims are being drawn into *daʿwa* efforts in a number of different contexts. Some are attracted to the teachings of conservative "missionaries" from countries like Pakistan or Saudi Arabia, and are being schooled in the most effective ways to preach Islam to others in the American context. Others are active in organizations such as the Muslim Student Association (MSA), which for years has served on college campuses to bring young Muslim students into contact with each other and to provide access to various facilities on campus. In a conversation with me in May, 2001, Altaf Hussein, president of MSA, described how he and his colleagues were deeply involved in *da'wa* of a very different sort. For them, *da'wa* specifically had to do with meeting together with youth of different religious traditions to talk about topics of common interest, or working together to address issues of community concern. In such contexts, *da'wa* is indirect, the possible fruit of open and honest communication among young people. On a growing number of college and university campuses, Muslim, Jewish, and other students now regularly meet together for *halal*/kosher meals, giving them other informal opportunities to talk about the faith and practices of Islam.[8]

A number of social action movements carry out another kind of "internal *da'wa*." The Muslim Youth of North America (MYNA) organization, a subsidiary of ISNA, for example, holds national annual meetings and camps, as well as a range of local activities, to train youth in the right understanding of Islam and to help ensure that they remain active Muslims. Annual meetings of the ISNA feature workshops for youth dealing specifically with *da'wa*, underscoring its importance in the context of such activities as relief work and urban development. In addition, part of MYNA's directive is to provide appropriate contexts for Muslim young people to meet potential marriage partners, working to ensure that they do not leave the faith through intermarriage. The Inner-City Muslim Action Network (IMAN) in Chicago, which promotes a range of social action projects in the metropolitan area, also holds a biennial festival in Marquette Park, entitled "Taking it to the Streets." The festival features talks on Islam, food and entertainment, and according to its website, "provides an opportunity for non-Muslim community residents to come out and be around Muslims who are giving the message that we are part of the community and that in Islam we have a message which is the solution to all of humanity's problems."[9]

One of the topics of great interest to contemporary Muslims in America is the appropriateness of women for assuming different kinds of religious roles. Today, both women and men insist that educated women are integral to the task of calling others to follow Islam. This role becomes especially important when it comes to appealing to other women, and convincing them that Islam offers to women not oppression, but enhanced opportunities for fulfillment. Women's organizations exist to assist women who may be thinking about Islam by providing services, classes, social occasions, and the like. An organization called "Sisters United in Human Service, Inc., Working for the Pleasure of Allah" attempts to promote, support, uplift and serve human concerns "in the spirit of sisterhood."[10]

Women are increasingly active in the growing numbers of Islamic social welfare agencies, and efforts being made by Muslim communities and individuals to reach out to the needy.

Implicitly or explicitly, such efforts at social action contribute to the *da'wa* effort. In Los Angeles, for example, the University Muslim Medical Association (UMMA) Free Health Clinic, run by Muslim physicians and medical students, focuses on healthcare and social welfare for the gang-troubled area of south central Los Angeles. In many areas of America's inner cities, Muslims are making efforts to ensure that all citizens, Muslim or otherwise, receive adequate healthcare. The concerted efforts of the Nation of Islam to clean up neighborhoods and rid them of drugs and crime have been heralded for their success. All of these kinds of efforts serve to propagate the message that Islam is a religion of care and human concern, and to demonstrate an aspect of social awareness that may be very attractive to those looking for a combination of faith and action.

As *da'wa* efforts continue in the American context as a whole, targeted to both African and Caucasian Americans, other groups are also being identified as potential converts to Islam. Among them are Hispanics and Native Americans. Some Muslim proselytizers point to the natural affiliation of Islam with many parts of these respective cultures, particularly the emphasis on family and community over individuality, and the specifically defined roles for men and women. The first American Hispanics to convert to Islam were located in the barrios of cities in the northeast in the early 1970s. Primarily first generation Puerto Ricans generally affiliated first with African American mosques. Organized Muslim missionary efforts since then have concentrated on Latino populations in various parts of the United States, including the west coast. Many American Muslims have argued for increased efforts at providing basic Islamic instruction in Spanish, and for translating the Qur'an and other works into the Spanish language. Typical of the growing number of Muslim organizations devoted to *da'wa* in the Hispanic community are PIEDAD (Propagacion Islamica para la Educacion y Devocion de Ala'el Divino), Alianza Islamica in New York, and ALMA (the Asociacion Latina de Musulmanes en las Americas) in California (Smith 1999, 66–67).

Since the September 11, 2001, terrorist attacks in New York and Washington, there has been a concentrated effort among Muslims to "tell the story" of Islam, so that non-Muslims will be able to see that it is a religion of peace rather than terror, of compassion rather than violence. A great range of means have been devised for telling this story, including interviews with the media and the press, talks in local churches and civic organizations, messages on the web, instruction sessions in public schools, and local displays in institutions such as public libraries. "There is no dearth of opportunities for outreach," says Shaheen

Akhtar, in a typical article in the popular journal *Islamic Horizons*, describing how "Each town library offers displays of the month" (Akhtar 1999, 32–33). Muslim women and men are encouraged to continue to wear Islamic dress if that is their preference, and to use that outward symbol of pride in and identity with Islam as a means of telling the story.

The story-telling mode has long been an important vehicle for teaching and reenforcing the message of Islam to those who are already Muslim. "Storytelling is a powerful tool to connect today's children to their history," says Rukhsana Khan, "and to morals and principles that define what it is to be Muslim" (Khan 1999, 51). Others look to more popular media for communicating the message of Islam. Thaufeer al-Deen, author of "The Popular Mystery Novel *Da'wah*," notes that such typical vehicles for teaching what is required and forbidden in Islam as sermons and educational programs often lack effective contextualization and relevancy. He points to the use of technology as a more effective tool for reaching the majority of the population, noting that "Western ideas exude from product packaging, billboards, public attire, music, film, computer games . . . ." One popular literary genre, he believes, is the mystery novel or short story as a vehicle for teaching the essentials of Islam (al-Deen 1999, 47–48). The title of his article suggests that it can be an effective way of telling a story to non-Muslims.

The "Commodification" of Islam and Its Implications for *Da'wa*

Much of the spread of Islam, and of information about Islam, is carried out through various kinds of "commodification." Here, it is very difficult to draw the line between providing products, including various kinds of information, for persons who are already members of the faith, and using those products as a way of "advertising" Islam to potential converts. One has to assume that both purposes are being served, and that for persons considering whether or not to adopt Islam there is without doubt an appeal in having so many interesting and attractive products readily available. And available they are: at neighborhood markets and shops, in stalls at both local and national Muslim meetings, and through many different kinds of advertising, including magazines, journals, and online ready-to-order catalogs and many other sources. Here is only a small sampling of the kinds of products that are available and the general categories into which they fall:

Clothing. Both men and women can find all manner of dress available, from scarves, *hijabs* (head-coverings) and *kufis* (small caps for men), to long robes for both men and women. Some are ready-made, while others can be fitted to the individual customer. Islamic Boutique's "Islamic Clothing for the Muslim Woman," for example, "is dedicated to all Muslim women, to find fashionable Islamic clothing designed to comply with regulations of Muslim dress code" (Islamic Boutique). Although based in Cairo, Egypt, this online company advertises products in American dollars and regularly holds auctions for clothing and related accessories on E-Bay.[11] Islamic Boutique boasts a "big collection of *Abaya*, *Jilbab*, *Khimar*, *Niqab*," and includes weblinks with advice for Muslim and non-Muslim women about appropriate styles. "Seven Conditions for a Woman's Dress in Islam," for instance, is specifically aimed at "westerners seeking a knowledge and understanding of Islam" (Rahman).[12] By contrast, Shukr bills itself as "the leading Islamic fashion house" and "the first to introduce contemporary styled Islamic clothing for a new generation of Muslims" (Shukr). Its "Clothing for Women" section includes a variety of dresses in a range of natural and man-made fabrics, while "Clothing for Men" includes formal wedding suits in Turkish, Tashkent, Samarqand, and Manchester designs.[13] While outfits are sometimes fashioned for daytime use, often in gray or tan tones, others are specifically created for evening wear. Opportunities to dress both Islamically and stylishly are seemingly endless. Thus, Imported Islamic Fashions offers *hijabs*, *jilbabs*, accessories and more, while Al Hannah Islamic Clothing, mindful at once of its American market and of those who might need individualized styling, imports from Jordan "a loose-fitting Arabian over-garment [*abaya*], . . . meant to fit a wide range of plus sizes, from American size 16 women's–30 women's" (Al Hannah).[14] Though a number of these online companies use models to advertise their clothing products, nowhere are the faces of the models shown, in accordance with Muslim religious proscriptions against the figural representation of living beings.[15]

Health Products. "Don't Smile Without it," admonishes the manufacturer of Siwak, a tooth product designed to promote healthier gums, and he goes on to claim that his mixture is formulated with extract from the Miswak tree. Some historical background is important here, for siwak is the product said to have been used by Prophet Muhammad in cleaning his teeth.[16] In a similar fashion, Al-Istinja, Sunnah Hygiene reminds brothers and sisters that cleanliness is part of faith, and advertises its portable cleansing dispenser, so that one can keep clean at home, at work, and at school. Soaps, deodorants, shampoos, body oils, and a long list of other products designed to improve one's health "Islamically" are available for the conscientious Muslim. Such products make good gifts from Muslims to others who may be considering adopting Islam.

Food Products. Related to concerns of health, and one of the most important issues for American Muslims who wish to live Islamically, is the need to be able to observe Muslim dietary restrictions. Thus many of the products advertised for Muslims have to do with *halal* food, most specifically referring to the elimination of pork products and alcohol, but increasingly meaning meat that has been slaughtered in a religiously appropriate way. Recommended by the Islamic Food and Nutrition Council of America, such companies as Al Safa Halal Foods offer hand-slaughtered Zabiha beef and chicken to distributors like Safeway, Valu-Mart, Stop & Shop, Jewel, Winn Dixie and Waldbaums.[17] Many other "Islamic" food products are available, including *halal* sausages, pastrami, turkey ham, pizza toppings, jello, and marshmallows prepared appropriately from beef gelatin.

Religiously Educational Products. A number of accessories are provided to allow one to become more religiously literate, most importantly products having to do with the Qur'an and its interpretation for and adaptation to modern life. For example, Halalco Supermarket, of Falls Church, Virginia, offers the Qur'an in a range of technologically sophisticated forms. "An excellent gift idea," the "Digital Qur'an Reader" comes in Arabic with English and French translations. Among other selling points, it features "a built-in Speaker," enabling the devotee to simultaneously hear and read the scripture, "easy search for surahs and verses, [and] book-marking of surahs and verses that will be saved even after shutdown" (Halalco Supermarket). Halalco advertises the Qur'an on CD-ROM as well, as does the Chicago-based company, Micro Systems International, whose pitch argues that this format is "the best multimedia tool for learning the Qur'an today," bringing "a *new world of study and contemplation*, opening to everyone the word of God regardless of their own native language" (Micro Systems International; emphasis in the original). Also, numerous companies put out audio tapes featuring presentations by prominent Muslim speakers. One online retailer offers the thoughts of Dr. Abu Ameenah Bilal Philips, for example, whose biography and vocational career as a Muslim proselytizer represent a fascinating instance of the transnational nature of globalizing contemporary Muslim identity. Born in Jamaica, Philips grew up in Canada, where he "accepted Islam" (View Islam). He earned an MA in Islamic Theology from the University of Riyadh and a PhD in Islamic Studies from the University of Wales, taught Islamic Education and Arabic in private schools in Riyadh, Saudi Arabia, and lectured in Islamic Studies at Shariff Kabunsuan Islamic University, in Cotobato City, Mindanao, Philippines. Thence, Philips founded and directed the Islamic Information Center, Dubai, and the Foreign Literature Department of Dar al Fatah Islamic Press, Sharjah, both in the United Arab Emirates. A lecturer of Arabic and Islamic Studies at the American University in Dubai and at Ajman University, United Arab Emirates, his tapes range from theological reflections to practical advice on the everyday rights and responsibilities of the good Muslim.[18] Available titles include "A Lecture on Faith," "Spirit Possession," "The Message of Jesus Christ," "Proper Treatment of Husbands and Wives," and "Seven Habits of Truly Successful People." Titles like "Islamic Education and Establishing Islam in the West," "The Obligation of Da'wah," "Da'wah in Desert Storm," and "Da'wah to Non-Muslims" testify to the importance of missionizing in Philips's teaching.[19]

Children's and Family Entertainment Products. The Sound Vision Foundation provides ways to help children learn to speak and read Arabic, recite the Qur'an, master prayer, and generally become more Islamically adept under the rubric "helping tomorrow's Muslims today!" Located in Bridgeview, Illinois, this "Islamic Information and Products" company also promotes "Abu Saleh, World's first Muslim arcade game hero! Pumped with iman, strength, and wisdom!"[20] Tomorrow's Muslims, of course, may well be potential converts as well as the children of Muslim families. Fine Media Group (FMG), "the Internet's largest Islamic store," introduces movie hits of the year for children and family entertainment. For those who want to engage in family activities, a wide variety of games and puzzles are available, all with Islamic themes. Families can construct three-dimensional models of the Ka'ba in Mecca; fully assembled, they are more than two feet wide. Families can also quiz each other about Islamic history or facts of the faith, or play Islamic card games. "Mission: Survival" is an educational adventure game designed to preserve Islamic identity, cope with societal challenges, and reinforce Islamic values.[21] And for little girls unable to resist the "Barbie" doll phenomenon, NoorArt says "Move Over Barbie! Razanne is here." Razanne, according to the ad, means a woman who is beautifully modest and shy in the best Islamic manner, "a doll that is 'just like Mom'—one who could serve as a role model for young Muslims." Razanne is 12 inches tall and wears a solid color *jilbaab* (robe) and a white *hijab*. The scarf is removable so that the child can practice the correct way of putting it on.[22]

Financial Products. Muslim Investor lists a number of educational resources, many taught by Islamic scholars, which have been specifically designed to advise Muslims about investing according to Islamic regulations.[23] The Harvard Islamic Finance Information Program, for example, aims "to act as a point of convergence for information about Islamic banking, finance, and economics for academics, researchers, and industry professionals, . . . to develop an increased awareness and understanding of Islamic banking and finance both within the Muslim world and in the West, . . . [to] assist[s] research projects that investigate new trends, strategies, and methods, with particular emphasis on studies about how existing financing methods available in conventional banking and finance can be applied to their Islamic counterparts, . . . [and] to bring together industry professionals, *Shariah* scholars, and western academics to engage in discourse, both theoretical and practical, about the past progress and future prospects of the field of Islamic finance" (Harvard University). The Islamic Finance Network offers access to a mass of information, including Islamic business and financial news; "Netversity," which offers several professional certification programmes in Islamic business and finance; Maktabe Online, an electronic library of materials in Islamic economics, business, law, banking and finance; links to over a dozen online resource-centers and their newsletters and bulletins; and "Cyber Fatwa," which makes available a wide array of pronouncements by contemporary Muslim jurists and scholars on any number of issues having to do with Islamic banking, finance, and business (Islamic Finance). On a quite practical basis, Islamic Finance also provides links to Islamic banks, business directories, insurance companies, and investment analysts, both overseas and in the United States. For example, American financial institutions listed include the Amana Mutual Funds Trust, American Finance House, LARIBA Bank, Failaka Investments Incorporated, Takaful USA, MSI Financial Services Corporation, and Manzil USA.[24] In short, Muslim Americans and prospective converts to Islam may have every confidence that their particular financial concerns will be addressed by competent Muslim advisors, whether these concerns are of a personal or a professional nature.

Miscellaneous Products. Muslims can buy virtually any kind of product today with some kind of Islamic identifier on it. Islamic greeting cards and calendars, posters of Mecca and Medina or with the entire Qur'an printed on one large page, incense sticks, prayer rugs, *tashbih* prayer beads, *hasmi* kohl for the eyes, Qur'an stands, Zamzam jigsaw puzzles, coffee mugs, charts of the family tree of Prophet Muhammad, watches pointing to Mecca from any location without using a compass, and clocks calling out the time for prayer ("Don't pray when your remember," advertises CASIO, "pray when it is time to pray!"). If one wants to affirm one's Islamic identity, and also do a bit of *da'wa* by means of a bumper sticker, Halalco Books in Falls Church, Virginia, can provide stickers not only with verses from the Qur'an on them, but such encouraging affirmations as "Islam is the Way," "No Compulsion in Islam," "Islam Makes the Difference," "The Qur'an has the Answer," "Don't Get Caught Dead Without Islam," "Allah is Just a Prayer Away," "Welcome to Islam," and "I ♥ Islam."[25]

For persons who may be considering whether or not to adopt the religion of Islam, such a dazzling array of products affirming not only the superiority of Islam, but the physical means and the structural support to help one make the transition, can be enormously persuasive. "Here—just 'try it on' for awhile," Muslim merchants, as well as *da'wa* experts, appear to be saying, "and see if you don't like it." Meanwhile, of course, manufacturers, publishing companies, and webmasters are thriving in an environment in which there seems to be an almost endless hunger for the paraphernalia that are said to help one be a better Muslim—or at least a more outwardly affirming one. In a kind of two-way and mutually encouraging and productive movement, Muslims are using products directly for self-support and indirectly for *da'wa*, while American companies are waking up to the potential market not only among persons who are already Muslim, but also among those who might be persuaded to Islam by purchasing their products.

New Modes of Communication for *Da'wa*[26]

The closing years of the twentieth century introduced enormous change into the ways in which Americans and others around the world are able to communicate with each other. These new opportunities have not gone unnoticed by American Muslims, who have been particularly creative in bringing them to bear on the process of providing information about and propagating the faith of Islam. Most immediately apparent has been the rapid growth and variety of print materials. Translations of the Qur'an into all Western languages, and of texts and classics of Islamic law, history, and theology, are readily available from catalogs, Islamic bookstores (of which there are currently hundreds in America), and a range of other locales. The number of Muslim journals, representing a range of ideological perspectives, has increased enormously in recent years, including glamorous new magazines designed specifically for women. Most Muslim professional associations issue periodic publications. Virtually any kind of information a potential convert to Islam, or a Muslim already well-versed in the faith, might want is easy to come by. Most bookstores and other information houses also sell a huge variety of audiotapes on Islam, including recitations of the Qur'an, sermons, and lectures by Muslim leaders.

To date, Muslims have not made as much use of radio and television broadcasts to promote the dissemination of Islam, as have many Christian evangelical groups. That circumstance is changing, with sites like Webradio and WebTV. The Sound Vision Foundation, a communications wing of the ICNA, responsible for much of the educational material on Islam available in America, broadcasts news and information programs and daily talk shows through RadioIslam. The Islamic Assembly of North America (IANA), which is one of the most explicitly *da'wa*-oriented associations in the United States, provides daily live programs on IANA Radionet, including instructional sessions, sermons, documentaries, and children's entertainment. Television has not yet been used as widely as radio, although programs are increasingly available from Muslim countries in the Middle East, perhaps most notably the Al Jazeera news network, based in Qatar.

Hardcopy print, radio, and television are now being augmented at an almost staggering rate by the material on Islam available online. While no daily Islamic newspaper is available for purchase and delivery in hardcopy, viewers can find constant coverage without subscription on the Internet site *iViews.com.* Websites are often constructed to provide basic information about Islam, with clear instructions to the viewer as to how to make direct contact with a mosque or Islamic center for more detail. Many are set up with the specific purpose of doing *da'wa*, and make that clear in their listings. The Islamic Information and Da'wah Center in Toronto, for example, advertises that it provides over 2.3 gigabytes of Islamic knowledge.[27] DawaNet, which has chapters all over the United States, states that its purpose is "to establish a network of Muslims who are committed to inviting others to Islam through personal dawa efforts, assisting majsids and Islamic centers in living and strengthening their dawa programs, and educating Muslims in appropriate and effective methods of *dawa*."[28]

Because the field of e-technology is so relatively new, and because it is being developed so rapidly by so many Muslim organizations and individuals, it is difficult to assess which sites are reliable and which are not. Studies have estimated that currently there are more than a thousand sites on the Internet on which to get information about Islam. Perhaps the most comprehensive cyberspace site is *IslamiCity*, where the viewer can not only find information and products, but can also go into virtual mosques and shop from traditional-looking marketplaces. Whether or not it is true, as some claim, that the rising number of conversions of Americans to Islam is due primarily to the influence of the Internet, there is no question that Muslims are taking serious and immediate advantage of the opportunity to do *da'wa*, in all of its modes, through this medium.

This orientation to the future clearly entails an orientation toward the young. As I have already indicated to some extent, materials designed especially for children and youth glut the electronic market. Children can learn Arabic from the most elementary level on, play Islamic games online, and view films about Islam, famous Muslims, and Western converts to the faith. Songs, puppets, and various kinds of animation are carefully prepared as means of providing Islamic instruction, with many of the presentations designed for children's interactive participation. Muslim parents who may not wish to have their children viewing American programs ostensibly designed for children, but featuring violence and stereotyped imaging, have many alternative choices, including books, magazines, videos, and online programming. Such presentations are designed not only to instruct about Islam, but also to instill pride in Muslim children at being part of the worldwide community of Islam.

Da'wa and Muslim–Christian Dialogue

Before leaving the subject of *da'wa*, it may be important to turn for a moment to the question of conversion and Muslim–Christian dialogue in America. For the last quarter-century, one of the most interesting conversations taking place among Muslims, among Christians, and between Christians and Muslims, relates to what is called evangelization in Christian terminology and *da'wa* in Muslim terminology. Muslims who have been involved in Muslim–Christian dialogue have struggled with the question of whether or not it is appropriate for *da'wa* to be part of the conversation, just as Christians have worried about the relationship of evangelization to dialogue. In both cases opinions vary widely. Some Muslims are deeply convinced that any effort at *da'wa* must be strictly abandoned if dialogue is to be successful, and draw a clear line between Muslims who are seriously interested in interfaith conversation and those who are only interested in conversion. Others are persuaded that if one is not able to speak honestly and with conviction about one's deepest beliefs, there can be no effective dialogue, and if this stance constitutes *da'wa*, then so be it. In a private conversation with me, early in 2002, Qasim Sharief, African American *imam* of the Mohammed Islamic Center of Imam of Hartford, put it this way: "If I experience something that I think is good, then it is un-Islamic for me not to try to share it. . . . This is what Islam is. It may be perceived as proselytism, but we must tell you what we believe. God will ask us at the judgment, 'Why didn't you say so-and-so when you had the opportunity to do it?' I believe that the same integrity exists for Christians."

One of the reasons why many Muslims feel strongly that *da'wa* must remain at the door, so speak, is the concern that they recognize echoes of an older issue. That is to say, in the past dialogue initiatives have too often been made by Christians with the apparent purpose of trying to convert their Muslim partners. Others worry about the opposite reality, namely that some of their coreligionists may be interested in interfaith conversation only for the purpose of the promotion of *da'wa*. Still others feel that the intellectual integrity of the conversation and the purpose of the promotion of better common understanding will be compromised if each side is busy with the task of trying to convince the other. And still others are less certain that attempts to prohibit *da'wa* are possible, or even advisable, although they may worry about terminology. Prolific author and speaker, Jamal Badawi, insists that the Qur'an makes it incumbent on Muslims to convey the message of Allah in its final form to all humanity, but insists that "We are not talking here about conversion. I do not like that word." While Badawi does not use the term *da'wa*, however, it is quite clear from his writings that bringing others to an acceptance of Islam is what he is talking about (Badawi). Fawaz Damra, Imam of the Islamic Center of Cleveland and a longtime advocate of dialogue and interfaith relations, insists that "*Da'wa* can't stay outside the door. It takes integrity, courage and patience to speak honestly."[29]

Seyyed Hossein Nasr of George Washington University, one of the most articulate longtime participants in American interfaith dialogue, is among those who believe that *da'wa* and evangelization do belong in the dialogue, but he does so with very specific qualifications.[30] The problem, he says, is the historical relationship between Western Christian missionary activity and Western colonialism. Because of this history, many Muslims are suspicious of the dialogue. His point is to relate the Christian missionary movement of evangelism to the reality of the disparity of power and wealth between the West and most Muslim lands. Implicit in Nasr's narratives about Western Christian missionary activity is the assumption that until these realities are recognized, acknowledged, and discussed by Christians in the West, the issue of whether or not *da'wa* and evangelisim are appropriate at the dialogue table cannot be addressed at any other than a very superficial level. At the same time, though, many Muslims and Christians who have been about the dialogue endeavor for many years feel strongly that the issue of *da'wa* and evangelism, complicated as it is, must be addressed. It has been an essential ingredient in past relations between Muslims and Christians, they argue, and shows every sign of continuing to be influential in the religious responses of many members of both faiths today.

Concluding Remarks

The *da'wa* efforts that have been carried out particularly in the last decades of the twentieth century and the early years of the twenty-first have resulted in the visibility of Islam in public places in new and sometimes surprising ways. Mosques and Islamic centers of striking beauty and proportions are appearing in many American cities. Plans for a five-acre mosque and community center in Dade County, Miami, like many others across the United States, include offices specifically designed for the development of *da'wa* to the community (Kahera 2002, 110). Several airports, beginning with Denver International, now feature a mosque as part of their worship facilities. Muslims are taking part in public interfaith worship services and are even being asked to lead the prayer in political gatherings. Islamic and other organizations are calling to public attention cases in which Muslim employees, students, and others are not being given free access to practice their faith and are working to redress such concerns. In many ways it is "easier" to be Muslim in the United States than ever before.

At the same time, however, the well-documented rise in anti-Islamic feeling on the part of the American public, the anti-Muslim rhetoric of some Christian evangelicals and their increased efforts at evangelization of Muslims both in the United States and abroad, and the loss of some Muslim civil rights as a result of the American government's "war on terrorism" have made life painful for Muslim since September 11, 2001. Still, *da'wa* efforts continue, perhaps invigorated by these new challenges. The process of *da'wa* is not simply a linear one of action leading to result, but rather a kind of cyclical phenomenon, in which results lead to increased, more creative and more self-conscious efforts to find ways to enhance and sustain the Muslim community in America.

Identification and support of the different kinds and interpretations of *da'wa* is the by-product, one might say, of the coming of age of Islam. It is no longer the religion simply of a few immigrants and a few African Americans or other converts to a faith that is alien to the American scene, but one that many observers describe as the fastest growing religion in the West. Muslims are claiming their rightful place in the American context and urging that the United States be described religiously as Christian, Jewish, *and* Muslim. Some Muslims now publicly predict that it is only a matter of time before Islam is the dominant faith of the country. Others argue that the real goal is for members of all religions to live in harmony and understanding with each other. The call to Islam, whether public or private, is now an institutionalized part of the religious fabric of the United States. The attempts to promote better understanding of Islam, the encouragement of more faithful practice of Islam on the part of its adherents, and the conviction that the number of new converts accepting Islam is continually on the rise all serve to motivate the different kinds of activities that constitute *da'wa* in the West.

Notes

1. Forcing conversion is often referred to as *jihad*, or striving in the way of God. For Muslims the external *jihad* is considered of less merit than the internal struggle to subdue the forces of temptation within one's own soul.
2. The term is most accurately transliterated from the Arabic as *da'wa* or *da'wah*, although it may appear in a variety of other forms such as *dawa*, *dawah*, or *dakwah*.
3. See Malcolm X (1965). For a fascinating study comparing the religious visions of Muslim Malcolm X and Christian Martin Luther King, especially with respect to the history and situation of African Americans in the United States, see Cone (1991).
4. A meeting at which the author was present.
5. See the Institute of Islamic Information and Education website (http://www.iiie.net).
6. See, e.g., the article entitled "Zabiha Meat in U.S. Prisons: A Success Story!" on the Sound Vision Foundation's website (http://www.soundvision.com/Info/halalhealthy/zabiha.asp).

7. The American deputy of Shaykh Nazim al-Kibrisi, the leader of the Naqshbandi-Haqqani Order, is the controversial Shaykh Hisham Kabbani, criticized by many Muslims for having said that a major proportion of mosques in America are hotbeds of Islamic extremism.
8. Just as Jewish rabbinic *halakhah*, or religious law, includes a number of dietary provisions, so also does the Muslim religious law of *sharia*. Observant Jews thus keep *kosher*, from the Hebrew word meaning "right" or "proper," while Muslims observe the rules of *halal*, from the Arabic word meaning "allowed" or "lawful." Insofar as Muslims consider their traditions the right and natural heirs of divine revelations first expressed in Jewish scriptures, the dietary laws of the two traditions are quite similar.
9. See the Inner-City Muslim Action Network website (http://www.imancentral.org).
10. See the Sisters United in Human Service website (http://www.sistersunited.org).
11. See Islamic Boutique's website (http://www.islamicboutique.com)
12. The seven conditions are: Clothing must cover the entire body, [for] only the hands and face may remain visible (according to some *fiqh* schools); the material must not be so thin that one can see through it; the clothing must hang loose so that the shape/form of the body is not apparent; the female clothing must not resemble the man's clothing; the design of the clothing must not resemble the clothing of the nonbelieving women; the design must not consist of bold designs that attract attention; and, clothing should not be worn for the sole purpose of gaining reputation or increasing one's status in society (http:// www.islamfortoday.com/7conditions.htm). The targeting of westerners alluded to here is part of Islam for Today's website introduction.
13. See Shukr's website (http://www.shukronline.com/mens-suits.html).
14. See Islamic Market's website (http://www.islamicmarket.com), and Al Hannah Islamic Clothing's website link (http://www.alhannah.com/cgi-bin/guide.cgi?a;plussize).
15. Condemning idolatry, the Qur'an ascribes the Arabic term *musawwir*, or "maker of forms," only to God, while the Hadiths threaten painters with punishment on the Day of Judgement for not being able to breathe life into their creations, that is, in effect, for aspiring hubristically to divine creativity and having to fake it. Subsequent *sharia* law comes to associate the essence of life with the face and eyes in particular, and explicitly forbids their portrayal.
16. See, e.g., Bos (1993).
17. See the Islamic Food and Nutrition Council of America website (http://www.ifanca.org).
18. For these details about Philips, see "About Him: A Short Biography of Dr. Abu Ameenah Bilal Philips," on Islamic Online University's website (http://www.bilalphilips.com/abouthim/bio_summ.htm).
19. See, for example, the lists of Philips's tapes linked to the websites of Halalco Supermarket and Islam.com (http://www.halalco.com/audio_bp.html and http://www.islaam.com/audio/lectures/bp).
20. See the Sound Vision Foundation's website (http://www.soundvision.com).
21. See the Fine Media Group's website (http://www.finemediagroup.com).
22. See NoorArt's website (http://www.noorart.com).
23. See Muslim Investor's website (http://muslim-investor.com/mi/education.phtml).
24. See Islamic Finance's website link (http://islamic-finance.net/bank.html).
25. See the website of Halalco Books (http://www.halalco.com/ Islamic).
26. Much of the information in this section is credited to Lotfi (2002).
27. See "The Reign of Islaamic *Da'wah*," on the website of the Islamic Information and Da'wah Center (http://www.troid.org).
28. See DawaNet's website (http://www.dawanet.com).
29. Conversation with the author, March 30, 2001.
30. See, e.g., Nasr (1987).

CHAPTER NINE

THE SPREAD OF BUDDHISM IN THE WEST: MISSIONARY WORK AND THE PATTERN OF RELIGIOUS DIFFUSION

James William Coleman

Most of us are familiar with the missionaries who played such a critical role in the spread of various forms of Christianity outside the Western world. In the last 50 years, Buddhism has shown remarkable growth in the Western world, and it seems natural to wonder if such missionary work played a similar role in its expansion and to try to account for whatever differences there may have been. Such an analogy, however, is much more difficult to maintain than it appears. Scholars in the social sciences and humanities often pride themselves on their fairness, objectivity, and lack of cultural bias. But the same lexicon we use to proclaim those virtues is itself replete with eurocentric bias. The concept of "missionary work," for example, is deeply rooted in the European Christian experience. Almost everyone in the West is acquainted with the image of the bible-toting evangelist, suffering through the deprivations of life in the "Third World" in order to spread the word of God. Although we are a little less clear on what an Islamic missionary might be, it is not so hard to conjure up the image of a *mullah* struggling to do *da'wa* to spread the knowledge of the holy Qur'an to nonbelievers. But what exactly would a Buddhist missionary be like? If we are to apply a concept like missionary work to a non-Western tradition, we must pare off its Western, eurocentric connotations and strip it down to its bare essentials.

Our working definition cannot, of course, contain any reference to God or gods, since some branches of the Buddhist tradition make little use of such concepts. Likewise, faith and belief must be stricken, since many Buddhists, especially the Zen Buddhists who have been so influential in the West, see rigidly held beliefs of any sort to be a barrier to spiritual development. The most influential Korean Zen teacher in the West, Seung Sahn, for example, has frequently equated the enlightened state with the "don't know mind," free from preconceived ideas and beliefs or conditioned habitual responses.[1] Further, no reference can be made to "religious conversion," since such words imply the Western idea that one can belong only to a single religion, and that changing one's religious views involves turning from one religion to another. Many Asian societies, by contrast, lack this demand for religious exclusivity. Few Japanese, for example, would find a contradiction in holding themselves to be both Buddhist and Shintoist. Even here in the West, we find that many of those active in Buddhist groups still consider themselves to be Christians or Jews as well. What then are we left with after we perform this conceptual surgery? As a working definition, we can say that missionary work is an organized effort to persuade others to adopt a particular set of religious ideas or practices. Although we could certainly use other definitions, note that this one implies at least some degree of institutional support. Thus, one friend trying to persuade another friend about the value of her religious practice would not be included under the rubric of missionary work, unless her activities had formal support and encouragement from some religious group.

Religious Diffusion and Missionary Activity

With this definition in hand, we can turn to an examination of some of the sociological forces that shape the course of religious diffusion and the role played by missionary work in this process. An examination of the history of religion in the last 2,000 years shows us that there are three general paths for the diffusion of religion from one area or one group to another. The first is migration. When people move from one place to another, they usually bring their religion with them, and the growing tides of migration that are associated with the globalization of the world economy are making this phenomenon an ever more important factor in religious change. The rapid growth of Islam in western Europe in recent years is one typical example.

Second, there is contact and association. Obviously, people have to be exposed to the beliefs and practices of a religion before they can adopt them. Traditionally, this contact came directly from personal association with the practitioners of a particular religion. In this age of nearly universal literacy (at least in the wealthy nations) and explosive growth in the means of electronic communication, secondary exposure to religious ideas through the media of mass communication is becoming increasingly important. My own survey of the members of meditation-oriented Buddhist groups in the West, for example, found that most respondents developed an interest in Buddhism first by reading about it (Coleman 2001, 185–216).

Finally, there are various forms of coercion and material inducements for religious change. Such forces become particularly important when a religious group takes over the state apparatus of a society and uses it to advance their religious objectives. The most extreme case is, of course, "conversion by the sword," as occurred, for example, when invading Islamic armies sacked the Buddhist monasteries of India and slaughtered the monks. Coercion can also be simply by command, as when Roman Emperor Constantine ordered his troops to convert to Christianity. Coercion takes various economic forms as well. The great Islamic empires of the Middle East often levied a special tax on nonbelievers, thus offering obvious economic benefits for conversion to the official faith. Economic and social pressure can also be brought through rewards rather than coercion. Well-funded Christian missionaries from the West often offer their converts financial benefits and charity not available to nonbelievers, just as merchants and traders in colonial nations often found it to their economic advantage to accept the religious beliefs of their foreign rulers.

Missionary work does not play much of a role in the religious changes brought on by migration. But the mere presence of missionaries in a foreign culture can, like migration, significantly increase the channels for contact and association with people from their religious orientation, and the dissemination of various kinds of books and religious materials may increase their impact. Missionaries also utilize many forms of coercion and material inducements to pressure nonbelievers to accept their faith. This sort of suasion was often true, for example, of the Christian missionaries in areas subject to the colonial economic and political domination of the home nations of their sending missionary societies. Natives who accepted Christianity had access to schooling and those who stuck with their own indigenous religious traditions were denied valuable social contacts.

This observation is not to imply, however, that the three variables of migration, contact, and coercion are themselves sufficient to explain religious diffusion. The ideas, beliefs, and practices of a particular religious tradition, and the affinity they hold with the experiences and beliefs of existing status groups is, of course, another critical factor. Indeed, many religions are primarily tied up with the experiences and traditions of a particular ethnic group and have shown little tendency to spread to other ethnicities. Hinduism and Judaism are often cited as examples of such ethnic religions, but there are many, many others as well. In contrast to these ethnic religions are the so-called universal religions, which have to some degree or other shed the traditions of their country of origin and spread across the ethnic boundaries that divide our world. The three largest universal religions are Christianity, Islam, and Buddhism—a fact that makes an examination of the more recent spread of Buddhism especially interesting, since its roots are outside the Middle East, its ritual and doctrinal traditions do not originate in Abrahamic monotheism, and historically, it has had little to do with the West (Wach 1944, 309–310).

Patterns of Religious Diffusion

It is possible that the Buddhist foothold in the West is only a temporary anomaly of little long-term significance, but if, as seems more likely, Buddhism continues its present expansionary trajectory and establishes itself as a significant player on the Western religious scene, it will mark an historic watershed. For over a thousand years, the tides of religious diffusion have been almost exclusively from the West eastwards and southwards. From the seventh to sixteenth centuries, conquering Islamic armies brought monotheism to Persia, India, and the Eurasian steppes, and it spread from there to most parts of what is now Malaysia and Indonesia. And just as the Islamic explosion seemed to have spent its initial force, European colonialism brought Christianity to large parts of what was emerging as the periphery of the first truly global world system. In the sixteenth century, Jesuit missionaries enshrined Roman Catholicism as the one true faith in the "new world" as Spanish conquistadors crushed the traditional civilizations of South America, and eighteenth- and nineteenth-century Protestant evangelists likewise accompanied European colonial and imperial adventurers around the world into Africa, India, and China. Buddhism, on the other hand, was generally on the retreat during these centuries, most notably in its Indian homeland, where it was challenged by a resurgent Hinduism and militant Islamic invaders, and later by a very different Western ideology in communist East Asia.

Not only does the spread of Buddhism in the West mark a countercurrent in the tides of global influence, it is occurring under very different conditions from the historic growth of Christianity and Islam in their expansionist phases. Most obviously, Buddhism is not accompanying a dominating political power into its subordinate areas, as occurred in the last 1,000 years with various instances of Christian and Muslim expansion, but the other way around. Thailand, Burma, Tibet, Korea, and the other nations from which Buddhism first reached into the West, were all clearly in a peripheral position in the world system under the economic and political domination of the core Western powers. The one possible exception is Japan, which certainly counts now as a major economic power. But Japan was still recovering from the devastation of World War II and had not yet assumed the mantel of full core status at the time that it was to have its strongest impact on the American religious scene, during the 1950s and 1960s. This political reality meant that newly established Buddhist groups in the West could seldom draw on the same kind of financial resources and support that were often available to Christian missions in the "Third World." Similarly, Buddhism did not have the kind of cultural appeal that comes from being the representative of a more technologically advanced culture in a less developed or even preliterate area.

What, then, was the role of missionary work in the spread of Buddhism beyond its historic environments? As we shall see, the answer to that question is a complex one, requiring some understanding of the significant differences between the various kinds of Buddhist groups that have become popular in the West. In a recent study of this topic, *The Diffusion of Religion: A Sociological Perspective*, the sociologist and Western Christian missionary, Robert L. Montegomery (1996, 22), argued that missionary activity is a "necessary precondition" for religious diffusion, but this argument seems not to hold for many Buddhist traditions in the West. Some scholars have identified such a missionary strain within modern Buddhism. Martin Baumann, for example, describes the Ceylonese modernizer, Anagarika Dharmapal (1864–1933) as "the first global Buddhist missionary or propagandist," and the Maha Bhodi Society he founded as "the first inter-or transnational Buddhist organization" (Baumann 2002, 89). But, to look ahead, with one major exception, it seems fair to say that the relatively minor importance of missionary work in the spread of Buddhism to the West is yet another significant difference from patterns of Christian and Muslim diffusion.

The Varieties of Western Buddhism

Most westerners are just beginning to become accustomed to seeing beyond the image of Buddhism as some impossibly exotic foreign import. But there is still very little understanding among the general public of the major differences between the many Buddhist groups active in the West. Scholars, of course, have come up with a variety of different ways of making sense of the great diversity of the Western Buddhist experience. The most common distinction is between the "ethnic Buddhism" practiced by immigrants from Buddhist countries and the "convert Buddhism" practiced by native westerners.[2] While this typology accurately reflects the most important sociological divide among Western Buddhists, however, the term "convert Buddhism" is an unfortunate one. As time passes, an ever increasing number of these so-called converts will undoubtedly be the daughters and sons of Western Buddhists, and thus not converts at all. Moreover, many people who participate in ethnic Buddhist groups were not religiously active in their native lands, and thus are in some sense converts themselves. Moreover, there are some important differences among the varieties of

Buddhism practiced by Western "converts." Indeed, some westerners have actually adopted various forms of "ethnic Buddhism."

Jan Nattier has suggested a tripartite distinction between ethnic Buddhism, defined pretty much as I have indicated, and two other types of Buddhist groups that are composed primarily of native-born westerners. The first of these other types is "evangelical Buddhism," which, Nattier argues, has been *exported* to the West by Buddhist groups in Asia. The second type Nattier calls "élite Buddhism," by which she means those kinds of Buddhism that were *imported* by élite groups of westerners with enough time and money to allow them to devote themselves to meditation practice (Natteir 1998). These distinctions are useful in some ways, less so in others. To begin with, evangelical Buddhism is a rather unusual category, since it seems to contain only one group—Soka Gakkai. To label Soka Gakkai "evangelical" does point out the very significant differences between them and the other Buddhist groups whose membership is composed primarily of westerners. But to define the unique characteristics of Soka Gakkai solely in terms of its evangelism is highly misleading, especially since the group has significantly toned down its evangelical activities in recent years.[3] Likewise, the term "élite Buddhism" is misleading, though in a different way, for while the groups Nattier so designates have indeed attracted a significant number of affluent "élite" members, surveys of their memberships also shows a lot of lower income dropouts from the middle-class world of competitive materialism (Coleman 2001, 192–193). Moreover, surveys have also shown that Soka Gakkai attracts a disproportionate number of middle- and upper-middle-class adherents (Hammond and Machacek 1999, 36–54).

Since the category "evangelical Buddhism" apparently contains only one case, it would seem to make more sense to drop it altogether and simply refer to Soka Gakkai by its own name. On the other hand, there are numerous different groups under Nattier's rubric of "élite Buddhism." The most central characteristic they share may well be their strong emphasis on the importance of meditation practice, something absent in Soka Gakkai. So for the purposes of this chapter, at least, these groups will be referred to as meditation-orientated Buddhists, or "New Buddhists." This term has the advantage of acknowledging the fact that these meditation-oriented Western groups represent a distinctive new type of Buddhism, whereas groups in the other two categories adhere more closely to Asian traditions.[4]

These new Buddhist groups contain a diverse collection of differing styles, practices, and allegiances, with little in the way of overall organizational unity. Nonetheless, they share a number of important characteristics. In one way or another, all these groups represent an attempt to take the complex and sophisticated technology of spiritual practice, which in Asia is reserved primarily for the monastic élite, and to make it available to anyone who is willing to pursue it. But if we are to call this "spiritual technology" meditation, it is necessary to conceptualize it in a far broader way than is typical in the West. In addition to classic sitting meditation, which itself may involve a bewildering variety of techniques and approaches, there is walking meditation, working meditation, daily mindfulness, and rituals that, when practiced with full attention, become their own kind of meditation practice. A second common characteristic emphasized by all these groups is the belief in what is often known as *sila*, or ethical behavior. The ethical injunctions contained in the Buddhist Five Precepts—to refrain from killing, lying, stealing, improper sexual activity, and the use of intoxicants—are not conceived as absolute God-given rules of behavior, as are, for example, the Ten Commandments of Judaism and Christianity, but rather, as flexible guidelines for living a wholesome life. Nonetheless, there is also a firm conviction that kind and generous actions inevitably produce positive results, while actions based on greed, hate, and delusion produce pain and suffering. Finally, the third characteristic shared by these groups is the critical importance given to the development of wisdom. But as with so many Buddhist terms, wisdom often does not mean the same thing it does to most westerners. Most westerners likely conceive of wisdom as some kind of knowledge or intellectual understanding of the way things are. In Buddhism, wisdom might better be defined as the realization of emptiness—the direct experience of the world as an interconnected whole, without substantial independent entities, including our human selves.

Despite all these common characteristics, the new Buddhism evolving in the West can be divided into four distinct streams.[5] The first Buddhist tradition to win a significant number of Western converts came from Japan, and Zen Buddhism still remains the most popular among the new Buddhists. Like their Japanese and Chinese forebears, Western students of Zen tend to place great emphasis on discipline and dedicated practice. There is quite a bit of variation, but most Western Zen centers still carry on a good deal of ritual and maintain a fairly strictly enforced set of rules and standards, though this feature is certainly far less true among the Americans than their Japanese counterparts.[6] The second largest group of meditation-oriented Western Buddhists follows the Tibetan tradition.[7] Often called Vajrayana Buddhists, members of this group are less formal and rather more extroverted in style. At the same time, Vajrayana Buddhism often appears to be the most exotic to Western eyes. It has the most elaborate rituals, greatest sense of mystery, and by far the largest arsenal of meditative practices, which include the visualization of a range of terrifying, peaceful, and erotic deities. The third stream of this new Buddhism is often known as Vipassana. Vipassana has its roots in the ancient Theravadin tradition, but in the West its practitioners tend to be more secular than Zen and Vajrayana Buddhists, at least in the sense that they have fewer rituals, less elaborate symbolism, and less social distance between students and teachers.[8] Vipassana, especially as practiced on the west coast of the United States, also seems to draw more heavily from Western psychology.[9] Finally, there are a growing number of what might be called nondenominational groups, which are not affiliated with any of these three traditions, or conversely, are affiliated with more than one.[10]

Although ethnic Buddhism in the West also contains representatives from a wide variety of different traditions—Chinese, Japanese, Thai, Cambodian, and Vietnamese, among others—it seems fair to say that none of the major groups would disagree with the three fundamental values listed above. The difference is rather one of emphasis, in particular, questions having to do with the importance of a meditation practice for lay members. Ethnic Buddhists from Theravadin countries like Sri Lanka or Thailand might occasionally meditate, but meditation and other strict spiritual practices are seen as primarily a matter for monastics. Similarly, ethnic Buddhists from east Asia often focus on chanting or other ritual practices they feel will bring about a better rebirth, rather than on meditation. Underlying these distinctions is a very different overall orientation. The main focus of the new Buddhist groups is on the spiritual realization of their members, whereas the ethnic Buddhist groups are more concerned with meeting the social and religious need of the communities they serve.

Soka Gakkai is similar to the meditation-oriented Buddhists, in that their members are now both primarily composed of westerners. But Soka Gakkai practice centers on chanting, rather than meditation. Of course, chanting can be a meditative practice, and indeed, many meditation-oriented groups also do a considerable amount of chanting as well. Soka Gakkai conceives of chanting as more than just a path of meditative concentration, however; it is a profoundly powerful activity that will not only produce personal happiness, but also bring material benefits. And this brings us to a more subtle, but nonetheless important, difference between these two types of Western Buddhism. Whereas the new Buddhist groups certainly take no formal position on the matter, it is clear that most of them are rather skeptical about the value of Western materialism. They see an excessive concern with possessions to be a significant barrier to spiritual growth. Soka Gakkai, on the other hand, has very much come to terms with consumer culture, and even sees its chanting practice as a road to material success. As Kiyoaki Murata has pointed out, Josei Toda, the second leader of the movement, once described the *daigohonzon*, or "supreme object of worship," as a kind of "happiness machine" (Murata 1969, 107). "Your faith has only one purpose: to improve your business and family life," wrote Toda, so "Let's make money and build health and enjoy life to our hearts' content before we die!" (quoted in Murata 1969, 108).

Missionary Activity and the Spread of Buddhism in the West

With this background laid down, it is now possible to examine the role missionary work has played in the spread of Buddhism in the West. It is no surprise to find that missionary activity, at least when defined as we have above, played only a minor role in the spread of ethnic Buddhism in the West. The driving sociological dynamic was, of course, migration. However religious these immigrants were in their native lands, they came from cultures—or, among the second generation, were raised in families—steeped in the Buddhist tradition, and their participation in Buddhist groups seldom needed to involve any kind of real psychological reorientation. Rather, they were drawn into Buddhist groups seeking community support, spiritual guidance, and a familiar taste of home. The spiritual leadership of these groups has often been provided by priests or other functionaries sent out by Buddhist organizations in Asia. But their role has seldom been that of missionaries—that is, proselytizers consciously seeking to make converts—but rather, more sacerdotal, social, and spiritual. Interestingly enough, the Soto Zen sect of Japan has established a number of what it calls "Soto Zen Missions" in American cities with a significant population of Japanese Americans.[11] But despite the terminology they use, these groups do not focus their energies on proselytizing activities, but on meeting the social and spiritual needs of the Japanese American community they serve. Nonetheless, some of these ethnic Buddhist groups have certainly attempted to reach out to attract members from the wider community; they might offer meditation classes or lectures in English rather than an Asian language, for example. But such activities, if they occur at all, remain very much a secondary priority to meeting the needs of the ethnic community, and few of these groups have attracted large numbers of Western members.

The Buddhist groups whose membership consists primarily of native-born westerners present us with some interesting sociological contrasts. One might have expected missionary work to have played a very important role in the spread of these groups, but the actual facts of the matter present us with a much more mixed picture. While missionary evangelism did indeed play a vital role in the expansion of Soka Gakkai in the West, it has been of very little importance in the growth of meditation-oriented Buddhism. Nattier's work is useful for helping us to understand this difference. In her analysis of the spread of Buddhism in the West, she distinguishes three kinds of Buddhism: *baggage* Buddhism, which immigrants brought with them, as part of their cultural tradition (i.e., "ethnic Buddhism"); *export* Buddhism, which Asian missionaries introduced, as part of an intentional campaign to gain new members in the West (e.g., Soka Gakkai); and *import* Buddhism, which includes most of the meditation-oriented groups.

According to Nattier, " 'Import' in this case refers to what might be described as 'demand-driven' transmission: here Buddhism is actively sought out by the recipient" (Nattier 1998, 189). Whereas few westerners had even heard of Soka Gakkai before the start of its missionary activity, knowledge about Buddhism in general had been slowly spreading throughout Western nations for generations before it won any significant number of adherents. While Buddhism may have seemed impossibly exotic to many westerners, the idea that meditation might provide a way out of the confusion and uncertainty of modern life, and lead to a deep spiritual enlightenment, proved a very attractive one. People read about the shattering enlightenment experiences of the Zen monks and the mysterious transformative power of exotic Tibetan practices, and they began experimenting with meditation and seeking out Buddhist teachers to guide them on the path. Some westerners made the trek to the great Asian centers of monastic practice, while others gathered around teachers who came West to meet the needs of the growing number of ethnic Buddhists, or as part of the great Tibetan diaspora.

The first Buddhist tradition to make the leap to a Western audience was Japanese Zen. A Japanese Rinzai master, Soyen Shaku, spoke at the World Parliament of Religions in Chicago in 1893, and the writings of his student, Daisetz Teitaro Suzuki, introduced paradoxical Zen thought to many fascinated Western intellectuals. By the 1950s, most educated westerners had at least heard of Zen Buddhism, even though it continued to be seen as something strange and exotic. During that era, the young Bohemians of the "beat generation" took up Zen as a kind of intellectual talisman, as a challenge to existing Western views of things. The beginnings of this new interest in Buddhism are sometimes traced to the series of lectures Suzuki gave at Columbia University in the early 1950s, but its real origins have far deeper roots. The most influential figures in what came to be known as "Beat Zen"—Alan Ginsberg, Jack Kerouac, and Gary Snyder, among others—first encountered Buddhism in the library, not the lecture hall, although Suzuki's books were inevitably on their menu of readings.[12] There was something in the classical Zen texts that struck a deep chord among these young rebels. Even more than the jazz musicians the Beats idolized, the masters of Zen seemed to make their everyday lives a kind of improvised performance, acting out their realizations in the most surprising and unpredictable ways. The heroes in the Zen stories the Beats read not only seemed to stand completely outside the restraints of traditional morality; Zen itself provided an absolute perspective from which the standards of consumer society could only be judged as meaningless, arbitrary, and unreal. Zen soon became a powerful philosophical ally in the Beats' attack on the conformism of conventional society. Moreover, as Epicureans and far more than casual dabblers in drugs and alcohol, the Beats were drawn to the ecstatic descriptions of Zen *satori*, that sudden flash of profound awareness that seemed to them a kind of ultimate high.[13]

The next two decades saw something of a "Zen boom" when, for the first time, significant numbers of westerners began actual Buddhist practice. The Beats' original encounter with Zen was limited by the fact that there were virtually no Zen teachers active among westerners. But some dedicated people, like Beat poet Snyder, made the journey to Japan to study Zen at its source. In the late 1970s, back in the United States, Snyder joined up with Joanna Macy and Robert Aiken Roshi to found the Buddhist Peace Fellowship, an example of what Christopher S. Queen has recently called "engaged Buddhism," which "may be said to parallel the activism, if not the militancy, of other world religions, notably Judaism, Christianity, Islam and Hinduism" (Queen 2002, 341, 324). Other committed converts discovered teachers who had come to the United States to work in the Soto Temples that served California's Japanese American community, like Shunryu Suzuki and Hakuyu Taizan Maezumi, founders respectively of Zen centers in San Francisco and Los Angeles. By the time this first wave of enthusiasm died down, residential Zen centers had sprung up in most of the major urban areas of North America, and Zen had firmly established itself as a religious presence in the West.

The headwaters of the second stream of the new Buddhism are in the remote Himalayan mountains of Tibet. For centuries, Tibet was one of the most isolated countries on earth. But the Chinese conquest of the 1950s, and the brutal repression that followed, sparked a Tibetan diaspora that brought their culture, and especially their religion, onto the world stage.[14] A Gelugpa monk, Geshe Wangal, founded the first Tibetan monastery in the United States in New Jersey, in 1955. Other Tibetan teachers reached the West during the 1960s, but they did not establish much of an institutional presence for another decade. Fueled by a seemingly inexhaustible supply of charismatic Tibetans, epitomized in Tenzin Gyatso, the fourteenth Dalai Lama, with his combination of compassionate presence and political importance, Tibetan Vajrayana has become increasingly important on the Western Buddhist scene since the 1970s.[15] It is, of course, possible to characterize some of those Tibetan teachers as missionaries, since they did come to the West to help spread Buddhism. The Kagyu monk, Chogyam Trungpa Rinpoche, for example, built bridges between Tibetan Buddhist traditions and the American counterculture of the 1970s and 1980s, notably the Naropa Institute in Boulder, Colorado. Following Trungpa's death in 1987, his followers accompanied his son, Sakyong Mipham Rinpoche, to Halifax, Nova Scotia, to establish the headquarters of Shambala International, where Trungpa's teachings on "mindfulness–awareness meditation" continue as "a sectarian path of spiritual training that emphasizes the cultivation of fearless, gentle, and intelligent action in the world" (Shambhala). But to designate such activities as missionary in the sense of active proselytizing does not lead to a very accurate understanding of what Tibetan teachers like Trungpa actually did. Rather than trying to recruit followers or convert members of other traditions, these teachers all kept a very low profile. They made their teachings available to those who were interested, but made very little effort even to publicize themselves, much less to try to persuade skeptical westerners that they should switch to some new faith.[16]

The newest stream of meditation-oriented Buddhism in the West actually has the most ancient roots. Known in the West as Vipassana, this style of practice derives from the Theravadin tradition predominant in the southern parts of Asia, and most scholars would agree that it adheres more strictly to the Buddha's original teachings than any of the world's other Buddhist sects.[17] While there were a significant number of Asian Zen and Vajrayana teachers active in the West, that is not true of Vipassana. It was spread almost entirely by westerners who went to Thailand or Burma to seek out Buddhist teachings. As a result, the Vipassana style is the most secular and most Western, and it has the lightest cultural baggage from the east. As I have indicated, many Vipassana teachers, especially those on the west coast of the United States, are also heavily influenced by Western psychological thought and the therapeutic tradition it fostered.

The three central figures in American Vipassana—Sharon Salzberg, Joseph Goldstein, and Jack Kornfield—all went to Asia to study Buddhism. Moreover, they have remarkably similar backgrounds, strikingly so in the case of Goldstein and Kornfield. Although the two did not meet until later in life, both came from upper-middle-class, Jewish homes on the east coast, both attended Ivy League colleges in hopes of starting a professional career, and both came into first-hand contact with Buddhism while working as volunteers in the Peace Corps in Asia. Founding members of the Insight Meditation Society (IMS), Goldstein and Kornfield have published numerous books on Vipassana, notably the joint effort, *Seeking the Heart of Wisdom: The Path of Insight Meditation* (1987). Based in Barre, Massachusetts, the IMS is closely allied with the Spirit Rock Meditation Center, located in Marin County, California. By 2000, these meditation centers had spawned a nationwide network of well over 200 Vipassana retreats and affiliated groups, as well as a national periodical, *Inquiring Mind*, launched in 1984 (Fronsdal 2002, 286–288).[18] As the movement has grown, its understanding of the purpose of meditation has deepened. "In the earlier writings," according to Gil Fronsdale, "the rationale for ethical behaviour was mostly based on the personal benefits of pursuing the goal of liberation, while the later books place an emphasis on the benefits ethical behaviour has for others" (Fronsdal 2002, 301). The notion of interconnectedness lies at the heart of this shift. In Salzberg's words, "*Sila* works on all levels of our relationships: our relationships to ourselves, to other people, and to the environment around us" (Salzberg 1995, 172).

The history of the spread of Soka Gakkai in the West follows a very different pattern. The movement traces its roots back to the thirteenth-century Japanese prophet, Nichiren Daishonin (1222–1282). Nichiren was a unique figure in Buddhist history. Of all the world's major universal religions, Buddhism has been by far the most tolerant of divergent religious practices and viewpoints. But Nichiren declared his Buddhism to be the one true Buddhism, agitated for the state to make his version of Buddhism the official religion and to repress others, and in the fashion of Western millenarian movements, even warned of a coming disaster for Japan if it failed to follow his path.[19] Nichiren never achieved his political goals, but in 1930, Tsunesaburo Makiguchi founded the Soka Kyoiku Gakkai, or Value Creation Educational Society, first to reform Japanese education, then in the 1940s, to advance Nichiren's Buddhist ideas.[20] Outlawed for criticizing Japan's aggression in World War II, Soka Gakkai was revived by Josei Toda in 1945. It gained wide popularity in Japan as part of the "rush hour of the Gods" that occurred as the Japanese people tried to cope with the cultural disruption and physical deprivation that gripped the country following its disastrous defeat in the war (McFarland 1967). In 1964, Soka Gakkai started the political party, Komeito, or League for Clean Government, which has become a major force in Japanese politics and is currently part of Japan's ruling coalition.

Often more exclusive than other Buddhists, Nichiren's followers have nonetheless been more inclined to evangelism than those in other Buddhist groups. Soka Gakkai first entered the United States in the early 1950s.[21] The vast majority of its members in those early days were Japanese women who had married American servicemen and followed their husbands back to the United States. There was also a smattering of Japanese businessmen and students who were living in the United States. As might be expected, the membership was small and the organization had a very low profile. Unlike the meditation-oriented Buddhist groups, which are a very diverse collection of independent organizations with little in the way of centralized power, Soka Gakkai has a much more integrated organizational structure, similar to something like the Roman Catholic Church. Under its dynamic third leader, Daisaku Ikeda, Soka Gakkai launched a vigorous missionary campaign. The first targets were Japanese Americans. Soka Gakkai missionaries aggressively sought out new members, for example, by looking for Japanese names in the telephone book and calling them up to make contact. By 1963, there was a sufficient number of English-speaking members to hold discussion meetings in English, and the recruitment of non-Japanese members began in earnest. Using the same aggressive style of evangelism that had made them highly successful and highly controversial in Japan,

Soka Gakkai members approached people on the telephone, in the streets, on park benches, and in other public places, often debating religion and always trying to persuade their targets to come to a discussion meeting. This practice was known by its Japanese name, *shakubuku*, which translates roughly as "break and subdue." Soka Gakkai grew rapidly over the following years, and the new influx of Western members caused a major shift in its demographic base. In 1960, 96 percent of its members were of Japanese origin, making it a fairly typical example of "ethnic Buddhism." But by 1970, that number had dropped to only 30 percent, and Soka Gakkai was clearly in a category by itself (Machacek 2000, 287).

This aggressive style of recruitment, and the sudden change some family members noticed in the behavior of new Soka Gakkai members, began to give Soka Gakkai a reputation as some kind of cult. In the 1970s, media focus on dramatic abuses occurring in some new religious groups helped to create a general "anti-cult" sensibility in the West, and Soka Gakkai deftly changed tactics. Officially abandoning *shakubuku* in the mid-1970s, the organization took a much lower public profile. In place of *shakubuku*, they adopted a softer approach, known as *shoju*, or "gradual leading," which focuses on making recruits among the friends and family of existing members by showing the personal benefits Soka Gakkai brings to the lives of its members. Not surprisingly, the end of the era of *shakubuku* also saw the end of the rapid growth of the organization. Hammond and Machacek argue, however, that members brought in by the more gentle techniques have tended to show more long-term commitment to the organization (Hammond and Machacek 1999, 103–106). To consolidate this membership, and to further promote the movement's ideas on a worldwide basis, Ikeda founded Soka Gakkai International (SGI) in 1975. With "more than 12 million members in Soka Gakkai constituent organizations in more than 180 countries and territories around the world," SGI styles its interpretation of Buddhism as a means by which its adherents may "develop the ability to live with confidence, to create value in any circumstances and to contribute to the well-being of friends, family and community" (SGI-USA). The promotion of "peace, culture and education is central to SGI's activities," and the organization boasts its own educational network, including the Soka University campus in Aliso Viejo, California, numerous evangelizing and scholarly publishing ventures, and a range of cultural institutions, perhaps most notably the Tokyo Fuji Art Museum (SGI-USA).[22]

Understanding the Role of Missionary Work in the Western Diffusion of Buddhism

The fact that the ethnic Buddhist groups have not placed much emphasis on evangelism and missionary work is not difficult to understand. Indeed, it would have been more surprising if they had done so. When a religious orientation is identified with a particular ethnic group or ethnic community by its members, it naturally tends to have far less appeal to those who do not share that identity. Moreover, the members themselves often have little desire to bring outsiders with different ways and customs into what they consider to be a small enclave, perhaps far from home in a foreign land. At least initially, the very idea of converting outsiders to their religion may make no more sense than trying to turn westerners into Thais or Chinese.

The fact that meditation-oriented Buddhism has spread so widely in the West without any appreciable amount of missionary effort is more surprising, and requires some further explanation. We have already touched on the appeal Buddhist techniques of meditation have had for many westerners in an anomic age, rife with anxiety and personal insecurity. But why were the organized Buddhist groups so hesitant to follow up on this lead with an organized missionary campaign, as Christianity and Islam have done at various times in their histories? Part of the reason lies in the nature of Buddhism itself. Most of the Buddhist traditions active in the West lack what might be termed an "imperial ideology." While members of each group no doubt tend to see their own beliefs, approaches, and practices as superior to those of other groups, whether Buddhist or not, there is a general acceptance among all Buddhists of the idea that other faiths and traditions contain wisdom of their own, which can be of great value if it helps their members along the path of spiritual growth. The Dalai Lama, for example, has repeatedly discouraged his many admirers from being too quick to convert to Buddhism, reminding them that seeking after the exotic may cause them to miss the value of their own traditions.

Perhaps an even greater factor discouraging evangelism among the meditation-oriented Buddhist groups in the West is their attitude toward the practice of meditation itself. To most Western Buddhists—and perhaps even more so among Asian Buddhists—the practice of meditation is seen as difficult and demanding; it is recognized as something that not only requires a total individual commitment, but also as likely to present the most daunting kind of personal challenges on occasion. Members of most Western Buddhist groups would say that trying to pressure someone into following the path of Buddhist practice would be a complete waste of time, since they would lack the necessary kind of commitment. The general attitude is that people should come to Buddhist practice only when they are ready.

A third factor militating against evangelizing lies in the kind of status groups to which meditation-oriented Buddhist practice has had its greatest appeal. Most members of such groups tend to be middle-class, well-educated, and of highly liberal political persuasion. For example, the majority of the over 350 people who answered my survey of new Buddhist groups in the United States were not only college graduates, but also had some kind of post-graduate education as well, and the members of the Green Party substantially outnumbered the Republicans (Coleman 2001, 194–197). Many highly educated and politically progressive people have had negative experiences with conservative Christian evangelicals, and they tend to view evangelism, whether Buddhist or of any other kind, as something rather unsavory at its best, and as outright coercion at its most extreme.

How, then, do we account for the marked difference in Soka Gakkai? Part of the answer is historical and doctrinal. Right from the start, Nichiren Buddhists have tended to be much more convinced that theirs is the one true religion, and to be much more actively involved in evangelical activities. Moreover, because of its unique doctrines and practices, Nichiren Buddhism has not benefited as much from the kind of general intellectual interest in Buddhism that has helped other groups spread in the West. This difference is clearly shown in the survey data on Western Buddhists. When asked how they first became interested in Buddhism, 40 percent of the members of the new Buddhist groups I surveyed said it was from reading a book, and only 25 percent said it was from contact with friends and family, with another 9 percent professing it was from both (Coleman 2001, 199). By contrast, Hammond and Machacek's survey of Soka Gakkai members found that only one percent first encountered the group through "literature or publicity," while the vast majority encountered it through friends, acquaintances and family members (Hammond and Machacek 1999, 149). Another important difference lies in the nature of Soka Gakkai practice. Although it certainly takes a great deal of effort to memorize the chants Soka Gakkai members are expected to recite daily, it is not considered something difficult and demanding, but rather something that anyone can do. Similarly, Soka Gakkai members believe that the benefits chanting produces make it very easy for members to continue their practice.

It is also worthwhile to note that although Soka Gakkai still has a stronger emphasis on recruiting new members than most other Buddhist groups, it has moved much closer to the mainstream of Western Buddhism. Today, new members are usually brought in through what they call "warm contacts" with existing members, and not through the aggressive evangelism of its early days. Moreover, Soka Gakkai seems to be increasingly appreciative of the value of the other Western Buddhist groups with which it shares so many common perspectives. Part of the reason for these changes undoubtedly lies in the process of westernization all Buddhist groups have undergone in their new environment. A process of institutional and even personal maturation also seems to be involved, as Soka Gakkai has moved from a small sect to a large established denomination, and its youthful recruits have mellowed with the years. Soka Gakkai has also undergone a significant demographic shift moving away from its working-class immigrant base to a sociological profile composed of the same kind of highly educated, middle-class people that are attracted to the meditation-oriented Buddhist groups (Machacek and Mitchell 2000). Not surprisingly, as their demographics have converged, so too have their attitudes toward aggressive evangelism.

On the other hand, Soka Gakkai has been much more successful at attracting and retaining African American, Hispanic, and members of other minorities than the meditation-oriented Buddhist groups. According to Judith Simmer-Brown, "30 percent of SGI's members are non-white non-Asians" (Simmer-Brown 2002, 311). In addition, Simmer-Brown points out that in SGI, "diverse populations of men and women join together in practice, and women are currently stepping into a high percentage of leadership roles," making the movement "a rare example of an immigrant Buddhist tradition that has bridged the gap between populations of ethnic and convert men and women" (Simmer-Brown 2002, 311). In sum, it appears that the relatively minor role missionary activity played in the spread of Buddhism in the West can be attributed both to the fundamental differences between it and the Abrahamic monotheistic traditions, most notably Christianity and Islam in their expansionist phases, and the particular historical and sociological circumstances that marked Buddhism's arrival in the West. Soka Gakkai's exceptionalism stemmed primarily from its unique beliefs and traditions, but it does appear to be moving closer to the mainstream of Western Buddhism, as it adapts to new cultural environments.

Notes

1. See, e.g., Sahn (1982).
2. See, e.g., Seager, who makes extensive use of the concept of "convert Buddhism" (Seager 1999).
3. See, e.g., Soka Gakkai International-USA's website (http://www.sgi-usa.org).
4. For an interesting discussion of the issues involved in the classification of the different types of Buddhist groups in the West, see Prebish (1999). For more general works that include discussions of various "ethnic Buddhist" groups, see Prebish and Tanaka (1998), Prebish (1999), and Seager (1999).
5. There are many works on the history of the new Buddhism in the West. For the early history of Buddhism in the United States, see Tweed (1992). For an account of recent developments among the Buddhist communities in the United States, see Fields (1986). Batchelor (1994) includes discussions of Buddhism in Europe, while the essays collected in Prebish and Baumann (2002) explore Buddhism's global reach beyond its traditional centres in different parts of Asia.
6. For extensive access to the wide range of Zen Buddhist organizations in the United States, see DharmaNet's Zen Buddhist InfoWeb, which bills itself as "The Virtual Library of Online Zen Buddhist Associations, Monasteries & Practice Centers" (http://www.dharmanet.org/infowebz.html).
7. See, e.g., Diamond Way Buddhist Centers-USA's website (http://www.diamondway.org).

8. See, e.g., the California Vipassana Center's website (http://www.mahavana.dhamma.org).
9. See, e.g., the Vipassana Meditation Group of Long Beach's website (http://www.calirose.com/vipassana.html).
10. For a more detailed discussion of all these types of "new Buddhism" in the United States, see Morreale (1998) and Coleman (2001).
11. See, e.g., Zenshuji Soto Mission's website (http://www.zenshuji.org).
12. For studies of the Beats and Buddhism, see Tonkinson (1995).
13. For a classic, modern reflection on the nature of *satori*, see Daisetz Teitaro's "Satori, or Enlightenment," in Barrett (1956, 83–108).
14. For an historical overview of Buddhism in Tibet, see Kapstein (2000). For an introduction to the philosophy and practice of Tibetan Buddhism, see Ray (2000).
15. For a recent biography of the Dalai Lama, see Marcello (2003).
16. For an account of the development of Tibetan Buddhism in the United States, see Lavine (1998).
17. For an account of the Buddha's teachings, see Rahula (1974). For the history of Theravadin Buddhism, see Gombrich (1988), and for Theravadin Buddhism in south-east Asia, see Swearer (1996).
18. See the Insight Meditation Center's website (http://www.dharma.org) and the Spirit Rock Meditation Center's website (http://www.spiritrock.org).
19. For a representative account of Nichiren's teachings, see Montgomery (1991).
20. For an account of Soka Gakkai's origins, development, and ideas, see Metraux (1988).
21. For an account of Soka Gakkai in the United States, see Hammond and Machacek (1999).
22. See Soka University's website (http://www.soka.edu), and Tokyo Fuji Art Museum's website (http://www.fujibi.or.jp).

CHAPTER TEN

"IN EVERY TOWN, COUNTRY AND VILLAGE MY NAME WILL BE SUNG": HINDU MISSIONS IN INDIA AND ABROAD

Klaus K. Klostermaier

Introduction

Christian missionary activity in India has been a major irritant to many Hindus for more than a century: conversion to Christianity was seen as a betrayal of Indian identity, a rejection of the inherited age-old dharma, a "denationalization." India ceased issuing visas to foreign Christian missionaries from 1957 on, and several Indian states have since introduced legislations making conversion to Christianity a criminal offence. While Christians appeal to a section of the Indian constitution that guarantees freedom of religion, Hindus argue that conversion to Christianity entails social and cultural uprooting, causing social unrest and thus is unconstitutional.

In a fairly recent book, the well-known Indian industrialist, Ashok Chowgule, president of the Maharastra Pranth of the Visva Hindu Parisad, expressed a widespread Hindu opinion, critical of Christian missions:

> Except perhaps for ISKCON [International Society for Krishna Consciousness], none of the Hindu sects have a missionary character in the sense that Christianity has. . . . The lack of the missionary character is due to the pluralistic ethos of multiple ways of salvation. Until recently, Hinduism did not have a ceremony, which would initiate a non-Hindu into Hinduism. It was invented in the 19th century by Swami Dayananda Sarasvati as a reaction to the threat of the aggressive proselytizing programs of Islam and Christianity. (Chowgule 1999, 33)

It is true that modern Hindu missionary movements like ISKCON are largely imitating Christian missions in their proselytizing efforts. It is also true that

Hinduism throughout known history consisted of a multiplicity of different faiths. However, if we see "mission" as an effort to disseminate the teachings of a particular religion in order to win adherents, promising them substantial spiritual and social advantage over others, we can identify many instances of Hindu missions, both within India and outside: attempts to convince believers in other religions of the uniquely redemptive quality of specific teachings revealed to particular Hindu seers and sages.

Hindu Domestic Missions

Vedic Missions

Before the term "Hinduism" was introduced by English writers in the mid-nineteenth century, Indians used to designate their tradition as the *vaidika dharma* ("The Vedic Law") or as *sanatana dharma* ("The Eternal Law"). The authors of the Vedic hymns called their own people *aryas*, or "the Noble Ones," considering all others to be *anaryas*, or those who lacked these "noble" qualities. The blessings of the gods, which derived from the performance of Vedic rituals, were denied to *anaryas*, who did not therefore participate in the afterlife community of the *pitrs*, the ancestors dwelling blissfully on the moon. However, *anaryas* could become *aryas* by submitting to the Vedic social system and by adopting Vedic ritual. Many did so.

The traditional Vedic way of life was based on the observance of Vedic ritual connected with notions of pure and impure, the transmission of sacred lore by an unbroken chain of many generations of Brahmin scholar-priests and the division of society into four varnas.[1] It is an historical fact that this way of life spread gradually throughout the whole of peninsular India from the Vedic heartland in northwestern India. An ancient Indian tradition connects the sage Agastya, who is also believed to have been the author of the first Tamil grammar, with a Vedic mission to southern India. Agastya was sent to the Tamil country in response to a request by its rulers to have Vedic culture implanted in the south.[2] In the course of time, southern India became a very important and very conservative stronghold of Vedic learning and ritualism. There are numerous documented instances of Indian kings inviting individual *brahmin* teachers or groups of *brahmin* families to settle in their countries so that they might teach Vedic lore and ritual and by their example demonstrate the Vedic way of life. At one time, an attempt was made to duplicate in the south the names of the holy rivers and sites of northern India, in an effort to make it easier for people in the south to share in the redemptive effects of bathing in the sacred Ganges river, for example, or a pilgrimage to the holy city of Kasi (Varanasi), without having to leave their homeland.

During the last centuries before the Common Era, Vedic traditions lost ground to other spiritual movements. In his well-known pillar and rock edicts Emperor Asoka (ca. 273–232 BCE) recommended Buddhist ideals to his people. He also sent Buddhist missionaries to many countries for the well-being of the whole world. For about a thousand years thereafter Buddhism became the predominant religion of India, with Jainism a distant second. From the fifth century of the Common Era onward, however, Brahminic Hinduism began to reassert itself in Northern India under the protection of the Gupta dynasty, who held sway from the early fourth to the late sixth century. These centuries saw the final compilation of the celebrated Hindu epics, the *Mahabharata* and the *Ramayana*, as well as great advances in science, mathematics, and art. Freshly confident, Brahminic Hinduism generated its own vigorous missionary movements, which eventually brought the country back to its Vedic roots.[3] The new scriptures of the emerging Hinduism, the *Puranas*, recommended a return to the old faith not only by relating miracles and wonders wrought by Hindu gods and saints for the benefit of their devotees, but also by detailing the dire consequences of following other paths. In a vivid image, the *Visnu-puranam* calls the Hindu dharma a person's clothes; without *dharma*, one is naked and falls prey to demons. The text goes on to relate the story of King Satadhanu and his pious wife. Just by conversing with a Buddhist, so the story goes, the king reaps evil rebirths as a wolf, a dog, a vulture, a crow, and a peacock. He only assumes a human body again because of the prayers of his faithful Hindu wife, who had avoided all contact with the heretics (*Visnu-puranam* III. 18. 15 ff).

In the sixth century, there also arose in the deep south a movement of messengers of *Visnu-bhakti*: the Alvars, or "those immersed in God," began traveling around the country to spread their message of divine love, singing their Tamil hymns in praise of Visnu in temples and towns.[4] For at least three centuries, a succession of such god-intoxicated poets composed prayers and invocations that were eagerly accepted by large numbers of people, and that strengthened the cause of Vaisnavism in India immensely. It is noteworthy that amongst these Visnu missionaries there were women as well as low-caste people. They proclaimed a religion based on feelings coming from the heart, rather than on ritual codes. When the *acaryas* of the famous Visnu temple in Srirangam began recording these hymns in the tenth century, and had them recited at temple functions, they acquired official status and were treated as equal to the Vedic hymns. In these devotions, Visnu is exalted above all other deities, and personal salvation is promised to everyone who surrenders to him. This surrender to Visnu, or *prapatti*, became the most distinctive feature of Srivaisnavism; it entails exclusivity and uniqueness of faith, unfailingly guaranteeing salvation to devotees of Visnu. Nor was this kind of evangelizing zeal entirely peculiar to *Visnu-bhaktas*.

A little later, a parallel phenomenon appeared among the Saivas of South India: a group of 63 singer-saints, called the Nayanmars, helped to rekindle enthusiasm for Mahesa, the Great God Siva, through their fiery Tamil hymns. Like the Alvars, the Nayanmars traveled around the country, recruiting people for their faith community. According to tradition, one of these prophetic teachers, Jnana Sambandhar (Campantar), acceded to the pleadings of the Pandyan queen of Madurai in Tamil Nadu to persuade her husband, Arikesari Nedumaran, who had converted to Jainism, to return to Saivism. Sambandhar is even said to have induced the reconverted king to impale 8,000 Jains, who had refused to become Saivas. Stone carvings at the Saivite temple in Thiruvedagam, a small town not far from Madurai, vividly capture these events.

Sankara's Conquest of the Four Quarters

A spectacular instance of Hindu "inner mission" is offered by Sankaracarya, who lived between 788 and 820 CE, according to tradition.[5] In his writings, Sankara argues against virtually all the competing spiritual traditions and religious philosophies of the day. The *Sarirakabhasya*, his celebrated commentary on the *Brahma-sutra*, holds that to accept any of these wrong beliefs is to exclude oneself from liberation and to suffer deplorable loss (Gambhirananda 1965, I. 1. 1). The main opponents of Brahminic Hinduism in Sankara's time were Buddhists, and he is credited with having brought about the downfall of Buddhism as the main philosophy and religion of India. He sharply attacked Buddhist systems. He tried to prove their self-contradictory nature and the evil consequences of accepting them, refuting one by one the tenets of several Buddhist philosophical schools, comparing them to a pit dug in loose sand, which collapses upon itself.

Sankara also undertook a *dig-vijaya*, or "conquest of the four quarters," on which he met with and refuted representatives of other faiths and convictions. In the *Sankara-vijaya*, a hagiography of Sankara, his disciple Anantanandagiri describes in great detail the debates in which Sankara defeated not only Buddhists and Jainas, but also representatives of many Saiva and Vaisnava sects, as well as the followers of other deities, like the Ganapatyas and Saktas, and the proponents of various philosophical schools of thought (Veezhinathan 1971).[6] The work portrays encounters with representatives of over fifty different sects or religions, all of them deficient in Sankara's opinion, and incapable of leading a seeker to true *moksa*, or spiritual liberation, the ultimate goal of all humanity. In an introductory essay to this *Sankara-vijaya* T. M. P. Mahadevan, a former director of the Sarvepalli Radhakrishnan Centre for Advanced Study of Philosophy at the University of Madras, uses missionary language to characterize its contents. He speaks of Sankara "converting the adherents of different cult-beliefs and practices and schools of philosophy to the way of the Vedas and Vedanta" (Veezhinathan 1971, xii). According to Mahadevan, Sankara's aim was "to establish the supremacy of Advaita by showing that the other schools of thought are opposed to scriptural teaching and hence not valid" (Veezhinathan 1971, ix). To achieve this missionary goal, Sankara not only taught Advaita Vedanta, a rather esoteric philosophy of liberation, but he also composed hymns in honor of Visnu, Siva, and Devi, the great deities of popular Hinduism. In addition, he encouraged people to rebuild dilapidated temples, to regularly perform *puja*, and to maintain their ritual duties. Perhaps most significantly, Sankara introduced the still widely performed *pancayana-puja*, the simultaneous worship of the five deities Visnu, Siva, Devi, Ganesa, and Surya, which by its very nature accommodates a large number of devotees of different sects.

To consolidate his mission, Sankara established strategically located *mathas*, or monasteries, in the four corners of India, and organized the Dasanamis, an order of ascetics, consisting of ten branches, each distinguished by a different surname. These men were to spend their lives traveling the length and breadth of India, teaching people and encouraging them to practice Hindu traditions. In their view Advaita Vedanta alone was *siddhanta*, the complete and only truth. They were the authors of several treatises called *siddhi*, or "finally established ultimate truth," like Vimuktatma's thirteenth-century *Istasiddhi* and Madhusudana Sarasvati's sixteenth-century *Advaitasiddhi* (Sastri 1982; Sundaram 1980). In addition, his disciples continued Sankara's polemic against the many other religions still present in India. In the fourteenth century, for example, Madhavacarya, who headed the chief monastery of Sringeri, wrote a book on "comparative religion," the *Sarva-darsana-samgraha*, or "Review of All Systems of Philosophy," in which he ingeniously has each of 14 rival systems refuted by another rival system. The materialist Carvakas are refuted by Buddhists, the Buddhists by Jainas, the Jainas by Srivaisnavas, and so on, leaving Sankara's Advaita Vedanta triumphantly victorious (Cowell and Gough 1961). To this day, the successors to Sankaracarya, who call themselves *jagad-gurus*, or "world-teachers," as well as Sankaracaryas, spend most of the year touring their allotted districts, teaching, preaching, and encouraging the population to worship in the temples and to practice their religion.

Vaisnava Counter-Missions

The *acaryas* of Sri Rangam, ardent devotees of Visnu, were convinced that Sankara had got it all wrong. They set out to combat Advaita and Saivism by spreading their Visnu faith from their southern Indian base and establishing temples in northern India. Tradition usually places the ninth-century figure,

Natha Muni, at the head of this movement, since he collected the songs of the Alvars and gave them the status of *sruti*, or "revealed utterance." These Vaisnavas were fired by a sense of mission, too. Believing their teaching to be uniquely redemptive, they took care to warn their flocks of pernicious rival doctrines. Before explaining the actual content of his own teaching, for example, the greatest among them, Ramanuja (1017–1137), always deals with the errors of rival teachers. He does not mince words when discussing Advaita Vedanta, which he considered the main threat to the only true religion, *Bhagavata dharma*. Advaita, he says, "rests on a fictitious foundation of altogether hollow and vicious arguments . . . devised by men who were destitute of those particular qualities which the God-elect possess" (Thibaut 1904, 48. 39). Ramanuja thinks that the minds of the proponents of Advaita Vedanta are "darkened by the impression of beginning-less evil," that they "have no insight into the meaning of the words and sentences of revealed texts, and into the real purport conveyed by them," and that they lack the ability to argue according to the rules of logic (Thibaut 1904, 48. 39). Indeed, Ramanuja was convinced of the unique saving power of his Vaisnava faith. In his eagerness to share salvation with the masses, he is said to have broken traditional monastic discipline by announcing secret saving *mantras* from the top of a *gopuram*. By such a violation of vows he risked personal condemnation for the sake of the unredeemed millions. During his lifetime he had to flee for extended periods from his temple in Sri Rangam because Arimarthana, the ruling Pandyan king, had turned Saivite at the urging of Appar, a highly influential teacher and contemporary of Sambandhar. He became a militant Saivite missionary, demanding that everyone in his realm acknowledge the supremacy of Siva.

Madhva (1238–1317), perhaps the most uncompromising Vaisnava teacher, also known as Ananda Tirtha and Purnaprajna, criticized Ramanuja for what he considered a half-hearted rejection of Advaita Vedanta. Madhva traveled throughout India preaching a pure dualistic Vaisnava Vedanta (Dvaita). His followers denounced Sankara's Advaita Vedanta as "crypto-Buddhism," a form of teaching even more pernicious than the archenemy, "open" Buddhism.[7] But an even more ardent missionary spirit within the Hindu traditions was displayed by Caitanya (1486–1533). Born in Navadvip, a small town in what is today West Bengal, famous for its tradition of logic teachers, Caitanya became the founder of the last great *Vaisnava sampradaya*, Gaudiya Vaisnavism. Hagiography surrounding Caitanya makes his mission seem predestined. Even before his conversion, when he was still called by his birth name Nimai Pandit, he is reported to have said about himself: "I will become such a Vaisnava, that the whole world will flock to my door" (quoted in Majumdar 1969, 125). Later, on a visit to Gaya, when he was initiated by Isvara Puri, he heard a voice, saying: "You are the Lord of Vaikuntha descended to redeem humankind. You will dispense love and devotion all over the world" (Majumdar 1969, 133).

In fulfillment of these prophecies, Caitanya proclaimed the glory of Lord Krishna by singing and dancing in the streets. This *nagara-kirtana* became one of the hallmarks of Caitanya's new religion and one of the most effective mean of propagating it. He also instructed some early followers, Haridas and Nityananda, to "go to every house and preach that only Krsna is to be worshipped" (Majumdar 1969, 145). During Caitanya's time, however, Bengal was under the firm control of Muslim rulers and the Kazi of Navadvipa forbade Hindu missionizing. When Caitanya heard about this order, he arranged a protest march of all the men of Navadvipa and incited them to ransack and burn the house of the judge. The Kazi gave in and Caitanya continued to convert people to his new faith. Krisnadasa Kaviraja's *Caitanya-caritamrita*, a biography of Caitanya, mentions especially the conversion of such important scholars as Vasudeva Sarvabhauma. Caitanya traveled from Bengal to southern India to convert people and from there to Braj in the north, ecstatically dancing and singing in the streets of towns to communicate his message of the overlordship of Krishna.[8] Though of *brahmin* caste, he mixed freely with people from lower castes and members of other religions, who were considered outcasts, disregarding social and cultural barriers in the name of Lord Krishna's universal love, and predicting that his religion would one day be established in every town and village around the whole world. Selecting six of his closest disciples to settle in Vrindavana, he reactivated the ancient, forgotten holy places associated with Krishna's life and pastimes narrated in the *Bhagavata-purana*. These six *goswamis* established temples and composed books detailing the doctrines and rituals of Gaudiya Vaisnavism. They and their successors attracted ever more people to live in Vrindavana, spending their time in worship and contemplation of the *Krsna-lila*.

Hindu Missions under Muslim Rule and European Christian Dominance

At the time, when Ramanuja, Madhva, and Caitanya were actively propagating their religion, most of India was under Muslim rule. Influential Muslim clerics and ruling monarchs were quite aggressively promoting Islam. Under some Muslim rulers Hinduism was actively suppressed: thousands of temples were destroyed and many images smashed, sacred books were burned, and public Hindu processions were forbidden. Ramanuja had to leave Sri Rangam on several occasions because Muslim marauders ransacked the place. The population at large was put under pressure to accept the blessings of Prophet Muhammad's religion. A considerable portion of Hindus in northern India became Muslims.

It is hard to say whether they wanted to avoid the disadvantages of being *kafirs* in a Muslim country, or whether they genuinely considered the new religion superior to their old traditions. Members of the low castes would gain from the egalitarianism of Islam. Even then, as the examples of Ramanuja, Madhva, and Caitanya show, Hindus were actively spreading reinterpreted and revitalized Hindu traditions. Reconversions of Muslims to Hinduism were not uncommon under the Mughal emperor, Akbar the Great (1542–1605). His grandson, Shah Jahan (1592–1666), under whom a more orthodox faction of Islam gained the upper hand, forbade Hindu missionary activities. But even under his rule, there were a number of re-conversions to Hinduism, and a separate government department was established to deal with these (Schimmel 2000, 133). Poets and singers who proclaimed the greatness of Rama and Krishna—called collectively the Sants—moved freely through the villages and towns of Mughal India. Some, like Kabir, denounced the sectarianism of both Hindus and Muslims, and pleaded for the cultivation of sincere humanity and religiosity. Indeed, Kabir found acceptance from both Hindus and Muslims, and a dispute exists even today whether his background was Muslim or Hindu. But the Muslim conquest of India nonetheless made Hindus more aware of their distinctive identity and of the need to preserve their Hindu heritage by stricter observation of caste rules and by the compilation of encyclopedic Hindu works.

The rule of India by Muslim foreigners—Arabs, Turks, and Mongols—was broken not by a return of Hindu sovereigns, but by the advent of Christian foreign powers—Portuguese, Danish, French, and British—that from the late fifteenth century onward occupied increasingly large parts of the country. In 1498, the Portuguese landed on the west coast of India, occupying a piece of territory, which they called Goa, to which later were added territories in the north, Diu and Daman. The first European Christian colonial power to arrive in India, they expelled all Hindus who refused to become Roman Catholics and destroyed many Hindu temples.[9] In 1583, some Hindus took revenge and killed the Jesuit missionary, Rudolfo Aquaviva. This murder resulted in more reprisals against the Hindus. The Roman Catholic Inquisition of Goa became one of the most feared institutions in the Christian world, punishing not only Christians, but also Hindus for presumed breaches of Canon Law.

By contrast, the British East India Company did not at first allow Christian missions in its territories. Founded in 1600, the Company acquired factories in Surat on the west coast and in Hughli in Bengal. As one mission history puts it, however, "The officials of the East India Company were hostile to any kind of missionary enterprise, for they were afraid that educational progress and the opening up of new lines of thought would lead to general unrest, and create difficulties for the British administration in India" (Stewart 1961, 2). Expansion of the British

East India Company from Calcutta into the surrounding countryside increased contacts between Europeans and Hindus. Before long, though, pressure from the Church of England resulted in a change of policy, and in 1799, William Carey and his companions founded the Serampore mission under Danish protection, and Hindus found themselves exposed to active Christian proselytizing.

In Bengal, this encounter with the early British missionaries produced a new breed of enterprising, reform-minded representatives of Hinduism. The thoughtful Hindu aristocrat, Raja Ram Mohan Roy (1772–1833), initially found contact with the Christian Europeans stimulating; he enjoyed the opportunity to rethink his own tradition in the light of the teachings of Jesus.[10] But the Christian missionaries denounced his reflections on their own tradition and its scriptures, gathered in *The Precepts of Jesus*, as a kind of "Hinduized" Christianity (Ram Mohan Roy 1823). Undaunted, Ram Mohan Roy proceeded to found his own new religious community. The new movement, later called Brahmo Samaj, attempted to combine Upanisadic metaphysics with Christian ethics, and although it did not gain many followers, it became instrumental both for Hindu reform movements and for Hindu missionary activity.[11] On the other hand, Debendranath Tagore, an early associate of Ram Mohan Roy, saw in the Brahmo Samaj an opportunity to counteract Christian missions. Realizing that Christian missionaries attracted many people through their educational and charitable work, Debendranath Tagore began building up Hindu schools and spreading a new kind of modernized Hinduism through newspapers and book publications. He considered Christian missions a threat to India, and especially to Hinduism, which was mercilessly attacked and ridiculed in Christian publications. While Christian ministers anticipated the demise of Hinduism, Debendranath Tagore worked for its renewal and revival by establishing what, under the leadership of his son, Rabindranath, later became the world-famous "forest-university" of Shantiniketan, which he envisioned as a meeting place for the best of Eastern and Western traditions.

If the Brahmo Samaj tried to contain Christian missions by reforming traditional Hinduism and offering modern education outside the Christian missionary establishments, the Arya Samaj went one step further toward active Hindu missionizing. The movement's founder, Dayananda Sarasvati (1824–1883), spent three years studying in Mathura with the blind scholar Virajananda Sarasvati. At the end of his studies, Dayananda visited his guru to present him with his *dakshina*, or parting gift, in accordance with tradition. But Virajananda used the occasion to lay a commission upon his disciple:

> I want from you a new kind of dakshina. Promise me that you will, as long as you live, devote everything even give up your life, to the propagation in India of the books of the rishis and the Vedic religion. I will accept from you the fulfillment of that promise as my dakshina. (Jordens 1978, 38–39, citing Mukhopadhyay 1902, 192)

Dayananda went first to Hardwar, during a *Kumbha mela*, the ancient riverside sacred festival held every twelfth year in this city. There he told the assembled *sadhus* and pilgrims that their *tilakas* and their bathing in the Ganges were worthless, and that their holy book, the *Bhagavatam*, which contains stories about the life of Lord Krishna, was less a source of Vedic wisdom than a repository of immoral stories. In its place, Dayananda was intent on reintroducing the original, eternal religion of India and humankind, the *sanatana dharma*. In his own writings, for example, most notably the revised version of the *Satyartha prakasa*, he refutes Islam and Christianity as false religions.

As his translator, Ganga Prasad Upadhyaya, points out, Dayananda was very conscious of the ways in which Christian missionaries did "not hesitate to exploit the down-trodden-ness of the Hindus in their favor" by circulating "millions of tracts and booklets . . . in almost all Indian languages criticizing, condemning, caricaturing the religions of the Hindus" (Dayananda 1960, 685). In response, Dayananda mounted a spirited counterattack, arguing that as a self-professed religion of the book, Christianity must stand or fall according to the truthfulness of its scripture and the integrity of its proponents in adhering to the teachings of this scripture. Quoting at length from both the Old and New Testaments, Dayananda attempts to demonstrate the unreliability, particularism, and immorality of the Bible, as well as the hypocrisy of Christians who, for example, preach justice, and yet "when a black man is killed by a white man, he is for the most part declared not guilty and acquitted" (Dayananda 1960, 733). Dayananda concludes: "Who is there so unwise that he may give up his Vedic religion and accept the spurious religion of Christianity?" (Dayananda 1960, 753). Another chapter of *Satyartha prakasa* levels analogous charges against Islam and Muslims, while never losing an opportunity to advance the cause of the *sanatana dharma*. Dayananda cast his writings as "the preachings of a true preacher" (Dayananda 1960, 3). Dayananda also introduced *suddhi*, a purification ceremony, through which Muslims and Christians whose ancestors had been Hindus could return to the Hindu fold. While the Brahmo Samaj is of mainly historic importance and has few members today, the Arya Samaj remains alive and well, and in the course of time has spawned a number of assertive Hindu organizations, mainly through its educational institutions in northern India.[12]

Hindu Foreign Missions

Indian Expansion and Early Hindu Missions

In *Hindu America*, Chaman Lal offers interesting arguments for a long-lasting naval connection between India and Central and South America from ca. 500 BCE onwards (Lal 1960). He holds, and believes to have proofs, that much of Mextec and Mayan religion owes its origins to imported Hindu traditions, pointing to the markedly striking similarities between Mexican and Indian temple architecture. While plausible, these assertions still need more substantive evidence before they can be expected to find common acceptance.[13] On the other hand, there is no doubt at all about the colonial and cultural expansion of India toward Southeast Asia from the first century to the eighth or ninth centuries of the Common Era. In Hindu Colonies in the Far East, R. C. Majumdar, one of India's most eminent historians, collected ample materials relating to these Indian trading and colonizing adventures (Majumdar 1963). As far as we know, this Indian infiltration eastwards was a peaceful process of cultural and commercial expansion, which also included the spread of Hindu religious texts and rituals. Apart from abundant architectural and epigraphic Hindu (and Buddhist) remains all over Myanmar, Thailand, Laos, Cambodia, Vietnam, Malaysia, Indonesia, up to the Philippines, the languages of many of these countries and their living traditions still contain major Indian influences. Indian merchants and adventurers founded kingdoms and built temples in these regions, carried their sacred books and their deities into these new homelands, and transmitted their traditions and customs to the indigenous populations.

Throughout Southeast Asia one can find sculptures of Hindu deities and stone reliefs depicting Indian myths, often carved with the facial features and clothing styles of the local people, indicating the extent to which indigenous populations became acculturated to Hindu ways. Khmer, Cham, and other Southeast Asian dynasties justified their authority by claiming direct descent from Siva, Visnu, or Brahma and invoking the guardianship of these Hindu deities to maintain their rule. The area around Siem Reap, in Cambodia, for example, boasts over a hundred important temple sites, built by Khmer rulers between the ninth and thirteenth centuries. The most celebrated of these sites, Ankor Wat, was dedicated to Visnu by the twelfth-century Khmer monarch, Suryavarman II.[14] The main sanctuary consists of five towers, which symbolize the five peaks of Mount Meru, the abode of the gods and *axis mundi* of Hindu cosmology, while the outer gallery walls feature a huge *bas-relief*, narrating the mythological exploits of Hindu heroes and divinities. Similarly, in Vietnam, Cham dynasties adopted Hindu practices and beliefs, and used Sanskrit as a sacred language. From the late fourth to the thirteenth century, My Son served as the center of Cham religious life, and in 1985, excavations uncovered a *lingam* from the sanctuary of the earliest temple there, although in later centuries the Cham worshipped Shiva mostly in human form. Other important Cham Hindu relics include the seventh-century altar at Tra Kieu, which features several reliefs of scenes from the *Ramayana*; the sacred towers at Po Nagar, built as Hindu sanctuaries between the seventh and twelfth centuries; and the four brick towers at Po Klong Garai, which the thirteenth-century king, Jaya Simhabarman III, constructed as Hindu temples.[15]

Hindu missionaries made their way to Indonesia, too, and like the Southeast Asian mainland, several Indonesian islands possess significant reminders of ancient Hindu influence. The massive Hindu complex of Prambanan, in Java, for example, dates from the ninth century of the Common Era. Though long since abandoned and only benefiting from restoration in recent years, it consists of well over two hundred temples. Built by the Mataram king, Rakai Pikatan, the site includes three main sanctuaries for the Hindu *trimurti*: Visnu facing north, Siva in the center, and Brahma to the south. Reliefs illustrating scenes from the *Ramayana* decorate these sanctuaries, while smaller structures for the vehicles of the gods complement the main temples. There are famous indigenized Javanese versions of the *Ramayana* and the *Mahabharata*. The latter remained particularly popular in Java, where traditional shadow puppets are used to depict the timeless tale of conflict between two branches of a family descended from the gods. A favorite with the Indonesians is Arjuna, the victorious Pandava warrior, whose character resonates with indigenous Javanese notions of nobility, and whose fight for the righteous cause is in line with traditional Javanese ideas of justice. Several Javanese kings claimed direct descent from Arjuna; through Arjuna, they argued, they too were related to the supreme Hindu gods.[16]

A rich Hindu culture has been preserved on the island of Bali. There are traces of Hindu influence in Bali dating to the first century of the Common Era. In 1343, the Javanese Hindu king, Gajah Mada, conquered the island, which formally adopted the caste system, as well as a vast array of Hindu beliefs and practices. In indigenized forms, called *Agama Hindu Dharma*, or the "religion of Hindu teaching," and *Agama Tirtha*, or "religion of the holy places," this heritage persists to the present day in a plethora of rituals and festivals known collectively as *yadnya*, a term derived from Sanskrit *yajna*, "sacrificial rite."[17] Blending Hindu mythology and Balinese vernacular the *kecak* dance is the performance of scenes from the *Ramayana*. In a similar manner, the temple of Goa Gajah, near Ubud, mixes Hindu devotional practices with local folk traditions. Known locally as the Elephant Cave, this eleventh-century sanctuary is carved into a cliff face. It contains a statue of the Hindu elephant god, Ganesa, and altars holding a *yoni* and several *lingams*. According to Balinese legend, bathing in the two pools outside the cave keeps one young. Indian influence extended as far as the Philippine archipelago, where archaeologists continue to discover Hindu artifacts and popular performers revive vernacular adaptations of classical Hindu myths.

The Ramakrishna Mission

Narendra Nath Dutt (1863–1902), who under his monastic name Swami Vivekananda became world-famous through his arousing speeches at the World Parliament of Religions in Chicago in 1893, founded the "Ramakrishna Mission" to honor the memory of his spiritual master.[18] Ramakrishna Paramahamsa (1836–1886) had lived a life of renunciation and ecstatic meditation at the Kali Temple of Dakshineshwar, on the Ganges near Calcutta. The aim of the Ramakrishna Mission was not only to counteract the Christian missionary activities in India by opening up a number of schools and charities, but also to actively carry the message of Hinduism, as reinterpreted by Vivekananda, to the whole world. Vivekananda was convinced of the world-historic mission of Hinduism. Thus he wrote:

> We Hindus have now been placed, under God's providence, in a very critical and responsible position. The nations of the West are coming to us for spiritual help. A great moral obligation rests on the sons of India to fully equip themselves for enlightening the world on the problems of human existence. (Vivekananda 1982, 3. 139)

And:

> Once more the world must be conquered by India. This is the dream of my life. I am anxiously waiting for the day when mighty minds will arise, gigantic spiritual minds who will be ready to go forth from India to the ends of the world to teach spirituality and renunciation, those ideas which come from the forests of India and belong to Indian soil only. Up, India, and conquer the world with your spirituality. . . . Ours is a religion of which Buddhism, with all its greatness, is a rebel child, and of which Christianity is a very patchy imitation. (Vivekananda 1982, 3. 27–28)

During his visit to the United States Vivekananda founded the Vedanta Society of New York in 1894, devoted to the cultivation of Hindu religious teachings and spiritual service in the United States. This foundation was the first of a worldwide network of Vedanta Societies: by now there are 20 Vedanta Societies in the United States and many more in Argentina, Australia, Brazil, Canada, Fiji, France, Germany, Japan, Malaysia, Mauritius, Netherlands, Russia, Singapore, Spain, Switzerland, and the United Kingdom. The headquarters of the Ramakrishna Mission are at the Ramakrishna Math at Belur, just outside Calcutta. The Ramakrishna Mission teaches a kind of neo-Vedanta philosophy and promotes a religious universalism in line with Ramakrishna's vision. The mission insists, however, that it is not trying to convert non-Hindus to Hindu ways.[19]

The Caitanya Gaudiya Mission and ISKCON

The nineteenth-century revival of the Caitanya tradition in Bengal began with Kedarnatha Datta (1838–1914), a teacher and later government official.[20] Proficient in several languages and a prolific author, Kedarnatha Datta received the honorary title Bhaktivinoda Thakura from Vaisnava pandits in recognition of his lectures and writings. His best-known publications are *Sri Krsna Samhita* (1880), a Sanskrit treatise on devotion to Lord Krishna, and *Sri Caitanya Siksamrta* (1886), a Bengali work on the significance of Caitanya's teaching for the modern world. The nucleus of what later became known as the Neo-Caitanya Movement, Bhaktivinoda's following soon extended beyond his native region. Upon his death in 1914, Bhaktivinoda's son and disciple, Bimala Prasada (1874–1937), continued his father's work. Granted the title, Bhaktisiddhanta Sarasvati, in recognition of his vast learning, the son adopted the life of spiritual renunciation in 1918. Bhaktisiddhanta became editor of his father's journal, *Sajjana-tosani*, founded the Bhagavat Press to propagate Gaudiya Vaisnava literature, and expanded the movement throughout India by founding 64 Gaudiya Vaisnava monasteries, with the Caitanya Gaudiya Math in Mayapur, as headquarters.

Pursuing Bhaktivinoda's desire to fulfill Caitanya's dream of taking Gaudiya Vaisnavism's gospel of divine love beyond India, Bhaktisiddhanta encouraged some of his disciples to become overseas missionaries. In the 1930s, he sent his disciple Swami Bon Maharaj (1901–1982) on a preaching tour to England, Germany, and Japan, and asked the businessman, Abhay Caran De (1896–1977), to preach Gaudiya Vaisnavism in English through books and magazines. In 1944, Abhay Caran started *Back to Godhead*, an English fortnightly magazine, and in 1947, the Gaudiya Vaisnava society honored him with the title "Bhaktivedanta." He resolved the conflict between his vocation as a religious preacher and the demands of family life by separating from his wife in 1950 and taking shelter at the Radha-Damodar temple in Vrindavana, where he began working on an English translation and commentary on the 18,000-verse scripture, *Srimad Bhagavatam*, the main scripture of Gaudiya Vaisnavas. In 1959, Bhaktivedanta was initiated into *sannyasa*, the life of renunciation.[21]

After Bhaktisiddhanta's death in 1937, his immediate disciples were not able to agree on a successor and the movement split up under painful bickering and fighting. But Bhaktivedanta continued to follow his guru's mission, and in 1965, at the age of 69, he traveled to the United States aboard the *Jaladuta*, a cargo-ship of the Scindia Steamship Company. Bhaktivedanta knew hardly anything about the country to which he was carrying his mission; he had no connections, no money, nor even a residency permit. After spending a few weeks with his sponsors in Butler, Pennsylvania, to whom he had been recommended through an acquaintance in Mathura, he moved to New York, where, after some vicissitudes, he rented a cheap flat on the Lower Eastside. His English was heavily accented, and his dress was that of an Indian *sannyasi*, to which he added a heavy coat and a woolen cap. Discovering that all kinds of people, including religious preachers, set themselves up in Central Park to attract an audience, he likewise occupied a small area there and began singing his *kirtans*, accompanied by cymbals and hand-drums. It was the time of the hippies and the early drug scene, a counterculture for which India possessed some kind of mysterious attraction. Bhaktivedanta was soon surrounded by a group of young people, who listened to him half in bemusement and half out of genuine interest.

His first followers quickly discovered that Bhaktivedanta meant serious business. Not content with passive acquiescence in his chanting and seemingly exotic rituals, he demanded that his hippy audiences forswear drugs and sexual licentiousness, and even abstain from eating meat, smoking, and drinking alcohol. He did not offer any other inducements than the bliss of Krishna-consciousness. To everyone's amazement, hippies came in large numbers, staying to listen to lectures, especially on Sundays or feast days. Many young followers submitted to initiation, committing themselves to chanting 16 rounds of the Hare Krishna *mantra* daily, which helped to reinforce their adherence to the moral and spiritual principles of Gaudiya Vaisnavism. In 1966, Bhaktivedanta formally established the International Society for Krishna Consciousness (ISKCON), legally incorporated as a religion in Brooklyn, New York. In 1967, he started an ISKCON society in San Francisco. Soon there were dozens of temple-communities with hundreds of members, not only in New York and San Francisco, but also in Boston, Los Angeles, and other American cities.[22]

Encouraged by his success in North America, Bhaktivedanta traveled to England to set up an ISKCON center in London. Thence the movement spread across Europe, even to countries that were then still behind the Iron Curtain. It also reached Canada, Mexico and South America, Australia and New Zealand, eventually coming full circle, as it were, returning to India.

"Seven Purposes" constitute the common mission of all ISKCON branches:

1. To systematically propagate spiritual knowledge to society at large and to educate all people in the techniques of spiritual life in order to check the imbalance of values in life and to achieve real unity and peace in the world.
2. To propagate a consciousness of Krishna (God), as it is revealed in the great scriptures of India, Bhagavad-gita and Srimad-Bhagavatam.
3. To bring the members of the Society together with each other and nearer to Krishna, the prime entity, thus developing the idea within the members, and humanity at large, that each soul is part and parcel of the quality of Godhead (Krishna).
4. To teach and encourage the sankirtana movement, congregational chanting of the holy name of God, as revealed in the teachings of Lord Sri Caitanya Mahaprabhu.
5. To erect for the members and for society at large a holy place of transcendental pastimes dedicated to the personality of Krishna.

6. To bring the members closer together for the purpose of teaching a simpler, more natural way of life.
7. With a view towards achieving the aforementioned purposes, to publish and distribute periodicals, magazines, books and other writings. (ISKCON)[23]

To pursue these aims, the Bhaktivedanta Book Trust was founded in Los Angeles in 1968; today, it is one of the major sources of income for ISKCON. In 1970, Bhaktivedanta established a 12-member Governing Board Commission, to which he ceded executive authority upon his death in 1977. The Commission consults with branch presidents and other ISKCON leaders on all major policy matters, which are determined by democratic vote.

ISKCON's phenomenal growth around the world has not gone unimpeded, however. Resistance has come from outside the movement, and problems have arisen within it, as well. In the United States and in Europe, fundamentalist Christian anti-cult activists attacked the society, and in the former Soviet block, it was suspected to be an arm of the American government's Central Intelligence Agency. On the positive side, in 1977 members rejoiced when New York High Court Justice John S. Leahy declared ISKCON "a bona fide religion with roots in India that go back thousands of years."[24] But 1977 also saw Bhaktivedanta's passing, and his death brought to the surface rivalries between different groups within the organization, which further slowed its expansion. While most ISKCON members accepted the authority of the 11-member Governing Body Commission, others questioned it and started breakaway movements. In spectacular court cases, ISKCON members have been accused of illegal possession of weapons and even murder. Public opinion turned against the "Hare Krishna Movement," as it was popularly called. In recent times, the movement has been embroiled in intramural quarrels. The serious rift between the ISKCON Reform Movement (IRM) and the Governing Body Commission over the interpretation of Bhaktivedanta's last will and testament, for example, threatened the breakup of ISKCON, as do the claims of secessionist communities, like Kirtananda Bhaktipad's New Vrindaban Community, Bhaktivedanta Tripurari's Gaudiya Vaisnava Society, and Bhaktiprajnana's Kesava Gaudiya Matha. In 2003, Ravindra Swarupa Dasa, the President of the Governing Body Commission, feared the disintegration of ISKCON. In 2004 the IRM gained the recognition of a substantial number of ISKCON members and the split within the community seemed to widen.

Historically, though, ISKCON remains the largest and most successful Hindu missionary movement outside India. Accepted as part of the Gaudiya Vaisnava *bhakti* tradition, the over two hundred ISKCON centers around the world include temples, farms, restaurants, and schools, where the Vaisnava holy days and festivals are celebrated, and its principles of personal cleanliness, *prasadam* or healthy diet, ritual practices, moral etiquette, and strategies for spiritual proselytizing are cultivated. Specific membership figures are unavailable, but it is large enough to keep ISKCON involved in relief work in many countries. Some of its members with academic credentials actively seek dialogue with Christianity.[25] Initially, ISKCON emphasized the monastic ideal of *samnyasa*, but today married couples with families seem to constitute the major membership.

Western Converts as Hindu Missionaries

It is not known when the first westerners became Hindus. In spite of the orthodox assumption that one has to be born from Hindu parents in order to be counted a Hindu, exceptions have always been made for individuals who felt attracted to Hindu *samnyasa* and a life of meditation. The Englishman, Ronald Nixon (1898–1965), better known under his monastic name Krishna Prem, is one well-known example. A former World War I fighter pilot in the British Royal Flying Corps, Nixon took up a university teaching position in Lucknow and received initiation into Gaudiya Vaisnavism.[26] Together with his *guru*, Yasoda Mayi, the wife of the Vice-Chancellor of Banaras Hindu University, he moved in 1931 into a newly built Ashram near Mirtola, not far from Almora in the foothills of the Himalayas and lived there till the end of his life as librarian, cook, and temple-priest. His standing as a genuine Vaisnava was recognized by all and he was accepted as a religious teacher by the villagers, who arranged a grand burial for him when he died in 1965.

Another outstanding Western Hindu convert was Satguru Sivaya Subramuniyaswami (1927–2001), who also became one of the most effective Western Hindu missionaries in the West. Orphaned at age 11, he was raised by a family with strong connections to India. As a teenager, he trained in classical eastern and western dance and in yoga, becoming a leading dancer with the San Francisco Ballet Company at 19. In 1947 Subramuniya gave up his career in order to journey to India and to Sri Lanka, where he attached himself to a celebrated mystic, Satguru Siva Yogaswami. Yogaswami initiated Subramuniya into the Saiva Siddhanta tradition with the command: "Go round the world and roar like a lion. You will build palaces and feed thousands" (Srinivasan 2002). Advised by his guru not to preach till he was 30, Subramuniya returned to the United States and spent some years in meditation. In 1957, in San Francisco, he established the first Hindu temple in the United States, and in 1965, he founded the Himalayan Academy, a center for instruction in Hinduism, which in 1970 moved its headquarters to Kauai Aadheenam, a monastery and temple complex in Hawaii.[27] Subramuniya also founded the Saiva Siddhanta Yoga Order, a monastic community in the strict Saivite tradition of daily devotions, meditation, yoga, and service to humankind. From Kauai, the order's monks oversee the organization's international affairs, which are embodied in the Saiva Siddhanta Church. According to J. Srinivasan, Subramuniya "used the word Church because he thought that word would be more comfortable to Western ears" (Srinivasan 2002). At the same time, though an American, he felt a particular responsibility for Tamil Saivites in Sri Lanka, Mauritius, and Fiji, for whom, as the successor of Yogaswami, he was the hereditary spiritual leader.

The choice of Kauai as headquarters for his Hindu mission reflected Subramuniya's profound belief in the potential of Saiva Siddhanta for transcending differences between East and West. "I chose Kauai, the world's most remote land mass," he explained, "because I wanted to be close to my devotees in the East (Malaysia, Singapore, Sri Lanka, India and Mauritius) and close to my devotees in the West (Australia, Fiji, North America and Europe), while at the same time cloistered from the world at large" (Subramuniyaswami 2002 [1999]). The Hindu Academy trains Indian as well as non-Indian Hindu priests and monks, and Subramuniya was proud of the fact that "the best of the East and the best of the West have come together on the famed Garden Island of Kauai" (Subramuniyaswami 2002 [1999]). One feature of his mission was to take dozens of followers with him on tours to India as well as to Western and westernized countries. He became instrumental in building Hindu temples in Europe, Australia, and South Africa. Bridging East and West, he felt free to abandon those features of the Saiva Siddhanta tradition that he felt had become obsolete, yet insisted vigorously on pure Saivism, never leaving any doubt that he was living and teaching a Hindu tradition. What this approach meant he explored in more than 100 books and other publications, most notably *Dancing with Siva: Hinduism's Contemporary Catechism*. In the question-and-answer form of a traditional catechism, this work draws upon hundreds of Indian scriptural texts and sacred paintings to weave together a comprehensive picture of living Hinduism in a contemporary English style that is easily accessible to the lay reader, whether of Eastern or Western background (Subramuniyaswami 1993).

Subramuniya's missionary intentions are probably most clearly expressed in the founding, in 1979, of the monthly magazine, *Hinduism Today*, and in *How to Become a (Better) Hindu: A Guide for Seekers and Born Hindus*. The introduction to this guide distinguishes between compelled conversion and the voluntary adoption of a new religious life. "Hindu philosophy," Subramuniya argues, "is free from the missionary compulsion to bring the whole world into its fold in a kind of spiritual colonialism and cultural invasion" (Subramuniyaswami 2000). Instead, he talks of an "ethical conversion," which involves "the mandatory severance from any former faiths," and requires the "adoptee" "to go back to his prior religious leader, priest, rabbi, minister, imam, etc., and explain his change of belief, culture, etc., in a face-to-face meeting" (Subramuniyaswami 2000). There follows an express rationale for Subramuniya's mission:

> Many, I realized, had lived as Hindus in past lives, and now, born in the West, were merely rediscovering the religion of their soul. Having found it, they would be content with no other religion. To not provide a way for formal entrance to Hinduism would be to leave them between religions, stranded, in a sense, with no religion at all. (Subramuniyaswami 2000)

In a special initiation ceremony, such newcomers are given Hindu names and repeat "a verbal oath before God, Gods and guru and gathered devotees, promising to be eternally faithful to the principles of the Sanatana Dharma" (Subramuniyaswami 2000).

Hinduism Today sums up the global vision informing Subramuniyaswami's missionary agenda in these words:

1. To foster Hindu solidarity as a "unity in diversity" among all sects and lineages;
2. To inform and inspire Hindus worldwide and people interested in Hinduism;
3. To dispel myths, illusions and misinformation about Hinduism;
4. To protect, preserve and promote the sacred Vedas and the Hindu religion, especially the Nandinatha Sampradaya;
5. To nurture a truly spiritual Hindu renaissance.
6. To publish a resource for Hindu leaders and educators who promote Sanatana Dharma.

A thoroughly practical man, too, Subramuniya fully utilized modern technologies to advance this agenda. He initiated a desktop publishing enterprise, created an early online Hindu news service, and "required monks to be adept on Apple McIntosh computers" (Srinivasan 2002). *How to Become a (Better) Hindu* and *Hinduism Today* are now available on the worldwide web.[28]

Embodying East and West in person and in his teachings, Subramuniya represented Hinduism at many interreligious gatherings. In 1986 the World Religious Parliament in New Delhi honored him as one of five Hindu spiritual leaders outside of India who had done most to propagate Hinduism during the previous 25 years. In 1993 he was elected one of three Presidents of Hinduism at the Second World Parliament of Religions in Chicago. In 1994 he founded the Hindu Heritage Endowment to provide a source of permanent incomes for Hindu swamis and temples worldwide. In 2000, at the Millennium Peace Summit of World Religious and Spiritual Leaders, sponsored by the United Nations in New York, he received the U Thant Peace Award, a highly prestigious honor previously bestowed upon the Dalai Lama, Nelson Mandela, Mikhail Gorbachev, Pope John Paul II, and Mother Teresa. Shortly before his death, in 2001 Subramuniya designated Satguru Bodhinatha Veylanswami, the most senior monk of the Shaiva Siddhanta Yoga Order, as his successor.

The Jet-Set Hindu Missionaries

It is impossible in the context of this chapter to detail all the recent Hindu movements that have developed Western branches or that recruit Western members. The few that are mentioned are typical, but do not represent all of the branches of Hinduism that have established themselves outside India. From the mid-1960s onwards, the visits of prominent Hindu *swamis* to the United States became so frequent that people in India used to joke about the American *abhiseka*, or "anointment" as one of the new *adhikaris*, or "qualifications," of a respectable Hindu teacher. Many of these "jet-set" Hindu missionaries no longer preached the classical Hindu ideals of renunciation and meditation in forest retreats, but promised instant liberation and prosperity to anyone who subscribed to their teachings.

One of the best known of the new gurus is Mahesh Yogi Maharishi (1911–). He claims to have studied Advaita Vedanta for 13 years with Swami Brahmananda Saraswati, head of the Dasanami center at Jyotirmath, near Badrinath. In 1957, he started preaching in Madras, before long taking his message around the world. The Maharishi promulgated "Transcendental Meditation" (TM), a kind of yoga that dispenses with breathing exercises and other kinds of traditional practices, focusing instead on 15- to 20-minute periods of mental concentration, early in the morning and late in the evening, to dissolve stress and achieve a cyclical state of total relaxation. The Maharishi also claims to be capable of leading serious practitioners to the development of *siddhis*, or "supernormal powers," such as levitation and astral travel.[29] In spite of quite hefty charges for each level of instruction, the Maharishi found a large following and succeeded in establishing himself firmly in the colorful religious landscape of the United States. It helped enormously that the Beatles showed an interest in TM and descended by helicopter upon his Himalayan *ashrama*. To promote his ideas and to train teachers of TM, he established a "Maharishi International University" in 1971, which, in 1995, became "Maharishi University of Management": "gaining deep knowledge and experience has a powerful practical value—it enables every student to fully manage his or her life" (Maharishi University of Management Prospectus). In 1988, the Maharishi also formed the Natural Law Party (NLP), a worldwide political organization with branches in numerous countries.[30] Under the auspices of the "Maharishi Heaven on Earth Development

Corporation," the NLP came out with the ambitious plan to establish a world government in order to ensure peace and prosperity for all humankind. The TM movement claims a global following with over 1,000 centers, linked by the Maharishi Channel, which broadcasts the guru's teachings worldwide through a network of eight satellites.

A more conventional well-known Hindu movement is the Chinmaya Mission West, set up in 1975 in San Jose, California, by Swami Chinmayananda (1916–1993), with the help of Subramuniyaswami. Chinmayananda, after a career as journalist and political activist, began in 1949 to study Vedanta in Uttarkashi, in the Himalayas, with Swami Tapovan Maharaj (1889–1957). In 1961, he established Sandeepany Sadhanalaya in a suburb of Mumbai as a training center for Hindu missionaries.[31] For many years he held well-advertised lectures on the *Bhagavad-gita* in major Indian cities and undertook several world-tours. Chinmaya Mission West pledges "to provide to individuals from any background, the wisdom of Vedanta and the practical means for spiritual growth and happiness, enabling them to become positive contributors to society," a commitment expressed in a range of activities, from *Bhagavad-gita* chanting competitions to food and shelter for the homeless (Chinmaya Mission San Jose).[32]

Also comparatively well known are the Brahmakumaris, an order of women-ascetics, founded in 1937 by Dada Lekharaja (1877–1969), a Sindhi diamond merchant. Headquartered on Mount Abu, Rajasthan, India, the Brahmakumaris teach a westernized form of Hindu meditation known as Raj Yoga. In 1980, they affiliated with the United Nations as a nongovernmental organization to promote human rights, peace, and educational initiatives worldwide. With an international office in London, the movement now claims to have "more than 3000 educational centers and sub-centers in India and about sixty-six other countries, where education in Values, Human Resource Development, Meditation, Positive Thinking, etc, is imparted" (Brahmakumaris World Spiritual University).[33]

Another type of modern Hindu missionary organization is represented by the Ananda Marga, or "Path of Bliss," founded in 1955 by Prabhat Ranjan Sarkar (1921–1990), a former Indian Railways employee. It has spread from India around the world with the "twin yogic gospel of self-realization and service to humanity" (Ananda Marga). Based on the belief that "all creatures have a right to live in the world and develop according to their inherent nature," the Ananda Marga Universal Relief Team and the Ananda Marga Universal Relief Team Ladies, created in 1965 and 1977 respectively, have sponsored a wide variety of environmental awareness, disaster relief, and humanitarian projects around the world.[34] Though the organization has on occasion found itself embroiled in controversy, its current work in Burkina Faso, for example, includes programmes for assisted birthing, schools, HIV/AIDS awareness, reforestation, and sanitation and clean water supply (Ananda Marga, AMURT).[35]

Still more controversial in many ways is Bhagwan Shree Rajneesh (1931–1990), who later called himself Osho.[36] He attracted international attention and a worldwide clientele in the 1960s through the goings-on in is Ashram in Pune. Though Rajneesh was not born a Hindu himself, his organization was commonly identified as a modern Hindu movement. Drawing on Hindu, Jain, Zen Buddhist, Taoist, Christian, ancient Greek, and assorted other traditions, his teaching is neither consistent with traditional Hindu beliefs and practices nor acceptable to traditional Hindus. Facing problems in India, in 1981 his followers established a township near Antelope, Oregon. It was dissolved by court order in 1987. Rajneesh returned to die in Pune, where a somewhat subdued revival of the movement took place, and which serves as headquarters for about twenty meditation centers worldwide.

Over two million Hindus now live in the West, and information about a wide variety of events of interest to Western Hindus is widely available on the web and in numerous local, regional, national, and international periodicals and magazines. Leafing through *Hinduism Today*, for example, one can find dozens of advertisements from a great number of different Hindu sects and movements inviting non-Hindus to buy their literature, to join their celebrations, or to become members of their temple congregations. It often becomes difficult to distinguish between Hindu missions and the pastoral visits of Indian dignitaries to the Hindu diaspora. On the other hand, these diaspora communities attempt to keep their traditions alive not only by inviting Hindu representatives from India to preach to them, but also by building temples according to traditional Indian designs, the most spectacular likely being the recently completed Swaminarayan temple in London. While Hindu communities outside India normally do not proselytize among their non-Indian neighbors, they do invite their non-Hindu friends to join them for temple worship and spiritual teachings, and many respond.

Hindu Nationalism, Hindu Reform, World Hinduism

For many Indians, nationalism and religion became almost interchangeable terms since Bankim Chandra Chatterjee (1838–1894) wrote his *Bande mataram*, a hymn to the Goddess Mother India, which for some time served as India's national anthem. Dayananda and Vivekananda promoted the idea, too, but it was Aurobindo Ghose (1872–1950) who most ardently advocated the identity of the *sanatana dharma* with India as a nation. Krishna had promised in the *Bhagavad-gita* to appear again on earth to reestablish *dharma* when it was threatened by *a-dharma*. Inspired by this promise, the youthful Aurobindo sought to restore the rule of *dharma* in India.[37] Adapting Ramakrishna's devotion to Kali, he associated the Goddess with Mother India, and taught that *moksa*—"spiritual freedom"—was to be found by fighting for India's independence. Implicated in terrorist activities in 1908 and arrested by the British, he was thrown into prison in Calcutta on charges of sedition. He was shattered, thinking that the goddess for whose cause he had worked had failed to protect him. Following up studies of the *Upanishads* and the *Bhagavad-gita* with long hours of meditation and yoga, Aurobindo experienced visions in which Krishna told him not only that he would he soon be freed from prison, but that for the rest of his life his mission was to announce the *sanatana dharma* to the whole world. In 1909, in a famous speech to Uttarpara's "Society for the Protection of Religion," Aurobindo recounted Krishna's words:

> When it is said that India shall expand and extend herself, it is the Sanatana Dharma that shall expand and extend itself over the world. It is for the Dharma and by the Dharma that India exists. To magnify the religion means to magnify the country. (Aurobindo 2002 [1909])

For Aurobindo, India would be elevated over all nations for the sake of the *sanatana dharma*. In this sense, Hindu nationalism and the worldwide spread of Hinduism were inseparable.

Dharma became a highly emotionally charged term and a political weapon in the hands of Hindu nationalists.[38] In 1915, Pandit Mohan Malaviya (1861–1956) founded the Hindu Mahasabha, an organization committed to the preservation of traditional Hindu ways. Malaviya's contemporary, Vinayak Damodar Savarkar (1883–1966), coined the term "Hindutva," or "Hindu-ness," to express the inseparability of Hindu religion and Indian national identity (Savarkar 1923). In 1938, as president of the Hindu Mahasabha, Savarkar staunchly opposed British rule and Muslim ambitions with the battle cry, "Hinduize politics and militarize Hinduism" (Savarkar and Joshi 1967, 1). In its election manifesto of 1967 the Hindu Mahasabha declared that "Hindustan is the land of the Hindus from times immemorial," and that "Hindus have a right to live in peace as Hindus, to legislate, to rule, to govern themselves in accordance with Hindu genius and ideals and establish by all lawful and legal means a Hindu state, based on Hindu culture and tradition, so that Hindu ideology and way of life should have a homeland of its own" (cited in Rambachan).

Religious nationalists accused India's first Prime Minister, Jawaharlal Nehru (1889–1964), of establishing a government that was not just "secular," but positively anti-Hindu. Not only do Hindu nationalists accuse the Congress Party of India of having passed legislation contrary to dharma, but they also expect all the problems confronting contemporary India to disappear after the rule of *dharma* had been reestablished. Connecting with traditional ideas expressed throughout Hindu classical literature, from the epic poems to the *Puranas* and the *Sastras*, leaders of Hindu political parties continue to argue that natural calamities and misfortunes of all kinds are due to a violation and neglect of *dharma*. In 1992 a pamphlet issued by the Akhila Bharatiya Sant Samiti listed the well-known sins of secularism and concluded with some breathtaking assertions:

> After the rule of dharma has been re-established there will no longer be famine, poverty, ignorance, unemployment. The unity and integrity of the country will be safeguarded. Corruption, immorality, lawlessness and insecurity will be eradicated.[39]

Often Hindu nationalist politicians speak of their goals in eschatological terms as *Rama rajya* instead of Hindu *rastra*. Marked by justice and righteousness as well as bounty and prosperity for all, the rule of Rama as described in *Valmiki's Ramayana* embodies an ideal state of rule of *dharma*, in both senses of the word "state."[40] Others extol the role of Krishna as statesman, affirming his historicity and praising his rule as "not based on force but on renouncing, truth, compassion, justice, and humanity" (Gautami 1966, 87). "His only aim," according to Lantusinha Gautami, "is universal wellbeing" (Gautami 1966, 89).

Many Hindus share the belief that they are a chosen people and that they have a god-given mission to the rest of the world. This missionary spirit is especially alive among the members of the Rashtriya Swayamsevak Sangh (RSS), or "National Volunteer Association," founded in 1926 by Keshav Balram Hedgewar (1889–1940), a member of the Hindu Mahasabha.[41] Understanding "Hindu society as 'Janata Janardana'—god incarnate," the RSS aims "to activise the dormant Hindu society, to make it come out of its self-oblivion and realise its past mistakes, to instill in it a firm determination to set them right, and finally to make it bestir itself to reassert its honour and self-respect so that no power on earth dares challenge it in the days to come" (Rashtriya Swayamsevak Sangh). Madhav Sadashiv Golwalkar (1906–1973), the second *sarsanghachalak*, or "supreme leader," of the RSS spelled out the significance of this sense of mission for the world at large:

> It is the grand world-unifying thought of Hindus alone that can supply the abiding basis for human brotherhood, that knowledge of the Inner Spirit which will charge the human mind with the sublime urge to toil for the happiness of mankind, while opening out full and free scope for every small life-specialty on the face of the earth to grow to its full stature.
>
> This knowledge is in the custody of Hindus alone. It is a divine trust, we may say, given to the charge of the Hindus by Destiny. And when a person possesses a treasure, a

> duty is laid upon him to safeguard it and make it available for the welfare of others. (Golwalkar 1964)

"Verily this is the one real practical world mission, if ever there was one," concludes Golwalkar (Golwalkar 1964).

In recent years, the Visva Hindu Parisad (VHP), or "World Council of Hindus," has often led the way in the pursuit of this "one real practical world mission." Established in Bombay in 1964 by a group of prominent Hindus led by Golwalkar and Swami Chinmayananda, the VHP adopted the Vedic motto, *Dharmo rakshati rakshitah*, or "*dharma* protected will protect." The organization's symbol is the banyan tree, which spreads out its aerial root system far and wide. Advocating a kind of ecumenical Hinduism and engaging Hindus in religious and cultural activities, the VHP derives much of its inspiration from past and present leaders of the RSS and produces a large amount of literature spreading Hindutva in India and abroad.[42] The VHP insists that it is a Hindu sociocultural organization and not a Hindu political party, like the Shiv Sena and the BJP, which it often supports but also frequently criticizes, when it disagrees with their policies.[43] The VHP recognizes the existence of many millions of Indians "living in slums and backward colonies in urban areas" and "scheduled castes and other backward communities living in rural areas [and] suffer[ing] from discrimination, hatred, untouchability" (Vishva Hindu Parishad, "In the Service of [the] Poor"). Overseas, the VHP has gained great influence among expatriate Indians. The Vishva Hindu Parishad of America declares itself "inspired by the same values and ideals as those followed by Vishva Hindu Parishad of Bharat," though a "distinct, legally separate and operationally independent non-profit organization in its own right within the USA" (Vishva Hindu Parishad of America, "Relationship with VHP Bharat"). Its "vision for the Hindu society is rooted in the sacred soil of Hindu Dharma" (Vishwa Hindu Parishad of America, "Relationship with VHP Bharat"). Rejecting the proselytizing of the Christian Churches, who want to convert Hindus to Christianity, many new Hindus emphasize that theirs is a "dharmic," not a "religious" mission. Thus Chaturvedi Badrinath argues that the notion of "Hinduism" as a "religion" is an "invention of Christian missionaries" and that Hindu *dharma* "is a secular view of life, not a 'religious' one" (Badrinath 1993, 3). "Religion is by nature divisive," Badrinath asserts, "dharma unites" (Badrinath 1993, 5).

The major opposition to missionary Hindu nationalism today comes from the Dalits, organizations representing about 200 million former untouchables, outcastes, members of "scheduled castes" or whatever names were given to the lowest strata of Hindu society, as well as tribals and Muslim and Christian converts from these groups. Caste Hindus did not consider Dalits part of the *varnasrama-dharma* and took them for granted as providers of low-status services. Denied ambitions, which conflicted with their supposed betters, the Dalits became the preferred targets of foreign missionaries, who built churches and schools for them and helped them in many other ways, economically and culturally.[44] Bhimrao Rama Ambedkar (1891–1956) was perhaps the most celebrated recipient of such assistance. Born an "untouchable" Mahar, with the support of Christian missionaries Ambedkar studied economics and law in the United States and the United Kingdom and, as a member of the Constituent Assembly, played a key role in drafting the Indian Constitution.[45] At the same time, however, Ambedkar openly rejected Hinduism. In 1937, he burned a copy of the *Manu-smrti*, or "Laws of Manu," upon which the caste system is based, and in 1956, he publicly embraced Buddhism, along with thousands of fellow Mahars. While Mahatma Gandhi renamed untouchables "Harijans," or "children of God," and wished to include them in the lowly *sudra* caste, Ambedkar demanded the abolition of caste altogether.[46] Ironically, however, today's Dalit leaders promote a new caste identity theory to repudiate Hindu nationalism. In uncompromisingly strong language, for example, *Dalit Voice*, whose masthead reads "The Voice of Persecuted Nationalities Denied Human Rights," rails against "the entire bullshit built by our 'Hindu nation' heroes [and] their drummer boys in the 'national' toilet papers and academic circles" (Rajashekhar 1997, 3). For such Dalits, Hindu nationalism is Brahminism, which they totally reject. "India is not a 'nation,' " writes V. T. Rajashekhar, the editor of *Dalit Voice*, "but a conglomeration of 'nations' in which the basic building brick is CASTE (*jati*)" (Rajashekhar 1997, 3).

Although today many Hindus insist that theirs is a *sanatana dharma*, an eternal tradition, not a religion founded by a historic personality, it is an undeniable fact that *dharma* has changed dramatically over the centuries. In classical times, there was the *Dasavatara dharma parisad*, an expert body with authority to change Hindu law. This body no longer exists, but as we have seen, strong personalities in the nineteenth and twentieth centuries have changed what others believed to be irrefutable aspects of Hindu *dharma*. Encounters with Muslim and Christian traditions in India and the worldwide spread of Hindu teachings and practices have been important factors in such processes. Even in the early nineteenth century, Ram Mohan Roy was not alone in recognizing that to appeal to modern Indians, let alone to westerners, Hinduism must change. This reformed Hinduism would have to project an image that did not clash with modern democratic ideals of economic, social, and political equality and justice. In tune with such ideals, many recent exponents and reformers of Hinduism have campaigned successfully to bring about significant changes in Hindu traditions.

Passed in 1929, for example, the Child Marriage Restraint Act ended *bala vivaha*, or "child marriage," by prescribing a minimum age of 18 for girls and 21 for boys for contracting marriage. Likewise, numerous influential Hindu individuals and groups have spoken out against the persistence of *sati*, the self-immolation of wives, outlawed by the British in 1829. It was further condemned in the Sati Prevention Act, passed in 1987 "to provide for the more effective prevention of the commission of sati and its glorification and for matters connected herewith or incidental thereto" (India Bare Acts).[47] In 1984, the VHP convened a *Dharma samsad*, or "*dharma* parliament," in Delhi, claiming to revive an institution with the power to enact official changes in *dharma*, which had been dormant since Emperor Harsha (590–647). Some VHP leaders also have openly questioned the usefulness of caste divisions and have suggested the abolition of the multitude of often mutually competing *sampradayas* within Hinduism.

The Child Marriage Restraint Act and the Sati Prevention Act share a determination to reform Hindu tradition in one particularly crucial area; both pieces of legislation are concerned with the position of women in Hindu society. Traditional Hindu *dharma* disadvantaged women in many ways, despite the recognition bestowed upon some female saints such as the ninth century's Antal, the only woman among the 12 Alvars, or the sixteenth century's Mirabai, who had composed over two hundred verses devoted to Krishna. Recognizing the importance of women in all religions, both Ram Mohan Roy's Brahmo Samaj and Dayananda's Arya Samaj included women's groups and invited women to take active roles in reforming Hinduism. Some twentieth-century women saints, like Anandamayi, achieved recognition among all strata of Hindu society. The still living Jnanananda Saraswathi (born 1929) daily receives and counsels hundreds of devotees—male and female—in her Gnana Advaitha Peetham, near Chennai (Madras).[48] The BJP has a "Women's Wing" and the VHP has a women's affiliate, the Durga Vahini, and many of its members have outdone the men in their zeal and activism.

From the Vedic *risis* and the Upanisadic *acaryas* to great thinkers like Sankaracarya, Hindus throughout the ages believed themselves to have a "mission." In modern times, Aurobindo Ghose and Sarvepalli Radhakrishnan have continued this tradition, persuasively recommending Hindu ideas and ideals as solutions to the problems of the contemporary world. Hindus are also convinced that their ancestors thousands of years ago had discovered the most profound laws of nature that modern science is rediscovering in the West just now. Given the pluralistic nature of Hinduism as a whole, and its tendency to split up into numerous sects, the Hindu missionary influence is multidimensional and will not likely result in large-scale conversions to a "Hindu Church," entailing a total social reorientation and integration into a doctrinally or ritually uniform organization.

Still, large numbers of Western converts seem prepared to accept Hindu monastic lifestyles, submitting to a complete change in outlook and behavior, and Hindu missions will certainly continue to affect the religious thinking and devotional spirituality of non-Hindus all over the world.

Notes

1. Traditionally, Hindu society consisted of four *varnas*, usually (incorrectly) translated as "castes": the *brahmin* or priestly caste, the *ksatriya* or warrior and ruler caste, the *vaisya* or merchant and craftsman caste, and the *sudra* or servant caste. The members of the three higher castes were entitled to receive initiation, symbolized by the sacred thread that had always to be worn. *Upanayana*. or "initiation," was considered a "second birth" and thus the members of the three higher castes were known as *dvi-jatis*, or "twice-born." The large number of Indians who for a variety of reasons found themselves excluded from these, were deemed *Ati-Sudras*, below the lowest caste and termed *asprhyas*, untouchables, association with whom would make a caste member ritually impure.
2. A series of wall paintings in the Minaksi temple at Madurai depicts the exploits of Agastya. See Dessigane, Pattabiram, and Filliozat (1960, fascicle 2, plates XXXV and XXXVI).
3. There is a tradition in India, articulated by Bhimrao Ramji Ambedkar among others, that the majority of the outcastes—about a fifth of India's population—are the descendants of former Buddhists, who were not readmitted into the Hindu fold. See, e.g., Borale (1968, 62–63) and Keer (1971, 420–424).
4. For details of this movement, see Meenakshisundaran (1965), especially chapter 5, "Alvars and Nayanmars."
5. Modern Western scholarship assigns him to the seventh century of the Common Era, but some Hindu scholars hold the opinion that he lived before the Buddha, ca. 700 BCE.
6. There is a debate about the authorship of this hagiography. The main issue seems to have to do with the purportedly mistaken identification of Anantanandagiri's *Sankara-vijaya* with a biography of Sankara by the thirteenth-century writer, Anandagiri, which no longer survives. Mahadevan himself makes this identification. On the question of authorship, see Burnell (1880, 96). Also, though there is little doubting the basic facts of the *dig-vijaya*, scholars have questioned the reliability of the text's detailing, most notably attributions of supernatural powers to Sankara. On this matter, see Wilson (1977, 14).
7. For a modern biography of Madhva, see Tapasyananda (1981), and for a study of his thought, see Sharma (1981).
8. Caitanya's encounters with representatives of other religions in southern India are described in "Madhya Lila," the second part of Kaviraja's *Caitanya-charitamrita*.
9. There had been extensive contacts between India and ancient Western cultures up to the third century of the Common Era. Large hoards of Roman coins were found on both India's west and east coasts, for example, but the Romans made no attempt to expand these trading posts into colonies or to spread Roman religion. Like the Indians, they believed in many gods and liberally adopted the deities of other cultures.
10. For an engaging presentation of Ram Mohan Roy's experiences here, see Parekh (1927).
11. On Ram Mohan Roy and the origins and history of Brahmo Samaj, see Parekh (1929) and Kopf (1979).
12. For the history of Arya Samaj, see Lajpat Rai (1991).
13. This hypothesis is not as fantastic as may appear. In a foreword to Lal's book, as great an authority as Robert Freiherr von Heine-Geldern (1885–1968), whom many regard as the

founder of modern southeast Asian ethnology, offers evidence for pre-Columbian contacts between Asia and America (Lal 1960).

14. On Khmer civilization and Ankor Wat, see Giteau (1976).
15. On Cham civilization, see Boisselier (1963) and Tran Ky Phuong (1993).
16. On Hindu beliefs and practices in Java, see Fowler, Cale, and Bartlett (1974).
17. On Hindu beliefs and practices in Bali, see Hospital (1984) and Pringle (2004).
18. For an account of the life and teachings of Vivekananda, see Sen (2000).
19. For the history and aims of the Ramakrishna Mission, see Beckerlegge (2000), and for an account of the Ramakrishna movement in the United States, see Jackson (1994).
20. For an account of the life and teachings of Kedarnatha Datta, see Dasa (1999).
21. For a recent biography of Bhaktivedanta, see Goswami (2002).
22. The story of the beginnings and of the spread of the International Society for Krishna Consciousness (ISKCON) is told in great detail by one of its earliest American members, Satsvarupa dasa Goswami (2002).
23. Every website officially associated with ISKCON lists the society's "Seven Purposes." They also appear in documents establishing the legal status of the organization and its branches in different jurisdictions around the world. See, for example, "An Act for the Incorporation of the International Society for Krishna Consciousness (ISKCON) Trinidad and Tobago Inc. and for matters incidental thereto," which the House of Representatives of the Republic of Trinidad and Tobago passed into law in 1998 (Trinidad and Tobago).
24. See, e.g., the website of Vasu Murti (http://www.all-creatures.org/murti/asource-01.html).
25. On ISKCON and interreligious dialogue, see, e.g., Acharuparambil (1996) and Klostermaier (1996).
26. In *Initiation into Yoga: An Introduction to the Spiritual Life*, Krishna Prem provides a fascinating description of his adoption of Hindu devotional life, and Madhava Ashish's foreword gives a brief account of his teacher's life. See Prem (1976). For a fuller biography of Krishna Prem, see Roy (1968).
27. See the Himalayan Academy's website (http://www.himalayanacademy.com).
28. In another vein, according to Srinivasan, Subramuniya "had a sign put up in San Francisco suggesting that tithes could be put on credit cards" (Srinivasan 2002).
29. See Mahesh Yogi (1963) for a full account of TM. For a biography of Mahesh Yogi, see Mason (1994), and for an analysis of his teaching, see Campbell (1975).
30. See, e.g., the website of the Natural Law Party in the United States, which claims to be "the fastest growing new political party in America," with quite a sophisticated "50-Point Action Plan to Revitalize America" (http://www.natural-law.org/introduction/index.html and http://www.natural-law.org/platform/50_point_summary.html).
31. For the life of Chinmayananda, see Krishnakumar (1999).
32. For an inside history of the Chinmaya Mission, see Chidananda and Ramani (2001).
33. For an inside history of the Brahmakumaris, see Hodgkinson (1999). Walliss offers a sociological analysis of the organization as a new religious movement (2002).
34. At the time of writing, the website of the Ananda Marga Universal Relief Team Ladies was under construction.
35. One controversy had to do with allegations that Ananda Marga devotees were involved in acts of terrorism from India to Australia. See, e.g., Molomby's account of the "Ananda Marga Three," who were convicted of, then pardoned for the bombing of a Commonwealth Heads of Government Regional Meeting at Sydney's Hilton Hotel, in 1978 (1986).
36. For a brief biography of Rajneesh, see Fox (2002). For a posthumously published "autobiography," ghosted from thousands of hours of recorded talks, see Osho (2000).
37. For a brief biography of Aurobindo Ghose, see Heehs (1989).
38. For a critical account of Hindu nationalism, see Bhatt (2001).

39. During a visit to Vrindavana, I received a copy of this Hindi pamphlet from Swami Muktananda, the Secretary General of the Akhila Bharatiya Sant Samiti. The pamphlet carries the title, *Akhil Bharatiya Sant Samiti ka lok-cetana abhiyan*, and has no date. The quote is the last paragraph of column 6 of the pamphlet, which consists of one folded up sheet, divided into six columns. The translation is mine.
40. According to traditional historians, Rama ruled in Ayodhya, Uttar Pradesh, about 3000 BCE. In the sixteenth century, the Mughal emperor, Babur, built a mosque, the Babri Masjid, on the site of a temple marking the birthplace of Rama. In 1990, Lal Krishna Advani persuaded fellow nationalists in the Bharatiya Janata Party (BJP), which is closely allied to the RSS, to campaign for a new Ram Mandir in Ayodhya. In 1992, RSS activists destroyed the mosque, and the party announced intentions to begin construction of the Ram Mandir in 2004.
41. For an analysis of the Rashtriya Swayamsevak Sangh, see Embree (1994).
42. For an analysis of Visva Hindu Parishad, see van der Veer (1994). See also VHP's main website (http://www.vhp.org).
43. See the websites of Shiv Sena (http://www.shivsena.org) and the Bhartiya Janata Party (http://www.bjp.org), where the former argues "that whatever may be our religion, whatever may be our form of worship, our culture is Hindu," and the latter defines Hindutva as "cultural nationalism . . . not a religious or theocratic, concept" (Shiv Sena, Bhartiya Janata Party). On controversies surrounding the Hindutva agenda, see Lochtefeld (1996) and Ludden (1996).
44. For the history of the Dalits, see Mukherjee (1988) and Deliège (1999).
45. On Ambedkar's career as a jurist, see Biswas (1993).
46. On Ambedkar and the Dalit movement, see Omvedt (1994). The late medieval Gujarati poet, Narsi Mehta, coined the name "Harijan" for the children of the *devadasis*, young women sold into temple service as dancers. These children had no legal father other than God.
47. In Hindu mythology, Sati, the wife of Dakhsha, was so overcome at the death of her husband that she cast herself onto his funeral pyre.
48. On Jnanananda's teaching, see White (1980).

CHAPTER ELEVEN

ARTICLES OF FAITH: INTERNATIONAL RELATIONS AND "MISSIONARY" SCHOLARSHIP

J. Marshall Beier

The idea of the mission evokes a host of highly mythologized images in the popular imaginary: birchwood chapels, adobe compounds, and wilderness cathedrals, all of them populated by black-robed priests dispensing the requisites of salvation. Rather less familiar as sites of missionary work are the lecterns of the contemporary university, academic journals, and the associated conduits through which Western society's most privileged knowledge is transmitted. In the first instance, none of these is typically turned to the project of enlarging the ranks of Christendom. But any such objection might suggest too limited an understanding of missionary discourse: the missionaries who have for centuries worked to spread the Gospel to the non-European world have also been vehicles for myriad other material and ideational dimensions of Western culture. Besides the Christian faith, so much else has been borne along in the material and discursive practices of the mission that it turns out to have inhabited a much more expansive terrain in the colonial encounter than is sometimes appreciated. So diverse were the functional equivalents of the pulpit in this regard that the agents of the mission happen also to have included a great many people who might not have recognized their own role in the dissemination of Western values and ways of life. It would seem, then, that a much more inclusive conception of the mission and missionary is in order—one that does not confine our gaze to the "black robes" and others who answered the messianic impulse to shepherd the souls of "savages," but which includes also the more secular practices of those who have sought converts to more mundane aspects of Western habits of mind and practice.

Understood more broadly, the mission appears less as an institution, or even a particular cadre, than as a wide assortment of acculturative practices. It is thus that it can be said to have included not only the emissaries of various Christian churches, but also the sundry agents of state and civil society who were directly involved in the making of modern individuals among the Indigenous peoples of the Americas and elsewhere. Typically, this called for the severing of traditional ties of kinship and the destruction of forms of political community based on, for example, consensus decision-making. Toward these ends, Christian missionaries and the colonial and advanced colonial state have mutually engaged in consciously conceived assimilative practices whose explicit aim has been to "civilize" "savage" peoples, in part by working to disaggregate communities and foster a decidedly liberal form of individualism.[1] To be sure, it is the state that has usually played the most conspicuous part in this, insisting upon it in deference to its own administrative and juridical needs, and not infrequently backing this up through recourse to the varied coercive means at its disposal. In this sense, social assimilation has required cultural assimilation in order that knowable individuals might be made accountable under the law, become parties to contracts, and otherwise be made compatible with the broader social fabric of the settler state.[2] Similarly, it is not at all insignificant that the propagation of Christianity has tended to turn vitally on the inculcation of faith at the level of the individual—disposition whose origins reside most famously in St. Augustine's privileging of individual over communal sin.[3] Here, then, is the foundational sense in which liberal ideologies and the mission are no strangers to one another, for each abhors the collective, valorizing individualism instead.

A particular focus of many of the essays in this volume has been to explore the budding nexus between Mission Studies, Cultural Studies, and Postcolonial Studies. The focus of this chapter, however, is rather different. Instead of considering how we might think about missions from a new disciplinary standpoint, I propose to reflect upon the missionary qualities increasingly in evidence in a discipline itself—one that has shown precious little interest in postcolonialism and none at all in missiology. In particular, I will consider the ways in which liberal-inspired scholarship in disciplinary International Relations manifests as an important component of the ideational dimension of a much larger missionary enterprise with global reach.[4] And as we shall see, there are important senses in which this phenomenon can be read as a latter-day articulation of the "white man's burden." This chapter, therefore, inquires into the ways in which (neo)liberal International Relations scholarship merges with the material textualities of globalizing neoliberalism and is articulated through hegemonic structures in ways that make it susceptible of treatment as a missionary discourse. A secondary aim is to highlight the indeterminacies inherent in this synthesis and thereby to denaturalize its central claims and commitments. Before proceeding, however, a brief introduction to disciplinary International Relations is in order.

The State of the Discipline in the Discipline of the State

There is considerable danger in presuming to speak for—or even of—one's disciplinary home. In particular, it is difficult to avoid the violence of sweeping generalizations, reducing a complex and varied intellectual terrain to a handful of claims that belie much in the way of the nuance of their own contexts. Readers who may have little or no acquaintance with International Relations are therefore cautioned that my aim here is merely to sketch some of the broad strokes of the discipline, and only to the extent necessary to enable the more particular argument briefly outlined above. Having issued this caveat, however, I venture to say that disciplinary International Relations lends more readily—and perhaps less problematically—to generalization than might be the case where other areas of academic endeavor are concerned. This readiness owes much to the fact that it is a field that might best be described as introverted, having shown very little inclination to take note of developments elsewhere in the academy, even when they might bear directly on its own subject matters.[5] Without much in the way of conceptual infusions from beyond its own disciplinary boundaries, International Relations has exhibited quite a remarkable degree of consensus about its appropriate subject matter(s) and, no less, its accepted theoretical framework(s). This assertion is not to say that "novel" empirical cases have not been treated by some scholars; nor is it to deny that feminist, post-structuralist, and other "critical" voices have been raised. But these voices have largely been relegated to the margins of the discipline, whence the important challenges they bring frequently go unheard by the "mainstream." In any event, it is significant that they remain very much what they were recognized as more than a decade ago: dissident voices.[6]

As I have argued elsewhere, one thing that can fairly be said of International Relations is that it has been overwhelmingly, even pathologically preoccupied with the state (Beier 2002). This preoccupation has much to do with the circumstance that, as reflected in the theoretical commitments that dominated it for much of the latter half of the twentieth century, the academic discipline is simultaneously a field of practical political endeavor. Founded in the aftermath of World War I, International Relations was initially characterized by a liberal-inspired faith in the building of better structures of international governance as articulated most famously in the much celebrated—and equally maligned—Fourteen Points of the United States' President Woodrow Wilson. Believing that inflexible war plans, lack of democratic accountability, and reliance upon "power balancing" through a system of shifting alliances had caused the European great powers to blunder into a war that none seemed to have wanted, early theorists of international politics argued that future wars might be avoided through proactive measures aimed at promoting peaceful interaction. Instead of simply institutionalizing conflict in deference to the preservation of an inequitable stability, then, international grievances should be taken seriously and addressed cooperatively before they could result in war. Put to the test, however, this prescriptive advice failed quite spectacularly. In particular, the League of Nations proved a monumental disappointment, and even the appeasement of Nazi Germany did nothing to prevent the outbreak of another catastrophic war in Europe. Disillusioned with its founding perspective, International Relations redirected its focus from structure to agency and embraced political realism.

The first comprehensive articulation of this new perspective came in the form of British historian Edward Hallett Carr's devastating critique of the misguided hopes and schemes of the interwar period (Carr 1940). But it was in the United States, where its best-known exponent was Hans Morgenthau, that political realism took hold and grew most dramatically. Arguing that the first generation of theorists had erred in engaging the world as it ought to be, rather than how it is, Morgenthau called for a positivist science of international politics that could generate policy-relevant advice (Morgenthau 1985, 3–17). Interestingly, however, this new "scientific" approach was founded upon an unverifiable proposition: extrapolating from Thomas Hobbes's account of life in the state of nature, political realists posited the nature of states as essentially egoistic and violence-prone. Analogous to Hobbes's state of nature, they argued, there exists an international anarchy wherein, having no global leviathan to hold them all in awe, each state must provide for its own survival in a zero-sum competition for power with all others.[7] Accordingly, they counseled that violent conflict cannot be avoided and urged not only that policymakers recognize this fact, but also that they undertake, as their highest calling, to enhance the military wherewithal of the state in order to ensure its survival. In short, in the bleak world of realist imagining, the best that can be hoped for is to "manage" conflict well enough to prevail.

This political realism played quite well in the United States at the dawn of the Cold War. It appealed to American policymakers because it provided a theoretical rationale for pursuing a more active role in world politics, and many were inclined to do just that, having found the United States to be the most powerful nation in the world in the aftermath of World War II. Generous funding of realist scholarship in the United States thus fueled an explosive growth of International Relations, quite out of all proportion with anything else in the world. As Martin Hollis and Steve Smith have noted, the result was that International Relations became overwhelmingly American and overwhelmingly realist as well (Hollis and Smith 1990, 40–41). Indeed, reflecting on these developments some years later, one prominent scholar was moved to call the field "an American social science" (Hoffman 1987). Just as significantly, an apparently good fit between political realism and the policymaking climate in the United States has given American scholars of International Relations an extraordinary degree of access to and input in the making of foreign policy. Henry Kissinger is far from alone in trying his hand at the direct formulation and administration of American foreign policy, and many other International Relations scholars have offered advice as "expert citizens." This phenomenon has both fed and been fed by a system that, in Stanley Hoffman's words, "puts academics and researchers not merely in the corridors but also in the kitchens of power" (Hoffman 1987, 12).

If political realism's emphasis on state agency and the imperative pursuit of military power seemed to many to accord well with the world of the Cold War, the years since have seen a growing sense of discontent with a perspective that seems as unduly limited as it is limiting. Challenges have come from many quarters, but ironically it is a reinvigorated liberalism that seems the most widely accepted of the contenders. Though they do not engage political realism as foundationally as, for example, critiques mounted along epistemological lines, the new liberals do raise important objections at the level of ontology. In particular, they reject the realist zero-sum account of human social interactions, opting instead for faith in positive-sum outcomes of cooperative action. And while they retain a view of the state as central to the focus of International Relations, the new liberals are increasingly keen to consider the roles played by, among others, intergovernmental organizations, transnational corporations, nongovernmental organizations, and a presumed emergent global civil society. Perhaps most importantly, their insistence on the promise of cooperation introduces the possibility of a politics imbued with the emancipatory potential of a "progress" in place of the dismal world of managed conflict given us by the political realists. Together with the influence enjoyed by International Relations scholars in certain policy circles, however, this optimism all too easily manifests itself as a messianic impulse to urge liberal values and practices upon others in order that they too might enjoy the rewards they promise. In this way, the new liberal agenda works violences of its own.

Missionary Voices, Liberal Promises

That the new liberalism has grown in popularity since the end of the Cold War seems *apropos* its unmistakably triumphalist overtones. The collapse of the Soviet bloc and the subsequent dramatic, if imperfect, spread of capitalism into its former domains appeared to many to signal the fulfillment of what might be described as something of a liberal prophecy, at least implicitly foretold at the nexus between a foundational notion of progress and an abiding faith in the superiority of market capitalism and liberal democracy over other forms of economic and political organization. The transformative events of the late-1980s and early 1990s lent spectacularly well to the view that, in sum, Western social, political, and economic forms represent the pinnacle of possible human achievement in the almost evolutionary manner of a neo-Hegelian telos. To the extent, then, that it could be claimed that the United States had "won" the Cold War, it was the triumph of liberal values that was brought into sharpest relief. Moreover, abjuring any suggestion that the present moment be taken to be a transient stage in a still unfolding process of historic change, Francis Fukuyama proclaimed the "end of history" (Fukuyama 1989). Fascism and communism having been roundly discredited, Fukuyama argued that a "post-historical" period was emergent in the West, born in the realization that there are no significant contradictions, in a Hegelian sense, in human life whose resolution resides only beyond the pale of modern liberalism (Fukuyama 1992). Accordingly, historic struggle and transformation of the sort conceived in Hegelian dialectics had at last been deprived of their motor-force.

If Fukuyama looked favorably upon what he proposed as the emergent post-historic condition of the West, he was rather less sanguine about the rest of the world: "Clearly," he lamented, "the vast bulk of the Third World remains very much mired in history, and will be a terrain of conflict for many years to come" (Fukuyama 1989, 15). True enough, the liberal foundations of his thesis necessarily bespeak the inevitability of a universal transcendence of history. But, for the time being at least, the "non-Western" world of Fukuyama's imagining remains a prisoner of its own enduring condition of historic struggle. And to the extent that this condition might bring this non-Western world into conflict with the West, there is an important sense in which the West itself is as yet unable to entirely fulfill the promise of its own supposed post-historicity. In short, lest the point be missed, the time has not yet come for swords to be beaten into ploughshares. Complementing Fukuyama, then, is Robert Kaplan's dire warning of "the coming anarchy," a gloomy narrative taking all manner of human pathology in West Africa, complicated by a strained natural environment, as prototypical of a broader trend toward the unraveling of essential social fabric (Kaplan 1994).[8] Though his account of an imminent slide into the anarchic abyss is profoundly at odds with Fukuyama's predictions, Kaplan clearly shares the view of the West as the most orderly of humanity's environs. And if there is prescriptive advice to be gleaned from his account of the future, it surely resides in the intimation that contemporary Western ways of life are such that they mitigate against this trend. Social fabric, it seems, is cut from varying grades of cloth, and in terms of the practical pursuit of the good life, it might therefore also be said that Western ways of life are superior, perhaps even more "civilized."

In the canon of Western social theory, Hobbes's "man in the state of nature," who for want of sound social arrangements of governance lives a life that is "solitary, poor, nasty, brutish, and short," embodies the essence of the savage (Hobbes 1968, 186). Indeed, Hobbes appealed directly to the most novel of Europe's contemporary others in arguing the plausibility of his account of life in the state of nature: "[T]he savage people in many places of *America*, except the government of small Families, the concord whereof dependeth on naturall lust, have no government at all; and live at this day in that brutish manner, as I said before" (Hobbes "1968," 187). Hobbes thus echoed claims already made in travelogues authored by the conquerors of the Americas, to the effect that the indigenous peoples encountered there lived under decidedly inferior forms of community, if they did not lack community altogether.[9] In similar fashion, both Fukuyama and Kaplan give us the sense that inferior social and political arrangements characterize the realms beyond the West. And neither betrays any doubt that this inferiority is at the root of whatever problems and pathologies they associate with the "non-West." At the very least, poorer social and political arrangements are identified as an obstacle to transcending these problems and pathologies. Kaplan puts it thus:

> We are entering a bifurcated world. Part of the globe is inhabited by Hegel's and Fukuyama's Last Man, healthy, well fed, and pampered by technology. The other, larger, part is inhabited by Hobbes's First Man, condemned to a life that is "poor, nasty, brutish, and short." Although both parts will be threatened by environmental stress, the Last Man will be able to master it; the First Man will not. (Kaplan 1994, 60)

It is especially noteworthy that the discursive construction of this dichotomy in terms of "First Man" and "Last Man" suggests a continuum from a primitive to an advanced condition—a disposition that implicitly advances the notion of a differential and hierarchically ordered evolutionary progress.

Of course, no discourse of savagery so framed endures long without inspiring a missionary impulse amongst those who imagine it their calling to make converts of their others. In the case of the Christian missionaries who followed the advance of Europe's colonial frontiers through the so-called Age of Discovery and beyond, the aim of spiritual salvation was served by determined efforts to implant Europe's monotheistic faith commitments in place of indigenous traditions that were regarded as paganistic. But Christianity could not simply be grafted onto everyday practices of indigenous derivation with which they were often incompatible. Consequently, "conversion" necessitated the remaking of ways of life more generally, such that a secular "civilizing" mission became one with the ecclesiastical undertaking. With specific reference to southern Africa, John L. Comaroff and Jean Comaroff have described this phenomenon as a campaign to convert the indigenous population "not just into a congregation of Protestants, but also into a modernist 'nation' of propertied, properly-embodied, right-bearing, right-minded individuals" (Comaroff and Comaroff 1997, 118). The liberal overtones of this assertion are quite unmistakable, not least in the implicit assumption of the superiority of European sociopolitical arrangements. Moreover, it fits neatly with secular measures designed, for example, to further the private empropertyment of individuals and thereby to hasten their settlement on separate plots of land. In turn, this agenda worked to entrench the household in place of larger communal formations as the primary unit of social organization, remaking in Europe's image, albeit imperfectly, everything from traditional ties of kinship to the division of labor.[10] Their pernicious effects notwithstanding, however, it is important to note that such schemes were typically altruistic in conception and born of a genuine faith in the superiority of the "civilized" life over its "savage" negative counterimage. Indeed, such was the sense of responsibility bound up in the civilizing mission that it could be constructed, even bemoaned, as "the white man's burden."

Emblematic of the civilizing mission that attended the colonial encounter, the idea of the "white man's burden" has its contemporary analogue in the founding assumptions of liberal theory and practice. Here something comparable to the dichotomy between "civilized" and "savage" can be read from an unflagging confidence in Western sociopolitical arrangements as the penultimate harbingers of "the good life." For their part, liberal-inspired International Relations theorists do not seem at all reticent about participating directly in the reproduction of this binary opposition and the discursive constructions of self and other that ultimately sustain it. And this lack of reticence represents the most fundamental sense in which this increasingly influential body of scholarship bears quite unambiguously missionary overtones.

The resurgence of democratic peace theory in the 1990s is a case in point. With its origins in Immanuel Kant's pamphlet, *Perpetual Peace* (1795), contemporary democratic peace theory holds that liberal democracies are less prone to making war than other states. For Kant, the best hopes for an enduring peace lay in the confluence of democratic accountability and a republican constitution. As regards the former, he anticipated that a moderating effect upon any contemplation of war would issue from an enfranchised citizenry who, as the bearers of the costs of war, would "weigh the matter well, before undertaking such a bad business" (Kant 1972, 122).[11] In itself, this hesitation could be expected to make democracies more inclined toward pacifism than autocratic states whose unrestrained rulers, not being similarly accountable to their people, were free to "decide on war for the most trifling reasons" (Kant 1972, 123). Of course, this reluctance for "such a bad business" also meant that democracies could not hope for emancipation from war altogether, since they would remain vulnerable to the unscrupulous predations of nondemocratic states. In their relations with each other, however, they could be expected to enjoy peaceful interaction and therefore to suffer the harmful effects of war relatively less than others. And even if, notwithstanding all of these factors, democratic states should ever be given to outwardly aggressive inclinations of their own, Kant reasoned that a republican constitution should be equally supportive of peace, since the rights enshrined therein, vindicated as natural and universal, must be guaranteed for all of humanity if their validity was to be upheld. A democratic republic, then, would be logically and morally bound by an obligation to the citizens of other states as much as to its own. In the last analysis, the notion of a "cosmopolitan right" was not only possible, in Kant's view, but inevitable as "a complement of the unwritten code of law—constitutional as well as international law—necessary for the public rights of mankind in general and thus for the realization of perpetual peace" (Kant 1972, 124).

Whatever its merit, this primarily monadic account of the elements promoting peace does not yet suggest how it is that a generalized, perpetual peace might come about. The first hints of this idea are found in Kant's discussion of important material interests that go beyond the concern of an enfranchised citizenry to avoid the costly enterprise of war wherever possible. Put simply, war is disruptive of commerce so that those who war less are likely to enjoy greater overall prosperity, having wisely harnessed their national treasure to more propitious ends. At any rate, for being more regularly at peace they will suffer less in the way of death and destruction, both of which are disruptive of industry. The advantages of a peaceful disposition, therefore, are materially tangible to a degree that should be obvious to all. And these advantages, according to Kant, manifest as a powerful general incentive to maintain the peace: "Hence, states find themselves compelled—not, it is true, exactly from motives of morality—to further the noble end of peace and to avert war, by means of mediation, whenever it threatens to break out, just as if they had made a permanent league for this purpose" (Kant 1972, 157). Of course, already finding themselves less frequently at war and being more amenable toward cooperation by virtue of their very constitutions, democratic republics should more easily accommodate themselves to this imperative. And herein resides the dyadic component of Kant's thesis: more readily avoiding war and benefiting from less dislocation and greater prosperity as a result, these democracies furnish a model for emulation by other states. Once the whole of the world has been remade in their image, a perpetual peace will reign.

Importantly, Kant explicitly rendered this prophetic vision as an evolutionary progression whose terms are ordained by nature, though not without suggesting that it might still be hastened by our own purposeful interventions:

> In this way nature guarantees the coming of perpetual peace, through the natural course of human propensities: not indeed with sufficient certainty to enable us to prophesy the future of this ideal theoretically, but yet clear enough for practical purposes. And thus this guarantee of nature makes it a duty that we should labour for this end, an end which is no mere chimera. (Kant 1972, 157)

Inasmuch as it is not imagined that democracy will flower everywhere in the same instant—it must, after all, be spread by emulation—there is a decidedly missionary flavor to this allusion to "duty." At the very least, the treatment of the democratic republic as the most advanced form of political community seems to map comfortably over the binary opposition between "civilized" and "savage" so characteristic of European colonialism.[12] And in complementary fashion, the notion of an inevitable "progress" quite unambiguously reduces communities otherwise constituted to a primitive condition ultimately to be transcended, if only through the uninspired workings of emulation. Even if we absent any impulse to actively "convert" others, then, there is an implicit claim that democratic states will by example lead other sociopolitical worlds to transform themselves.

These pretensions are no less palpable in neo-Kantian democratic peace theory. Here, too, they typically evade reflexive scrutiny, easily hardening into ontology. That is, in neo-Kantian thinking, the idea of progress and the belief in the superiority of liberal democracy seem on the verge of acceptance as truisms in their own right. Indeed, many contemporary exponents of the basic Kantian thesis have evinced a level of faith in its core claims that may have precious few parallels in the social sciences today. The renowned International Relations scholar, Jack S. Levy, for example, has ventured to say that the "absence of war between democratic states comes as close as anything we have to an empirical law in international relations" (Levy 1989, 270). Elsewhere, others have claimed that "[s]cholars of contemporary international relations are nearing consensus that democratically governed states rarely go to war with each other or even fight each other at low levels of lethal violence" (Ember, Ember, and Russett 1992, 573). Even a prominent critic of this Kantian optimism concedes that "the theory has acquired the status of a received truth" (Cohen 1994, 207). To be fair, even the most enthusiastic adherents to the thesis are usually careful to point out that the *sources* of the apparent disinclination of democracies to fight one another are not at all a settled matter. It might well be that statistical evidence can be offered in support of the democratic peace thesis but, as Steve Chan argues, this evidence varies widely, even to the extent of contradicting the thesis. The historical timeframe selected for analysis makes a difference, for example, as does the question of whether or not colonial conquest counts as war—an unresolved question that returns us to the earlier matter of what counts as a legitimate form of political community (Chan 1984). And as Cohen points out, the way in which war and democracy are themselves defined can affect the outcome of analysis (Cohen 1994).

In spite of these and other caveats and critiques, however, the democratic peace thesis has been very much in vogue since the end of the Cold War, and all the more confident in its pretensions amidst a general Western triumphalism. At the same time, its appeals to material prosperity as an impetus to the spread of the democratic peace have resonated with globalizing neoliberalism. A firm belief in liberalized trade as an important force for peace was intimately bound up in Kant's concern that rights be made to accompany the movement of people and goods across state boundaries (Kant 1972, 142, 157).[13] Contemporary liberal International Relations scholars have maintained and extended this synthesis, arguing that well-developed international trade relations result in conditions of interdependence that make war a less viable instrument of diplomacy. After all, as Bruce Russett points out, one's rational self-interest is scarcely served by bringing ruin upon a foreign land that is also a valued export market or a needed source of raw materials (Russett 1998, 374). Of course, the conditions requisite to the building of initial economic prosperity are still typically associated with liberal democracy, such that all the essentials of Kant's thesis are reproduced. Democracy enables both peace and prosperity that, in turn, secure one another. Likewise, the explicitly normative or prescriptive component of Kant's *Perpetual Peace* remains very much intact, to the extent that liberal International Relations scholars counsel purposeful efforts to promote liberal democracy where it has yet to take hold.[14] And it is important to note that it is *liberal* democracy that is the focus of the theory and theoretical inquiry, not some other form.[15] Thus, as Miyume Tanji and Stephanie Lawson point out, "[t]he idealism underlying the 'democratic peace' thesis . . . aims at the universalization of what is, at base, a culturally specific model of democracy developed in the West" (Tanji and Lawson 1997, 140).

Significantly, the "democratic peace" is also conceived as being articulated through and between territorial states. Like liberal democracy itself, contemporary expressions of the democratic peace thesis are operationalized through the state to the exclusion of other forms of political community. It is, in the first instance, the creation of a peaceful disposition within and through the singular state that makes up the monadic part of the Kantian thesis; an account of peaceful relations between states is offered up in the dyadic component. In light of the missionary impulse bound up in the democratic peace thesis, this enduring emphasis on the state repeats the assimilative violences of colonialism, sweeping aside non-Western forms of political community and participating in the ideational (re)production of that which supplanted them. Together with the essential privileging of individualism over communalism, this repetition is reminiscent of the discursive framing of the earlier "civilizing" mission exalted as the "white man's burden." Interestingly, it also signals the failure of democratic peace theorists to affect a break from political realism's preoccupation with the state—a lapse that, according to Tarak Barkawi and Mark Laffey, has greatly limited their imaginings of the possible sources of the peace they seek to explain (Barkawi and Mark Laffey 1999, 17).

As conspicuous as the similarities may be, however, more is needed if meaningful parallels are to be drawn between this liberal democratic and earlier "civilizing" missions. In particular, a consciously conceived, practical political project must be identifiable. As it happens, this sort of project is very much in evidence, too. Former United Nations Secretary General, Boutros Boutros-Ghali, for example, repeatedly linked peace to the promotion of liberal democracy and free market forms of economic development, and throughout his term in office, worked to make these commitments central to the development programming of the United Nations.[16] His successor, Kofi Annan, has been faithful to this legacy. In the United States of the 1990s, the view that democracies are peaceful strongly influenced the foreign policy of President Bill Clinton's administration, which, under the heading of "Defense," determined to "support the advance of democracy elsewhere" with the expressed purpose of "building a durable peace" (Clinton 1994).[17] As John M. Owen has put it, "[f]or the United States and the United Nations in the 1990s, liberal peace [was] taken as a law upon which foreign policy and conflict resolution may be based" (Owen 1997, 228). Official rhetoric accompanying more recent efforts to install new liberal democratic governments in Afghanistan and Iraq signals that both the United Nations and the United States administration of President George W. Bush remain committed to these principles. In these and other hegemonic structures of global governance through which it is articulated and translated into concrete political action, the democratic peace thesis has its functional equivalents of the mission.

Complementing and completing the account of "the good life" to be had from the embrace of Western political values and commitments is the economic prosperity associated with the practices and production of Western material culture. Just as the missionary diffusion of Christianity went hand in hand with the inculcation of European ways of life more generally, so too the liberal democratic faith, inextricably bound together with fidelity to free market economic principles, comes in tandem with the valorized practices of individualized consumerism. Though the material accoutrements of Western ways of life might be far from universally attainable, consumer goods ranging from fashionable garments to cellular phones—and, no less, the corporate logos they bear—are now widely recognized symbols of the comforts and conveniences of life in the affluent west. Indeed, for many non-westerners these markers of Western material culture have become virtually synonymous with the enjoyment of "the good life." At the same time, they are tangible exemplars of the rewards said to await those who would, for a time at least, suffer the dislocations and deprivations of rapid democratization and neoliberal economic restructuring. The proposition that prosperity follows from the freeing of trade and the unfettered workings of market forces has, of course, long been central to liberalism. By the latter part of the twentieth century, however, the advent of "structural adjustment policies" and a host of similar disciplining practices bound up in what Stephen Gill has termed "the new constitutionalism" had to all intents and purposes transformed this inherently normative claim from a matter of neighbourly advice to a kind of moral obligation for much of the developing world.[18] Highly fetishized, the material textualities of missionary liberalism—Western consumer goods and their attendant semiotics—manifest as a powerful discursive buttress to these practices. Thus, we see again that, in ways analogous to the promise of spiritual salvation held out by Christian missionaries, peace and prosperity are put on offer to those who are faithful to the liberal creed. Underscoring the interconnectedness of these conditions in the formulations of missionary liberalism, one commentator has gone so far as to suggest that states become peaceful toward one another when they are host to McDonalds restaurants.[19]

Conclusion: Missionary Scholarship

In the settler states of the Americas, the state itself was directly complicit in the often ruthless acculturative practices of an advanced form of the mission: the church-run residential schools that operated well past the middle of the twentieth century and whose explicit purpose was the assimilation of indigenous children. Along with measures like legal prohibitions against the practice of such key indigenous rites as the Sun Dance of the Great Plains peoples, which was banned in the United States in 1904, this particular complicity is paradigmatic of the significant role played by the state in support of the missionary enterprise. For their part, Christian missionaries were, as we have seen, directly involved in secular acculturation. In similar fashion, the institutions of Western global governance and liberal-inspired scholars of International Relations are mutually implicated in contemporary practices of missionary liberalism. While the former are most readily associated with the practical implementation and maintenance of liberal prescriptions, the latter easily harness the discursive authority of their privileged voices to the ideational dimension of the project. They are credentialed experts backed up by an abiding general faith in positive science, and they speak the voice of certain knowledge in much the same way as earlier bearers of revealed religious truth.

Contemporary liberal international theory is thus identifiable as a "missionary" discourse in several important respects. Most fundamentally, it has an essential doctrine of core propositions and ontological commitments from which it abstracts promises of material and somatic salvation. Neoliberal economic theory holds out assurances of development and prosperity and prescribes particular—and often painful—means and limitations within which to realize these ends. Likewise, democratic peace theory promises material betterment, even as it claims to foreclose the very possibility of war amongst those who would keep the liberal democratic faith. The powerful proselytizing textualities of liberal International Relations scholarship, besides being influential in policy circles, contribute to the naturalization of neoliberal political commitments. In this sense, such textualities are one with their everyday material counterparts—the global dissemination of corporate names and logos and the conflation of this phenomenon with the spread of "the good life." Indeed, this synthesis is eagerly acknowledged by liberals themselves, who regard it as strong evidence supporting the validity of their claims to the inseparability of peace and prosperity from a very particular account of progress defined by the spread of liberal democratic and *laissez-faire* market principles, even to the extent of linking peaceful international relations to the global proliferation of McDonalds restaurants. But whatever its indeterminacies, the inherent altruism of this perspective should be neither overlooked nor denied, notwithstanding that it might belie the distinctly neocolonial quality of the "new constitutionalism." Emancipatory hope resides in the idea that the evolutionary schema suggested by Fukuyama's "end of history" thesis might be purposefully manipulated so as to hasten the "advancement" of peoples apparently forgotten by "progress." The liberally inclined may thus read globalization optimistically and celebrate a soon-to-be homogenized world in which peace and prosperity should be guaranteed by shared values and interpenetrated interests.

The missionary impulse of liberal international relations theory would amount to little more than an academic curiosity, however, were it unable to find direct expression through a "mission" of its own. Institutional equivalents of the mission are discernable as liberal international theory is articulated through United States foreign policy, while the likes of the International Monetary Fund, the World Bank, and the World Trade Organization variously articulate and enforce neoliberal economic policy prescriptions by dint of which the atonement of the "developing" world is to be effected and its deliverance from deprivation and conflict assured. And what makes apt these parallels with "traditional" missions is the access to policymaking circuits enjoyed by International Relations scholars. During the Cold War, political realists in the United States were intimately involved in the making of foreign policy. Robert Keohane, a pioneering theorist of the new liberalism in International Relations, made clear two decades ago that the liberal project was no less committed to shaping political practice:

> We study world politics because we think it will determine the fate of the earth. Realism makes us aware of the odds against us. What we need to do now is to understand peaceful change by combining multi-dimensional scholarly analysis with more visionary ways of seeing the future. (Keohane 1983, 533)

Hoffman's "relays between the kitchens of power and the academic salons" remain well intact, even if the theoretical fashions in those "salons" have begun to change somewhat since the end of the Cold War (Hoffman 1987, 12). Indeed, in February 2001, the prominent liberal International Relations scholar, Michael Doyle, who specialized in teaching and research in democratic peace theory at Princeton University, was appointed Assistant Secretary General and Special Advisor to the Secretary General of the United Nations.[20] It seems that in International Relations the boundary between theory and practice is still not at all clear. Through institutional sites of "missionary" practice, the liberal discourses of academic International Relations merge with the multifarious textualities of globalizing neoliberalism, both giving shape to and reconfirming the conduct and reproduction of hegemonic political narratives. In the end, then, voices from the lectern and articles (of faith, it turns out) in scholarly journals may better exemplify the reach of missionary liberalism than—and yet are of a piece with—the appearance of a McDonalds in Moscow or Beijing.

Notes

1. On the secular dimension of this phenomenon, see, e.g., Johnson (1974). On parallel Christian missionary practices, see Craig (1997).
2. The itinerant ways of the Native peoples of the Northern Great Plains of North America, for example, had to yield to a more sedentary existence at fixed addresses before they could be made meaningfully accountable under the laws of the settler state. See Hannah (1993) and Biolsi (1995).
3. See, famously, Augustine's *Confessions* (1981).
4. Reference to "International Relations" as opposed to "international relations" is an accepted way of distinguishing between the academic discipline and its subject matters.

5. In discussing the parceling of knowledge within disciplinary boundaries more generally, Dogan has seen fit to single out International Relations as an extreme example, calling it "a quasi-independent domain" (1997, 432).
6. On dissident thought in International Studies, see Ashley and Walker (1990).
7. For Hobbes on the state of nature, see *Leviathan* (Hobbes 1968, 183–188).
8. In what he calls "a premonition of the future," Kaplan argues that "West Africa is becoming *the* symbol of worldwide demographic, environmental, and societal stress, in which criminal anarchy emerges as the real 'strategic' danger. Disease, overpopulation, unprovoked crime, scarcity of resources, refugee migrations, the increasing erosion of nation-states and international borders, and the empowerment of private armies, security firms, and international drug cartels are now most tellingly demonstrated through a West African prism. West Africa provides an appropriate introduction to the issues, often extremely unpleasant to discuss, that will soon confront our civilization" (Kaplan 1994, 46; emphasis in the original).
9. Hobbes, who had never seen the Americas for himself, could rely only on accounts borne in the travelogues of those on the leading edge of European colonialism—accounts that were deeply imbued with the enabling knowledges of conquest and settlement.
10. In the United States, e.g., the General Allotment Act (1887) sought precisely these ends in ways that were ultimately disastrous for indigenous peoples. According to Stephen Cornell, "[b]y distributing tribal lands to tribal members, assigning each allottee a tract of homestead size, and granting US citizenship to allottees, the [General Allotment] Act set out to destroy tribe as territorial, economic, and political entity" (Cornell 1988, 33).
11. Michael W. Doyle glosses Kant's assertion: "Unlike monarchs, citizens are not able to indulge their aggressive passions and have the consequences suffered by someone else" (Doyle 1993, 186).
12. Indeed, Kant makes direct recourse to this dichotomy in his "Second Definitive Article of Perpetual Peace," likening the "lawless liberty" of "savages," who, in his formulation, seem quite clearly to reside beyond the pale of reason, to the inclinations of the sovereign, whose appetites are untempered by reason and a proper sense of obligation to uphold the natural rights of the other (Kant 1972, 130–131).
13. According to W. B. Gallie, "for Kant, as much as for Adam Smith and his disciples, free movement of men and goods was an essential facet of a peaceful and civilized world" (Gallie 1978, 27).
14. See, e.g., Owen (1997, 228–229), and Russett and Oneal (2001, 282–305).
15. Owen, for example, is quite clear that the democratic peace should not be expected to emerge where democracy is illiberal (Owen 1994, 98–99). A noteworthy exception in the literature is Ember, Ember, and Russett, who do consider indigenous polities such as that of the Yanomami people of Amazonia. At the same time, though, they find this form of democracy lacking for want of what are recognizable as liberal values and institutions. Unfortunately, in support of their conclusions, Ember, Ember, and Russett rely entirely upon questionable ethnographic accounts of the peoples they discuss, without apparently being aware of more recent theoretical developments in anthropology. In particular, they depend upon Napoleon Chagnon's increasingly controversial work on the Yanomami, the veracity of which has been seriously called into question by scholars like Brian R. Ferguson (1990).
16. See, e.g., Boutros-Ghali (1992, 1995, and 1996).
17. Clinton went on to offer the full gamut of neo-Kantian promises: "Democracies don't attack each other, they make better trading partners and partners in diplomacy" (Clinton 1994).
18. According to Gill, "[t]he new constitutionalism can be defined as the political project of attempting to make transnational liberalism, and if possible liberal democratic capitalism, the sole model for future development" (Gill 1995, 412).

19. The so-called Golden Arches Theory of Conflict Prevention belongs to Thomas L. Friedman, who points out that no two counties have ever gone to war with one another after they both became "McDonalds countries," and argues that sustaining a McDonalds restaurant requires an affluent and mature middle class whose members will not wish to bear the costs of war (Friedman 1999, 195–217).
20. Doyle succeeded Harvard University's John G. Ruggie, another prominent International Relations scholar.

CHAPTER TWELVE

AFTERWORD: GLOBAL CONVERSIONS

Peter van der Veer

By definition, world religions have always been expanding over the globe and have been a major part of the formation of world civilizations. This expansion has also always been intertwined with histories of trade and conquest as well as with those of learning and education. Since 1800 religious expansion is part and parcel of the spread of modernity. Finally, in today's world it is directly connected to the contemporary process of globalization. The study of conversion and of the globalization of religion gives us an excellent vantage point from which to study these larger transformations. This opportunity has often not been sufficiently realized for reasons that are closely related to these transformations themselves. Secularist assumptions about secular progress and the decline of religion have hindered the development of an adequate understanding of the importance of religion in the modern world.

While it is hard to miss the continuities in the global history of conversion it is equally difficult to miss the breaks, discontinuities, and differences. What we call modern is certainly conceptualized as a break with the past, with tradition, and as a celebration of newness. The concept of "the modern" emphasizes simultaneously difference from the past and from that which is found outside of one's own cultural domain. These things are connected to the extent that those who are living elsewhere, outside of the West, are often conceptualized to live in the past, outside of modernity. The modern, then, is seen to have a specific location in the Western world and more specifically in the European Enlightenment and the carriers thereof. Jonathan Israel has argued that there was a radical underground European Enlightenment between 1650 and 1750 that has been generally regarded as marginal to the wider Enlightenment, but he sees that as central. In his view "the Enlightenment—European and global—not only attacked and severed the roots of traditional European culture in the sacred, magic, kinship and hierarchy, secularizing all institutions and ideas, but (intellectually and to a degree in practice) effectively demolished all legitimation of monarchy, aristocracy, woman's subordination to man, ecclesiastical authority, and slavery, replacing these with the principles of universality, equality, and democracy" (Israel 2001, vi). Whatever one may think of such a grand view of the history of the European enlightenment, it strikes us that it emphasizes a process of expansion and conversion from a radical margin within Europe. The history of modernity in Europe is a history of conversion to ideas that were once marginal and radical and, *pace* Israel's focus on a European history of ideas, that history is intimately related to the encounter with civilizations and religions elsewhere.

To study global conversion would, in my view, imply that one is aware of a field of interactions that produces modern religion as well as modern secularity in the West and elsewhere (see van der Veer 2001). If one accepts that the coming of modernity, broadly conceived, is indeed the great transformation that Israel and others think it is, then one should take into account that it is a process that is of long duration, in principle always unfinished and riddled with contradictions. The notion that an already finished, modular modernity is shipped from Europe to the rest of the world is contrary to historical evidence. In studies of encounters between Europe and the rest of the world, one often finds an opposition between an internal and an external perspective. The internal account is that there is already an internal historical process of expansion and modernization taking place that is, as it were, fulfilled by the encounter with Western modernity. One may note here the concept of "fulfillment" that is taken from Christian theology. The external account is that one finds in that encounter an imposition of modern ideas on traditional worlds and thus a conquest of the native mind by modern ways of thinking, including Christian and secular ones.

Both such accounts contain valuable elements, but one may consider studying these encounters as a set of interactions in which internality and externality are tropes in the representation of such encounters. This observation is certainly not to say that this phenomenon takes place in a harmless world outside of a history of power, but that again, the signification of power and resistance to it are so much part of the process that is studied. The histories that precede these encounters are sometimes subsumed in colonial or missionary archives and marginalized or even erased, but these cultural traditions are not powerless or fruitlessly resisting from the margins; they are quite central to world history. This centrality is immediately evident in the case of Asia, which was at the heart of the world economy until 1800 or so, and is already returning to that position in our period.

An interactional perspective has a number of implications for the study of conversion. First of all, at the highest level of generalization, we are all coeval and in the process of becoming modern. The missionaries who bring modern Christianity to the rest of the world are being converted themselves. It is certainly not the case that they carry a stagnant and moribund Christianity from a secularizing world to a still enchanted world. Surely, they are themselves experiencing the transformation of religion at home and they bring that experience to bear on their understanding of their own endeavors in their mission fields. Simultaneously their encounter with the traditions of the people they try to convert also has an impact on their understanding of their own beliefs and practices.

Second, the emergence of modern missionary activity from the late eighteenth century creates a religious public at home that supports the activity and is also transformed by it (see van Rooden 1997; see also Hofmeyer in this volume). I would argue that the rise of a muscular, imperial Christianity in Britain in the nineteenth century is directly related to the representation of missionary activity as heroic and adventurous. The site for this form of Christianity is not primarily church or chapel, but the public school and the novel (see Griffiths in this volume). At the same time the missionary project is responded to by a number of religious groups in the mission field, who are challenged by it to come up with their own modern institutions for education and social welfare. While in Britain a whole genre of pamphlet literature and popular novels depicts the heroic encounter with such native barbarisms as widow-immolation, in India a genre of apologetic literature as well as of radically anti-Christian pamphlets emerges.

Third, the simultaneous emergence of the nation-state and the colony has some significant implications for the location of religion. Modern Christianity in a number of nation-states in Europe, such as Britain and Holland—both significant recruiting grounds for missionaries—becomes nationalized. That is to say, religious differences between Protestant and Roman Catholic Christians, and between different Protestant denominations, are subsumed under the rubric of national unity toward threatening neighbors, but significantly also toward the colony. The nation-state develops a number of secular institutions that undercut the public authority and power of religious institutions. One has to see this development as a long-term process since the real decline of the public significance of religion in Britain and Holland only takes place after World War II with the rise of the welfare state. This process is obviously of great importance to the location of religion in society. Contrary to what is often assumed, religion in nineteenth-century Europe appears to become more significant in civil society in terms of the active mobilization of people, despite its decline in scientific and intellectual circles and despite the competition with secular ideologies such as liberalism and socialism. Unlike the United States, Britain and Holland do not have such a sharp separation of church and state, so this process of religious mobilization was and continues to be stronger in the former case. At the same time, we find a shift in the location of religion in the colony. A religious public sphere emerges in which a number of so-called revivalist movements mobilize people and resources for the modernization of religious traditions and especially education.

When one interprets conversion to Christianity in the modern period as a conversion to modernity, one argues, in effect, that conversion is a crucial aspect of the transformation of Christianity into a modern, global religion (see van der Veer 1997). This transformation happens not only to Christianity but also to other religions, such as Buddhism, Hinduism, and Islam. With the imperial integration of the world system Buddhism evolves into a modern, text-based religion that becomes part of the nationalist ideology of countries like Sri Lanka, Burma, and Thailand. Orientalist technologies of knowledge, deployed by philologists of the Pali Text Society and spiritualist missionaries of the Theosophical Society, are crucial in new understandings of tradition and historicity. Revivalist movements tend to oppose syncretistic folk religion in very much the same terms as Christian missionaries oppose Buddhism as essentially non-modern.

Hinduism is often seen as a natural given, growing straight from India's soil. In the premodern period, however, it has expanded into a mixture of settled agriculture, trade, and conversion, in ways similar to those of other civilizations. In the modern period, Hindu missionaries adopt the new techniques of education and social welfare that are deployed by Christian missionaries. Their view of conversion is intricately related to a nationalist politics of numbers, made possible by colonial census operations and a new system of political representation. Hindu missionaries of the Arya Samaj interpret conversion as *shuddhi*, that is, a Hindu ritual of purification of those who had been converted to "foreign" religions, such as Islam and Christianity. Continued conversion to the latter religions is interpreted as a direct threat to Hindu majoritarian dominance and violently opposed. The Arya Samaj also sends its missionaries to all the places where Indian indentured laborers are working, such as Mauritius, Fiji, South Africa, and the Caribbean. The current activities of the Vishva Hindu Parishad (World Hindu Council), targeting both non-Hindu tribal populations within India as well as the Indian diaspora, are to a considerable extent the successor to these nineteenth-century projects of Hindu nationalism (see Klostermeier in this volume).

In Africa and Asia, Islam is obviously the great rival of Christianity in attempting to win the hearts and souls of "heathen" populations. The colonial powers were constantly afraid of the threat Pan-Islamism, a supposedly anticolonial secret network centering on the Ottoman Empire, posed to their hegemony. Pan-Islamism was more a colonial anxiety than a reality, however, despite short-lived movements like the Indian Khilafat movement. Of far greater significance is that Islam developed a number of modernist as well as traditionalist movements in the nineteenth century that aimed at transforming religious tradition. Many of these movements were involved in developing new curricula both for the clergy and for the laity while embracing modern science and technology. Revivalism often took the shape of converting Muslims with syncretic practices to a more scripture-based Islam.

Other movements, like the Indian Tablighi Jama'at, originating in the 1920s, target primarily Muslim populations by inviting them to do their Muslim duties, such as daily prayer, without much emphasis on textual knowledge (see Smith in this volume). Their method of propagation of the pure faith resembles that of evangelical movements, such as the Jehovah's Witnesses or the Mormons, by going from door to door summoning people. With Islam as with Christianity we see the dialectic of the global and the national very clearly. While these movements have their origin within a certain national space and address issues of nationalism explicitly, they are at the same time involved in cosmopolitan projects enabled by histories of migration and education. As world religions they have always ideologically focused on the world as mission field, but the ideological and practical meaning of the term "world" has obviously changed significantly in the modern period.

When all these religions globalize and modernize, what happens to their traditions? Modernity is often seen as a break with religious tradition. The theory of secularization puts forward that the modern world is gradually becoming disenchanted and that religion becomes more and more insignificant in public life while it may still play a marginal role in private life. This argument can only be upheld if one maintains that West-European societies, such as Holland and Britain after World War II, are the only societies that are truly modern and that the rest of the world is becoming more and more non-modern. While such an argument would be absurd, one still needs to acknowledge that modernity implies a rupture and thus a significant transformation of religion. It is also important to see that political ideologies, such as liberalism and socialism, have emerged as significant rivals of religion in the public sphere. To some extent these ideologies can be seen as transmutations of religion. They contain a certain redemptive myth in their emphasis on progress and liberation. That myth meant that liberals and Christian missionaries joined forces in the British Empire in their project to usher in modernity and free the heathens from their superstitions. This assertion is not to say that the secular is a mask for religion, but that secular and religious ideologies have some utopian elements in common.[1]

Moreover, one has to emphasize that these modern ideologies are emerging in response to the same conditions as modern Christianity does. Certainly, liberals, socialists, fascists, and other adherents to secular ideologies have often tried to get rid of religion precisely because they are competing in the same arena, but they have been markedly unsuccessful in the long run while religion has not declined but expanded. The ideological depiction of religion as "backward," "irrational," "unscientific," "conservative," or even "reactionary" by these secular movements has led to a whole range of religious apologetics aimed at showing the full compatibility of religion with modern life and especially science. At different historical moments, however, spokesmen for various religions have pronounced against the spirit of the times, against certain secular arrangements regarding the family, sexuality, and so on and so forth. In those instances, it is not the case that religions are not fully modern, but that they answer modern questions from traditions that are different from secular traditions. It seems to me that issues of authority and representation are crucial in these approaches to tradition.

Structures of authority are central to interpretations of religion and this phenomenon is a key issue in any missionary project. The relative autonomy of local authority toward central authority is always contested and addressed by religious institutions in terms of orthodoxy. Such conflicts are always clearest in the case of the strongest central authority, such as that of the Roman Catholic Church. The famous dispute of "Chinese Rites" between the Jesuits and Rome had important effects throughout the world, notably in China and India, the largest mission fields in terms of numbers. But such conflicts arise in religions that do not have these centralized structures of authority, too. In Islam, for example, for a long period there have been strong arguments against the Sufi practice of revering saints, while such practices have clearly been crucial in conversion to Islam in many parts of the world.

Perhaps the main thing to observe here is that modern means of communication, modern arguments for literate lay audiences, and new forms of education have transformed the sites of authority and their range in significant ways. An interesting development in all these religions is that of a process of individualization in which individual belief instead of social conformism is the basis of correct religious behavior. To be a "true" Muslim is more a personal choice and a matter of internal conversion than the result of social pressure. It is here that we can understand the success of such movements as the Tablighi Jama'at, the Pentecostals, and the Visva Hindu Parishad, since they produce kinds of "born-again" Muslims, Christians, and Hindus. This development is further enhanced by the expansion of Web sites where self-appointed experts on Islamic, Christian, and Hindu thought and behavior teach their version. Here we see new spheres of communication and debate created, in which the traditional interpreters of the tradition play a diminished role. In such debates, it is not "liberal religion" that is prevalent. Rather it is the more literalist or even fundamentalist arguments that are dominant.

When imperial encounters have indeed been as fundamental to the development of modern religion in both colonies and imperial metropoles as I have argued, then decolonization has to be seen as a major shift. The independence struggle against the colonial powers had often made use of religious symbolism, religious organizations, and religious institutions to mobilize large sections of the population. At the same time, this religious mobilization tended to pit one religious community against another, especially in the context of a democratic politics of numbers. A sad example is the history of South Asia, where Hinduism and Islam, and Hinduism and Buddhism, were pitted against each other in the formation of modern nations. A major nationalist question in the former colonies was and is the assumed indigenous or foreign origin of a particular culture or religion. Christianity, a minority religion in the new nation-states of Asia, had to indigenize itself and did so quickly. In large parts of Africa and in Latin America where Christianity is a majority religion, it became a part of the core identity of the nation in the same process of nationalization of religion that occurred in large parts of Europe.

After decolonization, Christianity has become a marginal presence in the secularized public life of such European colonial metropoles as France, England, and Holland. At the same time, it continues to be a major public presence in the former colonies. One can well argue, as Philip Jenkins has done, that there is a New Christianity with its center not anymore in the North but in the South (Jenkins 2002; see also Cox in this volume). The global interactions that count today are not between colonial metropoles and colonies any more, but between the United States and the rest of the world. After decolonization, the United States has taken over the central role in the modernization of the world from the former empires. And again, religion is central to the process. While the focus in discussions of world politics is commonly on the role of the United States as bringer of democracy and liberal values—however interpreted—the role of American missionaries in the postcolonial period is often forgotten. However, it is the rise of American Fundamentalism in the postcolonial period that is of utmost significance to struggles between Roman Catholics and Protestants in Latin America, and between Christians and Muslims as well as Christians and Hindus in other parts of the world. Pentecostalism and Charismatic Roman Catholicism seem to be the answers to both the indigenization of Christianity and the new opportunities of globalization.

Many students of religion in different parts of the world have observed that world religions adapt themselves to local circumstances. Indigenization, then, is the current phase of this process of adaptation. In theological terms, local religion is understood as a *preparatio evangelica.* I think that the picture of adaptation may be too easily interpreted as one of accommodation and tolerance. First, we have here long-term histories in which the local and the global are not two static poles of an interaction, but dynamic aspects of one and the same process. In Islam, Christianity, Buddhism, and Hinduism, there is a constant pressure to develop orthodoxy and condemn aberrations as heresy. Instead of adaptation we observe constant struggle between Sunis and Shias, Sufis and Ulama, Roman Catholics and Protestants, Buddhist monks and spirit priests. These configurations bear family resemblances that cannot be subsumed within a formal Weberian model.

Second, I do not think that the current forms of indigenization are a simple continuation of the older forms of adaptation. Indigenization is often interpreted in the literature as a recapturing or revival of traditional forms of religion in which proto-scientific or simply false practices of magic and especially healing are connected to texts and textual interpretations that are discarded by modernist interpretations of the same. In Christianity, for example, references to spiritual healing and spirit exorcism that modernists consider to be backward form a bridge with local practices. The successful practices of spirit exorcism of Bishop Emmanuel Milingo of Lusaka constitute one of the best illustrations of this phenomenon; these Roman Catholic Christian rituals connected very well with witchcraft beliefs in Africa. The question of indigenization is thus a rather complex one that has to be considered in the light of the significant shift of the location of religion under modern conditions. The mean element in this shift is the rise of the authority of science and the need for liberal believers to accept the central role of science in modern life and for so-called traditionalists or fundamentalists to conceptualize the dominance of science in the modern world.

There is a philosophical tradition from David Hume to Ernst Gellner that argues that the absolutist claims of religion on knowledge made scientific progress impossible till the Enlightenment was able to discard these claims. This Enlightenment tradition has inspired the thesis of the secularization of the European mind. It goes like this: for the development of modern life it is necessary to separate the domain of techno-science from religious belief. In his celebrated essay, "Religion as a Cultural System," Clifford Geertz sees science and religion as distinct perspectives (Geertz 1973, 111–112). In his response to Geertz, Talal Asad has pointed out that from the nineteenth century onward "religion is indeed now optional in a way that science is not. Scientific practices, techniques, knowledges, permeate and create the very fibers of social life in ways that religion no longer does. In that sense, religion today is a perspective (or an 'attitude,' as Geertz sometimes calls it), but science is not" (Asad 1993, 49). The secularization thesis allows one to avoid the question of the rationality of religious belief by arguing that religion is *sui generis*. But the problem is that the effects of techno-science on daily life can never be avoided. They will therefore be addressed by religious (and other) traditions and we cannot simply dismiss these encounters as backward attempts to adjust to modern life.

If one assumes the existence of historically and culturally different traditions one has to engage the question of universal rationality. One answer to that question has been to say that there are religious forms of knowledge that give rational answers to empirical questions. This response is a traditional, relativistic argument in anthropology from Sir Edward E. Evans-Pritchard to Robin Horton. The issue here is whether the "rationality" of these answers is to be judged in terms of the traditions themselves or in terms of Western enlightened views. In the latter case, one often finds other traditions "lacking," deficient in some ways or "mixing" the new and the old, denying the creativity of religious traditions in their confrontation with techno-scientific developments. In my view, religious traditions, as long as they are a vital part of social life, respond to social developments (some of which are the result of techno-scientific progress) in their own terms. This recognition raises the problem of a certain un-translatability of distinctions (such as, for example, that of belief *versus* knowledge) that are crucial for establishing rationality in Western traditions. After Michel Foucault, many authors have argued that such questions cannot be raised without taking the relation between power and knowledge into account. Some forms of knowledge and some languages are more powerful than others, and that not only in terms of their explanatory capacity, but also in terms of their institutional contexts.

Often the sociological awareness of these institutional contexts leads to an untenable societal holism. For Jürgen Habermas, for instance, the project of Enlightenment entails that the rationality of science and universal morality replaces religion in the organization of everyday life. He rejects the celebration of fragmentation in postmodernism and sees the modernist project of the Enlightenment to restore some kind of unity as incomplete. "In sum," writes Habermas with prophetic confidence, "the project of modernity has not yet been fulfilled" (Habermas 1981, 12).[2] The notion that religion signified the unity and totality of life before modernity seems to me a stereotypical, romantic representation of the holism of "premodern" life. It fits a sociological approach to society, as found in structural-functionalism, which sees society as a system with subsystems. Sociological (and political) discourse about integration and about norms and values that hold a society together belong to this way of thinking. In my view, we should approach social phenomena and historical change from the standpoint of the history of power relations, with an emphasis on the production of knowledge by movements and institutions. Then it seems clear that science and technology, as produced in universities and industries, have become very powerful in producing knowledge that affects people's lives, and that churches and religious movements have no role anymore in the production of this kind of knowledge. This would imply that they can continue to be creative forces in shaping social life and creating religious dispositions, including responses to scientific and technological changes, but that they are no longer the institutional sites for the creation of such changes. While this view definitely indicates the marginalization of religious institutions in the production of important knowledge, it does not imply a marginalization in social and political life.

Let me illustrate this position with the development of science and Christianity in contemporary American society. There is no doubt that the research institutions in the United States are major sites of the production of scientific and technological knowledge in the contemporary world. At the same time, a Gallup poll in the mid-1970s showed that over one-third of adult Americans (50 million Americans) described themselves as "born-again," that is, as having experienced "a turning point in your life . . . when you committed yourself to Jesus Christ and felt that the Bible is the actual Word of God and is to be taken literally, word for word" (Harding 2000, 19). Do these two facts—scientific productivity and religious fundamentalism—conflict as aspects of one society? No, they do not, except for the debate about creationism and evolutionism, which is marginal to most science. Even the fact that so many Americans are biblical literalists does not seem to affect their participation in the scientific and technological activities in their society. Does this imply that there is a separation of spheres that are relatively autonomous? Only in the sense that laboratories and churches are different sites of the production of knowledge and that these knowledge have different effects, but not in the sense that they can be reified as separate spheres.

The relative irrelevance of science for religious doctrine and *vice versa* does not marginalize the public role of religious institutions and movements in the United States. Jerry Falwell's Moral Majority was perhaps the most important political movement in the United States in the 1980s. The support it gave to the military–industrial complex in its Christian patriotism has been of crucial importance to the funding of scientific research for military purposes and that includes the development of the Internet. The development of the new Interactive Computer Technology (ICT) has been and will be overwhelmingly dependent on military research. Moreover, the Moral Majority made ample use of technological advances in communication and consumption (telemarketing, television, theme parks, and so on and so forth) to broadcast their message about the literal truth of the Bible. This trend continues in the 1990s with the full use of the new ICT by these movements. What is particularly striking is the extent to which these movements occupy the same terrain as secular humanist movements, with a similar flexibility and versatility. They are not outside modernity, but fully part of it.

One of the terrains in the encounter of religion and science in the colony is that of the indigenization of science. Major attempts are made to show that the project of science is in direct continuity with that of religion. While this trend becomes quite central in a colonial and imperial domain like India, it is always available in the margins of the British metropole in movements like Theosophy. The power of science is such that it has to be embraced and people are quite eager to do so, but not without challenging the notion that science is a Western way of thinking and intricately connected with Christianity. The missionary encounter takes place precisely in this field, since the major tool of conversion is education. Since missionary education is the best avenue for social mobility, there is often not much choice for aspiring groups who want to participate in the emerging world of science and technology. Missionary education, however, raises the issue of religious textuality in all sorts of ways, from the teaching of the Bible to the teaching of English literature, sometimes under quite controversial conditions (see Scott in this volume). The modern transformation of Hinduism, Buddhism, and Islam is directly related to the influence of Orientalist philology and the rise of new understandings of history and questions of origin.

Another terrain of the encounter between religion and science is that of magic (Meyer and Pels 2003). More than religion, magic is science's Other, "a spurious science," to use Sir James Frazer's words. In the modern period, missionaries of the various world religions have been very much involved in trying to purge religions from magic. With Max Weber they have understood the modern transformation as an *Entzauberung*, a disenchantment of the world, not as an *Entgötterung*, a decline of religion. This evolutionist optimism, however, has to be tempered with several considerations. First of all, what is science and what is pseudoscience is not so clear. For instance in Frazer's own period, Charles Darwin's cofounder of evolution theory in biology, Alfred Wallace, was a keen occultist experimenter, as were many of his contemporaries. One can perhaps accept Bruno Latour's observation that the history of science is a continuous purification of magical creativity and experimentation. What was valid once becomes superstition later.

Second, it seems to be a psychological truism that what one pushes out vehemently comes back to haunt you. In her study of the Ewe in Ghana, Birgit Meyer shows that it is the assault on African traditional spirits and witchcraft by German Protestant missionaries that gives an enhanced power to the devil among the converted. In another way, it can be argued that extreme bureaucratic rationalization in Germany, Europe's most modern state before World War II, enabled a genocidal witch hunt that has no parallel in world history. And third, modernity creates its own magic, especially in the sphere of commodity fetishism, as Marx saw very clearly. The way in which global capital mystifies and hides social relations of production creates, in Marx's view, a form of false consciousness, and again, this phenomenon represents a dark side of modernity. If one focuses more on patterns of consumption, the phantasmagoric identification with a world of things appears as magical as the cargo cults of Oceania. The huge shifts and crises in the world economy also produce uncertainties that are addressed in various ways by business gurus and lotteries, rather than by a science of economics that fails to predict.

In conclusion, I want to propose that world religions are at large in a way that they have never been before. There are a modern Christianity, a modern Islam, a modern Hinduism, and a modern Buddhism that are almost unrecognizable if one were to look at any of these developments from the viewpoint of someone in the eighteenth century. Today, these religions are clear continuations of their nineteenth-century predecessors, but they belong to a postcolonial world with different centers and peripheries, different forms of migration and communication, different forms of representation. They continue to be vital aspects of contemporary life, whether secular intellectuals like it or not.

Notes

1. See also Talal Asad on this point (Asad 2003, 22).
2. For a response to Habermas, see Lyotard (1983, 71–82).

BIBLIOGRAPHY

About him: A short biography of Dr. Abu Ameenah Bilal Philips. Islamic Online University. http://www.bilalphilips.com/abouthim/bio_summ.htm.

Acharuparambil, Daniel. 1996. Hinduism in interreligious dialogue. *ISKCON Communications Journal* 4.1. http://www.iskcon.com/icj/4_1/acharu.html#top.

Adams, Ron. 1984. *In the land of strangers: a century of European contact with Tanna, 1774–1874.* Canberra: Australian National University Press.

African Tidings. No. 64, January 1885. Universities Mission to Central Africa Archives. London: Rhodes House Library.

Agur, C. M. 1903. *Church history of Travancore*. Madras: E. Masillamani.

Akhtar, Shaheen. 1999. Introducing Islam in Massachusetts. *Islamic Horizons*. January/February: 32–33.

al-Deen, Thaufeer. 1999. The popular mystery novel *Da'wah. Islamic Horizons* July/August 1999: 47–48.

Al Hannah Islamic Clothing. http://www.alhannah.com.

Alison, Sir Archibald. 1833–1842. *History of Europe during the French Revolution*. 10 vols. Edinburgh: William Blackwood; London T. Cadell.

American Board of Commissioners for Foreign Missions. Rufus Anderson to the Zulu Mission, June 16, 1842. Section 2.1.1, vol. V, Archives of the American Board of Commissioners for Foreign Missions. Houghton Library, Harvard University.

American Board of Commissioners for Foreign Missions. Lewis Grout to Rufus Anderson, April 16, 1847. Section 15.4, vol. V, Archives of the American Board of Commissioners for Foreign Missions. Houghton Library, Harvard University.

American Board of Commissioners for Foreign Missions. James Churchill Bryant to Rufus Anderson, May 10, 1849. Section 15.4, vol. IV, Archives of the American Board of Commissioners for Foreign Missions. Houghton Library, Harvard University.

American Board of Commissioners for Foreign Missions. General letter for 1850. Section 15.4, vol. IV, Archives of the American Board of Commissioners for Foreign Missions. Houghton Library, Harvard University.

American Board of Commissioners for Foreign Missions. William Ireland, Annual report of Ifumi for the year ended June 1856. Section 15.4, vol. IV, Archives of the American Board of Commissioners for Foreign Missions. Houghton Library, Harvard University.

American Board of Commissioners for Foreign Missions. Andrew Abraham to Rufus Anderson, October 25, 1859. Section 15.4, vol. V, Archives of the American Board of Commissioners for Foreign Missions. Houghton Library, Harvard University.

American Board of Commissioners for Foreign Missions. Umvoti annual report for the year ended May 18, 1864. Section 15.4, vol. VI, Archives of the American Board of Commissioners for Foreign Missions. Houghton Library, Harvard University.

American Board of Commissioners for Foreign Missions. Josiah Tyler to Rufus Anderson, September 30, 1864. Section 15.4, vol. VII, Archives of the American Board of Commissioners for Foreign Missions. Houghton Library, Harvard University.

American Board of Commissioners for Foreign Missions. Annual report to secretary N. G. Clark, June 7, 1867. Section 15.4, vol. VI, Archives of the American Board of Commissioners for Foreign Missions. Houghton Library, Harvard University.

American Board of Commissioners for Foreign Missions. Josiah Tyler to N. G. Clark, December 4, 1868. Section 15.4, vol. VII, Archives of the American Board of Commissioners for Foreign Missions. Houghton Library, Harvard University.

American Board of Commissioners for Foreign Missions. M. Pinkerton to N. G. Clark, January 6, 1873. Section 15.4, vol. VIII, Archives of the American Board of Commissioners for Foreign Missions. Houghton Library, Harvard University.

American Board of Commissioners for Foreign Missions. D. Rood to N. G. Clark, November 10, 1876. Section ABC: 15.4, vol. VIII, Archives of the American Board of Commissioners for Foreign Missions. Houghton Library, Harvard University.

American Board of Commissioners for Foreign Missions. Annual letter for 1880. Section 15.4, vol. VIII, Archives of the American Board of Commissioners for Foreign Missions. Houghton Library, Harvard University.

American Board of Commissioners for Foreign Missions. Minutes of annual meeting of the American Zulu Mission, June–July 1890. Section 15.4, vol. XIV, Archives of the American Board of Commissioners for Foreign Missions. Houghton Library, Harvard University.

American Zulu Mission. Minutes of mission meetings, September 14, 1864. Case 1, 1/1/2, Papers of the American Zulu Mission. Natal Archives, Petermaritzburg.

American Zulu Mission. Minutes of a mission meeting, Durban, January 25, 1865. Case 1, 1/1/4, Papers of the American Zulu Mission. Natal Archives, Petermaritzburg.

American Zulu Mission. Minutes of a mission meeting, May 31, 1865. Case 1, 1/1/4, Papers of the American Zulu Mission. Natal Archives, Petermaritzburg.

American Zulu Mission. Minutes of a general meeting of the mission, February 13, 1867. Case 1, 1/1/4, Papers of the American Zulu Mission. Natal Archives, Petermaritzburg.

American Zulu Mission. Paper read before the mission by Gertrude Rachel Hance, December 1880. Case 12, 111/3/1, Papers of the American Zulu Mission. Natal Archives, Petermaritzburg.

Ananda Marga Universal Relief Team [AMURT]. http://www.amurt.net/homepage/index.html.

Ananda Marga Universal Relief Team Ladies [AMURTEL]. http://www.amurtel.org/.

Ananda Marga. http://www.anandamarga.org/nh.htm.

Anderson, Patricia J. 1991. *The printed image and the transformation of popular culture, 1790–1860*. Oxford: Clarendon.

"Anon." 1892. The Indians of western Canada. *The Colonist* 6.10: 2.

Anthony, E. A. n.d. *The buried Bible and the conversion of England to Christianity*. London: London Missionary Society.

Armstrong, Jeannette. 1998. The disempowerment of First North American Native peoples and empowerment through their writing. In Daniel David Moses and Terry Goldie, eds. *An anthology of Canadian native literature in english*. 2nd edn. 239–242. Toronto: Oxford University Press.

Arnold, Thomas K. 1839. *Henry's first Latin book*. London: J. G. & F. Rivington.

Arnstein, Walter L. 2001. *Britain yesterday and today, 1830 to the present*. 8th edn. Boston, MA: Houghton Mifflin.

Asad, Talal. 1993. *Genealogies of religion*. Baltimor, MQ: Johns Hopkins University Press.

Asad, Talal. 2003. *Formations of the secular: Christianity, Islam, modernity*. Palo Alto: Stanford University Press.

Ashcroft, Bill, Gareth Griffiths, and Helen Tiffin. 1989. *The empire writes back: Theory and practice in post-colonial literatures*. London: Routledge.

Ashley, Richard K. and R. B. J. Walker. 1990. Speaking the language of exile: Dissident thought in international studies. *International Studies Quarterly* 34.3: 259–268.

Augustine of Hippo. 1981 [1961]. *Confessions.* Trans. R. S. Pine-Coffin. Harmondsworth: Penguin Books.

Aurobindo, Sri. 2002 [1909]. Uttarpara speech. *Splendour [sic].* http://www.splendourindia.org/splen_aug2002/uttarpara.htm.

Badawi, Jamal. Bridge Building between Christian and Muslim. IslamiCity Mosque. http://islam.org/Mosque/Bridge.htm.

Badrinath, Chaturvedi. 1993. *Dharma, India and the world order: Twenty-one essays.* Edinburgh: St. Andrew's Press.

Barkawi, Tarak and Mark Laffey. 1999. The imperial peace: Democracy, force and globalization. *European Journal of International Relations* 5.4: 403–434.

Barman, Jean, Yvonne Hébert, and Don McCaskill. 1986. The legacy of the past: An overview. In Jean Barman, Yvonne Hébert, and Don McCaskill, eds. *Indian education in Canada, Volume 1: The legacy.* 1–22. Vancouver: University of British Columbia Press.

Barrett, David, ed. 1982. *World Christian encyclopedia: A comparative survey of churches and religions in the modern world, A.D. 1900–2000.* Nairobi; New York: Oxford University Press.

Barrett, David, George T. Kurian, and Todd M. Johnson, eds. 2001. *World Christian encyclopedia: A comparative survey of churches and religions in the modern world.* New York and Oxford: Oxford University Press.

Barrett, William, ed. 1956. *Zen Buddhism: Selected writings of D. T. Suzuki.* New York: Doubleday and Company.

Barringer, Tim and Tom Flynn, eds. 1998. *Colonialism and the object: Empire, material culture and the museum.* London and New York: Routledge.

Basu, Baman Das. 1923. *Rise of the Christian power in India.* 5 vols. Calcutta: M. C. Sarkar.

Batchelor, Stephen. 1994. *The awakening of the west: The encounter of Buddhism and western culture.* Berkeley, CA: Parallax.

Baumann, Martin. 2002. Buddhism in Europe: Past, present, prospects. In Charles S. Prebish and Martin Baumann, eds. *Westward dharma: Buddhism beyond Asia.* 85–105. Berkeley, CA: University of California Press.

Baxter, Richard. 1994 [1650]. In Christopher Pipe, ed. *The saints' everlasting rest [or, A treatise of the blessed state of the saints in their enjoyment of God in glory: Wherein is shewed its excellency and certainty, the misery of those that lose it, the way to attain it, and the assurance of it, and how to live in the continual delightful foretastes of it, by the help of meditation: Written by the author for his own use].* London: Hodder and Stoughton.

Bayly, Susan. 1989. *Saints, goddesses and kings: Muslims and Christians in south Indian society, 1700–1900.* Cambridge: Cambridge University Press.

Bebbington, David W. 1982. *The nonconformist conscience: Chapel and politics, 1870–1912.* Boston, MA: Allen & Unwin.

Bebbington, David W. 1989. *Evangelicalism in modern Britain: A history from the 1730s to the 1980s.* London: Unwin Hyman.

Beckerlegge, Gwilym. 2000. *The Ramakrishna Mission: The making of a modern Hindu movement.* Delhi: Oxford University Press.

Beidelman, Thomas O. 1982. *Colonial evangelism: A socio-historical study of an East African mission at the grassroots.* Bloomington: Indiana University Press.

Beier, J. Marshall. 2002. Beyond hegemonic state(ment)s of nature: Indigenous knowledge and non-state possibilities in international relations. In Geeta Chowdhry and Sheila Nair, eds. *Power, postcolonialism and international relations: Reading race, gender and class.* 82–114. London: Routledge.

Berlin Missionary Society. 1866. *Berliner missionsberichte* 27: 51–52.

Berlin Missionary Society. 1880. *Berliner jahresbericht der gesellschaft* 27–29.

Bhabha, Homi K. 1985. Signs taken for wonders: Questions of ambivalence and authority under a tree outside Delhi, May 1817. *Critical Inquiry* 12: 144–165.

Bhabha, Homi K. 1994. *The location of culture*. New York: Routledge.

Bhagavad Gita: A new translation. 2000. Trans. Stephen Mitchell. London: Rider.

Bhaktivedanta, Swami Prabhupada. 1970. *The nectar of devotion: A summary study of Srila Rupa Goswami's bhakti-rasamrta-sindhu*. New York: Bhaktivedanta Book Trust.

Bhartiya Janata Party. BJP philosophy: Hindutva (cultural nationalism). http://www.bjp.org/philo.htm.

Bhartiya Janata Party. http://www.bjp.org.

Bhatt, Chetan. 2001. *Hindu nationalism: Origins, ideologies and modern myths*. New York: Oxford University Press.

Biolsi, Thomas. 1995. The birth of the reservation: Making the modern individual among the Lakota. *American Ethnologist* 22.1: 28–53.

Birrell, C. M. 1874. Bunyan's personal pilgrimage. In William Howie Wylie, ed. *The book of the Bunyan Festival; a complete record of the proceedings at the unveiling of the statue given by his grace, the Duke of Bedford, June 10, 1874, with an historical sketch by the Rev. J. Brown*. 79–109. London: James Clarke & Co.

Biswas, A. R. 1993. Dr. B. R. Ambedkar, the jurist of modern India. In K. N. Kadam, ed. *Dr. B. R. Ambedkar: The emancipator of the oppressed*. 20–79. Bombay: Popular Prakashan.

Blair, Hugh. 1783. *Lectures on rhetoric and belles lettres*. 2 vols. London: W. Strahan; T. Cadell.

Blanchot, Maurice. 1973. *The step not beyond*. Trans. Lycett Nelvon. New York: State University of New York Press.

Boisselier, Jean. 1963. *La statuaire du Champa: Recherches sur les Cultes et l'Iconographie*. Paris: Adrien-Maisonneuve.

Bokwe, John Knox. n.d. *Ntsikana: The story of an African hymn*. Lovedale: Lovedale Press.

Bolton, Geoffrey. 1981. *Spoils and spoilers: Australians make their environment, 1788–1980*. Sydney: George Allen & Unwin.

Bompas, William Carpenter. 1888. *Diocese of the Mackenzie River*. London: SPCK.

Bonnemaison, Joel. 1994. *The tree and the canoe: History and ethnogeography of Tanna*. Honolulu: University of Hawai'i Press.

Borale, P. T. 1968. *Segregation and desegregation in India: A socio-legal study*. Bombay: Manaktalas.

Bos, Gerrit. 1993. The *Miswak*, an aspect of dental care in Islam. *Medical History* 37: 68–79.

Boutros-Ghali, Boutros. 1992. *An agenda for peace: Preventive diplomacy, peacemaking and peace-keeping*. New York: United Nations.

Boutros-Ghali, Boutros. 1995. *An agenda for development, 1995; with related United Nations documents*. New York: United Nations Department of Public Information.

Boutros-Ghali, Boutros. 1996. *An agenda for democratization*. New York: United Nations Department of Public Information.

Brahmakumaris World Spiritual University. http://www.brahmakumaris.org.in/home.htm.

Brewer, Ebenezer Cobham. 1848. *A guide to the scientific knowledge of things familiar*. London: Jarrold & Sons.

Bristow, Joseph. 1991. *Empire boys: Adventures in a man's world*, London: HarperCollins.

Brontë, Charlotte. 1981 [1847]. *Jane Eyre*. New York: Bantam Books.

Brookes, Edgar and Colin de B. Webb. 1965. *History of Natal*. Pietermaritzburg: University of Natal Press.

Brown, Callum G. 2001. *The death of Christian Britain: Understanding secularisation 1800–2000*. London and New York: Routledge.

Brown, John. 1900. *John Bunyan: His life, times and work*. London: Isbister.

Bryant, Alfred T. 1929. *Olden times in Zululand and Natal: Containing earlier political history of the Eastern-Ng̃uni clans, etc*. London: Longmans & Co.

Budden, Harry Douglas. 1923. *The story of Marsh Street Congregational church, Walthamstow*. Margate: Bobby & Co.

Bunyan, John. 1823 [1678, 1684]. *The pilgrim's progress*. Plymouth: J. Bennett.

Bunyan, John. n.d. (a) [1678, 1684]. *The pilgrim's progress*. London: Religious Tract Society.

Bunyan, John. n.d. (b) [1678, 1684]. *The pilgrim's progress*. London: Stirling Tract Enterprise.

Bunyan, John. 1776 [1678, 1684]. *The pilgrim's progress*. Part 1. London: W. Oliver.

Burnell, Arthur C. 1880. *A classified index to the Sanskrit mss. in the palace at Tanjore*. London: Trubnor.

Burton, Antoinette M. 1994. *Burdens of history: British feminists, Indian women, and imperial culture, 1865–1915*. Chapel Hill: University of North Carolina.

California Vipassana Center. http://www.mahavana.dhamma.org.

Campbell, Anthony. 1975. *The mechanics of enlightenment: An examination of the teaching of Maharishi Mahesh Yogi*. London. Gollancz.

Campbell, James. 1995. *Songs of Zion: The African Methodist Episcopal Church in the United States and South Africa*. Oxford: Oxford University Press.

Campbell, John. 1842. *The martyr of Erromanga, or, the philosophy of mission, illustrated from the labours, death, and character of the late Revd. John Williams*. London: John Snow.

Carey, William. 1792. *An enquiry into the obligations of Christians, to use means for the conversion of the heathens in which the religious state of the different nations of the world, the success of former undertakings, and the practicability of further undertakings, are considered*. Leicester: Printed by Ann Ireland.

Carr, Edward Hallett. 1940. *The twenty years' crisis, 1919–1939: An introduction to the study of international relations*. London: Macmillan.

Carter, Paul. 1988. *The road to Botany Bay: An exploration of landscape and history*. New York: Knopf.

Carter, Sarah. 1990. *Lost harvests: Prairie Indian reserve farmers and government policy*. Montreal and Kingston: McGill-Queen's University Press.

Chakrabarty, Dipesh. 1992. Post-coloniality and the artifice of history: Who speaks for "Indian" pasts? *Representations* 37: 1–26.

Chan, Steve. 1984. Mirror, mirror on the wall . . . Are the freer countries more pacific? *Journal of Conflict Resolution* 28.4: 617–648.

Chidananda, Swami and Rukmani Ramani. 2001. *The call of the conch: The history of the Chinmaya movement*. Mumbai: Central Chinmaya Mission Trust.

Chinmaya Mission San Jose. http://www.chinmaya-sanjose.org.

Chowgule, Ashok. 1999. *Christianity in India: The Hindutva perspective*. Mumbai: Hindu Vivek Kendra.

Church Missionary Society. 1860. *Church Missionary Gleaner*. London: Seeley.

Church Missionary Society. 1866. *Church Missionary Gleaner*. London: Seeley.

Church Missionary Society. 1899. *Proceedings of the Church Missionary Society for 1898–1899*. London: C[hurch] M[issionary] S[ociety] House.

Clinton, William Jefferson. 1994. 2nd state of the union address to congress, January 25, 1994. The American Presidency. University of California, Santa Barbara. http://www.polsci.ucsb.edu/projects/presproject/idgrant/sou_pages/clinton2su.html.

Cnattingius, Hans. 1952. *Bishops and societies: A study of Anglican colonial and missionary expansion, 1698–1850*. London: SPCK.

Cohen, Raymond. 1994. Pacific unions: A reappraisal of the theory that democracies do not go to war with each other. *Review of International Studies* 20.3: 207–223.

Cohn, Bernard S. 1996. *Colonialism and its forms of knowledge: The British in India*. Princeton, NJ: Princeton University Press.

Coke, Thomas. 1808–1811 [1971]. *A history of the West Indies, containing the natural, civil, and ecclesiastical history of each island; with an account of the missions instituted in those islands, from the commencement of their civilization; but more especially of the missions which have been established in that archipelago by the society late in connexion with the Rev. John Wesley*. London: F. Cass.

Coleman, James William. 2001. *The new Buddhism: The Western transformation of an ancient tradition*. New York: Oxford University Press.

Colenso, Bishop John William to Theophilus Shepstone, 5 March 1868. Colenso Papers. Killie Campbell Africana Library. Durban.

Collini, Stephan. 1999. Grievance studies: How not to do cultural criticism. *In English pasts: Essays in history and culture*. 252–268. Oxford: Oxford University Press.

Comaroff, Jean and John. 1991. *Of revelation and revolution. Vol. 1: Christianity, colonialism, and consciousness in South Africa*. Chicago, IL: University of Chicago Press.

Comaroff, John L. and Jean. 1997. *Of revelation and revolution: Christianity, colonialism, and consciousness in South Africa. Vol. 2: The dialectics of modernity on a South African frontier*. Chicago, IL: University of Chicago Press.

Cone, James H. 1991. *Martin & Malcolm & America: A dream or a nightmare*. Maryknoll, NY: Orbis Books.

Coombes, A. E. 1994. *Re-inventing Africa: Museums, material culture and the popular imagination*. New Haven, CT: Yale University Press.

Cooper, Frederick and Ann Laura Stoler, eds. 1997. *Tensions of empire: Colonial cultures in a bourgeois world*. Berkeley, CA: University of California Press.

Copley, Antony. 1997. *Religions in conflict: Ideology, cultural contact and conversion in late-colonial India*. Delhi: Oxford University Press.

Cornell, Stephen. 1988. The transformations of tribe: Organization and self-concept in Native American ethnicities. *Ethnic and Racial Studies* 11.1: 27–47.

Cowell, E. B. and A. E. Gough, trans. 1961 [1904]. *The Sarvadarsanasamgraha of Madhavacharya*. Varanasi: Chowkhamba Sanskrit Series Office.

Cox, Jeffrey. 1997. Religion and imperial power in nineteenth-century Britain. In Richard Helmstadter, ed. *Freedom and religion in the nineteenth century*. 339–372. Stanford, CA: Stanford University Press.

Craig, Robert. 1997. Christianity and empire: A case study of American Protestant colonialism and Native Americans. *American Indian Culture and Research Journal* 21.2: 1–41.

Crosby, Alfred W. 1986. *Ecological imperialism: The biological expansion of Europe, 900–1900*. Cambridge: Cambridge University Press.

Cutt, Margaret Nancy. 1979. *Ministering angels: A study of nineteenth-century evangelical writing for children*. Wormley: Five Owls Press.

Dalitstan. *Dalit Voice*. Fortnightly. Bangalore. http://www.dalitstan.org/voice.

Darian-Smith, Kate, Liz Gunner, and Sarah Nuttall, eds. 1996. *Text, theory, space: Land, literature, and history in South Africa and Australia*. London: Routledge.

Dasa, Shukavak N. 1999. *Hindu encounter with modernity: Kedarnath Datta Bhaktivinoda, Vaishnava Theologian*. Los Angeles, CA: Sri Publications.

Davin, Nicholas Flood. 1879. *Report on industrial schools for Indians and half-breeds*. Ottawa: n.p.

DawaNet. http://www.dawanet.com.

Daws, Gavan. 1980. *A dream of islands*. New York: W.W. Norton & Co.

Dayananda Sarasvati. 1960. *The light of truth: English translation of Swami Dayananda's* Satyartha prakasha. Trans. Ganga Prasad Upadhyaya. Allahabad: Kala Press.

de Alwis, Malathi. 1997. The production and embodiment of respectability: Gendered demeanors in colonial Ceylon. In Michael Roberts, ed. *Sri Lanka: Collective identities revisited*. Vol. 1: 105–143. Colombo: Marga Institute (Sri Lanka Center for Development Studies).

Deliège, Robert. 1999. *The untouchables of India*. Trans. Nora Scott. Oxford: Berg.

Dening, Greg. 1991. A poetic for histories, transformations that present the past. In Aletta Biersack, ed. *Clio in oceania: Toward a historical anthropology*. 347–380. Washington, DC: Smithsonian Institution Press.

de Santis, Solange. 2003. Church reacts to native boycott. *Anglican Journal*. http://anglicanjournal.com/129/05/canada01.html.

Dessigane, R., P. Z. Pattabiram, and Jean Filliozat, eds. 1960. *La légende des jeux de Civa à Madurai: D'après les textes et les peintures*. Pondicherry: Institut français d'indologie.

DharmaNet's Zen Buddhist InfoWeb. http://www.dharmanet.org/infowebz.html.

Diamond Way Buddhist Centers-USA. http://www.diamondway.org.

Dickens, Charles. 1853. *Bleak House*. London: Bradbury.

Dirks, Nicholas B. 1988. *The hollow crown: Ethnohistory of a little kingdom in south India*. Cambridge: Cambridge University Press.

Dirks, Nicholas B. 1996. The conversion of caste: Location, translation, and appropriation. In Peter van der Veer, ed. *Conversion to modernities: The globalization of Christianity*, 115–136. New York: Routledge.

Doddridge, Philip. 1847 [1745]. *The rise and progress of religion in the soul: Illustrated in a course of serious and practical addresses suited to persons of every character and circumstance: With a devout meditation, or prayer, added to each chapter*. Edinburgh, London: Thomas Nelson.

Dogan, Mattei. 1997. The new social sciences: Cracks in the disciplinary walls. *International Social Science Journal* 49.3: 429–443.

Doyle, Michael W. 1993. Liberalism and international relations. In Ronald Beiner and William James Booth, eds. *Kant and political philosophy: The contemporary legacy*. 173–203. New Haven, CT: Yale University Press.

Eliade, Mircea. 1959. *The sacred and the profane: The nature of religion*. Trans. Willard R. Trask. New York: Harcourt, Brace Jovanovitch.

Elliot, Elisabeth. 1987. *A chance to die: The life and legacy of Amy Carmichael*. Grand Rapids, MI: Fleming H. Revell.

Elliott, William. 1895. A Random visit to Coqualeetza (Indian) Institute. *The Missionary Outlook* September, 135.

Ellis, William. 1838. *History of Madagascar*. 2 vols. London: Fisher.

Ellis, William. 1870. *The Martyr Church: A narrative of the introduction, progress and triumph of Christianity in Madagascar*. London: John Snow.

Ellis, William. 1876. *Faithful unto death: The story of the founding and preservation of the martyr church of Madagascar*. London: John Snow.

Ember, Carol R., Melvin Ember, and Bruce Russett. 1992. Peace between participatory polities: A cross-cultural test of the "democracies rarely fight each other" hypothesis. *World Politics* 44.4: 573–599.

Embree, Ainslie T. 1994. The function of the Rashtriya Swayamsevak Sangh: To define the Hindu nation. In Martin E. Many and R. Scott Appleby, eds. *Accounting for Fundamentalisms: The dynamic character of movements*. 617–652. Chicago, IL: University of Chicago Press.

Esherick, Joseph. 1987. *The origins of the Boxer uprising*. Berkeley, CA: University of California Press.

Etherington, Norman. 1978. *Preachers, peasants and politics in southeast Africa*. London: Royal Historical Society.

Etherington, Norman. 1983. Missionaries and the intellectual history of Africa: A historical survey. *Itinerario* 7: 116–143.

Etherington, Norman. 1988. Natal's black rape scare of the 1870s. *Journal of Southern African Studies* 15.1: 36–53.

Fast, Vera K. 1979. A research note on the journals of John West. *Journal of the Canadian Church Historical Society* 21: 30–38.

Ferguson, R. Brian. 1990. Blood of the leviathan: Western contact and warfare in Amazonia. *American Ethnologist* 17.2: 237–257.

Fields, Rick. 1986. *How the swans came to the lake: A narrative history of Buddhism in America. Rev. edn*. Boston, MA: Shambhala.

Fine Media Group. http://www.finemediagroup.com.

Forrester, Duncan B. 1980. *Caste and Christianity: Attitudes and policies on caste of Anglo-Saxon Protestant missions in India*. London: Curzon Press.

Forster, E. M. 1924. *A passage to India*. London: E. Arnold.

Foucault, Michel. 1977. *Discipline and punish: The birth of the prison*. New York: Pantheon Books.

Foucault, Michel. 1982. The subject and power. In Hubert Dreyfus and Paul Rabinow, eds. *Michel Foucault: Beyond structuralism and hermeneutics*. Brighton, UK: Harvester Press.

Foucault, Michel. 1984. *The Foucault reader*. Edited by Paul Rabinow. Harmondsworth, Middlesex: Penguin Books.

Foucault, Michel. 1988. *Politics, philosophy, culture: Interviews and other writings, 1977–1984*. New York: Routledge.

Fowler, George A., Roggie Cale, and Joe C. Bartlett. 1974. Java: A garden continuum. Hong Kong; Tulsa: Amerasian.

Fowler, Loretta. 1996. The Great Plains from the arrival of the horse to 1885. In Bruce G. Trigger and Wilcomb E. Washburn, eds. *The Cambridge history of the Native Peoples of the Americas. Volume I: North America*. 2 Parts. 1–55. Cambridge: Cambridge University Press.

Fox, Judith M. 2002. *Osho Rajneesh*. Salt Lake City, UT: Signature Books.

Fraser, Donald. 1914. *Winning a primitive people: Sixteen years' work among the warlike tribe of the Ngoni and the Senga and Tumbuka peoples of Central Africa, by Donald Fraser . . . with an introduction by John R. Mott . . . with 27 illustrations & 2 maps*. London: Seeley, Service & Co.

Freeman, Joseph John and David Johns. 1840. *A narrative of the persecution of Christians in Madagascar with details of the escape of the six Christian refugees now in England*. London: John Snow.

Friedman, Thomas L. 1999. *The lexus and the olive tree*. New York: Farrar, Straus, Giroux.

Fronsdal, Gil. 2002. Virtues without rules: Ethics in the insight meditation movement. In Charles S. Prebish and Martin Baumann, eds. *Westward dharma: Buddhism beyond Asia*. 285–306. Berkeley, CA: University of California Press.

Fukuyama, Francis. 1989. The end of history? *National Interest* 16: 3–18.

Fukuyama, Francis. 1992. *The end of history and the last man*. New York: Free Press.

Gallie, W. B. 1978. *Philosophers of peace and war: Kant, Clausewitz, Marx, Engels, and Tolstoy*. Cambridge: Cambridge University Press.

Gambihirananda, Swami, trans. 1965. *Brahma-sutra bhasya of Sankaracarya*. Calcutta: Advaita Ashrama.

Gardiner, Allen. 1836. *Narrative of a journey to the Zoolu country, in South Africa . . . undertaken in 1835*. London: W. Crofts.

Gautami, Lantusinha. 1966. "Dharmangka." Special volume no. 40 of *Kalyanakalpataru*. Gorakhpur: Gita Press.

Geertz, Clifford. 1973. Religion as a cultural system. In Clifford Geertz, ed. *The interpretation of cultures; selected essays*. 87–125. New York: Basic Books.

Geschiere, Peter. 2001. Shaka and the limits of colonial invention. *African Studies Review* 44.2: 167–176.

Gill, Stephen. 1995. Globalisation, market civilisation and disciplinary neoliberalism. *Millennium* 24.3: 399–423.

Gill, William Wyatt. n.d. *Gems from the coral islands*. Philadelphia, PA: Presbyterian Board of Publication.

Gill, William Wyatt. 1880. *Selections from the autobiography of the Rev. William Gill*. London: Yates and Alexander.

Gilmont, Jean-François. 1999. Protestant reformations and reading. In Guglielmo Cavallo and Roger Chartier, eds. *A history of reading in the west*. Trans. Lydia G. Cochrane. 213–237. Cambridge: Polity Press.

Giteau, Madeleine. 1976. *The civilization of Angkor*. Trans. Katherine Watson. New York: Rizzoli.

Gladstone, John Wilson. 1984. *Protestant Christianity and people's movements in Kerala: A study of Christian mass movements in relation to neo-Hindu socio-religious movements in Kerala, 1850–1936*. Trivandrum: Seminary Publications.

Gnanadason, Aruna, ed. 1990. *The future of the church in India*. Nagpur: National Council of Churches in India.

Golwalkar, Madhav Sadashiv. 1964. *Bunch of Thoughts*. Bangalore: Vikrama Prakashan. Available online through Hindu Books Universe. http://www.hindubooks.org/bot/contents.htm.

Gombrich, Richard. 1988. *Theravada Buddhism: A social history from ancient Benaresto modern Colombo*. New York: Routledge.

Gordon, George. 1859. Letter to the London Missionary Society, 6 December, 1859. Council for World Mission, South Seas, Box 27, folder 4(D). School of Oriental and African Studies, London.

Goswami, Satsvarupa Dasa. 2002. *Srila Prabhupada-Lilamrta*. 2 vols. Los Angeles, CA: Bhaktivedanta Book Trust.

Gow, Bonar A. 1979. *Madagascar and the protestant impact: The work of British missionaries, 1818–95*. London: Longman and Dalhousie University Press.

Grafe, Hugald. 1990. *The history of Christianity in Tamilnadu from 1800 to 1975*. Bangalore: Church History Association of India.

Graham, William A. 1987. *Beyond the written word: Oral aspects of scripture in the history of religion*. Cambridge: Cambridge University Press.

Green, Samuel G. 1899. *The story of the Religious Tract Society for one hundred years*. London: Religious Tract Society.

Gresko, Jacqueline. 1986. Creating little dominions within the Dominion: Early Catholic Indian schools in Saskatchewan and British Columbia. In Jean Barman, Yvonne Hebert, and Don McCaskill, eds. *Indian Education in Canada, Volume 1: The Legacy*: 88–109. Vancouver: University of British Columbia Press.

Griffiths, Gareth. 2001. Appropriation, patronage and control: The case of the missionary text. In Gerhard Stilz, ed. *Colonies, missions, cultures in the English-speaking world*: 12–23. Tübingen: Stauffenberg Verlag.

Griffiths, Gertrude. 1920. *The great adventure: Three scenes*. London: London Missionary Society.

Guha, Ranajit. 1982. On some aspects of the historiography of colonial India. In Ranajit Guha, ed. *Subaltern Studies I*. 1–8. Delhi: Oxford University Press.

Gunson, Niel, ed. 1974. *Australian reminiscences & papers of L. E. Threlkeld, missionary to the aborigines, 1824–1859*. 2 vols. Canberra: Australian Institute of Aboriginal Studies.

Guy, Jeff. 1983. *The heretic: A study of the life of John William Colenso, 1814–1883*. Johannesburg: Ravan Press; Pietermaritzburg: University of Natal Press.

Habermas, Jürgen. 1981. Modernity versus postmodernity. *New German Critique* 22: 3–15.

Haggard, Rider H. 1887a. *She*. New York: N. L. Munro.

Haggard, Rider H. 1887b. *Allan Quatermain, being an account of his further adventures and discoveries in company with Sir Henry Curtis, Bart, Commander John Good, R.N., and one Umslopogaa*. London: Longman & Co.

Halalco Books. http://www.halalco.com/Islamic.

Halalco Supermarket. http://www.halalco.com/digitalquran.html.

Hammond, Phillip E. and David Machacek. 1999. *Soka Gakkai in America: Accommodation and conversion*. New York: Oxford University Press.

Hannah, Matthew G. 1993. Space and social control in the administration of the Oglala Lakota ("Sioux"), 1871–1879. *Journal of Historical Geography* 19.4: 412–432.

Hannington, James. 1886. *Peril and adventure in Central Africa; being illustrated letters to the youngsters at home, by the late Bishop H, with illustrations from original sketches by the Bishop, and a biographical memoir*. London: Religious Tract Society.

Hardgrave, Robert L. 1968. Breast cloth controversy: Caste consciousness and social change in south Travancore. *Indian Economic and Social History Review* 5.2: 171–187.

Hardgrave, Robert L. 1969. *The Nadars of Tamilnad: The political culture of a community in change*. Berkeley, CA: University of California Press.

Harding, Susan. 2000. *The book of Jerry Falwell: Fundamentalist language and politics*. Princeton, NJ: Princeton University Press.

Harper, Susan Billington. 2000. *In the shadow of the Mahatma: Bishop V. S. Azariah and the travails of Christianity in British India*. Grand Rapids, MI; Richmond, Surrey, UK: W. B. Eerdmans; Curzon Press.

Harvard University. Harvard Islamic Finance Information Program. http://www.hifip.harvard.edu/About.asp?Action=Objectives.

Hawthorn, Harry Bertram, ed. 1966–1967. *A Survey of the contemporary Indians of Canada: Economic, political, educational needs and policies*. 2 vols. Ottawa: Indian Affairs Branch.

Heathcote, R. L. 1976. Early European perceptions of the Australian landscape. In George Seddon and Mari Davis, eds. *Man and landscape in Australia: Towards an ecological vision*. 29–46. Canberra: Australian Government Publishing Service.

Heehs, Peter. 1989. *Sri Aurobindo, a brief biography*. Oxford: Oxford University Press.

Hermansen, Marcia. 2000. Hybrid identity formations in Muslim America: The case of American Sufi movements. *The Muslim World*. 90.1 and 2: 158–197.

Hewitt, Gordon. 1949. *Let the people read: A short history of the United Society for Christian Literature*. London: United Society for Christian Literature.

Highway, Tomson.1998. *Kiss of the Fur Queen*. Toronto: Doubleday.

Hilton, Boyd. 1988. *The age of atonement: The influence of evangelicalism on social and economic thought, 1795–1865*. Oxford: Clarendon Press.

Himalayan Academy. http://www.himalayanacademy.com. Kapaa, Hawaii.

Hinduism Today. http://www.hinduism-today.com. Kapaa, Hawaii.

Hobbes, Thomas. 1968 [1651]. *Leviathan*. New York: Penguin.

Hodgins, J. George, ed. 1893–1908. *Documentary history of education in Upper Canada, from the passing of the Constitutional Act of 1791 to the close of the Reverend Doctor Ryerson's administration of the education department in 1876*. 28 vols. Toronto: L. K. Cameron.

Hodgkinson, Liz. 1999. *Peace and purity: The story of the Brahma Kumaris: A spiritual revolution*. London: Rider.

Hodgson, Janet. 1980. *Ntsikana's great hymn: A Xhosa expression of Christianity in the early nineteenth century eastern Cape*. Cape Town: Centre for African Studies, University of Cape Town.

Hoffman, Stanley. 1987. *Janus and Minerva: Essays in the theory and practice of international politics*. Boulder, CO: Westview Press.

Hofmeyr, Isabel. 2001. Metaphorical books. *Current Writing* 13.2: 100–108.

Hofmeyr, Isabel. 2002. How Bunyan became English: Missions, translation and the discipline of English literature. *Journal of British Studies* 41.1: 84–119.

Hofmeyr, Isabel. 2004. *The portable Bunyan: A transnational history of* The Pilgrim's Progress. Princeton: Princeton University Press.

Hollis, Martin and Steve Smith. 1990. *Explaining and understanding international relations*. Oxford: Clarendon Press.

Holmes, Janice. 2000. *Religious revivals in Britain and Ireland, 1859–1905*. Portland, OR: Irish Academic Press.

Holy Bible containing the Old and New Testaments. Authorized or King James version.

Hospital, Clifford. 1984. *The righteous demon: A study of Bali*. Vancouver: University of British Columbia Press.

Hotchkiss, Willis R. 1903. *Sketches from the dark continent*. London: Headley Bros.

Howley, Aimee and Richard Hartnett. 1992. Pastoral power and the contemporary university: A Foucauldian analysis. *Educational Theory* 42.3: 271–283.

Hudson, D. Dennis. 2000. *Protestant origins in India: Tamil evangelical Christians, 1706–1835*. Grand Rapids, MI: Wm. B. Eerdmans.

Hulme, Peter. 1986. *Colonial encounters: Europe and the native Caribbean, 1492–1797*. London: Methuen.

I[nternational] S[ociety] [for] K[rishna] CON[sciousness]. "ISKCON's mission: The seven purposes of ISKCON." http://www.iskcon.com/about/mission.html.

India Bare Acts. The commission of sati (prevention) act, 1987. http://www.helplinelaw.com/bareact/index.php?dsp=sati1987#a1.

India Today. Weekly. New Delhi. http://www.indiatoday.com/itoday/20040216/index.html?

Inner-City Muslim Action Network. http://www.imancentral.org.

Insight Meditation Center. http://www.dharma.org.

Institute of Islamic Information and Education. http://www.iiie.net.

"Iota." 1891. The government and Indian education. *The Week* 8.24: 378–379.

Islamic Bookstore. http://islamicbookstore.com.

Islamic Boutique. http://www.islamicboutique.com.

Islamic Finance. http://islamic-finance.net.

Islamic Food and Nutrition Council of America. http://www.ifanca.org.

Islamic Information and Da'wah Center. The reign of Islaamic da'wah. http://www.troid.org.

Islamic Market. http://www.IslamicMarket.com.

Israel, Jonathan. 2001. *Radical enlightenment: Philosophy and the making of modernity, 1650–1750*. Oxford: Oxford University Press.

Jackson, Carl T. 1994. *The Ramakrishna movement in the United States*. Bloomington, IN: Indiana University Press.

Jacobs, Laverne. 1996. The Native church: A search for authentic spirituality. In James Treat, ed. *Indigenous voices on religious identity in the United States and Canada*. 236–240. New York: Routledge.

Jaenen, Cornelius J. 1986. Education for Francization: The case of New France in the seventeenth century. In Jean Barman, Yvonne Hébert, and Don McCaskill, eds. *Indian Education in Canada, Volume 1: The Legacy*. 45–63. Vancouver: University of British Columbia Press.

Jaine, Linda. 1991. Industrial and residential school administration: The attempt to undermine indigenous self-determination. *Journal of Indigenous Studies/La revue des études indigenes* 2.2: 37–48.

Jamison, Stephanie W., and Michael Witzel. 2003. "Vedic Hinduism." In Arvind Sharma, ed. *The study of Hinduism*. 65–113. Columbia, SC: University of South Carolina Press.

Jeffrey, Robin. 1994. *The decline of Nayar dominance: Society and politics in Travancore, 1847–1908*. New Delhi: Vikas Publishers.

Jenkins, Philip. 2002. *The next Christendom: The coming of global Christianity*. Oxford: Oxford University Press.

Johnson, Ronald M. 1974. Schooling the savage: Andrew S. Draper and Indian Education. *Phylon* 35.1: 74–82.

Johnston, Basil H. 1988. *Indian school days*. Toronto: Key Porter Books.

Jordens, J. T. F. 1978. *Dayananda Sarasvati: His life and ideas*. New Delhi: Oxford University Press.

Kaeppler, Adrienne. 1978. *Cook voyage artifacts in Leningrad, Berne, and Florence museums*. Honolulu: Bishop Museum.

Kahera, Akel Ismail. 2002. *Deconstructing the American mosque: Space, gender, and Aesthetics*. Austin, TX: University of Texas Press.

Kant, Immanuel. 1972 [1795]. *Perpetual peace: A philosophical essay*. Trans. M. Campbell Smith. New York: Garland Publishing.

Kaplan, Robert D. 1994. The coming anarchy: How scarcity, crime, overpopulation, tribalism, and disease are rapidly destroying the social fabric of our planet. *Atlantic Monthly* 273.2: 44–76.

Kapstein, Matthew. 2000. *The Tibetan assimilation of Buddhism: Conversion, contestation, and memory*. New York: Oxford University Press.

Kaviraja, Krishnadasa. 1962. *Sri Caitanya-charitamrita*. Trans. Sanjib Kumar Chaudhuri. Calcutta: Oriental Press.

Keer, Dhananjay. 1971. *Dr. Ambedkar: Life and mission*. Bombay: Popular Prakashan.

Kennedy, Dan [Ochankugahe]. 1972. In James R. Stevens, ed. *Recollections of an Assiniboine chief.* Toronto: McClelland and Stewart.

Kent, Eliza F. 1999. Tamil bible women of the Zenana Missions of colonial south India. *History of Religions* 39.2: 117–149.

Kent, Eliza F. 2004. *Converting women: Gender and Protestant Christianity in colonial South India.* New York: Oxford University Press.

Kenyatta, Jomo. 1942. *My people of Kikuyu, and the life of Chief Wangombe.* London: United Society for Christian Literature.

Keohane, Robert O. 1983. Theory of world politics: Structural realism and beyond. In Ada W. Finifter, ed. *Political science: The state of the discipline.* 503–540. Washington, DC: American Political Science Association.

Khan, Rukhsana. 1999. Storytelling—a tool of education. *Islamic Horizons.* May/June: 5.

Kipling, Rudyard. 1901. *Kim.* London: Macmillan.

Klostermaier, Klaus. 1996. The soul and its destiny: Christian perspectives. *ISKCON Communications Journal* 4.1. http://www.iskcon.com/icj/4_2/4_2klostermaier.html and http://www.iskcon.com/icj/4_2/4_2klostermaier2.html.

Kooiman, Dick. 1989. *Conversion and social equality in India: The London Missionary Society in south Travancore in the 19th Century.* New Delhi: Manohar.

Kopf, David. 1979. *The Brahmo Samaj and the shaping of the modern Indian mind.* Princeton, NJ: Princeton University Press.

Kraniauskas, John. 2000. Hybridity in a transnational frame: Latin-americanist and postcolonial perspectives on cultural studies. *Nepantla: Views from South* 1.1: 111–137.

Krishnakumar, Radhika. 1999. *Ageless guru: The inspirational life of Swami Chinmayananda.* Mumbai: Eeshwar.

Lahore Missionary Conference. 1863. Report of the Punjab missionary conference held at Lahore in December and January, 1862–1863. Ludhiana: American Presbyterian Mission Press.

Lajpat Rai, Lala. 1991. *The Arya Samaj: An account of its origin, doctrines, and activities.* New Delhi: Reliance Publishing House.

Lal, Chaman. 1960. *Hindu America, depicting the imprints of Hindu Culture on the two Americas.* Bombay: Bharatiya Vidya Bhavan.

Larson, Piers M. 1997. "Capacities and modes of thinking": Intellectual engagements and subaltern hegemony in the early history of Malagasy Christianity. *American Historical Review* 102.4: 969–1002.

Latourette, Kenneth Scott, 1958–1962. *Christianity in a revolutionary age: A history of Christianity in the nineteenth and twentieth centuries.* 5 vols. New York: Harper.

Lavine, Amy. 1998. Tibetan Buddhism in America: The development of American Vajrayana. In Charles S. Prebish and Kenneth K. Tanaka, eds. *The faces of Buddhism in America.* 99–115. Berkeley, CA: University of California Press.

Lawry, Walter. 1850. *Friendly and Feejee islands: A missionary visit to various stations in the South Seas in the year 1847.* London: Gilpin.

Lawry, Walter. 1851. *A second missionary visit to the Friendly and Feejee islands in the year MDCCCL.* London: Mason.

Laws of Manu. 1991. Trans. Wendy Doniger and Brian K. Smith. New York: Penguin Books.

Lawson, Barbara. 1994. *Collected curios, missionary tales from the South Seas.* Montréal: McGill University Libraries.

Leigh, Samuel. 1818. *Leigh's new picture of London.* London: Samuel Leigh.

Levy, Jack S. 1989. The causes of war: A review of theories and evidence. In Philip E. Tetlock et al., eds. *Behavior, society, and nuclear war.* 209–233. New York: Oxford University Press.

Lincoln, Bruce. 1989. Discourse and the construction of society: Comparative studies of myth, ritual and classification. New York: Oxford University Press.

Livingstone, David. 1857. *Missionary travels and researches in South Africa: Including a sketch of sixteen years' residence in the interior of Africa, and a journey from the Cape of Good Hope to Loanda on the west coast; thence across the continent, down the River Zambesi, to the eastern ocean.* London: J. Murray.

Livingstone, David. 1963. In I. Schapera, ed. and intro. *Livingstone's African Journal, 1853–1856.* 2 vols. London: Chatto & Windus.

Livingstone, David. 1865. *Narrative of an expedition to the Zambesi and its tributaries; and of the discovery of the lakes Shirwa and Nyassa. 1858–1864.* London: J. Murray.

Lochtefeld, J. G. 1996. New wine, old skins: The Sangh Parivar and the transformation of Hinduism. *Religion* 26: 101–118.

London Missionary Society. Madagascar Incoming Correspondence. Box 5, 1834–1840, Folder 3, July 28, 1838. CWM, London Missionary Society Papers, School of Oriental and African Studies, University of London.

Lotfi, Abdul Hamid. 2002. Spreading the word: Communicating Islam in America. In Yvonne Y. Haddad and Jane I. Smith, eds. *Muslim minorities in the West: Visible and invisible.* 3–24. Walnut Creek, CA: Altamira Press.

Louis, Wm. Roger, editor-in-chief; Alaine Low, assistant editor. 1998–. *The Oxford history of the British empire.* Oxford: Oxford University Press.

Ludden, David, ed. 1996. *Making India Hindu: Religion, community and the politics of democracy in India.* Delhi: Oxford University Press.

Lutz, Hartmut. 1991. *Contemporary challenges: Conversations with Canadian Native authors.* Saskatoon: Fifth House Publishers.

Lyotard, Jean-Francois. 1983. Answering the Question: What is postmodernism? In Ihab Hassan and Sally Hassan, eds. *Innovation/Renovation,* 71–82. Madison, WI: University of Wisconsin Press.

Machacek, David. 2000. Organizational isomorphism in SGI-USA. In David Machacek and Bryan Wilson, eds. *Global citizens: The Soka Gakkai Buddhist movement in the world.* 280–298. New York: Oxford University Press.

Machacek, David and Kerry Mitchell. 2000. Immigrant Buddhists in America. In David Machacek and Bryan Wilson, eds. *Global Citizens: The Soka Gakkai Buddhist movement in the world.* 259–279. New York: Oxford University Press.

Mackay, John A. 1886. Extracts from the annual letters: Saskatchewan. *Christian Missionary Intelligencer and Record* 36.2: 317.

Maharishi University of Management. http://www.mum.edu/introduction/history.html.

Mahesh Yogi, Maharishi. 1963. *The science of being and art of living.* New Delhi, New York: Allied Publishers.

Mainkar, Trimbak Govind, ed. 1978. *Sarva-darsana-samgraha of Sayana-Madhava.* Poona: Bhandarkar Oriental Research Institute.

Majumdar, Asoka Kumar. 1969. *Caitanya: His life and doctrine.* Bombay: Bharatiya Vidya Bhavan.

Majumdar, Ramesh Chandra. 1963. *Hindu colonies in the far east.* Calcutta: K. L. Mukhopadhyay.

Malcolm X. 1965. *The autobiography of Malcolm X.* With the assistance of Alex Haley. Introduction by M. S. Handler. Epilogue by Alex Haley. New York: Grove Press.

Maples, Chauncy. 1882. *The Magwangara raid upon Masasi.* Zanzibar: Universities Mission Press.

Marcello, Patricia Cronin. 2003. *The Dalai Lama: A biography.* Westport, CT: Greenwood Press.

Marsden, Samuel. 1836. Letter to Lay Secretary, February 29 1836, CMS Mission Books.

Martin, Sandra. 2001. Finding joy beyond the rage. *Globe and Mail* October 5: R1, R8.

Marty, Martin E. and R. Scott Appleby, eds. 1991. *The fundamentalism project; a study conducted by the American Academy of Arts and Sciences.* Chicago, IL: University of Chicago Press.

Mason, John Cecil Strickland. 2001. *The Moravian church and the missionary awakening in England, 1760–1800.* Woodbridge, Suffolk, UK; Rochester, NY: Royal Historical Society/Boydell Press.

Mason, Lowell. 1834. *The Manual of the Boston Academy of Music*. (Edited translation of G. F. Kuebler's *Anleitung zum Gesang-Unterrichte in Schulen*.) Boston, MA: n.p.

Mason, Paul. 1994. *The Maharishi: The biography of the man who gave transcendental meditation to the world*. Shaftesbury: Element.

Mateer, Samuel. 1871. *The land of charity: A descriptive account of Travancore and its people*. London: Snow and Co.

Mateer, Samuel. 1883. *Native life in Travancore*. London: W. H. Allen.

Mathews, Basil Joseph and Arthur E. Southon. 1922. *Yarns on heroes of the deep*. London: United Council for Missionary Education.

Mathews, Basil Joseph. 1932. *Yarns on heroes of the day's work*. London: Edinburgh House Press.

Maxwell, David. 2001. Sacred history, social history: Traditions and texts in the making of a southern African transnational religious movement. *Comparative Study of Society and History* 43.3: 502–524.

Mbembe, Achille. 2001. Introduction. *African Studies Review* 44.2: 1–14.

McFarland, Horace Neill. 1967. *The rush hour of the gods: A study of new religious movements in Japan*. New York: Macmillan.

McGillivray, Anne. 1997. Therapies of freedom: The colonization of Aboriginal children. In Anne McGillivray, ed. and intro. *Governing childhood*. 135–199. Aldershot: Dartmouth.

McMurrich, W[illiam] B[arclay]. 1872. Industrial schools. *Canadian Monthly and National Review* 2.5: 424–428.

McMurrich, W[illiam] B[arclay] and Emmerson Coatsworth. 1872 [1908]. Report to the Toronto School Board [of a tour of Industrial Schools in Massachusetts and New York, with a view to their introduction in Ontario]. In J. George Hodgins, ed. *Documentary history of education in Upper Canada, from the passing of the Constitutional Act of 1791 to the close of the Reverend Doctor Ryerson's administration of the education department in 1876*. 28 vols. 23: 275–285. Toronto: L. K. Cameron.

Meenakshisundaran, T. P. 1965. *A history of Tamil literature*. Annamalainagar: Annamalai University.

Megill, Allan. 1995. "Grand narrative" and the discipline of history. In Frank and Hans Kellner Ankersmit, eds. *A new philosophy of history* 151–173. Chicago, IL: University of Chicago.

Metraux, Daniel Alfred. 1988. *The history and theology of Soka Gakkai: A Japanese new religion*. Lewiston, NY: Edwin Mellen Press.

Meyer, Birgit. 1999. *Translating the devil: Religion and modernity among the Ewe in Ghana*. Edinburgh: Edinburgh University Press.

Meyer, Birgit and Peter Pels, eds. 2003. *Magic and modernity: Interfaces of revelation and concealment*. Palo Alto: Stanford University Press.

Micro Systems International. http://www.quran.com.

Miller, D. M. 1948. Missionary Methods. *Congo Mission News*. January.

Miller, James R. 1989. *Skyscrapers hide the heavens: A history of Indian–White relations in Canada*. Toronto: University of Toronto Press.

Miller, James R. 1996. *Shingwauk's vision: A history of Native residential schools*. Toronto: University of Toronto Press.

Million, Dian. 2000. Telling secrets: Sex, power and narratives in Indian residential school histories. *Canadian Woman Studies/Les cahiers de la femme canadienne* 20.2: 92–104.

Milloy, John S. 1999. *A national crime: The Canadian government and the residential school system, 1879–1986*. Winnipeg: University of Manitoba Press.

Mitchell, W. J. T., ed. 1994. *Landscape and power*. Chicago, IL: Chicago University Press.

Moffat, Robert. 1842. *Missionary labours and scenes in South Africa*. London: John Snow.

Moffat, Robert. 1855. *Visit to Moselekatse, king of the Matabele, by Rev R. Moffat, communicated to the London Missionary Society, with map*. London: W. Clowes and Sons.

Moffat, Robert. 1876. *Scenes and services in South Africa: The story of Robert Moffat's half-century of missionary labours*. London: John Snow & Co.

Molomby, Tom. 1986. *Spies, bombs and the path of Bliss*. Sydney: Potoroo Press.

Montegomery, Robert L. 1996. *The diffusion of religion: A sociological perspective*. Lanham, MD: University Press of America.

Montgomery, Daniel B. 1991. *Fire in the lotus: The dynamic Buddhism of Nichiren*. London: HarperCollins.

Morgenthau, Hans. 1985. *Politics among nations: The struggle for power and peace*. 6th edn. New York: Alfred A. Knopf.

Morreale, Don. 1998. *The complete guide to Buddhist America*. Boston, MA: Shambhala.

Morris, Alexander. 1991 [1880]. *The treaties of Canada with the Indians*. Saskatoon: Fifth House.

Mukherjee, Prabhati. 1988. *Beyond the four varnas: The untouchables in India*. Delhi: Motilal Banarsidas.

Mukhopadhyay, Devendranath. 1902. *Virjanandacharit*. Trans. into Hindi by Ghariram. Agra: n.p.

Muller, Carol Ann. 1999. *Rituals of fertility and the sacrifice of desire: Nazarite women's performance in South Africa*. Chicago, IL: University of Chicago Press.

Murata, Kiyoaki. 1969. *Japan's new Buddhism: An objective account of Sokagakkai*. New York: Walker/Weatherhill.

Murray, A. W. 1863. *Missions in western Polynesia*. London: John Snow.

Murti, Vasu. The writings of Vasu Murti. http://www.all-creatures.org/murti/asource-01.html.

Nandakumar, R. 1996. The missing male: The female figures of Ravi Varma and the concepts of family, marriage and fatherhood in nineteenth-century Kerala. *South Indian Studies* 1.1: 54–82.

Narasingha, P. Sil. 1998. *Ramakrishna revisited: A new biography*. Lanham, MD: University Press of America.

Nasr, Seyyed Hossein. 1987. *Traditional Islam in the modern world*. London: K. Paul International.

National Defence [Canada]. 2003. *Religions in Canada*. Ottawa: Directorate of Military Gender Integration and Employment Equity.

Nattier, 1998. Who is a Buddhist? Charting the landscape of Buddhist America. In Charles S. Prebish and Kenneth K. Tanaka, eds. *The faces of Buddhism in America*. 183–195. Berkeley, CA: University of California Press.

Natural Law Party [United States]. http://www.natural-law.org/introduction/index.html and http://www.natural-law.org/platform/50_point_summary.html.

Neff, Charlotte. 1994. The Ontario Industrial Schools Act of 1874. *Canadian Journal of Family Law/Revue canadienne de droit familial* 12.1: 171–208.

Net cast in many waters; sketches from the life of missionaries. 1866–1896. 31 vols. London: n.p.

NoorArt. http://www.noorart.com.

O'Connor, Daniel. 1990. *Gospel, raj and swaraj: The missionary years of C. F. Andrews, 1904–14*. Frankfurt am Main, Bern, New York, Paris: Peter Lang.

Oddie, Geoffrey A. 1975. Christian conversion in the Telegu country, 1860–1900: A case study of one Protestant movement in the Godavery-Krishna delta. *Indian Economic and Social History Review* 12.1: 61–79.

Offor, George. n.d. Memoir of John Bunyan. In *The Works of John Bunyan*. vol. 1. Edinburgh: The Banner of Truth Trust.

Offor, George. 1847. Introduction to *The Pilgrim's Progress*. London: Hanserd Knollys Society.

Offor, George. 1866. Introductory memoir to *The Pilgrim's Progress and other Works of John Bunyan*. Edinburgh: William Mackenzie.

Omvedt, Gail. 1994. *Dalits and the democratic revolution: Dr. Ambedkar and the Dalit movement in colonial India*. New Delhi: Sage Publications.

Osho [Bhagwan Shree Rajneesh]. 2000. *Autobiography of a spiritually incorrect mystic.* New York: St. Martin's Press.

Owen, John M. 1994. How liberalism produces democratic peace. *International Security* 19.2: 87–125.

Owen, John M. 1997. *Liberal peace, liberal war: American politics and international security.* Ithaca, NY: Cornell University Press.

Owens, J. M. R. 1974. *Prophets in the wilderness: The Wesleyan mission to New Zealand, 1819–27.* Auckland: Auckland University Press.

Parekh, Manilal C. 1927. *Rajarshi Ram Mohan Roy.* Rajkot: Oriental Christ House.

Parekh, Manilal C. 1929. *The Brahmo Samaj: A short history.* Rajkot: Oriental Christ House.

Parliamentary Papers. 1859. Copies of the official papers sent from India touching the recent disturbances in Travancore. India Office, August 5, 1859. Session II, XXV, No. 158.

Pascal, Blaise. 1847 [1656]. *The provincial letters; a new translation with historical introduction and notes by T. M'Crie.* Edinburgh: n.p.

Paton, James. 1965 [1889]. *John G. Paton: Missionary to the New Hebrides.* London: Banner of Truth Trust.

Patten, John A. and Edward Shillito. 1935. *The martyr church and its book.* London: British and Foreign Bible Society and London Missionary Society.

Patterson, George. 1882. *Missionary life among the cannibals: Being the life of John Geddie, first missionary to the New Hebrides; with a history of the Nova Scotia Presbyterian mission on that group.* Toronto: James Campbell.

Pearce, Susan M., ed. 1989. *Museum studies in material culture.* London: Leicester University Press.

Pedersen, Susan. 1986. Hannah More meets Simple Simon: Tracts, chapbooks, and popular culture in late eighteenth-century England. *Journal of British Studies* 25.1: 84–113.

Peril and Adventure in Central Africa: Being Illustrated Letters to the Youngsters at Home by the late Bishop Hannington RTS London: n.d.

Perez, Eugene. 1977. *Kalumburu: The Benedictine mission and the Aborigines, 1908–1974.* Wyndham, WA: Kalumburu Benedictine Mission.

Petition to the Right Honorable the Governor in Council from the Shanars of South Travancore. *Bombay Standard.* February 11, 1859.

Petrone, Penny, ed. 1983. *First people, first voices.* Toronto: University of Toronto Press.

Phiri, Desmond Dudwa. 1975. *Charles Chidongo Chinula.* Lilongwe: Longman.

Porter, Andrew. 2003. Introduction. In Andrew Porter, ed. *The imperial horizons of British Protestant missions, 1880–1914.* 1–13. Grand Rapids, MI: William B. Eerdmans.

Posten, Larry. 1991. Da'wa in the west. In Yvonne Y. Haddad, ed. *The Muslims of America.* 125–136. New York: Oxford University Press.

Posten, Larry. 1992. *Islamic da'wa in the west.* New York: Oxford University Press.

Prakash, Gyan, ed. 1995. *After colonialism: Imperial histories and postcolonial displacements.* Princeton, NJ: Princeton University Press.

Pratt, Mary Louise. 1992. *Imperial eyes: Travel writing and transculturation.* London and New York: Routledge.

Prebish, Charles S. 1999. *Luminous passage: The practice and study of Buddhism in America.* Berkeley, CA: University of California Press.

Prebish, Charles S. and Kenneth K. Tanaka, eds. 1998. *The faces of Buddhism in America.* Berkeley, CA: University of California Press.

Prebish, Charles S. and Martin Baumann, eds. 2002. *Westward dharma: Buddhism beyond Asia.* Berkeley, CA: University of California Press.

Prem, Krishna. 1976. *Initiation into yoga: An introduction to the spiritual life.* Foreword by Madhava Ashish. London: Rider.

Pringle, Robert. 2004. *A short history of Bali: Indonesia's Hindu realm.* London: Allen Unwin.

Punjab C[hurch] M[issionary] S[ociety] Native Church Council. 1883. Report of the seventh meeting of the Punjab CMS native church council held at Jandiala, December 29–30, 1882. Amritsar: n.p.

Punjab C[hurch] M[issionary] S[ociety] Native Church Council. 1898. Report of the 21st annual meeting of the Punjab CMS district native church council, Amritsar, April 11–13, 1898. Lahore: n.p.

Punshon, W. Morley. 1882. Lectures. In *John Bunyan*. London: T. Woolmer.

Queen, Christopher S. 2002. Engaged Buddhism: Agnosticism, interdependence, globalization. In Charles S. Prebish and Martin Baumann, eds. 2002. *Westward dharma: Buddhism beyond Asia*. 324–347. Berkeley, CA: University of California Press.

Radhakrishnan, Sarvepalli. 1927. *The Hindu view of life; upon lectures delivered at Manchester College, Oxford, 1926*. London: Allen & Unwin.

Radhakrishnan, Sarvepalli. 1932. *An idealist view of life . . . Being the Hibbert Lectures for 1929*. London: Allen & Unwin.

Radhakrishnan, Sarvepalli. 1947. *Religion and society*. London: Allen & Unwin.

Rafael, Vicente. 1988. *Contracting colonialism: Translation and Christian conversion in Tagalog society under early Spanish rule*. Ithaca, NY: Cornell University Press.

Rahman, Syed. Seven conditions for a woman's dress in Islam. Islam for Today. http://www.islamfortoday.com/7conditions.htm.

Rahula, Walpola. 1974. *What the Buddha taught*. 2nd rev. and exp. ed. New York: Grove Press.

Rajashekhar, V. T. 1997. Editorial. *Dalit Voice* 16.24: 3.

Rambachan, Anantanand. 2001. The co-existence of violence and non-violence in Hinduism. *Current Dialogue* 39. http://www.wcc-coe.org/wcc/what/interreligious/cd39-05.html.

Rashtriya Swayamsevak Sangh. Mission and vision. http://www.rss.org/New_RSS/Mission_Vision/Why_RSS.jsp.

Ray, Reginald A. 2000. *Indestructible truth: The living spirituality of Tibetan Buddhism*. Boston, MA: Shambhala Publications.

Redhead, Thomas W. 1848–1849. *The French Revolution from 1789 to 1848*. 3 vols. Edinburgh: W. and R. Chambers.

Religious Tract Society. 1846. *Forty-seventh annual report*. London: Religious Tract Society.

Rennell, James. 1800. *The geographical system of Herodotus examined and explained by a comparison with those of other ancient authors, and with modern geography . . . .* London: G. & W. Nicol.

Report of the Third Decennial Missionary Conference, 1892–93. vol. 1. Bombay: Education Society's Steam Press, 1893.

Richmond, Legh. 1811. *The Dairyman's Daughter*. London: W. Kent.

Ridgwell, Harold A. 1921. *Heroes in Madagascar*. London: Marshall, Morgan and Scott.

Rig Veda: A metrically restored text with an introduction and notes. 1994. Holland, Gary B. and Barend A. van Nooten, eds. Cambridge, MA: Harvard University Press.

Robbins, Joel. 2004. *Becoming sinners: Christianity and moral torment in a Papua New Guinea society*. Berkley, CA: University of California Press.

Robertson, H. A. 1903. *Erromanga; the martyr isle*. London: Hodder and Stoughton.

Robertson, William. 1749. *The history of the reign of the emperor Charles V*. 3 vols. Dublin: Wm. Watson & Thomas Ewing; Samuel Watson.

Roy, Dilip Kumar. 1968. *Yogi Sri Krishnaprem*. Bombay: Bharatiya Vidya Bhavan.

Roy, Ram Mohan. 1823. *The precepts of Jesus: The guide to peace and happiness, extracted from the books of the New Testament ascribed to the four evangelists*. London: Unitarian Society.

Russett, Bruce. 1998. A neo-Kantian perspective: Democracy, interdependence, and international organizations in building security communities. In Emanuel Adler and Michael Barnett, eds. *Security Communities*. 368–394. Cambridge: Cambridge University Press.

Russett, Bruce and John R. Oneal. 2001. *Triangulating peace: Democracy, interdependence, and international organizations*. New York: W.W. Norton & Company.

Rutherdale, Myra. 2005. Metaphors of domestication in British Columbia missions. In Alvyn Austin and Jamie S. Scott, eds. *Canadian Missions, Indigenous Peoples: Representing Religion at Home and Abroad*. Toronto: University of Toronto Press.

Ryerson, Egerton. 1898. *Statistics respecting Indian schools, with Dr. Ryerson's report of 1845 attached*. Ottawa: Government Printing Bureau.

S[oka] G[akkai] I[nternational]-USA. http://www.sgi-usa.org.

Sahn, Seung. 1982. *Only don't know: The teaching letters of Zen Master Seung Sahn*. San Francisco: Four Seasons Foundation.

Said, Edward W. 1978. *Orientalism*. New York: Pantheon Books.

Said, Edward W. 1993. *Culture and Imperialism*. New York: Knopf.

Said, Edward W. 1995. Contra mundum. *London Review of Books* 17.5: 2–23.

Said, Edward W. 1999. *Out of place: A memoir*. New York: Vintage Books.

Salzberg, Sharon. 1995. *Lovingkindness*. Boston, MA: Shambhala.

Samson, Jane. 1998. *Imperial benevolence: Making British authority in the Pacific Islands*. Honolulu: University of Hawai'i Press.

Samson, Jane. 2001. Ethnology and theology: Nineteenth-century mission dilemmas in the south Pacific. In Brian Stanley, ed. *Christian missions and the enlightenment*. 99–122. Grand Rapids, MI: William B. Eerdmans.

Sandilands, A. 1955. Making hymns in Africa I & II. *Books for Africa* 25.1: 3–5, 27–29.

Sankey, Ira David. 1874. *Sacred Songs and Solos*. London: Morgan & Scott.

Sanneh, Lamin O. 1989. *Translating the message: The missionary impact on culture*. Maryknoll, NY: Orbis Books.

Sanneh, Lamin O. 1993. *Encountering the west: Christianity and the global cultural process: The African dimension*. Maryknoll, NY: Orbis Books.

Sastri, Ananta Krishna. 1982. *Advaitasiddhi of Madhusudanasarasvati, with the commentaries Gaudabrahmanandi, Vitthalesopadhyayi, Siddhivyakhya of Balabhadra, and critical summary called Caturgranthi by Ananta Krishna Sastri*. Delhi: Parimal.

Savarkar, S. S. and G. M. Joshi, eds. 1967. *Historic Statements of V. D. Savarkar*. Bombay: Popular Prakashan.

Savarkar, Vinayak Damodar. 1969 [1923]. *Hindutva; who is a Hindu?* Bombay: Veer Savarkar Prakashan.

Schama, Simon. 1995. *Landscape and memory*. New York: A. A. Knopf.

Schimmel, Annemarie. 2000. *Im Reich der Großmoguln*. München: C. H. Beck.

Schlossman, Steven. 1995. Delinquent children: The juvenile reform school. In Norval Morris and David J. Rothman, eds. *The Oxford history of the prison: The practice of punishment in western society*. 363–389. New York: Oxford University Press.

Schreiner, Oliver. 1883. *The story of an African farm*. 2 vols. London: Chapman & Hall.

Scott, Jamie S. 2001. Mapping the sacred across postcolonial literatures. In Jamie S. Scott and Paul Simpson-Housley, eds. *Mapping the sacred: Religion, geography and postcolonial literatures*. xv–xxxiii. Amsterdam and Atlanta: Editions Rodopi BV.

Scott, Jamie S. 2005. Cultivating Christians in colonial Canadian missions. In Alvyn Austin and Jamie S. Scott, eds. *Canadian Missions, Indigenous Peoples: Representing Religion at Home and Abroad*. 21–45. Toronto: University of Toronto Press.

Seager, Richard Hughes. 1999. *Buddhism in America*. New York: Columbia University Press.

Secretary for Native Affairs. Inspector Mann, List of required books for native schools, January 15, 1865. Folio NA 1/1/15, Secretary for Native Affairs Papers. Natal Archives, Petermaritzburg.

Secretary for Native Affairs. Dr. Mann to Theophilus Shepstone, April 27, 1865. Folio NA 1/1/15, Secretary for Native Affairs Papers. Natal Archives, Petermaritzburg.

Secretary for Native Affairs. Joseph Jackson Jr. to Theophilus Shepstone, July 6, 1868. Folio NA 1/1/18, Secretary for Native Affairs Papers. Natal Archives, Petermaritzburg.
Seddon, George and Mari David, eds. 1976. *Man and landscape in Australia: Towards an ecological vision*. Canberra: Australian Government Publishing Service.
Sen, Amiya P. 2000. *Swami Vivekananda*. New York: Oxford University Press.
Sen, Makhanlal, trans. 1965. *Ramayana, from the original Valmiki*. Calcutta: Rupa & Co.
Shambhala. http://www.shambhala.org.
Sharma, B. N. K. 1981. *History of the dvaita school of vedanta and its literature*. Delhi: Motilal Banarsidass.
Shastri, Anantakrishna, ed. 1982. *Advaitasiddhi of Madhusudana Sarasvati, with the commentaries of Gaudabrahmanandi, Vitthaleopadhayi of Balahadra, and a critical summary called Caturgranthi, by Anantakrishna Shastri*. Delhi: Parimal.
Shattuck, Cynthia. 1999. *Hinduism*. Upper Saddle River, NJ: Prentice Hall.
Shingwauk, Augustine. 1991 [1872]. *Little Pine's Journal: The appeal of a Christian Chippeway chief on behalf of his people*. Sault Ste. Marie: Shingwauk Reunion.
Shiv Sena. http://www.shivsena.org.
Shiv Sena. Profile. http://www.shivsena.org/profile.htm.
Shourie, Arun. 1994. *Missionaries in India: Continuities, changes, dilemmas*. New Delhi: ASA Publications.
Shukr. http://www.shukronline.com.
Sibbes, Richard. 1998 [1630]. *The bruised reed*. Edinburgh: Banner of Truth Trust.
Simmer-Brown, Judith. 2002. The roar of the lioness: Women's dharma in the west. In Charles S. Prebish and Martin Baumann, eds. *Westward dharma: Buddhism beyond Asia*. 309–323. Berkeley, CA: University of California Press.
Sisters United in Human Service. http://www.sistersunited.org.
Smith, Donald B. 1987. *Sacred feathers: The Reverend Peter Jones (Kahkewaquonaby) and the Mississauga Indians*. Lincoln, NE: University of Nebraska Press.
Smith, Jane I. 1999. *Islam in America*. New York: Columbia University Press.
[Smith, Sydney]. 1808. Publications respecting Indian missions. *Edinburgh Review* 12.23: 151–181.
Society for the Propagation of the Gospel in Foreign Parts. Allan Tönnesen to the Secretary of the Society for the Propagation of the Gospel, July 1, 1863. Folio E13, Archives of the United Society for the Propagation of the Gospel in Foreign Parts. Rhodes House, Oxford University.
Society for the Propagation of the Gospel in Foreign Parts. W. Illing to Secretaries of the Society for the Propagation of the Gospel, n.d. Folio D37, Archives of the United Society for the Propagation of the Gospel in Foreign Parts. Rhodes House, Oxford University.
Society for the Propagation of the Gospel in Foreign Parts. Bishop John William Colenso to secretaries of the Society for the Propagation of the Gospel in Foreign Parts, May 9, 1857. Folio D8, Archives of the United Society for the Propagation of the Gospel in Foreign Parts. Rhodes House, Oxford University.
Society for the Propagation of the Gospel in Foreign Parts. Joseph Barker journal, entry for July 7, 1859. Folio E5, Archives of the United Society for the Propagation of the Gospel in Foreign Parts. Rhodes House, Oxford University.
Society for the Propagation of the Gospel in Foreign Parts. William K. Macrorie to W. T. Bullock, September 16, 1869. Folio D 37, Archives of the United Society for the Propagation of the Gospel in Foreign Parts. Rhodes House, Oxford University.
Society for Propagation of Gospel to Foreign Parts. William Chesson [Secretary to the Aborigines Protection Society], Bishop John William Colenso to Frederick. November 1, 1875. Folio Z, Archives of the United Society for the Propagation of the Gospel in Foreign Parts. Rhodes House, Oxford University.
Somerset, C. E. 1890. Indian industrial schools. *Missionary Outlook* 20: 131.

Sound Vision. http://www.soundvision.com.
Spirit Rock Meditation Center. http://www.spiritrock.org.
Srinivasan, J. 2002. Hindu spiritual leader—a Californian—dies in Hawaii. *South Asian Outlook*. January. http://www.southasianoutlook.com/sao_back_issues/january_2002/satguru.htm.
Stables, William Gordon. 1900. *Allan Adair; or Here and There in many Lands*. London: Religious Tract Society.
Stables, William Gordon. 1906. *Wild life in sunny lands; a romance of butterfly hunting*. London: Religious Tract Society.
Stevens, Christine. 1994. *White man's dreaming: Killalpaninna Mission, 1866–1915*. Melbourne: Oxford University Press.
Stewart, Wilma S., ed. 1961. *The Story of Serampore*. Serampore: Council of Serampore College.
Stoler, Ann Laura. 1995. *Race and the education of desire: Foucault's history of sexuality and the colonial order of things*. Durham NC: Duke University Press.
Stoler, Ann Laura. 2002. *Carnal knowledge and imperial power: Race and the intimate in colonial rule*. Berkeley, CA: University of California Press.
Stringer, Isaac O. 1911. The Chootla Indian School, Carcross, Yukon Territory. Series 6-A (printed), Box 23. Isaac O. Stringer Papers. General Synod Archives [Church of England]. Toronto, Canada.
Subramuniyaswami, Sivaya. 1993. *Dancing with Siva: Hinduism's contemporary catechism*. Hawaii: Himalayan Academy.
Subramuniyaswami, Sivaya. 2000. *How to become a (better) Hindu: A guide for seekers and born Hindus*. Hawaii: Himalayan Academy.
Subramuniyaswami, Sivaya. 2002 [1999]. Autobiography: The making of a master. *Hinduism Today*. April, May, June. http://www.hinduismtoday.com/archives/2002/4-6/16-25_autobiography.shtml
Sundaram, P. K., ed. 1980. *Istasiddhi of Vimuktatman*. Sanskrit text. Madras: Swadharma Swaarajya Sangha.
Sundkler, Bengt. 1976. *Zulu Zion and some Swazi Zionists*. Oxford: Oxford University Press.
Suzuki, Daisetz Teitaro. 1949 [1934]. *An introduction to Zen Buddhism*. London: Rider & Company.
Swearer, Donald. 1996. *The Buddhist world of southeast Asia*. Albany, NY: State University of New York Press.
Tanji, Miyume, and Stephanie Lawson. 1997. "Democratic peace" and "Asian democracy": A universalist–particularist tension. *Alternatives* 22.1: 135–155.
Tapasyananda, Svami. 1981. *Sri Madhvacarya, his life, religion and philosophy*. Madras: Sri Ramakrishna Math.
Tarlo, Emma. 1996. *Clothing matters: Dress and identity in India*. Chicago, IL: University of Chicago Press.
Thibaut, George, trans. 1890–1904. *The Vedanta-Sutras with the commentary by Sankarakarya (pt. 3. The Vedanta-Sutras with the commentary of Ramanuja)*. Sacred Books of the East. vols. 34, 38, 48. Oxford: Clarendon Press.
Thomas, Nicholas. 1991. *Entangled objects: Exchange, material culture, and colonialism in the Pacific*. Cambridge, MA: Harvard University Press.
Thomas, Nicholas. 1994. *Colonialism's culture: Anthropology, travel and government*. Oxford: Polity Press.
Thompson, E[dward] P[almer]. 1964 [1963]. *The making of the English working class*. New York: Pantheon Books.
Thompson, E[dward] P[almer]. 1993. *"Alien Homage": Edward Thompson and Rabindranath Tagore*. Delhi; New York: Oxford University Press.
Thorne, Susan. 1999. *Congregational missions and the making of an imperial culture in nineteenth-century England*. Stanford: Stanford University Press.

Thwaites, R. G. 1896–1901. *The Jesuit Relations and allied documents; travels and explorations of the Jesuit missionaries in New France, 1610–1791.* 73 vols. Cleveland, OH: Burrows Bros. Co.

Tims, John W. 1909. Evangelizing the Canadian Indians. *Church Missionary Review* June: 344–350.

Titley, E. Brian. 1986. Indian industrial schools in western Canada. In Nancy M. Sheehan, J. Donald Wilson, and David C. Jones, eds. *Schools in the west: Essays in Canadian educational history.* 133–153. Calgary: Detselig Enterprises.

Tonkinson, Carole. 1995. *Big sky mind: Buddhism and the Beat generation.* New York: Riverhead.

Tran Ky Phuong. 1993. *Cham ruins: Journey in search of an ancient civilization.* Hanoi: Gioi.

Trinidad and Tobago, Republic of House of Representatives, Third Session of the Fifth Parliament. An Act for the incorporation of the International Society for Krishna Consciousness (ISKCON) Trinidad and Tobago Inc. and for matters incidental thereto. *Legal Supplement Part C to the Trinidad and Tobago Gazette, vol. 37, no. 121, 24th June, 1998.* No. 17 of 1998. http://www.ttparliament.org/bills/house/1998/b1998h17.

Turner, George. 1861. *Nineteen years in Polynesia: missionary life, travels and researches in the islands of the Pacific.* London: J. Snow.

Tweed, Thomas. 1992. *The American encounter with Buddhism, 1844–1912.* Bloomington, IN: Indiana University Press.

United Free Church of Scotland Mission. 1873. Young to James Allison, November 23, 1872. Section 7748/67, United Free Church of Scotland Mission Archives. National Library of Scotland, Edinburgh.

United Presbyterian Church. 1890. *Missionary record of the United Presbyterian Church.* October. Edinburgh: Oliphant.

Van der Veer, Peter. 1994. Hindu nationalism and the discourse of modernity: The Vishva Hindu Parishad. In Marty and Appleby, eds. *Accounting for Fundamentalisms: The dynamic character of movements.* 653–668. Chicago, IL: University of Chicago Press.

Van der Veer, Peter, ed. 1997. *Conversion to modernities: The globalization of Christianity.* New York: Routledge.

Van der Veer, Peter. 2001. *Imperial encounters: Religion and modernity in India and Britain.* Princeton: Princeton University Press.

Van Rooden, Peter. 1997. Nineteenth-Century representations of missionary conversion and the transformation of western Christianity. In Peter van der Veer, ed. *Conversion to modernities: The globalization of Christianity,* 65–89. New York: Routledge.

Veezhinathan, N., ed. 1971. *Anantanandagiripranitam srisankaravijayam.* Intro. T. M. P. Mahadevan. Madras: Centre of Advanced Study in Philosophy, University of Madras.

View Islam. http://www.bilalphilips.com/abouthim/bio_summ.htm.

Vipassana Meditation Group of Long Beach. http://www.calirose.com/vipassana.html.

Vishnu-puranam. 1962. Sanskrit and Hindi. Gorakhpur: Gita Press.

Vishva Hindu Parishad. http://www.vhp.org.

Vishva Hindu Parishad. In the service of poor. http://www.vhp.org/englishsite/d.Dimensions_of_ VHP/aSewa/NSNS/intheserviceofpoor.htm.

Vishwa Hindu Parishad of America. Relationship with VHP bharat. http://www.vhp-america.org/whatvhpa/standrelation.htm.

Viswanathan, Gauri. 1989. *Masks of conquest: Literary study and British rule in India.* New York: Columbia University Press.

Viswanathan, Gauri. 1998. *Outside the fold: Conversion, modernity, and belief.* Princeton, NJ: Princeton University Press.

Vivekananda, Swami [Narendranath Datta]. 1982. *The complete works of Swami Vivekananda.* 8 vols. Calcutta: Advaita Ashram.

Wach, Joachim. 1944. *Sociology of religion.* Chicago, IL: University of Chicago.

Waghorne, Joanne Punzo. 1989. From robber baron to royal servant of God? Gaining a divine body in south India. In Alf Hiltebeitel, ed. *Criminal Gods and Demon Devotees: Essays on the Guardians of Popular Hinduism*, 405–426. Albany, NY: State University of New York Press.

Waghorne, Joanne Punzo. 1994. *The raja's magic clothes: Re-visioning kingship and divinity in England's India*. University Park, PA: Pennsylvania State University Press.

Walliss. John. 2002. *The Brahma Kumaris as a "reflexive tradition": Responding to late modernity*. Aldershot: Ashgate.

Ward, W. R. 1994. The evangelical revival in eighteenth-century Britain. In Sheridan Gilley and W. J. Shiels, eds. *A History of Religion in Britain: Practice and belief from pre-Roman times to the present*. 252–272. Oxford: Oxford University Press.

Ward, William. 1815–1818. *A view of the history, literature, and religion of the Hindoos: Including a minute description of their manners and customs, and translations of their principal works*. 2 vols. Serampore: Mission Press.

Wasylow, Walter J. 1972. History of Battleford Industrial School for Indians. M.Ed thesis. Saskatoon: University of Saskatchewan.

Watts, Newman. 1934. *The romance of tract distribution*. London: Religious Tract Society.

Wesleyan Methodist Missionary Society. General school schedules of the Natal District. Archives of the Wesleyan Methodist Missionary Society. University of London.

Wesleyan Methodist Church in Canada. 1846. Minutes of the annual conferences of the Wesleyan Methodist Church in Canada, 1824–1845. Toronto: Anson Green.

Wesleyan Methodist Missionary Society. Schedules of financial state of day schools. Synod Minutes 1848–1876. Archives of the Wesleyan Methodist Missionary Society. University of London.

Wesleyan Methodist Missionary Society. Joseph Gaskin to the Secretaries of the Wesleyan Methodist Missionary Society, November 5, 1860. Archives of the Wesleyan Methodist Missionary Society. University of London.

Wesleyan Methodist Missionary Society. Jesse Pilcher to George Osborn, March 4, 1863. Archives of the Wesleyan Methodist Missionary Society. University of London.

Wesleyan Methodist Missionary Society. Joseph Jackson Jr., January 1, 1864. Archives of the Wesleyan Methodist Missionary Society. University of London.

Wesleyan Methodist Missionary Society. James Langley to William B. Boyce, October 26, 1868. Archives of the Wesleyan Methodist Missionary Society. University of London.

Wesleyan Methodist Missionary Society. Joseph Jackson Jr. Report of two students in the Indaleni circuit, 1871. Synod Minutes. Archives of the Wesleyan Methodist Missionary Society. University of London.

Wesleyan Methodist Missionary Society. R. Hayes to the Secretaries, September 1, 1876. Archives of the Wesleyan Methodist Missionary Society. University of London.

Wesleyan Methodist Missionary Society. Schedule of subordinate paid agents, 1876. Archives of the Wesleyan Methodist Missionary Society. University of London.

Wesleyan Methodist Missionary Society. Thomas Kirkby to Thomas Kilner, August 16, 1880. Archives of the Wesleyan Methodist Missionary Society. University of London.

West, John [Reverend]. 1967 [1824]. *The substance of a journal during a residence at the Red River colony, British North America, in the years 1820–1823*. Vancouver: Alcuin Society.

West, Martin. 1975. *Bishops and prophets in a black city: African independent churches in Soweto, Johannesburg*. Cape Town: David Philip.

Whatever 101 is. Champion to Hill, August 28, 1837. Folio 10/1, Wesleyan Missionary Papers. Natal Archives. Petermaritzburg.

White, Charles S. J. 1980. Mother guru: Jnanananda of Madras. In Nancy Auer Falk and Rita M. Gross, eds. *Unspoken Worlds: Women's religious lives in non-western cultures*. 43–56. San Francisco, CA: Harper & Row.

Wilberforce, William. 1797. *A practical view of the prevailing religious system of professed Christians, in the higher and middle classes in this country, contrasted with real Christianity*. Dublin: B. Dugdale.

Williams, C. Peter. 1994. British religion and the wider world mission: Mission and empire, 1800–1940. In Sheridan Gilley and W. J. Sheils, eds. *A history of religion in Britain: Practice and belief from pre-Roman times to the present*. 381–405. Cambridge, MA, and Oxford: Blackwell.

Williams, Charles. 1888. *A bi-centenary memorial of John Bunyan, who died A. D. 1688*. London: Baptist Tract and Book Society.

Williams, John. 1837. *A narrative of missionary enterprises in the South Sea Islands; with remarks upon the natural history of the islands, origin, languages, traditions and usages of the inhabitants*. London: John Snow.

Willis, Jane. 1973. *Geniesh: An Indian girlhood*. Toronto: New Press.

Wilson, Edward F. 1890a. Anthropology in Canada. *The Canadian Indian* 1.1: 2–3.

Wilson, Edward F. 1890b. The Indian of today. *The Canadian Indian* 1.2: 28–29.

Wilson, Horace Hayman. 1977 [1861]. *A sketch of the religious sects of the Hindus*. New Delhi: Cosmo Publications.

Wilson, J. Donald, ed. 1986. "No blanket worn in school": The education of Indians in nineteenth-century Ontario. In Jean Barman, Yvonne Hebert, and Don McCaskill, eds. *Indian Education in Canada, Volume 1: The Legacy*. 64–87. Vancouver: University of British Columbia Press.

Wilson, James. 1966 [1799]. *A Missionary voyage to the southern Pacific ocean, 1796–1798*. Graz, Austria: Akademische Druck.

Wilson-Carmichael, Amy. 1904. *Things as they are: Mission work in southern India*. London: Morgan and Scott.

"Wood, J. Claverdon" [Thomas Carter]. 1911. *Sinclair of the scouts; or with bayonet and barricade in West Africa*. London: Religious Tract Society.

Yalman, Nur. 1963. On the purity of women in the castes of Ceylon and Malabar. *Journal of the Royal Anthropological Institute of Great Britain and Ireland* 93.1: 25–58.

Yate, William. 1970 [1835]. *An account of New Zealand; and of the formation and progress of the Church Missionary Society's mission in the northern island*. Shannon: Irish University Press.

Yesudas, R. N. 1975. *A people's revolt in Travancore: A backward class movement for social freedom*. Trivandrum: Manju Publishing House for Kerala Historical Society.

Zenshuji Soto Mission. http://www.zenshuji.org.

INDEX